W9-AWT-503

Culture, Ideology, and World Order

STUDIES ON A JUST WORLD ORDER

*Toward a Just World Order, edited by Richard Falk, Samuel S. Kim, and Saul H. Mendlovitz

*Toward Nuclear Disarmament and Global Security: A Search for Alternatives, edited by Burns H. Weston, with the assistance of Thomas A. Hawbaker and Christopher R. Rossi

*International Law and a Just World Order, edited by Richard Falk, Friedrich V. Kratochwil, and Saul H. Mendlovitz

*The United Nations and a Just World Order, edited by Richard Falk, Samuel S. Kim, Donald McNemar, and Saul H. Mendlovitz

*Culture, Ideology, and World Order, edited by R.B.J. Walker

*Available in hardcover and paperback.

About the Book and Editor

Culture, Ideology, and World Order
edited by R.B.J. Walker

Contemporary discourse about human affairs is largely grounded
in the specific historical experience and interests of a few dominant societies. This poses an important challenge to all those who
urge that we need to adopt a global perspective on modern political
life, whether in terms of international relations, comparative and
developmental politics, international political economy, world order
studies, or general social and political theory. In terms of
"culture," we must then face the problem of ethnocentrism; in terms
of "ideology," we must contend with the complex problems of the relationship between discourse and the broader patterns of social,
economic, and political power and evaluate the way in which appeals
to alternative cultural traditions inform strategies of resistance
to the prevailing international order.

This volume of essays underlines the centrality of these themes
in modern international affairs, presenting an important context in
which to understand recent debates in international political theory
in general and speculations about the character of a just world order
in particular.

R.B.J. Walker is assistant professor of political science at
the University of Victoria. He was Visiting Fellow at the Center of
International Studies, Princeton University, from 1977 to 1979 and
at Australian National University in 1978. Dr. Walker is author of
Political Theory and the Transformation of World Politics (1980).

STUDIES ON A JUST WORLD ORDER, NO. 5

Culture, Ideology, and World Order

edited by R.B.J. Walker

WESTVIEW PRESS / BOULDER AND LONDON

Studies on a Just World Order

All rights reserved. No part of this publication may be reproduced or transmitted in any form or by any means, electronic or mechanical, including photocopy, recording, or any information storage and retrieval system, without permission in writing from the publisher.

Copyright © 1984 by Westview Press, Inc.

Published in 1984 in the United States of America by Westview Press, Inc., 5500 Central Avenue, Boulder, Colorado 80301; Frederick A. Praeger, President and Publisher

Library of Congress Catalog Card Number: 84-50599
ISBN: 0-86531-678-3
ISBN: 0-86531-679-1 (pbk.)

Composition for this book was provided by the editor
Printed and bound in the United States of America

10   9   8   7   6   5   4   3   2   1

For Susan, Johanna and Caitlin

Contents

Preface xi

PART 1. INTRODUCTION
  1. East Wind, West Wind: Civilizations, Hegemonies,
      and World Orders, *R.B.J. Walker*. 2

PART 2. CULTURES, ECONOMIES, AND STATES
  2. The Moving Cultural Frontier of World Order:
      From Monotheism to North-South Relations,
      Ali A. Mazrui. 24
  3. Race in International Relations, *R. J. Vincent* . .44
  4. Civilizations and Modes of Production: Conflicts
      and Convergences, *Immanuel Wallerstein* 60
  5. The Advanced Capitalist State and the
      Contemporary World Crisis, *Joseph Camilleri*. . . .70

PART 3. HEGEMONY, RESISTANCE, AND REASSERTION
  6. Dependence in a Unified World, *Celso Furtado* . . .98
  7. The Occultation of Egypt, *Anouar Abdel-Malek* . . 124
  8. Oppression and Human Liberation: Toward a Third
      World Utopia, *Ashis Nandy*. 149

PART 4. IDEOLOGY AND WORLD ORDER DISCOURSE
  9. World Politics and Western Reason: Universalism,
      Pluralism, Hegemony, *R.B.J. Walker* 182
 10. On Marxian Thought and the Problem of
      International Relations, *R. N. Berki* 217
 11. The Discourse of World Order, *Mark Blasius* . . . 243
 12. Social Forces, States, and World Orders: Beyond
      International Relations Theory, *Robert W. Cox*. . 258

PART 5. CULTURE, IDEOLOGY, AND PEACE
 13. Contemporary Militarism and the Discourse of
      Dissent, *R.B.J. Walker* 302
 14. Peace in an Age of Transformation, *Rajni Kothari* 323

Selected Bibliography 362
About the Contributors. 365

Preface

    Contemporary analyses of human affairs are largely grounded in the specific historical experience and interests of a few dominant societies. This poses an important challenge to all those who sense a need for a more cosmopolitan or global perspective on modern political life. This challenge may be posed in terms of "culture" and therefore of ethnocentrism and nationalism, or in terms of "ideology" and thus of the complex relationship between particular discourses and other forms of social, economic, and political power. In either case, it demands a sensitivity to the way in which appeals to alternative cultural and theoretical traditions can inform strategies of resistance to the prevailing international order.

    This collection of essays is intended to encourage a greater concern with this set of problems. It has grown out of my own attempt to come to terms with the theoretical and philosophical traditions that have informed contemporary analyses of international politics within the West. The adequacy of such analyses has been questioned frequently and from many points of view. Yet it has seemed to me that neither the fairly obvious dangers of parochialism in theorizing about global events nor the ideological implications of our inherited traditions of thought in this area have received anything like adequate attention.

    In putting this collection together, I have been all too aware of the theoretical difficulties that accompany the concepts of both culture and ideology as well as of the wide range of substantive matters that could be addressed. Consequently, I have been less concerned to develop a consistent theoretical perspective than to draw attention to the often sharply contrasting ways in which cultural and ideological themes have been treated in the literature on international politics. My aim has been to provoke questions and critical discussion rather than to offer definitive analyses of particular issues. However, the essays are structured around what seems to me to be one inescapable theme--the tension between universalist and pluralist conceptions of human affairs. The way in which the universal validity of the discourses of

dominant groups is both claimed and challenged has long
been central to critical social and political thought.
It is particularly significant for the analysis of
international politics which is so often torn between the
priority of global structures and necessities on the one
hand and the particular interests of states on the other.

    This volume has developed out of an ongoing research
project on international political theory begun while I
was a Visiting Fellow at the Center of International
Studies, Princeton University. Additional stimulation has
come from participation in the World Order Models Project
Working Group on Culture, Power and Global Transformation
as well as from faculty and students at the University of
Victoria. Research has been supported by what is now the
World Policy Institute in New York which awarded me a
Transnational Academic Program Fellowship in 1981-82. I
am indebted to a great many people for encouragement and
assistance, most particularly to Richard Falk, Susan
Gordon, Saul Mendlovitz and Sherle Schwenninger.

R.B.J. Walker

Culture, Ideology, and
World Order

PART 1

Introduction

CHAPTER 1

East Wind, West Wind: Civilizations, Hegemonies, and World Orders

R.B.J. Walker

I

Cultural and ideological themes have been invoked with increasing regularity in the analysis of international affairs. Whether addressing Islamic radicalism, strategies of autonomous development, resurgences of nationalism, debates over human rights or international law, critiques of the monopolization of communications media by the industrialized states, attempts to demystify Western notions of economic growth and political development, or calls for a dialogue of cultures in the creation of an emerging global society, it now seems less useful than ever to view global tensions only in terms of explicitly economic and military structures.

The essays in this volume are brought together to underline the importance of cultural and ideological issues in contemporary world politics and to point toward some of the complex theoretical difficulties that arise once they are taken seriously. The essays derive from a variety of theoretical and doctrinal viewpoints, yet they all engage in one way or another with an issue that has to be confronted in any attempt at understanding world politics with even a minimum of critical sensitivity. Although many analysts now agree that it is necessary to examine world politics as a totality and to adopt a global perspective on human affairs, contemporary discourse about world politics is still grounded in the specific experience and interests of particular historically and geographically delimited societies, not to mention classes in those societies. Viewed in terms of "culture," this gives rise to the problem of ethnocentrism, the tendency to assume the superiority and universal nature of one's own cultural values. Viewed in terms of "ideology," it appears as a form of political power: assumptions of cultural superiority play a part in the domination of the strong over the weak. Some observers have begun to suggest that we are entering an epoch that will be characterized increasingly by a clash of civilizations and a decline of the current hegemony of Western cultural forms. This in turn gives rise to enquiries into ways in which ethnocentrism might be transcended, in which cultures might meet in a creative dialogue about future possibilities. Other observers, emphasizing the more critical concept of ideology rather than that of culture, seek to unravel the ways in which specific concepts and discourses have played an essential role in maintaining the dominant position of the West in the world.

To suggest that culture and ideology are crucial for analysis of world politics is not necessarily to take an idealist position on the matter. On the contrary, it is important to recognize that ideas, consciousness, culture, and ideology are bound up with more immediately visible kinds of political, military, and economic power.[1] But it is all too tempting to lapse into the kind of crude reductionism in which culture, ideology, and so on are treated as mere epiphenomena determined by something supposedly more fundamental. Indeed, the very assumption of a clear-cut division between a realm of "ideas" and one of "matter" can itself be seen as an ideological form associated with historically specific traditions of Western philosophy and science. Almost the entire development of the concept of ideology has in fact centered on ways of overcoming the debilitating effects of simplistic dualistic formulations of the political role of ideas and of associated notions of determinism.

Lapses into crude reductionism are common enough both in the conservative schools of *realpolitik* and in the more deterministic brands of international political economy. Some might argue that blunt analytical tools are all we need to illuminate the crude "realities" of world politics. But then, students of this subject are sharply divided about precisely what these realities are--a states system, a world economy, a world society, or some combination of each. In the face of such divergent conceptions, it is wise to be skeptical about any simplified representation of the nature of things--especially one that would eliminate the effects of human consciousness.

Nevertheless, to suggest that culture and ideology are important is to enter into a complex theoretical universe. Part of the intention of bringing these papers together is precisely to suggest that, despite the generally pragmatic and policy-oriented nature of most analyses of world politics, this is a realm that poses a range of difficult issues at least as significant as those raised by life within sovereign states, the usual focus of attention for social and political theory. As concepts, "culture" and "ideology" are themselves historically and sociologically specific, bringing with them meanings and implications that may require careful handling. Ideology, after all, has often become something "they" have--a doctrine, inevitably false, that has to be overcome by the guarantors of truth. And culture, like civilization, becomes something "we" have, distinguishing us from the barbarians outside. In the context of international politics, such concepts merely add to what is already a wide range of difficulties confronting any analyses of an emerging world order. And in the context of the development of social and political theory in general, they invite a renewed emphasis on such perennial themes as the opposition between the "one" and the "many," the "universal" and the "plural." For the conventional view of world politics has largely been pluralist and, indeed, relativist in inspiration, a matter of the continuous collision of the particular interests of supposedly autonomous states. More recently, the relativity of Western claims to universality has become the target of Third World criticism of the global hegemony of the modernized industrial states. In both cases, we are confronted by powerful challenges to the commonly voiced hopes for a form of political organization that expresses and embodies the universality of humankind.

It is this underlying tension between universalist aspiration and the claims of pluralistic relativism--a tension that has always been central to an understanding of world politics--that has emerged once again with renewed insistency in the literature on world order. It is a tension that has found a great number of historical articulations. In the Western tradition, perhaps the most important formulation was the contrast between the universalizing Enlightenment and pluralizing Romanticism. The Third World, we may recall, once began at the Rhine. Historically we find resonances of contemporary discussions in the contrast between the philosophies of, for example, Kant and Herder and in the relations between modernizing Europe and the Ottoman Empire. Much of the discussion of contemporary world order is still preoccupied with the dynamics of the spread of and resistance to a universalizing West. It therefore seems appropriate to approach the issues raised in recent analyses of culture and ideology in modern world politics in terms of this underlying historical and philosophical problematic, which can be invoked in a number of different ways.

II

For many observers, the necessity of taking some kind of global perspective on human affairs is no longer in doubt. From the broadest speculation about the future of humankind to more technical analyses of biospheric equilibrium, international political economy, or various world systems, the emphasis on a global context has come to be a major theme underlying all kinds of commentaries on the modern human condition.[2] It is possible--indeed necessary--to be intensely skeptical about the specific contribution of any particular school of thought, but the general point has probably been made decisively enough.

However, because a global perspective challenges some of the more fundamental categories of thought within which human activity has come to be understood in the West, the implications of its adoption certainly are in doubt. The concept of politics, for example, becomes problematic. Viewed retrospectively, modern conceptions of the nature of politics have emerged in the context of the European state. Even though considerable variety and development can be found within this context, as a whole our present understanding of politics differs substantially from that which characterized, say, the Hellenic *polis* or the world of St. Thomas Aquinas. The development of the European nation-state was a phenomenon without precedent. Conceptions of politics appropriate to it, while drawing on the experience of the preceding social formations, emerged in the specific historical context of a transition from a feudal to a capitalist mode of production and the associated closing of territorial space. It is precisely the novelty of this transition, this movement to modernity, that becomes the focus of any serious attempt to understand modern political life. For some, following Marx, the transition can be portrayed in terms of a novel principle of social organization--the wage-labor-capital relation. Others, drawing more on Weberian themes, have been more concerned with the restructuring of consciousness. But whatever the substantive explanation or the variations in detail between different historical perspectives, our modern understanding of political life is tied inextricably to the experience of the post-Renaissance European state. As Perry Anderson has put it in a penetrating study, "the Renaissance remains--despite every criticism and revision--the crux of European history as a whole: the double moment of an equally unexampled expansion of space and recovery of time. It is at this point, with the rediscovery of the Ancient World, and the discovery of the New World, that the European state system acquired its full singularity."[3]

To suggest that it is necessary to take a global perspective on human affairs is thus to throw into question the continuing vitality of political forms specific to the European state. It is to raise the possibility that whereas the most difficult and important issues in social and political thought since Machiavelli have been concerned with life within sovereign states, they now increasingly concern the possiblity and character of life on a single planet.

III

It is also now clear enough that Western social and political thought is in the midst of considerable uncertainty and possibly significant transformation. Gone are the days when the social sciences could confidently pretend to imitate the physical sciences or appeal to some timeless methodological formula in order to condemn the recalcitrant ideologues or metaphysicians. Instead we witness a widespread sense of ambivalence about the kinds of assumptions that have guided the study of human activity for most of this century. The tale is usually told in terms of deeper difficulties within the traditions of Western philosophy, particularly those traditions preoccupied with epistemology. It is said, for example, that we have fallen too deeply into the grips of eighteenth-century empiricism, Cartesian or Kantian dualism, or mechanistic materialism and atomism; that we have not learned carefully enough from Hegel, Marx, Nietzsche, pragmatism, phenomenology, structuralism, or other attempts to escape the twin demons of objectivism and subjectivism.

Certainly this story captures much of what is most creative and fertile in modern sociopolitical thought. But it has one obvious and major deficiency. It tends to concern itself only with the intricacies of European or Western philosophy; to assume that a more authentic account of human experience would be possible if only we could discover some way out of the maze constructed by Descartes, Kant, Hegel, and the rest. For all the sophistication of much of the discussion of this issue, and for all the insistence that we take account of the specific historical and social grounding of philosophy in general and claims to universality in particular, the limited context of the contemporary debate tends to get obscured. The West is not the world. European philosophy is not the only discourse attempting to give meaning to human experience. The problems confronting modern industrial societies are not entirely the same as those facing most of humanity, although they are undoubtedly structurally related. In an age in which many of the major forces that shape the modern world are international or global in scope, the most obvious characteristic of recent discussions of the restructuring of social and political theory may well be its parochialism.

There is a well-known and all-pervasive response to this sort of complaint, one that comes in much the same form from widely divergent doctrinal positions. It is the response implicit in the unilinear view of history in which the West merrily leads the rest of the world down the road to modernity. Western philosophy is thus assigned a universal stature, and parochial traditionalisms are recommended to transcend their own limitations with this philosophy. Some simply think this is a good thing. Others evoke a tragic sense of loss reminiscent of Weber's portrayal of the "disenchantment of the world." We may progress or we may "progress." But from the universal histories of the Enlightenment down to those more recent scenarios of global salvation that have liberalism or socialism in the starring role, this attitude has been questioned too infrequently.

There has also been resistance to this response. Some, reacting to a presumed loss of innocence, have idealized the primitive, the exotic, the foreign. Others have claimed to see the imminent collapse of Western civilization, one of many such collapses among the cycles of history. More recently, resistance has taken the form of a critique of the ideological and cultural forms assumed by the global hegemony of the industrialized powers. Theories of "development," for example, are said to be a mere mask for the realities of "underdevelopment." The universalization of parochial social and political concepts thereby appears as part of a system of stratification, one in which poorer states are integrated into a global division of labor organized by, and to the advantage of, the dominant powers. More recently still, with the economies of the industrialized world in shock and with the forceful assertion of other civilizational traditions in the Middle East and elsewhere, it no longer seems inevitable that Western societies will continue to hold the initiative in human affairs. "East Wind prevails over West Wind" is an aphorism attributed to Mao, but it echoes in many languages in an increasingly complex world.

Out of sensitivities about the parochialism and ethnocentrism of the Western traditions of social and political theory in a global context, there has developed a substantial interest in other civilizations. Joseph Needham's attempt to come to terms with China and Marshall Hodgeson's work on Islam[4] are now well known and very important recent enterprises of this sort, but they are part of a much broader tendency. It is now remarkable only that this interest has not percolated very far into the debates about theoretical and methodological assumptions in the social sciences. For what seems to be the most important feature of Western social and political theory is that it is faced by internal and external critique simultaneously. The long-entrenched claims to universality made by Western sociopolitical theory and philosophy appear to be increasingly vulnerable both on their own terms and on those of other civilizational traditions that are able to assert themselves in the modern world.

However, it is one thing to say simply that we must escape the parochial, cease being ethnocentric, and be open to other civilizations. This can be a misleadingly seductive rhetoric. After all, the pitfalls of

relativism or eclecticism are always waiting for the
critics of a presumed universal reason. It is quite
another thing to come to terms with the full implications
of what a sensitivity to other civilizations might mean
for social and political theory as we know it.

IV

In contrast with those who urge the necessity of
adopting a global perspective on human affairs, most
theorists of world politics are always quick to point out
that we in fact live in a deeply fragmented world, with
very little room for common agreement on the most basic
necessities of coexistence. Schopenhauer's dictum that
states exist like hedgehogs in a bag captures the
prevailing tone quite nicely. And there are enough
contemporary examples of conflict and brutality to drive
the point home. The conventional image of international
politics evokes a devious Machiavellianism or a Hobbesian
state of nature, a version of original sin or a
biologically induced lust for power. There may be rules
of the game that allow for some degree of coexistence, or
even, at times, for some kind of community of nations.
Yet, in the end, the key rule of the game is the presumed
legitimacy of war. Once upon a time, war may have been
merely the sport of kings. Now there are fewer and fewer
observers who give us a good chance of surviving the
logic of the war system for much longer. A similar hard-
boiled cynicism characterizes the professional view of
relationships between rich and poor states, or of the
degradation of planetary ecology. The strong exact what
they can, the weak grant what they must; the individual
national interest always takes precedence over any common
human interest.

This stark, conventional view often comes as a shock
to those socialized within the cocoon of modern Western
societies. In order to understand international affairs
it becomes necessary to undergo a sort of ritualized
deflation, a critique of the prevailing liberal values
that, if directed at intrastate affairs, might even be
thought subversive. Despite almost daily reminders, it
is not always easy to comprehend the extent to which,
say, the American way of life depends on the brutal
exercise of power beyond its borders, on the underwriting
of corruption and naked aggression on a global scale.

This form of selective vision is particularly
endemic to the citizens of dominant powers. But it is a
selectivity that is itself part of the basic structure of
the modern state system. Within states, it is possible
to envisage a perfect social order. Being perfect, the
vision is easily assumed to be exportable to all other
states--with a little persuasion from economic or
military forces if necessary. The possession of

"civilization" justifies the conquest of "barbarism."
Such is one way to empire. But in a states system,
perfection can remain relative; it develops in a variety
of national forms. The tendency toward empire is
thwarted by the fragmentation of power and the creation
of structures that maintain some kind of order among
contending forces.

In the broad historical context, states systems have
been the exception and empires have been the norm. Since
the sixteenth century, the modern world has organized
itself principally as a states system, although rarely
have strong elements of empire been absent. The result
has been the development of two distinct, though closely
related, traditions of discourse about human affairs. On
the one hand, there has been a concern with the
possibility of creating a better human existence within
national boundaries. Whatever the differences among the
multiple forms of modern social and political thought,
they almost all take the single national unit for
granted. On the other hand, there is international
political theory, characterized mainly by its silence.
Its concern is with the mere space between states and
with the construction of the fragile order that is a
precondition for loftier ambitions within the secure
confines of the state.

If the distinction is drawn sharply enough, several
important consequences follow. To begin with, it
suggests a series of differentiations of political life.
Foreign policy becomes a matter of expediency and order,
while domestic policy is tempered by considerations of
justice. Public participation becomes limited in
external affairs; only a special elite--the great
statesmen, the diplomats sent abroad to lie on behalf of
their country--can hope to defend the "national interest"
without succumbing to popular sentiments or conceptions
of justice derived from civil society. More
significantly, the distinction leads, in the present era,
to an important contradiction. The logic of the state
system seems liable to get us all blown to bits. It
therefore seems reasonable to seek ways of transcending
this logic, to recognize that as inhabitants of one
planet we all have something in common. That is, we
ought to overcome pluralism in favor of universalism.
But of course there is no shortage of claimed
universalisms and no shortage of crusaders who would be
happy to impose them on everyone else. Against a
universalizing empire, the appropriate response is
pluralistic nationalism. In some ways the state system
threatens annihilation; in others it seems to be the only
plausible defense against an incipient world empire.

Yet to see these two traditions of discourse as
strictly separate is deeply illusory. They participate
in a fundamental tension, a contradiction or perhaps a
dialectic. To put it bluntly, in the context of the

state, Western social and political thought has pursued universalisms of one kind or another while international politics has been the realm where pluralism and relativism have remained the dominant values. Or to qualify the comparison somewhat, where mainstream theorists of international politics underline the diversity of human experience and pursue the consequences of relativism, historicism, and nationalism into forms of unmediated conflict, their critics argue for the essential unity of humankind and seek means of institutionalizing a common policy that will remove the need for war. For theorists of civil society, exactly the reverse is the case. Universalist themes—particualrly those crystallized in the Enlightenment—dominate, and those who celebrate diversity are shunted off to the periphery of Romanticism, anarchism, subjectivism, or literature.

International events now impinge more and more on everyday life. It becomes impossible to engage in any political activity without coming to terms with the global context of contemporary human existence. The issues of disarmament and development have become particularly prominent concerns. Recognition of the dangers of military escalation has mobilized considerable mass action. The poverty of most of the world's population has come to gnaw insistently at the conscience of the industrialized nations.

In the conventional view, both movements are misguided. The realities of power politics require negotiation from strength. Northern wealth will eventually trickle down South and, in any case, inequality is an unfortunate fact of life. It is no good, this argument goes, trying to carry over images and assumptions from civil society into international politics. Universalist assumptions of a global harmony and community are inappropriate for a realm of fragmented power. The bottom line of international politics is order and survival, not justice and progress. The usual response to this position is to suggest that it is precisely the global community whose survival is at stake; that we are no longer talking about international order but world order; that we need to start thinking about global unity, about universals, about humankind as a whole. And, of course, some begin to believe that they are in possession of just the right universals, just the right values appropriate for all humankind. Praise God and pass the ammunition, they say again.

V

It does not take much persuasion to become convinced that we are in fact all in a global crisis together. Despite the conventional pluralist view of international

politics, the argument for universalism is increasingly
urgent. It is necessary only to consider in a little
more detail some of the issues at stake in what have
probably been the two most insistent themes in popular
discussions of international politics--disarmament and
development.
There is presently particular concern about the
dangers inherent in the massive and escalating
militarization of the world. The conventional argument
has always been that if one wants peace, one should
prepare for war. The standard response to this argument
has been that preparations for war themselves induce war.
With the advent of nuclear weapons the debate gets rather
more complex. In a system of autonomous states there is
little or no community, merely divergent interests and
powers. Peace is attained by processes of power
balancing and rules of accommodation. War is the central
mechanism of system change. But with nuclear weapons,
war as a mechanism of change becomes counterproductive.
And so we have come to live in an era of deterrence, of
mutual assured destruction, of second strike capability;
a transition from an age in which war was, at best, a
continuation of policy by other means to an age in which
the prevention of war becomes a precondition for the
continuation of policy. At the center of the
international system, therefore, the conventional means
of change has been blocked, and we have been treated
instead to oscillating periods of Cold War and detente,
and the deflection of superpower conflict to peripheral
regions. But the forces that generate change have
remained as strong as ever.
In the most recent period, the whole concept of
deterrence has seemed to be on the brink of
disintegration. The reasons for this are quite
complicated, but the general issues have become fairly
well known. The doctrine of mutual assured destruction
promises stability through the ability of each major
power to use its so-called second strike capacity to
annihilate the other even if it is itself attacked first.
Yet, even if the basic premises of this doctrine are
accepted, there are a number of nasty jokers in the game.
Quantitative assessments of capability may become less
important than paranoid or crusading beliefs about the
enemy held by those who count. Moreover, deterrence
depends to a large extent on the credibility of the
threat to retaliate, and it is not always easy to make a
credible threat to retaliate against aggression at the
margins of the system, the defense of Western Europe
having been particularly important in this respect. Thus
it becomes necessary to develop other, more credible but
less violent weapons to deal with limited incursions.
But then, being less violent, these weapons become easier
to use, thereby risking the possibility of escalation
into full-scale conflict. Furthermore, there is always

the internal dynamic of the development of military technology itself. In the present era this dynamic has tended to emphasize the increasing offensive accuracy of missile systems, raising the possibility that, at some point in the escalating spiral, one state will find itself in a technologically favorable position to make a first strike, thereby completely undermining deterrence. All these problems with the logic of deterrence--not to mention the socioeconomic interests that also influence arms production--have quite properly generated a concern that in spite of the success of deterrence in preventing general war so far, it offers no long-term guarantee of security; it may even contribute to long-term instability.

It is possible to work out a parallel picture of the logic of the structures that generate concern with Western notions of development in a so-called Third World. Against a background of a conception of liberal economics based on Ricardo's principle of comparative advantage, and the conception of development as a series of stages concocted out of a make-believe version of British economic history, we can find many alternative accounts of the logics of underdevelopment, of unequal exchange, of neo-colonialism, and of the restructuring of the global division of labor in response to the internationalization of capital. These analyses may be supplemented by more descriptive accounts of the aggressive power of multinational corporations in undermining unsympathetic governments, the use of foreign aid as a form of blackmail, and the dumping of surplus or dangerous products on Third World states.

Both of these themes, disarmament and development, are very familiar. They now play a significant role in the political consciousness of Western industrial societies and lead to frequent assertions of the need to adopt a more global perspective on human affairs. Each is an exceptionally complex issue. It is difficult enough to acquire even an elementary grasp of the dynamics of the modern arms race or the structures of international economic relations. But the greatest difficulty of all arises from their being considered separately, as two separate systems that organize two different kinds of social activity. The themes of disarmament and development lead us back into two different traditions of discourse. Military affairs are discussed in terms of international *politics*, particularly in its most relativistic geopolitical form, while discussions of development emerge mainly from the realm of international and developmental *economics*.

The tendency to separate politics and economics has been one of the main characteristics of twentieth-century liberal thought. It has been particularly important in conventional thinking about international politics. Here it has taken the form of a distinction between the "high" politics of diplomatic and military relations and the "low" politics of social and economic affairs. "National interest" therefore comes to be abstracted from particular socioeconomic interests within or across states. The game of international politics then becomes simply a mechanical affair between autonomous powers. As with the old histories told as tales about kings and queens, ·broader socioeconomic structures and transformations can then be conveniently ignored.

One symptom of this dilemma that arises from time to time in popular discussions is the presentation of the relationship between development and militarization in strictly either/or terms: guns or butter. But even President Eisenhower knew better when he warned of the dangers of military-industrial complexes. The interests of the armaments industry are not obviously identical with the interests of a nation as a whole. In relations between states, military hardware has become one of the major commodities of international trade. Domestically, military expenditures have come to be important instruments of economic as well as foreign policy. To discuss the issues of military escalation and economic development as separate issues is in fact to participate in a discourse that embodies a particular form of ideology, one portraying economic and political issues as essentially distinct. Without some account of the relations between militarization and economic policy, analysis becomes partial and cooptable. Advocates of peace can condemn militarization as such without coming to terms with the socioeconomic consequences of militarization. After all, condemnation of war is easy. Condemnation of socioeconomic structures that support a comfortable, middle-class life-style may be somewhat more difficult, but it may well amount to the same thing. Sympathy for the poor is readily available, but it is more difficult to absorb the idea that poverty is at least partly perpetuated by the wealth of those who sympathize.

The same general theme may be pursued in many other ways, but the outcome is more or less the same: in trying to understand the dynamics of modern world politics it is necessary to adopt a view of the totality. The argument is made variously in terms of the need to examine the "world system," "world order," "war system," "planetary politics," or some other inclusivist concept. But whether in terms of popular images of "spaceship Earth" and "global village" or of more sophisticated accounts of global interdependence or internationalizing capital, analyses of particular aspects of world politics inevitably struggle toward some image of the whole.

Thus in the face of a fragmented state system that threatens to explode, and of analyses of world politics that seem to be only partial, invocations of a more universalist perspective have come to make a serious challenge to the conventional traditions of pluralism. We live in a world that increasingly seems to be both integrated and vulnerable to one swift cataclysm. Analytically it becomes essential to examine the world as a totality. Ethically it becomes essential to think in terms of some global human interests.

Unfortunately, it is not entirely clear how the totality is to be understood or what those global interests are. The dilemma has always been most explicit in terms of the prevalence of nationalist sentiments in the modern world:

> The key question for the rationality of nationalism is the question of how far in such an integrated world it is correct for the inhabitants of different territories to see their interests, cultural, economic or political, in zero-sum terms, as matters in which the gain of one is necessarily the loss of another. There is really no surviving tradition of thought which provides at all a plausible method of answering this question with any confidence or generality, though in different ways, liberal international trade theory and Marxist political rhetoric both pretend brazenly from time to time to be able to do so.
>
> And the stumbling bemused idiom of thought which looks most realistic in its insistence on the idiocy of defining all interests in zero-sum terms--that deep terror that we may be systematically destroying in the pursuit of our several short-term interests the global ecology which offers our only habitat--this idiom has no boundaries to teach us its realities in modern daily life (because its only boundary is the globe itself) and controls no governments, compelled to enforce its definition of our common interests. If it does now constitute the conventional wisdom of the species as a whole, it is a conventional wisdom without a trace of political power at its disposal.[5]

VI

It is this tension between the pluralist logic of the state system and the potential that arises for universal destruction when statist geopolitical formations occur in the context of twentieth-century military technology that generates the characteristic categories of contemporary debate about international politics. The debate is usually formed in terms of a perpetual dialogue between "realists" and "utopians," a terminology that is itself a reminder of the dominance of pluralist state interests over aspirations toward any common human interest.

Yet the contrast is inevitably overdrawn. It has already been suggested, for example, that there has been both a strong complementarity within international political theory between pluralist and universalist traditions, and an underlying continuity between theories of international affairs and those of civil society. Similarly, the fragmented state system as we have come to know it originated in Europe, and the very name Europe suggests an underlying unity in which fragmentation could occur. Thus, in place of the usual image of international anarchy, Europe could be understood as a "society" of states tolerating each other's existence: "not Holy Wars but the adjustment of frontiers; unity in an agreement about independence rather than continental solidarity."[6] The same general theme has been taken up in a number of different ways with respect to the contemporary international system. Fragmentation, it is argued, occurs within the broader unity of an emergent cosmopolitan culture, one rooted in science and technology (not to mention capital accumulation), rather than the largely Christian natural law of Europe. Taking this theme seriously, it is possible to reverse the figure/ground relationship between universalism and pluralism so that the major issues of international politics arise not from geopolitical fragmentation but precisely from the dominance of a particular form of universalist integration.

The extent to which such a cosmopolitan culture has taken hold has been a matter of considerable debate. The question permeates a large part of substantive research on modern world politics. The general theme has been that the developing patterns of industrialization, trade, and communications characteristic of the twentieth century have begun to create an embryonic world society in which the state plays a subordinate role. It is a theme with many different variations, but the crucial issue concerns whether the visible indicators of such a change point toward some authentic universal community of humankind or toward the hegemonic imposition of parochial values in some form of world empire.

Suspicions that the real dynamic at work here is one of hegemony find one expression in the critique of many modern forms of "cultural imperialism." For much of humankind, culture is increasingly something that arrives in cans. Extraordinarily high proportions of information processing and image production in the developing states are of American origin. Donald Duck has become a symbol of oppression almost on a par with the dreaded multinational corporation. International law, for all that it embodies the universalist hopes of Western liberals, appears as merely a consecration of the will of the great powers. Invocations of human rights lean more toward the specifically Western version that emphasizes individual freedom rather than socioeconomic well-being.

Perhaps the most powerful recent expression of this theme is Edward Said's influential polemic against "Orientalism." For Said, the very attempt by the West to understand the non-West--and specifically the Middle East--has resulted in a pervasive hegemonic discourse, an integral element of Western domination.

> Under the general heading of knowledge of the Orient, and with the umbrella of Western hegemony over the Orient during the period from the end of the eighteenth century, there emerged a complex Orient suitable for study in the academy, for display in the museum, for reconstruction in the colonial office, for theoretical illustration in anthropological, biological, linguistic, racial, and historical theses about mankind and the universe, for instances of economic and sociological theories of development, revolution, cultural personality, national or religious character. Additionally, the imaginative examination of things Oriental was based more or less exclusively upon a sovereign Western consciousness out of whose unchallenged centrality an Oriental World emerged, first according to general ideas about who or what was an Oriental, then according to a detailed logic governed not simply by empirical reality but by a battery of desires, repressions, investments, and projections.[7]

For Said, the essential dynamic that has been at work here has involved a systematic objectification of "the Other." Elevating reason, masculinity, and order within its own culture, the West projected a stereotype of an Orient characterized by passion, femininity, and chaos. The Orient became a place of inscrutable, mysterious, sensuous but inferior people, suitable for rule by the dominant "civilized" powers. Thus in a modern theoretical idiom derived from the writings of Antonio Gramsci and Michel Foucault, we have one more indictment of the bigotry and ignorance of the "lords of human kind,"[8] a reworking of the dialectic of master and slave, or even that of Prospero and Caliban. Said's indictment became particularly resonant in the context of a variety of challenges to modernity or Western dominance in the Middle East in the past decade, whether in terms of the Iranian revolution, petropower, or the plight of the Palestinians. But despite a certain overdose of rhetoric, the point is of considerable general importance.

This kind of analysis is particularly useful in clarifying the dangers of making any simple ontological distinction between the essential character of the Orient or Occident. Neither Western nor Oriental philosophical traditions, for example, admit of any easy overall characterization. There is in both a considerable

diversity of traditions. In any case, the very attempt
to understand a tradition of thought is itself subject to
a complex subjection of historical texts to the
epistemologies and political interests of the present.
Yet Said's success in raising this issue simultaneously
highlights a persistent stumbling block. For he candidly
admits that it is difficult to grasp another culture
without misrepresentation and distortion. It is thus not
clear how Orientalism is to be avoided. Furthermore, in
criticizing the essentializing discourse about the Orient
produced in the West, Said tends toward an essentialist
portrayal of the West itself; "Orientalism in reverse."[9]
It is not clear how this is to be avoided either.

In fact, beyond the powerful polemical and
demystifying character of this kind of analysis, we come
up against the fundamental issue of how cultures can ever
meet. The critique of hegemonic universalism takes us
back to pluralism and relativism. It succeeds in
demystifying the way in which claims to universality are
grounded in power and in elucidating some of the
consequences of hegemonic discourse in contemporary
international events. But if we are all inevitably
caught in a continuous objectification of "the Other,"
then we are condemned to a perpetual confrontation but no
meeting: radical relativism is again on the horizon.

VII

Almost the entire literature on change in
contemporary world politics seems to fall into this
simple dichotomy between pluralist and universalist
perspectives. For the conventional or pluralist view,
change essentially implies a realignment of existing
structures, the strengthening and weakening of players in
the same game. For the universalists, the game itself is
dangerous and absurd, and its competitive struggles
between powers ought to be transcended in favor of a
cooperative community based on common principles. Some
contenders for the source of universal principles are
well known: Enlightenment rationalism, free trade, *Pax
Britannica, Pax Americana,* the Trilateral Commission,
capitalism, socialism, and so on. Given a universalist
starting point it is possible to assume that any
fundamental restructuring of the international system
would involve the development of international
institutions and structures modeled on those already
characteristic of the dominant states. Thus, just as
Europe, so recently at war, could transcend its petty
nationalisms in a common economic or even political
enterprise, so the other nationalisms, even those so
recently spawned in the retreat from colonialism, could
be transcended through integration into a supranational
community. But despite the undeniable scope of an

integrating international economy, nationalism is far from gone. Indeed it may well be increasing in potency. And in its present phase, it is in large part developing not within the universalizing structures of European culture or European political economy, but against the universalizing structures of the currently dominant powers. As K. J. Holsti has put it in an interesting study of the double movement toward integration and fragmentation in the contemporary international system,

> Weak, vulnerable societies and communities are not likely to favour schemes of economic or political integration if they predict that their implementation will lead to extensive foreign penetration, inequitable distribution of costs and rewards, and submerging of local life styles. To argue abstractly that integration increases the possibilities of peace is not likely to make much impact on those who see their language, religion, customs, or occupations threatened by foreign penetration.[10]

The argument thus cuts both ways at once. And what goes for the dynamics of contemporary international politics as a whole also seems to apply to many specific societies. Fouad Ajami's recent analysis of the "Arab Predicament," for example, takes up the familiar theme of a "fractured tradition," one caught between "the claims of authenticity and the realities of independence." "In societies of acute cultural dualism, the relatively modernized sectors lay claim to modernity and feel embarrassed about their more backward brethren. Meanwhile, the claim of the more traditional culture is that of orthodoxy and authenticity. But when the claims of the modernized sector become increasingly hollow, the traditions reassert themselves." For Ajami, it is precisely this that has recently given a certain "comparative advantage" to Islam, enabling it to "assert itself and its uniqueness at a time when technology is seemingly blurring distinctions between cultures, when models of development tantalize people with promises that in the end they fail to deliver." In Ajami's view, in fact, neither the reading of history as a simple march to modernity, nor as one that sees cultures obstinately refusing to be universalized, is adequate; "there is around us as much intoxication with machines and gadgets as there is cultural archeology--people busy trying to revalidate once discredited traditions and revive once-forgotten symbols. There is both a submission to a dominant culture and a revolt against it."[11]

VIII

There are many ways of cutting into the analysis of culture and ideology in political life. In the context of international politics, it has seemed to me to be most useful to pose the issues in terms of the dialectics of universalism and pluralism as a way of making some connections with other major aspects of international political theory. Indeed, given that international political theory has itself recently been the subject of a surge of interest and renewal,[12] it seems important to suggest that theoretical discourse about international politics could benefit substantially from an increased sensitivity to its own cultural horizons and ideological functions.

The essays that follow approach this theme from several different directions. Different essays will undoubtedly attract very different sympathies. Contradictions between essays may raise doubts and questions, encourage further speculation, and suggest other ways of posing the problem of future world order. At a time when there is such a disjunction between the importance of global political issues and the scarcity of serious consideration of what this implies for our inherited categories of understanding, the tensions embodied in these essays may encourage not only a more theoretically informed discourse about world order, but also one that is more critically aware of its own participation in the creation of a problematic present.

There are also many specific topics that are directly relevant to this theme. Some, like the resurgence of nationalism and the reassertion of Islam in the political life of some societies, have themselves been the subject of rapidly expanding literatures. No attempt has been made here to survey the wide range of cultural and ideological forces that are conspicuous in modern world politics. Rather, the intention has been to draw cultural and ideological questions further into the ongoing debates about contemporary world order and the possibilities of future transformation.

In pursuit of this goal, the essays are organized in four general groups. The first group focuses on the international system as a whole. These essays raise the general question of the importance of cultural issues in modern world politics and suggest widely contrasting responses to it. Ali Mazrui argues that the history of the international system has revolved around a deeply structured "moving frontier of cultural exclusivity." By contrast, R. J. Vincent's emphasis on the significance of "race" in modern world politics is highly qualified by his insistence on the priority of other factors. Immanuel Wallerstein's discussion of "civilizations" emphasizes their relationship to developing modes of production in a capitalist world economy. And Joseph

Camilleri addresses the underlying theme of the relation between universal and plural in terms of the tension between the central focus of international politics--the state--and the contemporary international division of labor. Although the theoretical orientations underlying these four essays are quite diverse, they all draw attention to the complex relationship between cultures, economies, and states as a critical point of departure.

The next group of essays focuses on particular states and cultures and on the way in which they seek to absorb and resist the hegemonic cultural forms of contemporary world order, to reassert other traditions, and to generate alternative visions of the future. Celso Furtado, unlike most other *dependencia* theorists, argues that it is futile to resist the cultural unification of the world being brought about by the modern system of communication and by the force of example of a high standard of living in industrialized countries. By contrast, Anouar Abdel-Malek countenances the renaissance of Egypt and the Arab-Islamic cultural area in the face of the penetrating impact of the West in general and the Camp David Accords in particular. And Ashis Nandy draws on the experience of India and the insights of Gandhi and cultural psychology in order to explore the close bond between the cultures of the imperial powers and those of the periphery.

International political theory itself is the focus of the third section. Here the essays explore both the way in which the issues of culture and ideology have been handled in the literature on international relations and the way in which international political theory itself can be considered as an ideological discourse. My own essay surveys some of the theoretical issues raised by recent challenges to the global hegemony of Western modernity and raises the problem of the cooptation of dissent. R. N. Berki poses the issues in terms of the difficulties encountered by the Marxian tradition in coming to terms with international relations in general and the "national question" in particular. Mark Blasius examines the term "world order" as a form of discourse, as a relationship of "power/knowledge" in the sense developed in the writings of Michel Foucault. And Robert Cox portrays the development of international relations theory in the context of the transition from *Pax Britannica* to *Pax Americana* and suggests that thinking about future world order requires a deeper understanding of the basic processes at work in the development of social forces and forms of state and in the structure of the global political economy.

The final section brings a number of these themes together in order to address the contemporary debates about peace and peace movements. My own analysis uses the universal-plural theme to examine the relationship between hegemonic and counter-hegemonic discourse in the

critique of contemporary militarism in the West.   Then
Rajni Kothari reflects on the possibilities of survival
in an age of transformation in terms of his long-standing
pluralist concern with the primacy of Third World
resistance to global hegemony in any strategy of global
transformation.   The dialectical motif is central.   To
pose an abstract opposition between universalism and
pluralism is to remain trapped in a timeless present,
within a universe of frozen essences, within a puzzle
that simply is.   Such puzzles are resolved only in
history, in the coming into being of some new integration
and differentiation through human practice.

My own view is that we are indeed in an era of very
rapid change; that we cannot hope to understand this
change only in terms of Western experience and
categories; that a dialogue of civilizations is therefore
essential; that it is misleading to view contemporary
events as evidence of either a process of universal
modernization or pluralistic fragmentation; that the
specific forms in which the dialectic between
universalism and pluralism will occur cannot be
understood apart from a continuing tension between the
state and the global economy; and that even allowing for
the importance of the state and the global division of
labor, cultural and ideological forms can often maintain
a certain autonomy from them, an autonomy with both
repressive and emancipatory potential.   Consequently, in
a global age it becomes necessary "both to acknowledge
the limitations of the Western-centrist conceptual
apparatus and sustain the demand for universalism."[13]   If
there are to be future world orders, a struggle with this
issue seems to me to be unavoidable.

NOTES

1.   In recognition that they have come to be
understood differently within different styles of
analysis, the concepts of "culture" and "ideology" are
used here in a fairly loose sense.   They are assumed to
be closely related to other terms like "consciousness"
and "subjectivity," and newer terms like "signification,"
"representation," and "discourse."   For a useful general
discussion, see Jorge Larrain, The Concept of Ideology
(London: Hutchinson, 1979).
2.   For sharply contrasting approaches to the
analysis of contemporary world politics, see as examples
Hedley Bull, The Anarchical Society: A Study of Order in
World Politics (London: Macmillan, 1977); Richard Falk,
Samuel S. Kim, and Saul H. Mendlovitz, eds., Towards a
Just World Order (Boulder, Colo.:   Westview Press, 1982);
and Samir Amin, G. Arrighi, A. G. Frank, and I.
Wallerstein, Dynamics of Global Crisis (New York:
Monthly Review Press, 1982).

3. Perry Anderson, *Lineages of the Absolutist State* (London: New Left Books, 1974), p. 422.

4. Joseph Needham, *Science and Civilization in China* (seven volumes in twelve parts) (Cambridge: Cambridge University Press, 1954-); M.G.S. Hodgeson, *The Venture of Islam,* 3 vols. (Chicago: University of Chicago Press, 1974).

5. John Dunn, *Western Political Theory in the Face of the Future* (Cambridge: Cambridge University Press, 1979), pp. 78-79.

6. R. J. Vincent, "The Factor of Culture in the Global International Order," in *Yearbook of World Affairs* (London: Stevens and Sons, 1980), p. 256.

7. Edward W. Said, *Orientalism* (New York: Pantheon, 1978), pp. 7-8.

8. V. G. Kiernan, *The Lords of Human Kind: European Attitudes to the Outside World in the Imperial Age* (London: Weidenfeld and Nicolson, 1969).

9. Sadik Jalal al-'Azm, "Orientalism and Orientalism in Reverse," *Khamsin* 8 (1981):5-26.

10. K. J. Holsti, "Change in the International System: Interdependence, Integration and Fragmentation," in O. R. Holsti et al., eds., *Change in the International System* (Boulder: Westview Press, 1980), p. 48.

11. Fouad Ajami, *The Arab Predicament* (Cambridge: Cambridge University Press, 1981), pp. 171-172.

12. *See* as examples W. B. Gallie, *Philosophers of Peace and War* (London: Cambridge University Press, 1978); Andrew Linklater, *Men and Citizens in the Theory of International Relations* (London: Macmillan, 1982); Michael Donelan, ed., *The Reason of States* (London: George, Allen and Unwin, 1978); James Mayall, ed., *The Community of States* (London: George, Allen and Unwin, 1982); Charles Beitz, *Political Theory and International Relations* (Princeton, N.J.: Princeton University Press, 1979); Stanley Hoffman, *Duties Beyond Borders* (Syracuse, N.Y.: Syracuse University Press, 1981); E.B.F. Midgely, *The Natural Law Tradition and the Theory of International Relations* (London: Elek Books, 1975); and R.B.J. Walker, *Political Theory and the Transformation of World Politics,* World Order Studies Program, Occasional Paper No. 8 (Princeton, N.J.: Princeton University, Center of International Studies, 1980).

13. Anouar Abdel-Malek, *Civilizations and Social Theory* (Albany: State University of New York Press, 1981), p. 26.

PART 2

Cultures, Economies, and States

The Moving Cultural Frontier of World Order: From Monotheism to North-South Relations

Ali A. Mazrui

DICHOTOMOUS FRAMEWORK OF WORLD ORDER PERCEPTIONS

The "us/them" confrontation is the most persistent theme in world order perceptions. The dichotomy can take a variety of forms--the native versus the foreigner, the friend versus the foe, the familiar versus the strange, the Orient versus the Occident, the East versus the West, the North versus the South, the developed versus the developing countries, and so on. This dichotomous framework of world order perceptions amounts to an iron law of dualism, a persistent conceptualization of the world in terms of "us" and "them." To what extent is this mode of thinking a product of culture? Is it inevitable? Are we prisoners of dualism?

My first proposition is that in most, if not all, parts of the world, the culture of *politics* (though not necessarily of economics) tends towards dualism. The "us" versus "them" tendency is, in the political arena, almost universal. It could be friend versus foe, supporter versus opponent, ally versus adversary, conformist versus dissident, loyalist versus other. The range of cultural examples is also wide--from Whigs and Tories to the tensions between Confucians and legalists in the Chinese political tradition.

Although a certain level of dualism is inescapable in political thinking, the *degree* of dualism is culturally relative: societies vary considerably in how they perceive the wider world, with some paradigms more dualistic than others. My more complicated thesis, therefore, is that paradoxically, monotheism is particularly dualistic, though not uniquely so. There is a tendency in monotheism to divide the human race between believers and unbelievers, between the virtuous and the

----

Reprinted by permission from *Alternatives: A Journal of World Policy* 7:1, 1981.

sinful, between good and evil, between "us" and "them."
In the monotheistic tradition, there is only one God,
with no rival, who commands all loyalty and all
obedience. The lines begin to be drawn precisely because
one is either for or against God.

In contrast, polytheistic religions like those found
in parts of Africa and Asia are more tolerant. To some
degree, this tolerance stems from the readiness to
accommodate additional gods: so what is an extra god
between friends? Hardly any religious wars were fought
in Africa before the intrusion of Islam and Christianity.
African traditional religions permitted different ethnic
groups to have their own gods, and divine plurality was
the order of the day.

Yet to suggest that all religions are either
monotheistic or polytheistic is to commit the sin of
dualism. Many religions in India and parts of Africa
incorporate both monotheistic and polytheistic elements.
And a religion like Zoroastrianism could be regarded as
diatheistic--having more than one but fewer than three
gods.

What is clear is that the Judeo-Christian-Islamic
paradigm is more dichotomous than the paradigms normally
encountered in polytheistic cultures. The three Middle
Eastern religions are also all monotheistic. Is there a
causal link between their tendency to dichotomize and
their monotheism? Is there a link between the powerful
idea of one universal God and the dangerous dualism of
"us" versus "them?"

A major purpose of this essay is to demonstrate the
strong tendency toward the paradigm of bipolarity which
is manifested in monotheistic dualism and to explore its
impact on contemporary world politics and international
relations. Our second concern is to try to demonstrate
that at the international level the class structure of
the world is often defined in cultural rather than
economic terms. The third thrust of our analysis is to
illustrate how, in the absence of world government, the
idea of "community" at the transnational level has come
to be defined in terms of shared values and culture
rather than shared political authority. There is indeed
a cultural theme at the center of the history of the
international system--complete with a moving frontier of
cultural exclusivity. Let us now turn to these theses in
greater detail.

THE ORIGINS OF SACRED ORDER

We mentioned earlier that the dual paradigm in world
order thinking has been shaped by two factors--by the
culture of politics, which tends to dichotomize, and by
the impact of monotheism on world culture. The two
ideas--culture of politics and monotheism--were fused in

the earlier versions of Judaism, Christianity, and Islam. God was conceived in the image of the king, often complete with a throne. Monotheistic thought in these three religions, then, not only anthropomorphized God but also royalized Him with terms like "majesty" and the "kingdom of God" central to religious discourse. The emphasis on the oneness of God tended to attract the kingly metaphor, a unique throne. The universe thus became one massive imperial order.

It would also seem that the God of these three monotheistic religions had a royal court of his own. The courtiers were angels, usually committed to continuous flattery of the king. Hymns and prayers emphasized that the king was almighty, omnipotent, omniscient, all-powerful--Glory be to God, Hallelujah! But, like most royal courts, God's court was not without intrigue. The only intrigue which had been recorded in *human* annals in any detail was the one which culminated in Satan's rebellion. Satan, jealous of the creation of Adam, finally found the will to rebel against the culture of constant flattery, constant prayer and devotion, and unmitigated submissiveness to the king. If the English poet John Milton, is to be believed, Satan was driven to conclude that: "Better to reign in Hell than serve in Heaven!"

The paradigm of dichotomy, so characteristic of the culture of politics, is captured in that line from *Paradise Lost*. Indeed, the very dichotomy of Heaven and Hell is part of the grand divide between rewards and sanctions which characterizes political authority. The notion of loyalty to the king leading to heavenly rewards, and treason to God leading to damnation and hellfire, was a stark polarization embedded in those earlier versions of monotheistic divine order.

Of the three religions we mentioned, Christianity tried to balance the majesty of God with the humbleness of His Son. The Prince of Peace was born in a stable, preached among the poor, and praised both poverty and humility. It was a measure of Jesus' sacrifice that He descended from the ultimate Royal House to mingle with the meek on earth and to die for them. For God to send His own Son to earth was a major act of policy, a political act of momentous importance. It had to be balanced with another major political act here on earth--the sentencing of Jesus to crucifixion. But here Christian dualism gets intermingled with the concept of trinity, posing problems of political authority. The idea of three-in-one and one-in-three provides us with God the Father, God the Son, and God the Holy Ghost. But one momentous Friday, God the Son was crucified. Was there a crisis of authority in the universe? Are we to say that for three cataclysmic days, when Jesus was dead, the universe as a whole was under the majesty of only two-thirds of God--one of which was a ghost? The tendency to think of the relationship between God and the universe in terms of majestic authority should have created a crisis of legitimacy for those three days when part of the king was dead.

Islam, a younger religion than Christianity but one which honors Jesus as a prophet, argues that trinity was an invention of overenthusiastic followers of Jesus; Jesus, Islam asserts, never claimed to be Son of God. Monotheism in Islam is uncompromising.

Islam is also uncompromising in the majesty it accords Allah. Since there is no equivalent to a prince in rags on earth, descending from Heaven, the majesty of the being is not tempered by the humility of an offspring. Islam, therefore, has a greater propensity for dichotomizing than Christianity.

Furthermore, the culture of politics has conditioned Islam more directly than it has affected Christian doctrine. This is partly because the founder of Islam, unlike the founders of most great religions, underwent upward political mobility in his lifetime and became a head of state. Whereas Jesus and Buddha were, according to their followers, princes who decided to descend to the level of the common people and to teach them uncommon things, Muhammad was a humble camel driver who lived to become head of state and to lay the foundations of an empire here on earth.

One consequence of Muhammad's upward political mobility was the need for a system of law and judicial order. The system thus devised was the Shari'a, the Islamic Law. Muhammad's political role stood in clear contrast to the role of Jesus, assumed as founder of Christianity. After all, if the main mission of a founder of a religion is self-sacrifice, with a crucifixion serving to underscore atonement, there is no need to devise an elaborate system of social and political control for society. On the contrary, Jesus' crucifixion was at best a judgment on the existing laws of a particular society; it was not a blueprint for an alternative judicial order.

The prophet of Islam, on the other hand, had to rule and exercise authority; the innocent had to be protected, the guilty had to be discouraged or punished, and society had to be strengthened. The Shari'a was born: a system of vice and virtue, crime and punishment, reward and sanction--that was at once one of the glories of Islam and one of its shackles. The trend towards dualism, so characteristic of monotheism and the culture of politics, was consolidated in Islam by the political success of the prophet Muhammad and his immediate successors.

Judaism is, of course, as monotheistic as Islam, and more so than Christianity, since Judaism is not as encumbered by the doctrine of three-in-one and one-in-three. The tendency towards dichotomizing and dualism is also strong in both Jewish history and Jewish doctrine.

It certainly conditions the Jewish paradigm of identity--
Jews on the one side, and Gentiles on the other.

The identity crisis of Jews confronting the rest of
the human race has taken a variety of forms over the
centuries and has been reinforced by the exodus from
Palestine, the general Jewish dispersal, and the
historical experience of discrimination and martyrdom.
Political Zionism in its modern manifestation was born
partly as a dichotomy between a Jewish "us" and a Gentile
"them." There had to be a Jewish state to protect the
Jews against the world. Hitler's holocaust vindicated
some of these Jewish fears. Zionism gathered
momentum--and Israel was born.

The tragedy of dichotomizing continued. Could not
Jews live in Palestine without partitioning the
territory? For the Jews, the answer was no--there had to
be a separate Jewish state. Of course, the
practicalities of creating a separate state were more
complicated than the doctrines. On balance, many
Zionists believed in a total dichotomy so that ideally
there would be no Arabs at all in the land of Israel. To
paraphrase Rudyard Kipling: "Jews are Jews and Arabs are
Arabs--and never the twain shall meet!"

But in practice there were too many Arabs still in
the land of Palestine. Even after partition, and the
efforts of many Zionist zealots to frighten Arab peasants
out of Israel, an Arab presence in the new land of the
Jews remained. The Zionist dichotomies failed to
accomplish complete purification.

Within Israel, the culture of politics was
influenced by the theocratic heritage of monotheism.
Jehovah was king. Citizenship in the Israeli state was
in part religiously defined and the law of Return of
Israel offered the embrace of citizenship to all those
professing the genuine Jewish faith all over the world.[1]

The general laws of Israel are, on the whole, in the
tradition of Western liberal democracy rather than
centralized theocracy. But the idea that the state is
under some kind of divine jurisdiction has influenced the
political culture of Israeli society; sometimes it is
accepted literally by right wing parties and movements,
and by leaders like Menachim Begin. Once again, the
dichotomizing tendency in the culture of politics,
combined with the anthropomorphic conception of God as
king within a monotheistic framework, have sharpened the
dualism of "us" and "them."

But to what extent have these tendencies affected
the wider international and world order? It is to this
transnational and global level of analysis that we now
turn.

TOWARDS GLOBALIZING THE SACRED ORDER

Of the three monotheistic religions under review in
this essay, Judaism has had a less direct impact on the
existing world order than Islam or Christianity.
Indirect Jewish influences have been diverse, ranging
from the impact of Jewish jurists and thinkers upon
international law to repercussions surrounding the
creation of Israel and the introduction of Jewish
elements to Islamic and Christian doctrines, to the
tantalizing question of whether Karl Marx was one of the
last of the Jewish prophets. There can therefore be
little doubt that Judaism has been a major contributory
force to the world of rules and ideas as we know it
today. But in terms of direct impact on the structure of
the world system as it exists, Christianity has been a
far more fundamental force, with Islam trailing
significantly behind as a secondary force.

In Islam, the trend towards dichotomizing at the
international level took the form of a division of the
world into *Dar el Islam* (the Abode of Islam) and *Dar el
Harb* (the Abode of War). The Abode of Islam was, by
definition, governed by shared values and principles and
by shared allegiance to that ultimate of all sovereigns,
God. Within the world of Islam, the rules of
intersocietal relations assumed the bonds of community.
Indeed, Muslims all over the world were supposed to
constitute an *Umma*--a community and a people--with the
culture of Islam serving as the bond of commonality.

As for the Abode of War, its meaning is close to
Thomas Hobbes's view, many centuries after the founding
of Islam, that where there is no shared sovereign,
conditions amount to a state of war. Every man is for
himself, with the persistent danger that the life of man
might become "nasty, brutish and short." Hobbes was
interested more in civil society than in the broader
world community as a whole, but his conception of the
state of war has often been internationalized. It has
indeed been suggested that the world system, in the
absence of a world government, is characterized by
conditions amounting to an immanent state of war. Under
this state, in Hobbes's terms, people need not actually
fight. The main question is whether, in the absence of
the leviathan and of shared rules, war is the final
resort. Similarly, *Dar el Harb* assumed that lands not
governed by shared principles, and not recognizing shared
allegiance to the one God, were potential theaters of
war.

Future Islamic jurists attempted to modify the
strong dichotomy in Islamic international law between *Dar
el Harb* and *Dar el Islam*. Intermediate categories were
sometimes devised, partly to allow for special alliances
between Islam and friendly non-Muslims, and partly to
accommodate the distinctive conditions in places like

India where Hindu and Muslim rulers constituted a complex pattern of subcontinental relationships.

The division of the world in this manner may be a living residual element in the political thinking of rulers like the Ayatollah Khomeini of Iran and Muammar Gaddafy of Libya. In less stark forms, the dichotomy may underlie even the more peaceful Islamic movements and the global Islamic conference that came into being in recent years. The "us" and the "them" persists as an aspect of Islamic political culture.

The dichotomous tendency of Islamic international law has its equivalent in Western international law. It is worth remembering that the origins of the present international system as a whole, including contemporary international law and its usages, go back to Europe and its culture. Originally, the polarized stratification of the world was, at least in part, religious. World order was for a while perceived as an order of Christian faith: international law was for Christendom. There was a time when community in Europe was defined, not merely in terms of shared values and culture, but also in terms of the supreme power of the Pope and, in a substantial part of Europe, of this Emperor or that one. In other words, communal ties included shared political and religious authority, which could be traced to some extent to Roman Emperor Constantine the Great's conversion to Christianity in the seventh century.

Much later, the Christian nations of Europe formulated rules of international conduct, but they perceived themselves as *Christian* nations. As B.V.A. Roling once put it:

> Those Christian Nations emanated from the spiritual unity prevailing in Western Europe before the Reformation. After the overthrow of the supreme power of Pope and Emperor and the acceptance of the concept of national sovereignty, the monarchs of Europe continued to consider themselves subject to God's Commandments and the law of nature . . . The Christian States considered themselves bound by Christian law. Christianity was the source of their standards. In addition, each determined the circle within which law should prevail: a different law, or none at all, held good for relations with heathens. Finally, Christianity was the justification of the domination of other peoples.[2]

Roling traces the legalistic dichotomy between Christians and "heathens" at least to the Lateran Council of 1139. This forbade, *sub anathema,* the use of the crossbow among Christian knights, *adversos Christianos et Catholicos*. It was accepted that Christian standards did not apply to heathens and heretics.

Roling also refers to an interesting early

illustration of germ warfare. In 1649-1650, *Christians* decided to use "pestilential vapors" against the Turkish in Crete. They sent a certain Dr. Michelangelo. His mission was to infect the Turkish army with his "quintessence of the pest." This exercise in biological warfare was rationalized officially at the time by the old crusading argument: ". . . The usual considerations do not apply to the Turks who are enemies by religion, treacherous by nature and who have betrayed your excellencies."[3]

Implicit in all this is once again a dichotomy--this time between the Abode of Christianity and the Abode of War, a mirror reflection of *Dar el Islam* and *Dar el Harb.* And underlying that dualism is once again a definition of community based on shared values and faith. In Shakespeare's *Henry the Sixth,* Gloucester suggests that a sacred order is "the only means to stop the effusion of Christian blood." Gloucester reflects:

> . . . I always thought
> It was both impious and unnatural,
> That such immanity and blood strife
> Should reign among professors of one Faith.[4]

Dichotomization between Christian nations and barbarians of other faiths has persisted in different forms in the Western world, albeit in subtle ways. A former Dutch prime minister is reported to have wondered in Parliament how a Muslim or Hindu could really grasp the essence of aggression--since this judgment, according to him, required the sensibilities of Christian culture. An American diplomat, engaged in the quest for a solution to Arab-Israeli conflicts in the 1950s, inadvertently drifted into advising the Jews and Arabs "to settle the conflict in a true Christian spirit."[5] More recently, many Christians in the West have probably discovered that their attitudes to the Ayatollah Khomeini in Iran are very similar to the attitudes their grandfathers held in the 19th century towards the abstract "Turk."

What these situations reveal is not merely the relevance of culture to international polarization but also its relevance to international stratification. Polarization is a horizontal divide, a cleavage and possible confrontation which could be between equals. Stratification, on the other hand, is a vertical divide--a confrontation between the privileged and the underprivileged, the dominant and the oppressed, the higher in status and the lower. Our examples reflect an earlier phase of culturally defined international stratification. Then the pecking order existed on the basis of who believed what, rather than on the basis of who owned what. The international class structure was culturally derived rather than economically based--at least in those earlier days when religious solidarity was an explicit foundation of what was later to become the Law of Nations.

SECULARISM AND THE CIVILIZATIONAL HIERARCHY

But the cultural frontier of Western international law had in fact been moving--redefining the class divide. Instead of international law being a law for Christian nations, it became for a while a law for civilized nations--one of the costs of the secularization of world order. It is arguable that modern race consciousness has its origins in the decline of religion in Europe, since to some extent the development of race consciousness paralleled the evolution of the nation-state. Religious tensions in Europe between Catholics and Protestants first culminated in the treaty of Augsburg in 1555, which fused religion with sovereignty. The religion of the prince was deemed to be the religion of the principality; the king's faith was the faith of the kingdom. This was the famous doctrine of *Cu ius Regio Eius Religio*.

In reality, the decision to equate the religion of the king with the religion of the kingdom was a principle of no interference in the various princes' internal religious affairs. But this *modus vivendi* broke down when Europe undercut the agonies of the Thirty Years' War. Out of that war emerged the Treaty of Westphalia, which laid the foundations of the modern state system and the principles of modern conceptions of sovereignty. This secularization of allegiance (to the State rather than through the Church) which came with Westphalia led to secularization of *identity*.

Out of this parallel development emerged new theories of racial gradation and ethnic stratification. But, in the ultimate analysis, the great divide was between the civilized and the uncivilized, defined both in terms of a pecking order of cultures and a pecking order of pigmentation. Even such a devout Western lover of liberty as John Stuart Mill could argue that "barbarians" had no rights except the right to be converted into nations as rapidly as possible. As for the application of international law, this once again required not only a horizontal homogeneity of values, but also vertical equality of civilization. According to Mill:

> There is a great difference between the case in which the nations concerned are of the same, or something like the same, degree of civilization, and that in which one of the parties to the situation is of a high, and the other of a very low, grade of social improvement. To suppose that the same international customs, and the same rules of international morality, can obtain between one

civilized nation and another and between civilized
nations and barbarians, is a grave error, and one
which no statesman can fall into, however it may be
that those who, from a safe and unresponsible
position, criticize statesmen . . . To characterize
any conduct towards the barbarous people as a
violation of the Law of Nations only shows that he
who so speaks has never considered the subject.[6]

This approach to the dichotomy between civilization and
barbarism was by no means unique to liberalism. It also
characterized the thinking of those founding fathers of
modern radicalism, Karl Marx and Friedrich Engels.
Engels was delighted by the French conquest of Algeria.
He regarded it as an important and fortunate development
in the whole progress of civilization:

And the conquest of Algeria has already forced
the Bays of Tunis and Tripoli and even the Emperor
of Morocco, to enter upon the path of civilization.
. . All these nations of free barbarians look very
proud, noble, glorious at a distance, but only come
near them and you will find that they, as well as
the more civilized nations, are ruled by the lust of
Cain, and only employ ruder and more cruel means.
And after all, the modern bourgeois, with
civilization, industry, order, and at least relative
enlightenment following him, is preferable to the
feudal lord or to the marauding robber, with the
barbarian state of society to which they belong.[7]

Engels' partner, Karl Marx, was more sophisticated in his
defense of British rule in India. Marx saw Western
imperialism as an engine of progress in Asia and Africa.
On 25 January, 1853, Karl Marx made the following
observation:

English interference [in India] . . . produced
the greatest and, so to speak the truth, the only
social revolution ever heard of in Asia. Now,
sickening as it must be to human feeling to witness
myriads of industrial, patriarchal and inoffensive
social organizations disorganized and dissolved into
their units, thrown into a sea of woes, and their
individual members losing at the same time their
ancient form of civilization and their hereditary
means of subsistence, we must not forget that these
idyllic village communities, inoffensive though they
may appear, had always been the solid foundation of
oriental despotism, that they restrained the human
mind within the smallest possible compass, making it
the unresisting tool of superstition, enslaving it
beneath traditional rules, depriving it of all
grandeur and historical energies . . . England, it

is true, in causing a social revolution in
Hindoostan, was activated by only the vilest of
interests, and was stupid in her manner of enforcing
them. But that is not the question. The question
is: Can mankind fulfill its destiny without a
fundamental revolution in the social state of Asia?
If not, whatever may have been the crimes of
England, she was the unconscious tool of history in
bringing about the revolution.

But then whatever bitterness the spectacle of
the crumbling of an ancient world may have for our
personal feelings, we have the right to exclaim with
Goethe:

Should this torture then torment us?
Since it brings us great pleasure?
Was not through the rule of Timur
Souls devoured without measure?

Karl Marx later formulated his own version of "the Dual
Mandate" in Asia:

England has to fulfill a double mission in
India: one destructive, the other regenerating--the
annihilation of all Asiatic societies, and the
laying of the material foundations of Western
society in Asia.[8]

The major difference between Karl Marx and Rudyard
Kipling, the author of "The White Man's Burden," is that
Kipling made a virtue out of the unintended constructive
consequences of imperialism, whereas Marx recognized the
developmental effects of British rule in India as
primarily amoral and incidental. Rudyard Kipling took
this developmental side effect of imperialism to a level
of self-righteousness.

What emerges from this comparison between John
Stuart Mill, on one side, and Marx and Engels, on the
other, is a shared belief in the superiority of Western
civilization and the shared conviction that the civilized
had a right to dominate and even exploit the barbarians.
Once again the dualistic paradigm was at
play--articulated, on one side, by a highly secularized
product of monotheistic Westernism (John Stuart Mill)
and, on the other, by a highly secularized product of
Hebraic intellectualism (Marx).

Cultural stratification did lay the foundations of
imperialism not just in Algeria and India but elsewhere
in Asia and Africa. Even as late as World War II,
Winston Churchill and Franklin Roosevelt could sign the
Atlantic Charter affirming the rights of peoples
everywhere to control their own destiny. And yet, the
same Churchill, when questioned in the House of Commons
in London soon after, could sharply differentiate between

the freedom of the Belgians under the Nazis--a freedom which needed to be encouraged--and freedom of the colonized peoples of the British Empire, which Churchill regarded as an entirely different matter. Not very long after, when confronted with the demands of India to become independent, Winston Churchill, the signatory of the Atlantic Charter with its ringing acknowledgment of the rights of self-determination, could nevertheless refuse to "preside over the liquidation of the British Empire."

Once again, the basic dichotomy between the "civilized" and the "uncivilized" was at play even if no longer articulated in those terms. Community and stratification were culturally defined once again.

THE PRINCE OF PEACE AT THE UNITED NATIONS

Because the term "civilized nations" was used to justify European imperialism, it began to decline in public usage with the rise of nationalism in Asia and Africa. The new assertiveness of the colonized peoples and their sense of dignity gradually discouraged Europeans from talking about them as "barbarians" and "heathens."

A related factor was the revolution in communications. When, in the 19th century, people like John Stuart Mill and Karl Marx discussed Indians, other Asians, and Africans as "uncivilized," they were sure that much of the conversation was almost exclusively among Westerners themselves. Literacy was still very low in Africa and Asia, and books written in England were not likely to constitute bedtime reading in the Orient. Nor were there news agencies that transmitted public utterances made in London or New York to radio listeners or to newspaper readers in Lagos or Bombay. In terms of blunt racialistic language, Europeans in the 19th century could comfortably speak their minds about nonwhite people without risking the embarrassment of reaction from those people. International eavesdropping in the 19th century was significantly more modest than it has since become.

By the time the United Nations Organization was formed in 1945, it no longer made sense to think of restricting membership to "civilized nations." It was also much too late to return to the old language of "Christian nations." Yet, in a sense, here was a partial return to Jesus as the Prince of Peace since the Charter of the United Nations designated the membership as "peace loving nations"--a concept first used in the Moscow Declaration on General Security on 30 October, 1943. But the United Nations' emphasis on peace went beyond the concept of "peace loving nations." Those who framed the Charter in 1945 first declared their determination to "save succeeding generations from the scourge of war,"

and then, only secondarily, to "reaffirm faith in
fundamental human rights, in the dignity and worth of the
human person, and the equal rights of men and women, and
of nations large and small."

Whether the framers of the Charter realized it or
not, their document betrayed a historic Christian
tendency to regard peace and "love" as an answer to the
scourge of war. Indeed, the English wording of "peace-
loving" encompasses the two most central concepts in
Christian ethics--precisely, peace and love. Justice, on
the other hand, is quite often a different framework of
reasoning. The ethic of turning the other cheek is
consistent with the pursuit of peace and love, but it may
seldom be consistent with the pursuit of social justice.

The God of Christianity has doctrinally been
regarded as a god of love, and his Son has been regarded
as a Prince of Peace. The God of Islam and Judaism, on
the other hand, has been more of a god of justice--ready
to invoke sanctions against violators and capable of
purposeful ruthlessness in defense of divine justice and
order.

When the French rose up in arms against their own
ancien regime in 1789, they wanted to tear down the
Church as well. They did tear down the monasteries that
had encouraged the poor to turn the other cheek while the
rich puffed their own cheeks in luxurious living. The
French Revolution was almost as anticlerical as it was
antimonarchical.

When the Russians overthrew their own Czarist
imperial system in the October revolution of 1917, they
were rebelling against their nobility in an idiom which
was also profoundly distrustful of religion. In the
poetry of Karl Marx: "Religion is a sigh of the
oppressed creature, the sentiment of a heartless world,
and the soul of souless conditions. It is the opium of
the people."

Both Czarist Russia and prerevolutionary France were
Christian countries. Popular rebellion against
injustice, therefore, encompassed rebellion against
religious institutions as well.

Iran, on the other hand, is a Muslim country.
Popular rebellion in 1979 against political injustice was
far from being simultaneously a rebellion against
religious institutions. On the contrary, the call to
revolution against the Shah was often couched in fervent
religious terms. The god of justice in Islam encouraged
at times resort to arms in defense of Muslim justice.
The god of love in Christianity, on the other hand, was
more comfortable with the doctrine of loving one's enemy
and turning the other cheek.

In reality, Christian nations (as distinct from
devout individual Christians) have never been all that
"peace-loving." Many use the idiom of Christianity to
disarm their own people, to "pacify" rebellious natives

and, thereby, to promote acceptance of imperial rule.
Even the idea of giving to Caesar what is Caesar's and to
God what is God's was often a call to obedience and
submission to Caesar--in the name of God! Similarly,
when the United Nations came into being, the language of
peaceful solutions was often invoked to legitimize a
status quo in which those already possessing might could
secure their privileges while the "have-nots" would be
encouraged to accept their lot for the time being.

The United States also used the concept of "peace-
loving nations" as a basis for excluding the People's
Republic of China from the United Nations for more than
20 years; China's seat on the Security Council, complete
with the big power veto that went with it, was allowed to
be occupied by Taiwan throughout that period. In debates
concerning the credentials of the People's Republic of
China for occupying that seat, the United States--year
in, year out--invoked the argument that the People's
Republic was not a "peace-loving nation," and was not
therefore the right "China" for the United Nations.
After all, so the argument went, Article IV of the United
Nations Charter restricted membership to those countries
which were "peace-keeping."

But as more and more countries from Africa and Asia
became members of the United Nations, a normative change
was discernible both in voting patterns and in the
emphasis placed on certain Charter provisions. For the
new nations of Africa and Asia, issues of social justice
were more important than issues of peace and war
prevention. The Prince of Peace at the United Nations
was demoted as the world body became culturally and
ideologically more diverse. Instead of trying to keep
out the People's Republic of China on the argument that
it was not peace-loving, the majority of the members were
now more inclined to keep out the Republic of South
Africa on the argument that it was guilty of gross
injustices. Even Israel has, from time to time, been a
target of demands for exclusion; but, in the Israeli
case, the basis for attack has rested on issues both of
peace and of social justice. Was Israel peace-loving
enough? This question echoed the earlier vocabulary of
the Messiah of Peace. Was Israel sufficiently respectful
of human rights and social justice? The second question
revealed the new concerns of the formerly colonized
nations of Africa, Asia and the rest of the Third World.

But issues of social justice go beyond colonialism,
racism and military occupation; they also include
economic dimensions. And here the tradition of
dichotomization has continued. Under the new dualism,
the world is perceived in terms of developed countries,
on one side, and developing countries, on the other.
From a world system involving Christians versus non-
Christians, civilized versus noncivilized, peace-loving
versus non-peace-loving, we have now entered the world of

development as the central divide in the configuration of the globe.

Outside the United Nations, issues of war and peace, of course, remain quite fundamental. UN Secretary-General Kurt Waldheim himself reminded the world in June 1980 that it was spending a million dollars a minute in armaments, and had acquired the capacity to destroy the human race ten times over. The imperative of being "peace-loving" had in this sense become more vital than in the days of the Prince of Peace. And yet, the causes of war were not simply attitudinal; they were also structural.

The most dangerous arena from the point of view of peace is the arena of East-West relations. This is a dichotomy within a dichotomy. The world of communism occupies one side, and the world of capitalism the other. Since each accuses the other of "war-mongering," the idiom of peace is characteristic of the rhetoric on both parts of the Northern hemisphere--Northwest (the capitalist world) and Northeast (the Soviet Union and its allies).

At the height of the cold war, the United States regarded the Soviet Union as fundamentally expansionist, and communism as fundamentally aggressive. At the beginning of the 1950s, the United States was sufficiently in control of the United nations to rally the world body in defense of the independence of South Korea. When the Security Council appeared paralyzed by the Soviet veto, the United States took the issue to the General Assembly, and successfully invented the idea of "uniting for peace." The world body became the banner for defense for South Korea against the incursion of North Korea and the Chinese, and entered a regional war in the name of world peace.

Since then, the United Nations has taken part in a variety of other situations of conflict, but not in the direct combatant role that it assumed in Korea. In defense of peace, major international assignments for the world body have ranged from involvement in the Middle East to efforts to save the Congo (now Zaire) from chaos, to Cyprus, to General Assembly censure of the Soviet invasion of Afghanistan.

But the United States and its allies have by no means monopolized the language of peace. The Soviet Union has managed to infuse both an ideology of revolution and a rhetoric of peace into the proceedings. A variety of recommendations have emerged from Moscow over the years concerning proposed principles of "peaceful coexistence." The Soviet Union has also often paid lip service to the goal of total and complete disarmament, though never with an adequate acceptance of the type of safeguards that would be needed to monitor such a process. The value of peace remains honored in words, though not always in deeds. The world needs peace as a moral ideal more than ever--since the world's very survival may depend upon it. But the stratification system of the globe is no longer conceived in terms of peace-loving nations on one side and peace-haters on the other. The central dichotomy has now become technological; it is between developed and developing.

It is to this last dichotomy that we now turn.

MONOTHEISM AND DEVELOPMENT

If one looks at the history of the international system in the last 600 years, there has been a transition from dualism based on faith to dualism based on know-how. The world which distinguished *Dar el Harb* from *Dar el Islam,* Christian nations from heathen, still puts emphasis on confessional credentials for participation within a communal system. But the world which distinguishes between developed and developing countries now invokes credentials of technical know-how and expertise.

If one looks at the geographical area designated in the 19th century by the term "civilized world," it still strongly coincides with what today is called the developed world; the barbarians and heathens of the 19th century are today the developing societies of Africa and Asia. And even if one went further back in time and looked at the word *Christendom* as conceived in the 17th century before the signing of the Treaty of Westphalia, one would be talking about a considerable fraction of what is today the industrialized world.

We may therefore say that the transition from religious dualism to civilizational dualism to the developmental dualism has been direct. Once we allow for the fact that Europeans populated and "developed" much of the Western hemisphere, it is apparent that these terms apply to approximately the same geographical areas across the centuries.

What lies outside the straight transition of religion, civilization and technology is the dualism of peace. It is as if this particular component was not really a stage in a transition from the seventh century but was rather a continuing subtheme in global history, whose latest incarnation includes the role of the United Nations in areas of human conflict.

And yet, in another sense, even the latest cleavage based on technology has its origins in the years when the cleavage was based on religion. Modern technology was born out of modern capitalism, and modern capitalism was in part born out of the same causes which gave rise to religious wars in Europe. The Protestant revolution helped transform the value patterns in the economic domain of behavior, not merely in the religious domain. I find the Weberian thesis substantially persuasive--that there is a link between the rise of capitalism and the Protestant ethic. Protestantism helped make what was previously the sin of "avarice" morally respectable. Indeed, the pursuit of worldly success was now deemed to be a good way of measuring whether one was in good standing with the King of Kings. Piety was not manifested merely in prayer, but also in work and business. The Calvinistic notion of God was particularly monarchical. Human beings were subjects of the Lord, and in need of Grace; their fates were often sealed within the doctrine of predestination. Nevertheless, this doctrine did not become another version of fatalism because it was accompanied by a doctrine suggesting that people must struggle to discover whether they are among the saved. Evidence of salvation could take the form of prosperity and material success. In other words, responding to one's calling was an important part of the quest for salvation.

In addition, the puritanical factor in Calvinism prepared the way for economic accumulation. On the one hand, the pious were encouraged to acquire more and more; but, on the other, they were not encouraged to consume more and more. "Make money, but do not spend it!"--this seemed to be the ultimate commercial imperative operating within the Protestant ethic. Given that life-styles were supposed to be austere, the alternatives open to those who made more money were: (1) to save the surplus, (2) to reinvest it, and (3) to do both simultaneously. With this accumulation of capital and entrepreneurial drive, the stage was set in Europe for a capitalist takeoff. And as the capitalist revolution matured, the industrial revolution got under way as part of a cumulative process of developmental change.[9]

But it was not merely the rise of capitalism with which Protestantism seems to have been linked; it was also linked with the rise of modern science. In England, the Royal Society, overwhelmingly Protestant by the 17th century, was also disproportionately *Puritan*. The men of science in England seemed to be nonconformists--the majority being neither Catholic nor Anglican. Cambridge University became more scientifically oriented than Oxford, partly because it was more nonconformist in religious composition. The origins of the scientific bias, displayed by Cambridge in the modern period, may well lie in that phase of high Puritan influence exhibited in the 17th century.

In the United States, too, the Puritan influence on the growth of the scientific spirit was considerable. Part of the influence came through Cambridge University in England, described in that period as the *alma mater* of the Puritans (of the 20 leading Puritan clergymen in New England, 17 were graduates of Cambridge, and only three of Oxford). However, its educational program also felt this Puritan influence. The sciences in the United

States were certainly upheld better in Protestant than in Catholic institutions; within Protestant circles, the Puritan bias towards scientificity stood out.[10]

If there was a heavy Protestant factor in the scientific revolution, on one side, and also a disproportionate Protestant factor in the rise of capitalism, on the other, the two processes together (the mating of science with the economy) helped to create a technological momentum. The world of faith had interacted with the world of technical know-how and laid the foundations for this latest dichotomy in the global structure--the dichotomy between the developed and the underdeveloped, the technically knowledgeable and the technically preliterate. Western civilization is still triumphant--but the credentials of supremacy are technological rather than spiritual.

Two major challenges to the West have now emerged, one of which echoes the old Crusades. Islam, which has been undergoing a new resurgence on the world scene, is one challenge. The other is Marxism, which has been making new converts in the global seminaries of values.

As it happens, Islam is of course militantly monotheistic; Marxism is self-consciously atheistic. This new bipolarity captures the contemporary predicament of Western civilization as a whole--which indeed exists somewhere "between the sacred and the secular, the monotheistic and the atheistic."

The Islamic challenge to the West, because of its very nature, is a challenge from the sacred. The Marxist challenge to the West attempts to be a challenge from the secular. Islam seeks to reintroduce God to international relations, a partial return to a sacred world order. Marxism seeks to subtract capital from international relations, a quest to reverse the Protestant revolution. Islam's challenge to the West is the challenge from the South; it is vertical, since leaders of Islam are overwhelmingly Southern. Marxism's challenge to the West is a challenge from the East; it is horizontal, since leaders of old Marxism are overwhelmingly Northern. Islam's challenge to the West betrays concern for cultural authenticity; the Marxist challenge is ultimately inspired by economic equity.

But in the final analysis, the world of Islam, the world of Marxism and Western civiliztion are interrelated systems of values and ideas. Islam's challenge of the West is a challenge from a cousin. Western values and Islamic ideas were both profoundly conditioned and influenced by Judaism. In addition, Western values and Islamic scholarship were conditioned and influenced by the civilization of ancient Greece.

Marxism, on the other hand, is a *child* of the West. Karl Marx and Friedrich Engels were themselves Westerners and their theories and ideas emerged out of Western intellectual and economic history. In that sense, the confrontation between Marxism and Western civilization is between a parent and the offspring; it is an intergenerational conflict in the realm of ideas and values.

Simultaneously, the center of the economic world is still basically monotheistic in culture. The greatest exporters of oil are Muslims; the greatest importers of oil are Christians. The exporters include Saudi Arabia, the heartland of Sunni Islam, and Iran, the heartland of Shi'a Islam, as well as a majority of the rest of the members of the Organization of Petroleum Exporting Countries. The greatest importers of oil include Western Europe and the United States. Japan remains the striking exception to the rule that the greatest capitalist countries are also of Christian cultural persuasion. Again, apart from Japan, ultimate ledership in technology continues to coincide with cultures that were originally Christian. In turn, their need for energy continues to link them with countries which are self-consciously Islamic.

Technology seems destined to be the last cultural frontier of the first two millennia of the Christian era. Only a few more years are left of the second millennium. Christianity itself has declined in its heartland; that is, in the Western world. And yet the cultures of monotheism continue to cast a shadow on world events. The center of the world economy is still Christo-Islamic. Monotheism as a doctrine may no longer condition behavior and perspectives directly, but the heritage of dualism persists. The latest cultural frontier between the "haves" and the "have-nots" is, in the ultimate analysis, technological.

CONCLUSION

We have sought to demonstrate in this essay that there is a hidden cultural agenda in world order problems which ranges from dogma (both sacred and secular) to international stratification. A particularly important perceptual factor is the tendency towards dualism in the mode of identification--the culture of "us" and "them." The tendency towards two opposing foci, thus, did not begin with the cold war the the division of the world between capitalists and communists, but goes back to that basic dichotomizing tendency which some cultures emphasize more than others.

Although the cultural frontier of world order has indeed been moving, monotheism, weakened by the decline of religion generally, continues to cast its shadow over international relations and world affairs. As Western civilization has become increasingly secularized, its two greatest challenges have been, on one side, militant monotheism (Islam) and, on the other, self-conscious atheism (Marxism). But, as we pointed out, Marxism, Western civilization and Islam are interrelated. The dialectic in Marxism is dualistic; so is the constant tension between good and evil in both Christianity and Islam. Thus the map of world power today is a map covered by Islam, Western civilization, and Marxist systems. All three cultural universes betray the historic and normative impact of monotheism and its derivative patterns of cognition. "In the beginning was the Word, and the Word was of God, and the Word was God."

NOTES

1. The Black Falasha Jews of Ethiopia were for a long time denied recognition as genuine Jews. The Law of Return did not apply to them for many years. But their status was changed progressively in the course of the 1970s. On the other hand, ethnic Jews from Eastern Europe, who are often complete atheists, have enthusiastic access under the Law of Return.

2. B.V.A. Roling, *International Law in an Expanded World* (Amsterdam: Djambatan, 1960), pp. 17-18.

3. Sir George Clark, *War and Society in the 17th Century* (Cambridge: Cambridge University Press, 1958), p. 88. Cited by Roling, ibid., p. 18.

4. *Henry the Sixth,* Part I, Act V, Scene 1.

5. For the references to the former Dutch prime minister and the American diplomat goof, see Roling, *International Law in an Expanded World,* pp. 21-22.

6. John Stuart Mill, "A Few Words on Non-Intervention," in *Dissertations and Discussions,* Volume 3 (London, 1967), pp. 153-158.

7. Friedrich Engels, article for the *Northern Star* (English Chartist Newspaper), Volume XI, January 22, 1848.

8. Consult Marx, "The Future Results of British Rule in India (August 8, 1853)," Schlomo Aveniri, ed., *Marx on Colonialism and Modernization* (New York: Doubleday & Co., Anchor Books, 1969), pp. 94-95; 132-134. I am also greatly indebted to my former student, Dr. Rovan Locke, for stimulation and bibliographical guidance on Marx's theories of cultural stratification.

9. Max Weber, *The Protestant Ethic and the Spirit of Capitalism* (New York: Scribners, 1977); see also R. H. Tawney, *Religion and the Rise of Capitalism* (New York: New American Library, 1954).

10. Consult Robert K. Merton, *Social Theory and Social Structure* (New York: The Free Press, 1967), pp. 574-605.

CHAPTER 3

Race in International Relations

R. J. Vincent

Like sex in Victorian England, it has been said, race is a taboo subject in contemporary polite society. Conflicts or attitudes that to the simpleminded might appear to be self-evidently racial are explained away as class-based, or as difficulties attending immigration, or as responses to special local circumstances. Certainly, race relations are not an area in which political reputations are easily made, and outspokenness on the subject seems to be the preserve of those who have little to lose, their having either departed the scene or not yet arrived at it.

Yet beneath this wish to talk about something else, and perhaps in part explaining it, lurk the largest claims for the factor of race in politics, and the direst of forebodings about the future of race relations. As early as 1903 W.E.B. Du Bois was already expressing the problem of the twentieth century as the problem of "the colour line," and this has been a theme of pan-African congresses to the present day. A recent British prime minister, not noted for his proneness to exaggerate, is reported as having said "I believe the greatest danger ahead of us is that the world might be divided on racial lines. I see no danger, not even the nuclear bomb, which could be so catastrophic as that."[1] These instincts of politicians are fortified by academic analysis. John Rex, one of the most prominent writers in Britain on race relations, has gone so far as to predict that "for the next few centuries the problems which will preoccupy men politically more than any other will be problems which they subjectively define as problems of race."[2] Hugh Tinker, in one of the very few works on race in international politics, concludes that "Today, transcending everything (including even the nuclear

----

Reprinted by permission from *International Affairs* 58:4, 1982.

threat) there is the confrontation between the races."[3]

This paper is confined to an assessment of the place of race in international relations, in so far as it is possible to distinguish, in this regard, domestic from international politics. In any event, it may be argued that it is to the history of international relations, during the imperial expansion of Europe over at least the last two centuries, that one needs to refer to understand the contemporary significance of race in both domestic and international society. This is a task that is attended to in the second part of this article, after an attempt to clear the problem of definition out of the way. The third part of the article is concerned with the possibility of explanation rather than that of definition, and it seeks to measure race against class and nation as forces in international politics. The conclusion, with the benefit of the discussion of explanation, aims to describe and to assess the impact of the factor of race in international politics.

THE DEFINITION OF "RACE"

In both domestic and international politics race is now thought above all to be about colour. Race relations in modern Britain are taken to concern whites and blacks, not different groups of whites. Similarly, in international relations, the most prominent racial issue is that between whites and blacks in Southern Africa. But this is a comparatively recent development. The notion of race was in the nineteenth century used much more generally to depict, it seems, almost any social group. Charles Kingsley, for example, said both that "there is no more beautiful race in Europe than the wives and daughters of our London shopkeepers," and that the "valiant peasants between Halifax and Cheshire" were "the finest race in England."[4] Kingsley here was departing from a rather narrower sense of race already established, and bearing a closer relation than his own ideas to contemporary usage: namely, race used not merely to describe any group of people, but to set apart people of common descent. European history, told from a racial point of view, might, by making use of this definition, include an account of Frankish aristocrats justifying their rule over a bastard proletariat of Celts and Mediterraneans in France, and of the myth of a Norman yoke in English historiography which depicted anything fine about England as derivative from an Anglo-Saxon past.[5] The same racial mythology was available in the relations among European nations: "this island race," "the unspeakable Turk," "the Hun is at the gate!" Usage in this arena was, in turn, a preface to the racialisation of the world.[6]

This racialisation came about, it may be argued,

because the expansion of Europe coincided with the elaboration of the idea of racial inequality. In nineteenth-century Europe, what is now called, pejoratively, racialism, was widely thought to have a scientific basis rather than being the instinct of blimps and fanatics. The idea of discrete racial types took firm root and became the dominant explanation both of the variety of cultures and of the hierarchy among them. It was possible on physiological grounds alone, said the French writer and diplomat Gobineau, to distinguish three great and clearly marked types, the black, the yellow, and the white, and to arrange them in a scale with the lowest, the negro, being hardly more than a mere brute, the yellow race committing none of the strange excesses so common among negroes but tending to mediocrity in everything, and at the top the white race gifted with energetic intelligence, perseverance, an instinct for order and a love of liberty.[7]

Less repellent to the modern reader and more sophisticated were the later nineteenth-century ideas of social evolution influenced by Herbert Spencer's analogy between societies and organisms, and Darwin's account of the survival of the fittest in the animal world. Benjamin Kidd wrote that the road along which man had come was strewn with the wreckage of nations, races and civilisations. Social systems, like individuals, were organic growths seeming to be governed by laws of health and development. They flourished until displaced by more efficient systems. Weaker races gave way to the stronger through the effects of mere contact.[8] "The gradual extinction of inferior races," wrote Sir Charles Dilke, "is not only a law of nature, but a blessing to mankind."[9]

Dilke's law of nature would now be interpreted as a piece of imperial conceit that misled a civilisation ahead in some areas of human endeavour into visions of manifest destiny to rule the world. Biology, in the twentieth century, has eschewed not merely the idea of a hierarchy among the races, but also that of race itself. It has dealt instead with statistics about populations. "There are no races," we are told, "but only clines--gradients of change in measurable genetic characteristics."[10] The conventional wisdom as now distilled by UNESCO has as much diversity within the so-called races as between them; no coincidence between races and blood groups; factors grouped together and said to be transmitted en bloc in fact passed on independently and in varying degrees of association; and cultural advance as a more profound factor in human evolution than genetic inheritance.[11]

Race, according to this view, is a scientifically obsolete concept, and cannot be commandeered in the service of this or that vision of society. Like much conventional wisdom, the consensus this commands is not complete. Writers such as Professors Eysenck and Jensen arouse controversy by finding that there are differences between racial groups measurable by their performance in intelligence tests.[12] But in regard to the question of definition, neither the conventional wisdom dismissive of race, nor the objection to it which seems to accept the old categories without question,is very helpful. The difficulty with the rejection of the concept of race is that it would afford us no purchase on the popular notion of race as part of everyday belief and experience and therefore a piece of political data whether we like it or not. The difficulty with the acceptance of the old categories, racial types such as Caucasoid, Mongoloid and Negroid, because they seem plainly to capture the reality of physical difference among the peoples of the world, is the danger of making too much of these obvious but superficial differences, so that description masquerades as explanation. To observe, when black rioters confront white police, that the conflict is racial, is crudely to describe one aspect of it. Class, to refer back to the beginning of this discussion, may indeed be a better explanation, or the pressures of living in an inner city, or problems associated with immigration, and so on. The racial label has added little to our comprehension, explaining everything and nothing. For this reason, although she goes too far, one understands Ruth Benedict when she writes: "In order to understand race persecution . . . To understand race conflict . . . we need fundamentally to understand *conflict* and not *race*."[13]

Ruth Benedict does go too far. It is race conflict as a sub-group of all conflict that we need to understand, and to mark off from other kinds of conflict. Otherwise we should merely be making something else explain everything and nothing. Race is at the same time a biological and a sociological notion. Races are not pure types, but populations differing from each other in the relative commonness of certain hereditary traits,[14] and thinking of themselves as socially distinct. The subjective element is crucial. "The White Man's Burden" was a racial attitude struck from above looking down. Negritude and Black Power were expressions coined in the attempt to get out from under. An examination of this process illuminates the place of race in contemporary international politics.

EUROPEAN EXPANSION AND THE EMERGENCE OF RACIALISM

The ascendancy of the peoples of Europe over those of Asia has been taken, in an important book, to be one of the marks of Western dominance in Asia from 1498 to 1945.[15] This dominance, which came to be rationalised in doctrine of racial superiority, can be said to have

applied generally in the relations between the European
and the non-European world in the nineteenth and into the
twentieth century. The Japanese were widely dismissed as
dishonest, getting along quite happily without religion
and thus at best semi-civilised.[16] One writer has said
that the general image of China during the same period
was one of a "depraved race governed by a despotic and
corrupt ruling class."[17] Despising the natives was the
orthodox attitude of the British in India during the
nineteenth century so that it was eccentric if not
bizarre to adopt any other attitude.[18] And Africans,
coming conventionally at the bottom of the European
racialist scale, became a standard of barbarism: Lord
Salisbury once declared the Irish to be as unfit for
self-government as Hottentots.[19]

Along with the confidence in white superiority went
a fear that the higher civilisation was under threat from
the lower in the tradition of Goths, Vandals, and
Tartars.[20] The "yellow peril," composed of Chinese and
Japanese, was such a threat. It had a military and
socio-economic aspect. Militarily, there was the fear in
the West from Kaiser Wilhelm II through to the allied
leaders during the Second World War and beyond that the
next great conflagration would take place between the
white and the yellow races. Economically and socially,
there was the fear that the cheaper race would starve out
the dearer.[21] The Chinese could outwork white men. In
this respect they were superior. The result was in the
United States the series of Exclusion Acts, and in
Australia the Commonwealth Immigration Restriction Act,
seeking to avoid the swamping of the white race by
denying access to competitors.

Nor was it just the yellow peril against which this
redoubt was to be fortified. The white race was "in
danger of social sterilization and final replacement or
absorption by the teeming coloured races."[22] If the
problem of the twentieth century was to be the problem of
the colour-line, then demographic trends suggested its
settlement in favour of the "rising tide of colour."

In view of the racial rhetoric of this kind that
accompanied the age of European ascendancy, it is not
perhaps surprising that the emergence from colonial
domination should have had a racial flavour. The colour-
consciousness of Africans or Asians, it has been argued,
stems from the dominance of Europeans who were conscious
of their whiteness. "The Negro," writes Fanon, "never so
much a Negro since he has been dominated by the Whites,
when he decides to prove that he has a culture and to
behave like a cultured person, comes to realize that
history points out a well-defined path to him: he must
demonstrate that a negro culture exists."[23] In the same
way, K. M. Pannikar writes of "European-ness" leading to
"Asian-ness."[24] And in his controversial *Orientalism,*
Edward Said speaks of a Western habit of making a

"binomial opposition" between ours and theirs, occidental and oriental, white and non-white in which the former terms were related to the latter as subject to object: we created them, white men designated the non-whites.[25]

It may be said that the practical effect of this racial discrimination on international politics was small. The self-consciousness about ethnicity involved in the shedding of colonial nomenclature in Mali, or Bangladesh, or Sri Lanka, or Zimbabwe might be a one-shot affair, celebrated in independence before the assumption of routine diplomacy. Viewed from underneath, or from the position of object in Said's binomial opposition, however, the matter seems to go deeper. Toussaint Louverture, the celebrated negro leader who, before his betrayal, brought St. Domingue to the verge of independence from France, is supposed to have said: "It is not a fortuitous concession of liberty, made to us alone, that we want, but a recognition of the principle that whether a man be red, black or white, he cannot be the property of any other man . . . the First Consul maintains slavery in Martinique, which means that he will make us slaves when he feels he is strong enough to do so."[26] More than a century later, the Jamaican founder of the Universal Negro Improvement Association (UNIA), Marcus Garvey, had similarly global objectives: to restore negro self-respect and to speak for negroes as one of the great constituencies of mankind.[27] His allowing himself to be elected "Provisional President of Africa" at a UNIA meeting in New York in 1920 was thought to be an allowable hyperbole given the importance of finding a spiritual home for the black diaspora.[28] And Nkrumah, actually on the continent of Africa, making the case for independence in the Gold Coast Legislative Assembly, referred to an historical Ghanaian Empire that had been a centre of civilisation long before the expansion of Europe:[29] the home was actual as well as spiritual.

The insistence on racial equality that lay behind these claims was the concern of the Japanese at the Paris Peace Conference. They wanted the clause of the League of Nations Covenant providing for religious equality broadened to cover racial equality, and so to legitimise their arrival as fully-fledged members of international society. At that time the great powers were not ready, mainly for domestic reasons, to accept the claim. At the end of the Second World War, a war in which a noxious racial doctrine had been worked out within the Western world, the United Nations Charter proclaimed the human rights and fundamental freedoms of all without distinction as to race, sex, language or religion. One writer has interpreted the Charter not as a minimalist arrangement for peace and security, but as nothing less than a global "Bill of Rights" which, by its enthronement of the principle of self-determination, required an end to racialism.[30] The interpretation of this doctrine and the examination of the extent to which practice can be said to have followed it, is a question for the concluding part of this paper. Meanwhile, there is the measurement of race as a force in international politics against other forces such as class and nation.

THE RELATIVE IMPORTANCE OF RACE IN INTERNATIONAL POLITICS

From an anthropological point of view, it might be said that the function of racialist doctrine during the period of European dominance was to legitimise it, and to order society in recognition of a racial hierarchy. A God-given mandate to rule meant that the Europeans were to appear God-like themselves in the eyes of the natives;[31] and if not quite God-like then, at least in the relationship of masters to servants, or, a common theme, parents to children. By reference to racialism, both parents and children were confirmed in their roles: Europeans sustained the will to govern; non-Europeans remained deferential. By the same token, the function of the doctrine of racial equality in the emergence from empire might be said to have been that of signalling that "we are as good as you." The children had grown up, and should now live on land of their own, enjoying the same right to self-determination as their erstwhile masters.

This anthropological view interprets race as a symbol of something else, such as universal structural patterns of dominance and dependence. But what of race as a reason for action rather than a rationalisation of it, as a motivating force in politics, domestic and international, rather than as a symbol manipulated on behalf of another thing? How does race as a social bond compare to the rival adhesives of class and nation?

Writing on "the principle of racial sovereignty," Ali Mazrui distinguishes at least five concepts of self-government involved in the politics of anti-colonialism: absence of colonial rule, sovereign independence, internal management of internal affairs, the consent of the governed, and government "by rulers manifestly belonging to the same race as the ruled."[32] But the greatest of these, says Mazrui, is the last, for it is ethnicity as a basis for legitimation that determines the interpretation of each of the other senses of self-government. Alongside the old European notion of the sovereign territorial state, there had to be placed the African and Asian notion of "peoples" recognisable in a racial sense as having a right to sovereignty. This is racial sovereignty. And it was on the assumption of "the inherent sovereignty" of each race, Mazrui says, that many leaders in the Afro-Asian world based their welcome of India's annexation of Goa at the expense of a colonial power of different racial stock.

The implications of this doctrine for international politics will be examined in the concluding section of this paper. It belongs here as an example of the force of ethnicity in contemporary politics. And it has a domestic aspect as well as an international one. It may be that the rise of ethnicity, and of the ethnic group in the United States, is an internal echo of the international movement towards decolonisation. Certainly, some writers have seized on the concept of ethnicity to account for the forces they interpret as being dynamic ones in contemporary society.[33]

The expression "ethnicity" is itself an interesting one, and one might be forgiven for interpreting the phrase "ethnic group" as the de-odourised form of "racial group." Generalised to apply to any group with a distinct cultural tradition, the vitality of ethnicity has been detected in the proliferation of ethnic conflicts from that between English and French speakers in Canada to tribal conflict in Nigeria, and including Northern Ireland, Belgium, Pakistan, Malaysia, Cyprus and the Soviet Union.[34] The salience of ethnicity, as compared to class, is explained partly strategically, partly in terms of what Americans call "affective ties" and partly very much more boldly in terms of some kind of a sea-change in world society.

The strategic explanation has an ethnic group as a better bet than a class in a contest to extract a deal from the state. From the point of view of the participants in the group, their membership is relatively small and visible, while the class is rambling and conjectural. From the state's point of view, "doing something for the Scots" is more obvious than doing something for the workers.[35] The second explanation has class as a cold category, ethnic affiliation as a warm one. Class is defined in terms of common interests, or of a common predicament, and has lost its revolutionary bite. Ethnicity defines interests in the terms of a group united by ties of language, culture and tradition.[36]

There is thirdly the grandiose notion that the old treatment of ethnic conflict as class conflict in disguise should be turned on its head. The argument here derives from Ralf Dahrendorf's treatment of social stratification in a well-known article on the origin of inequality.[37] Of the conventional explanations for social stratification, that of the institution of property seems particularly inappropriate in such countries as Israel, the Soviet Union and Yugoslavia, where private property has been "reduced to virtual insignificance."[38] Perhaps ethnicity is a better explanation of inequality in these societies, something that is more fundamental than class and having to do with some primordial attachment to tribe.[39]

Whatever the doubts about this rather inflated

notion, there is a plausible distinction between ethnic group and class as social forces. Race (for I am supposing it to be another word for ethnicity) and nation are more difficult to disentangle. For they are both "warm," both derive from a notion of something one is born into and stuck with, and each is frequently defined in terms of the other. A definition of "nation" found in a 1910 dictionary illustrates both the confusion and a way out of it:

> An extensive aggregate of persons, so closely associated with each other by common descent, language or history, as to form a distinct race or people, usually organized as a separate political state and occupying a definite territory.
> In early examples the racial idea is usually stronger than the political: in recent use the notion of political unity and independence is more prominent.[40]

Nation has become attached to state. We live in a world composed officially of nation-states. And this is seized upon by the champions of ethnicity. The very success of the idea of nation has enmeshed it in the global bureaucracy. If all states are nation-states then a focus for protest and change must be found elsewhere, and the ethnic group inherits the progressive connotation that the idea of nation enjoyed in the nineteenth century. The task now is to discover if this is true of race in contemporary international politics.

THE IMPACT OF RACE IN THE INTERNATIONAL ARENA

There is, in the language to which we are all becoming accustomed, a horizontal and a vertical dimension to the question of race in contemporary international politics. The horizontal dimension involves the relations of states in the ordinary everyday business of diplomacy. The vertical, sometimes called structuralist, dimension involves not merely the surface relations of notional equals, but the hierarchical arrangement of world society in which rich white states are said to exploit poor non-white ones, or, beyond the state, a white bourgeoisie is said to exploit a black proletariat.

We have noted above the inclination of some new states to announce a new name, on or before arrival in international society, that makes a point of their ethnic grouping. This, it was observed too, might make little difference from day two onwards. Indeed, it might be observed, it is the states that continue to make a point of their ethnic grouping after day two that constitute the exception rather than the rule--Haiti's absorption with its status as a negro republic in the Western hemisphere,[41] for example, or Liberia's position as the first independent black state in Africa. And yet, uniting many new states is the memory of what is taken to be racial oppression. It was, after all, well into this century, and not at the height of Victorian imperial enthusiasm, that Franklin Roosevelt put forward his schemes for the inter-breeding of European and Asian stock to produce a less delinquent Asian race, and Churchill thought in terms of "baboos," "chinks," and "Hottentots."[42] And if Churchill himself is counted in this regard as a Victorian,[43] then it is reasonable to suppose that the resentment felt by those who were the object of the kind of scorn he expressed might last at least as long.

Nor has the scorn that leads to the resentment disappeared. The presumption of Western superiority that led to the under-rating of the skill of the Japanese military during the Second World War[44] was featured still in the American attitude to the opposition during the Vietnam war. "The belief that one Marine was better than ten slopes saw Marine squads fed in against known NVA platoons, platoons against companies, and on and on, until whole battalions found themselves pinned down and cut off. That belief was undying . . ."[45] In the same way, the tendency persists, when the opposition is clearly formidable, to associate its strength with European support. Russian assistance to the Egyptians and to the Vietnamese is supposed to have provided the same stiffening as the Germans supplied for the Japanese during the Second World War.

This persistence of the idea of white superiority is matched by the continuation of the old fear that the poorer races will drive out the richer. Immigration laws in the predominantly white rich world might be said to be the expression of this fear. It is true that the blatant racialism of old immigation legislation such as that of Australia in the first decade of federation and of the United States in the 1920s has now moderated and that more recent law in the receiving countries has been more liberal. For instance, the notion in the United States that immigration law should be framed so as to exclude immigrants of "inferior racial stock" has now given place to the doctrine of the "plural mix" as the goal of legislation in this area.[46] But despite this recent liberalisation, it remains the function of immigration laws broadly to preserve the characteristics of established populations. In the plural mix some are more plural than others.

It is not then merely the memory of past oppression, but also the observation that the conviction of white superiority persists, that prompts the non-white world to continue to insist on the principle of racial equality. It is in this regard that we observed earlier the interpretation of the United Nations Charter as a global Bill of Rights proclaiming the self-determination of peoples. According to this view the mistake of the Western powers in taking peace and security to be the master purposes of the United Nations, is to fail to look beyond those values to "the dignity and worth of the human person" from which they derive their importance. Following this logic, it may be argued that the test for membership of the United Nations should not be the superficial requirement that a state be peace-loving, but the more fundamental demand that it be respectful of human dignity. On this ground, apartheid in South Africa is, for example, a "more flagrant failure of the test than territorial aggrandizement by the Chinese."[47]

The interpretation of the principle of self-determination which would justify, indeed require, the ending of apartheid is the doctrine of pigmentational self-determination that was discussed above--the idea that rulers and ruled should be of broadly similar racial stock. Africa for the Africans is a racial slogan. In its name much has been made at the United Nations of the demand for reform or revolution in South Africa. The spiritual home that Garvey saw to be necessary for negro dignity must now become a physical home that spans the continent.

Nor is this racial mode of thought the particular preoccupation of black Africans with their eyes turned to the imperial debris littering the south of their continent. When the Afro-Asian countries met for their first conference at Bandung, President Sukarno pronounced it the first intercontinental conference of coloured peoples in the history of mankind, and this racial self-consciousness has been carried into the General Assembly of the United Nations. It has even been said to have introduced an "additional dimension to the doctrine of non-intervention."[48] Saudi and Egyptian "intervention" in Yemen would be a domestic affair according to racial sovereignty, but an external violation of state sovereignty. Soviet or American intervention would be doubly illegitimate, offending against racial as well as state sovereignty.

The difficulty with this doctrine is that the frontiers of racial sovereignty are a good deal fuzzier even than those of state sovereignty, and the overlapping legitimacies produced by such a doctrine might lead to chaos. Ethnic groups within states can already affect international relations by bringing pressure to bear on their governments, or by providing a target for outside intervention, as for example in the relationship between American Jews and Israel, and French Canadians and France. And if ethnic solidarity across state frontiers were to be endowed with the same legitimacy as interstate alliances, so that some association for the advancement of coloured peoples took its place alongside the Warsaw

Pact, the implications for the maintenance of world order would be profound.

Yet it is only by thinking in terms of ethnic solidarity across state frontiers, some writers argue, that we can appreciate the place of race in world society. Their view is that the interstate level of analysis distorts the real place of race in world politics, and they require a global or at least a continental framework for its evaluation. There is first the doctrine of the indivisibity of black freedom and dignity: the idea that continued oppression of non-whites anywhere is an offence to their dignity everywhere. An example of this, we have seen, is the connection between the liberty of the American negro and African independence in what became a rich theme in pan-Africanist thought. And on the continent of Africa Tom Mboya said "As long as any part of Africa remains under European rule, we do not feel that Africans will be regarded in the right way."[49]

The idea of a global coincidence of interests among the coloured races connects, in another strand of racial thought, to a class analysis of world politics. "In the colonies," wrote Fanon, "the economic substructure is also a superstructure. The cause is the consequence; you are rich because you are white, you are white because you are rich."[50] More recently, Stokeley Carmichael joined class with colour in a structuralist account which asserted the existence of a Third World proletariat (of which the black American proletariat was part) ranged against a bourgeoisie of whites.[51]

In a third strand of thought about race in world society, the world political system has solidified, from the relative fluidity of class, into the rigidity of caste. Not merely, in this view, does it happen to be the case that the rich world is predominantly white, and the poor world predominantly coloured, but since the gap is widening between them it can be argued that world society displays the features of a caste-system; separation, division of labour and hierarchy.[52] Separation is not hermetic, but immigration laws universally maintain the characteristics of established populations. Where contact does take place White Brahmins oversee the Third World, black Harijans fulfil menial functions in the First World. The division of labour is the familiar one between white manufacturers and coloured primary producers. And hierarchy exists in virtue of the inequality of reward in this division, surplus value accruing to the manufacturers who then reinforce their position of superiority.

How is all this to be judged? Race, it has been suggested, in the horizontal relations of states, has had some part in the liberation from colonialism, continues to be part of the persona of some states, and has even added a new notion of ethnic self-determination to that

of national self-determination as part of the theory of
international society. This theory is the more
persuasive as notions of white superiority linger on, and
are not merely part of the memory of past oppression. In
multilateral diplomacy at the United Nations and
elsewhere, the call for racial equality is often heard,
and it is directed particularly at pariah states like
South Africa. In the vertical relations among classes in
world politics, the notion of ethnic self-determination
is given added point by the dramatic demonstration of the
position of the non-white races at the foot of a global
hierarchy.

There is, by virtue of this list, some reason to pay
more attention to the place of race in world politics
than is normally given in the textbooks. In particular,
it may be said that textbooks tend to be written by those
near the top rather than the bottom of the world
hierarchy, and that they are for that reason less
sensitive to the factor of race than if they were written
from underneath looking up. Nevertheless, it may be that
some of the claims for the importance of race in
international politics are exaggerated. The doctrine of
pigmentational self-determination is an African one,
hardly applicable to, say, Latin America, and brittle in
its application even to African politics. Just as the
doctrine of national self-determination has had a clear
run only in delegitimising colonial rule, so that of
ethnic self-determination seems unambiguously to apply
only to white minority rule in South Africa. Such
general headway as racial doctrine has been able to make
in international society seems limited to the protests
made against white racism characteristic of the United
Nations General Assembly. The idea of a global caste-
system is a striking metaphor, but its strength is sapped
by observation, among other things, of the
cosmopolitanism of the global diplomatic elite--something
more susceptible of class than caste analysis. If it is
objected that this elite is tiny and unrepresentative,
this is precisely the point: one would not expect, on a
caste analysis, to find Harijans among the Brahmins.

To measure the pronouncements about the prominence
of race in international relations with which this paper
began, one might apply the litmus test used by Bruce
Miller some twenty-five years ago.[53] Sceptical of the
view then (still) widespread that the next war would be a
race war between coloured and white people, he pointed
out that, to be correct, it would need to assume that
race relations were either more important than national
interests or had become the principal factor in them;
that peoples would be prepared to go to war against
discrimination against others; that racial discrimination
constituted a form of aggression; that states founded in
an atmosphere of release from racial oppression would
continue to find race a crucial factor; and that race

relations had enough drive behind them to set the machinery of war in motion. Like Professor Miller, I doubt that race has transcended everything.

And yet it is broadly true to say that the affluent and the hungry worlds stand on either side of a colour line, that the chances are that if you are white you are rich, and if non-white, poor.[54] This does not make of race, any more than it does of poverty, the stuff of international politics. But it does mean that the argument for change, for justice in international relations (in other words that the stuff of international politics ought to be different from what it now is), is likely to be presented as a claim for racial as well as for economic equality. The realist who calls the stuff of international politics today's response to yesterday's demand for justice, should have an eye for tomorrow.

NOTES

1. Quoted in Lord Caradon, "Race, Poverty and Population: (An Internationalist's View)," in Sir F. Vallatt et al., *An Introduction to the Study of Human Rights* (London: Europa, 1972), p. 54.

2. John Rex, *Race Relations in Sociological Theory* (London: Weidenfeld & Nicolson, 1970), p. 161.

3. Hugh Tinker, *Race, Conflict, and the International Order* (London: Macmillan, 1977), p. 135.

4. Quoted in Michael Banton, *The Idea of Race* (London: Tavistock, 1977), pp. 76-79.

5. *Ibid.*, pp. 15-22.

6. *Ibid.*, Chap. 3.

7. Arthur de Gobineau, *The Inequality of Human Races,* translated by Adrian Collins (London: Heinemann, 1915), pp. 205-207.

8. Benjamin Kidd, *Social Evolution,* 3rd ed. (London: Macmillan, 1902), pp. 31, 43, and 47.

9. Sir Charles Dilke, *Greater Britain* (London: Macmillan, 1870), p. 88.

10. Frank B. Livingstone, quoted in M. Banton and J. Harwood, *The Race Concept* (London: David & Charles, 1975), pp. 56-57.

11. From UNESCO's Moscow Declaration on Race, cited in Rex, *op. cit.*, pp. 2-4.

12. *See* Ralph Pettman, *Biopolitics and International Values* (New York: Pergamon, 1981), Chap. 3.

13. Ruth Benedict, *Race and Racism* (London: Routledge, 1942), pp. 147 and 151.

14. *See* L. C. Dunn, "Race and Biology," in Leo Kuper, ed., *Race, Science and Society* (UNESCO, 1975), p. 41.

15. K. M. Panikkar, *Asia and Western Dominance* (London: George Allen & Unwin, 1953), p. 12. The

pattern of the argument here is taken from my "Racial Equality and the Expansion of International Society," forthcoming in H. N. Bull and Adam Watson, *The Expansion of International Society.*

16. V. G. Kiernan, *The Lords of Human Kind* (London: Weidenfeld & Nicolson, 1969), p. 180.

17. Jerome Ch'en, *China and the West* (London: Hutchinson, 1979).

18. Kiernan, *op. cit.,* pp. 42-45.

19. Quoted in *ibid.,* p. 27.

20. Ch'en, *op. cit.,* p. 58.

21. Dilke, *op. cit.,* p. 192.

22. Lothrop Stoddard, *The Rising Tide of Colour: Against White World Supremacy* (London: Chapman & Hall, 1922), p. 298.

23. Frantz Fanon, *The Wretched of the Earth* (Harmondsworth: Penguin, 1967), pp. 170-171.

24. Panikkar, *op. cit.,* p. 494.

25. Edward Said, *Orientalism* (London: Routledge & Kegan Paul, 1978), pp. 227-231.

26. Quoted in Ralph Dorngold, *Citizen Toussaint* (London: Gollancz, 1945), pp. 147-148.

27. Richard Hart, "From Garvey to Black Liberation," *The Black Liberator,* July-September 1973, Vol. 2, No. 1, p. 24.

28. *Ibid.*

29. Kwame Nkrumah, *Autobiography* (London: Nelson, 1975), pp. 201 and 185.

30. Ali A. Mazrui, *Towards a Pax Africana* (Chicago: University of Chicago Press, 1967), ch. 8.

31. Kiernan, *op. cit.,* p. 50.

32. Mazrui, *op. cit.,* ch. 2.

33. *See* N. Glazer and D. Moynihan, eds., *Ethnicity* (Cambridge, Mass.: Harvard University Press, 1975).

34. Glazer and Moynihan, "Introduction" in *ibid.,* pp. 5-6.

35. *Ibid.,* pp. 9-11.

36. Daniel Bell, "Ethnicity and Social Change," in *ibid.,* pp. 165-170.

37. Ralf Dahrendorf, "On the Origin of Inequality Among Men," in Dahrendorf, *Essays in the Theory of Society* (London: Routledge & Kegan Paul, 1968).

38. *Ibid.,* p. 159.

39. Glazer and Moynihan, *op. cit.,* pp. 16-19.

40. *A New English Dictionary* (Oxford: Clarendon, 1910).

41. *See* Roy Prieswerk, "Race and Colour in International Relations," *Year Book of World Affairs* Vol. 24, 1970, p. 58.

42. Christopher Thorne, *Allies of a Kind* (London: Hamish Hamilton, 1978), pp. 5 and 8.

43. Lord Moran, quoted in *ibid.,* pp. 5-6.

44. *Ibid.,* p. 4.

45. Michael Herr, *Dispatches* (London: Pan, 1978),

p. 86.

46. Michael S. Teitelbaum, "Right versus Right: Immigration and Refugee Policy," *Foreign Affairs,* Vol. 59, No. 1, Fall 1980, p. 32.

47. Mazrui, *op. cit.,* p. 137.

48. *Ibid.,* pp. 38-39.

49. Quoted in Mazrui, *Africa's International Relations* (London: Heinemann, 1977), p. 216.

50. Fanon, *op. cit.,* p. 31.

51. Stokeley Carmichael, "Black Power and the Third World," in Tariq Ali, ed., *New Revolutionaries* (London: Peter Owen, 1969), pp. 98-101.

52. Mazrui, *op. cit.,* ch. 1.

53. J.D.B. Miller, "Racial Equality," unpublished paper delivered at the Institute of Commonwealth Studies, London University 1956.

54. *See* Trevor Huddleston, "Race Relations," a lecture given in Canterbury Cathedral, November 12, 1969, p. 4.

CHAPTER 4

Civilizations
and Modes of Production:
Conflicts and Convergences

Immanuel Wallerstein

> The main problem . . . is that of the dialectic
> of the specific (the factor of nationality, of
> national culture, of civilization) and the universal
> [the] syncretic civilization that will emerge out of
> the human species through the mediation of science
> and technology). In the first stage, the principal
> danger is not that of accentuating the dimension of
> nationality but rather that of imposing hegemonic
> molds that are asserted to be universal, and which
> will ensure, even more than previous ways, the
> denaturing of non-Western world civilizations,
> destined to be sub-products of technicality and
> productivism; economic, demographic, ethnographic
> reserves; an alienated underworld.

> Anouar Abdel-Malek[1]

This long quote catches the fact that behind the
central intellectual antinomy of the modern world, which
Abdel-Malek calls the "dialectic of the specific and the
universal," lie the parallel symbiotic dyads of barbarian
and civilized, non-Western and Western, periphery and
core, proletarian and bourgeois, the dominated and the
dominant, the oppressed and the oppressors.

None of these pairs of terms involve two separate
phenomena brought into (external) relationship with one
another. Rather the terms represent positions on a
continuum which are the outcome of a *single* process. The
creation of the one was the creation of the other--both
materially and ideologically. "Civilization gave rise to
barbarism," said Owen Lattimore.[2] And hegemonic forces
gave birth to social science. *Pax Britannica* ensured the

Reprinted by permission from *Theory and Society* 5:1, 1978.

intellectual triumph of the belief in
universals--universals that could be circumscribed and
tested, theorems that were defined as laws, realities
that became imperatives. Just as British power and
capitalist enterprise came to pervade the furthest
corners of the world, so did the presumptions about
universal truths come to pervade and define our
consciousnesses, our cosmologies, our moralities, our
scientific efforts.

It was not new that a civilization saw itself as
Civilization (singular), the center surrounded by
barbarisms. What was new was that this attitude was no
longer defended on the basis that it was *deduced* from a
God-given construction of reality; rather it was said to
be *induced* from existential experience. What before was
known metaphysically was now known rationally. Progress
resided in the fact that present and future inequalities
were now said to be merited inequalities, the consequence
of the presumedly autonomous inner efforts of
individuals.

The whole argument is so inherently preposterous and
implausible that it requires a wrench of our critical
faculties to appreciate that such ideas did not merely
receive *droit de cité* but very nearly expunged all
opposing views from the academy, on the grounds that they
were legacies of pre-rational thought. Such were the
glitter and the power of a capitalist world-economy in
its days of unself-questioning splendor that it was not
easy to gain a hearing for the other side.

Yet other side there was. Indeed, there were two
movements to refute this apotheosis of one particular
into the universal. The two movements represented two
different strategies of rebuttal. One riposte was to
argue that this particular was only one particular among
several or many. The other riposte was to argue that
this particular was not universal.

The distinction was subtle but full of implications.
The first movement asserted that civilization was a term
with a plural and no singular. There were *only*
civilizations. The second movement asserted that this
particular, which thought itself to be universal, was
only a transitory phase of human existence. The first
movement emphasized the cultural context of human
production, human activity; the second, the social
relations that underpinned them. The first movement led
to scholarly elaborations of alternative
civilizations--to Orientalism, in both its best and worst
senses. The second movement led to scholarly and extra-
scholarly effort to analyze and further the transitory
quality of the dominant world structures.

I do not suggest for a moment that these two schools
of thought were identical or even similar. But they both
started as reactions to (as well as expressions of)
dominant socio-ideological forces. And their paths have

crossed constantly in *praxis,* even when the actors involved have refused to admit it. And thus I should like to review the conflicts and convergences between these two anti-systemic *Weltanschauungen* and movements.

What is a civilization? An old question, and definitional games are not always fruitful. In this instance, however, we must be clear. The word "civilization" ought to be used to mean something different from and more than the term "culture" of long anthropological tradition; else, why have two terms? If so, it then must be something more than a set of collective norms and values of a particular group of any size in any place. Most of us tend in fact to use the word "civilizations" to describe only larger, more encompassing more enduring "cultural" phenomena. We speak of Western civilization, of Chinese civilization, of Indian civilization. In these three cases at least, we refer to phenomena asserted to continue for millenia, and this despite the fact that the Europe of the eleventh century and the twentieth, the China of the Sung dynasty and of today, the India of the Delhi Sultanate and today have only the most marginal similarities as social structures. And this statement would be a *fortiori* true if we pushed the comparisons back 3000 more years.

What is it then that permits us to speak of a "civilization?" There are, to start with, certain surface continuities. The language or languages spoken, while far from identical, are historically linked, such that contemporary languages can be said to be derived from earlier ones. But even there we stretch our imaginations. Outside linguistic influences have intruded in the interim. Many languages have been extinguished. If we are tracing linguistic heritages (say, English out of Romance and Germanic languages out of their Indo-European origins) we must also remember that there is a vast geographic shift. New York is indeed far from Athens.

Well, then, you may argue, it is less a relative epiphenomenon such as language than a broader cosmological unity as reflected in religion and philosophy which constitutes the continuity. I scarcely need to review both the similarities and the differences of ancient and contemporary cosmological views identified with these "civilizations." But let us note in passing that the cosmological lines are different from the linguistic ones--for example, it is frequently stated that contemporary Western thought has, at least in part, Hebraic roots, but clearly there is no linguistic link.

I could go on like this, but it is essentially a false path. There is no "essence" which defines a civilization. For each trait uncovered, one could list countless exceptions. There probably do not even exist any *dimensions* of definition common to all "civilizations." Rather, I think we should conceive of "civilizations" as historical mental constructs, created, dissolved, and recreated, as groups feel the need of asserting their particularity in a dyadic relationship with some other groups. "Civilization gave rise to barbarism," said Owen Lattimore. We could rephrase the same point: "One civilization gives rise to another civilization." One only exists in function of the other(s).

When groups seek to establish their particularities, they reinvent their histories. They look for "continuities" which at that moment in time will be congenial: linguistic, religious, philosophical, esthetic, racial, geographic. They endow artifacts with the status of prior moments in a progression. Needless to say, the civilizational past chosen by groups in the tenth century A.D. will have been quite different, perhaps radically different, from the civilizational past chosen by the twentieth-century groups who include particular tenth-century groups in their past.

Tradition is always a contemporary social creation. Civilizations are the way we describe our particularities in terms of millenial heritages. We are not free to be totally arbitrary. There must be some surface plausibility to the continuities asserted. They cannot, at least today, fly in the face of all the canons of empirical verification. But once that is said, there remains a vast gamut of pasts one can plausibly choose, a vast gamut of pasts that are in fact chosen. And of course conflicting interests argue for alternative pasts for the collectivity.

To say that civilizations are everchanging, very impermanent creations of contemporary groups is not to denigrate in any way their importance or their reality. No one who has ever travelled around the world, or read in the world's literature, has any doubt that there are significant differences between the world's diverse "civilizations." But when it comes to drawing the boundaries and defining the differences, we seldom agree with each other.

Let me now turn to "modes of production," a quite different concept from "civilization," having a separate intellectual heritage and enjoying a quite segregated but equally lively contemporary renaissance and debate. Here too I must make clear my position. A mode of production is a characteristic of an economy, and an economy is defined by an effective, ongoing division of productive labor. Ergo, to discover the mode of production that prevails, we must know what are the real bounds of the division of labor of which we are speaking. Neither individual units of production nor political or cultural entities may be described as having a mode of production; only economies.

Given this premise, I have previously argued that there are only four possible modes of production, only three of which have been known thus far in empirical reality. They are reciprocal mini-systems, redistributive world-empires, a capitalist world-economy, a socialist world-government.[3]

From my perspective, the key difference in these modes of production is found in the *productive* process. In reciprocal mini-systems, all able persons are direct producers, but the process of reciprocal exchange results in an unequal distribution of real surplus--which, given the technology, is always limited--in favor of a sub-group of direct producers, usually older males. The primary concern of the privileged groups is to ensure that there is a surplus at all.

In redistributive world-empires, there is a stratum of non-producers. The surplus generated by the direct producers is preempted in the form of tribute paid to the (imperial) ruling stratum. This tribute is collected by an armed bureaucracy. The interests of the ruling stratum *vis-à-vis* the armed bureaucracy lead them to try to limit the creation of surplus by the direct producers for fear that the armed bureaucracy will be able to appropriate enough to make them (or part of them) independent of the ruling stratum. The slogan might well be: "Enough but not too much."

In a capitalist world-economy, the surplus generated by the direct producers is preempted in the form of profit distributed *among* the bourgeoisie via the market, as modulated by the multiple state-structures which seek to affect market distribution. The interest of the bourgeoisie taken collectively is *always* the expanded (and unlimited) accumulation of capital, since the dynamics of the system mean that stagnation always leads to regression.

We can only guess how a socialist world-government would operate. Presumably its defining features would be production for use, equitable distribution, and a collectively agreed-upon balance of use-values. How these objectives would or could be structurally ensured is a matter of continuing debate.

I have reviewed this taxonomy very cursorily because I wish to see its relation to the concept of civilization. Historically, there have been countless mini-systems, a large but countable number of world-empires, a similarly large but countable number of world-economies (but only *one* that has survived and flourished for more than a brief period, that one being the modern world-system). A socialist world-government is an invention of the future.

Mini-systems have emerged and disappeared over the millennia. My guess is that few have survived for more than 150-200 years. We have virtually no direct knowledge of how they historically functioned. One of the ways (but only one) in which they disappeared was their incorporation into world-empires, at which point they ceased to be mini-systems with their own mode of production and became simply one more region producing surplus seized by the bureaucracy of a world-empire in the form of tribute.

Since world-empires operated structurally in a cycle of expansion and contraction, they were continuously abolishing mini-systems by absorbing them and later "releasing" zones within which new mini-systems could be created. World-economies were inherently much more unstable than world-empires, and were constantly either being converted into world-empires by conquest or disintegrating, allowing mini-systems to re-emerge.

Hence, up to about 1500, the history of the world was the history of the temporal co-existence of three modes of production--one without records, the mini-systems; one unstable and therefore transitory, the world-economies; one spectacular and encompassing, the world-empires. It is fundamentally the latter to which we now in retrospect give the name "civilizations." One of the reasons we do this is that each time a *new* world-empire was on the ascendant, it sought ideological legitimation by claiming a direct link with a prior world-empire, and in so doing it created certain continuities which we, the analysts of today, perceive as the distinguished features of that "civilization."

In the sixteenth century, a new phenomenon occurred which was to change the rules of the game. For the first time, a world-economy did not disintegrate but survived, and became the world capitalist system we know today.

The modern world-system changed the rules of the game in two ways. In the first place, the operation of the rules of world-empires led to long-term geographical expansion followed by geographical contraction. The rules of the capitalist world-economy (the expanded reproduction of capital) involved expansion but no contraction--periods of relative stagnation, yes; attempts of areas at tactical withdrawal, yes; but real contraction, no. Hence, by the late nineteenth century, the capitalist world-economy included virtually the whole inhabited earth, and it is presently striving to overcome the technological limits to cultivating the remaining corners: the deserts, the jungles, the seas, and indeed the other planets of the solar system.

This ceaseless expansion has meant that both mini-systems and world-empires have disappeared from the surface of the earth. Today there is only one social system and therefore only one mode of production extant, the capitalist world-economy. Does this mean that there is then only one civilization? Here we come to the second important change in the rules of the game. For the answer to my question is "yes" in one sense, and "quite decidedly no" in another.

On the one hand, something we might call "capitalist civilization" clearly dominates the thinking and action of rulers and ruled, oppressors and oppressed. It is the cosmology of "more," more of everything, more for everybody, but more particularly (or if necessary) for "me" or "us." There are seeming rebellions against this cosmology: "limits of growths" rebellions which often turn out to be hidden ways of defending the "more" of what is of interest to one group against the "more" of another group; "egalitarian" rebellions which often turn out to operate on the assumption that the route to equality is through more of the same, but this time for someone else, "us."

I do not need to develop this theme. The analysis of the pluses and minuses of capitalist civilization has dominated the literature, the philosophy, and the social sciences of the last century, if not of the last two. Nor am I even taking sides on what seems to me an historically pointless question: the progressiveness of capitalism. What is more to the point is to observe that capitalist civilization (singular) has bred modern nationalisms (plural).

When Western civilization sought to transform itself into civilization pure and simple by the Enlightenment trick of reifying capitalist values into secular universals, it was sure that not only God and history was on its side but that all rational men (by which was meant the elites throughout the system, including its periphery) would be on its side as well, at least eventually.[4]

Instead what has happened is that everywhere, and more and more, nationalist particularism has been asserting itself. Indeed, if there is any linear equation at all, it is the correlation of the expansion of capital, the uneven development of the world system, and the claims to differentiation by groups ever more integrated into the system--in dialectical vortex of centripetal and centrifugal forces.

How are these nationalisms we know so well and the civilizations of which we have been talking related? It is a question seldom posed, as far as I know. The confusion is simple when we deal with China, or India, or even the Arab world. (I say "even" because though there are multiple Arab nations or at least states today, nonetheless we talk of an "Arab nationalism.") But what of the large number of members of the United Nations whose claim to "civilizational" status is less widely accorded?

I have tried to think of an uncontroversial example, and I cannot. This in itself tells us something. I cannot think of an uncontroversial example of a present-day state that is clearly not the "heir" of a specific "civilization," because any example that might seem plausible to me--or to you--would probably give offense to the leaders and the intellectuals of the state in question. For, be it well noted: every state today, without exception, proclaims itself the continuation of a civilization, and in many (perhaps most) cases heir of a civilization unique to it.

One of the rare persons with the courage to tackle this issue was in fact Anouar Abdel-Malek who, at the VIIth World Congress of Sociology in 1966, distinguished varieties of nationalism on the Three Continents of Asia, Africa, and Latin America, singling out a category which he called "renascent nations," which were "those supported by a continuing millenary national tradition. . . ." He listed China, Egypt, Iran "principally," but also Turkey, Morocco, Vietnam, Mexico, Armenia. He said of these "nations" as compared to others in the Three Continents: "the coefficient of propulsion to development . . . cannot but be different."[5]

No doubt, but is the difference fundamental? I am not sure. The nationalisms of the modern world are not the triumphant civilizations of yore. They are the ambiguous expression of the demand both for participation in the system, assimilation into the universal, the elimination of all that is unequal and indeed different, and simultaneously for opting out of the system, adhering to the particular, the reinvention of differences. Indeed, it is universalism through particularism, and particularism through universalism. This is the genius and the contradiction of capitalist civilization which, precisely as it hurtles towards its undoing, becomes in the interim stronger and stronger.

Are renascent nations in a different position from "truly" new nations? Stronger perhaps, but different? Is not the real issue that we are all in the same boat, facing the same dilemma: that, within a capitalist world-economy, nationalism (and civilizational analysts as one expression of nationalism) is both the "ideology of weaker, less developed countries struggling to free themselves from alien oppression,"[6] (which are *all* countries and quasi-countries except the momentarily hegemonic one), and is also the ultimate expression of the form of rapacity that is peculiar to capitalism (power and privilege through unlimited growth)?[7]

If civilizations as a mode of legitimating new redistributive world-empires are no more, but civilizations as the epitome of contemporary cultural resistance within a capitalist world-economy are flourishing, what future do they have? Here we come not only to untrod ground, but to arenas about which thus far we have largely refused to think. If, as I believe is the case, we are living in the early moments of a long systemic change—the transformation of the capitalist world-economy into a socialist world-government—and if we think such a transition will probably be completed but not certainly, we ought to pose the following question: If the millenial particularisms we label "civilizations" have redefined themselves as *intra*systemic oppositional ideologies within a capitalist world-economy, will the transition to socialism complete the undermining of their material bases, or conversely provide them with the building-stones of true reconstruction?

It is not cowardice but wisdom to say we do not know the answer. In the first place, we really do not have more than the remotest idea of what a socialist world would look like in practice, and most certainly it would require a heroic leap of the imagination to envisage its cultural parameters. It is a bit like asking the burghers of thirteenth-century European city-states to sketch our twentieth-century world. Some might have risen to the challenge, but what they would have imagined might in turn seem hopelessly parochial to us.

What I think we may plausibly assert is that a socialist civilization will not be a cosmological mélange of a bit of this and that from everywhere. The ideas, the values, the world-views that will emerge from a socialist mode of production will lead in new directions, reflecting very different material premises from either classical world-empires or the capitalist world-economy.

Those who are hopeful share the vision of Marx: "from the realm of necessity to the realm of freedom." For Samir Amin, this means that:

> The direct apprehension of use-values is thus the bearer of diversity, not uniformity. In contrast to the uniformity brought about by capitalism's destruction of culture, here there is the richness of a rebirth of diversity. National diversity, doubtless, but also diversity that is regional, local, individual.[8]

I need hardly say that against this optimism the world is full of harbingers of doom.

The harbingers of doom reject the Enlightenment. The optimists fulfill it. This in itself might make us suspicious. Is socialism merely the last gasp of Western capitalism triumphant? And if it is, can we truly still see this as progress, as Marx saw British rule in India, and Engels French rule in Algeria? For me, surely not. There is, however, this to remember, in Tom Nairn's very perceptive words:

> History was to defeat the Western Philosophers. The defeat has been permanent. This is perhaps the true, larger meaning of Marxism's failure over the National Question.[9]

What is crucial in practice I think is to try to bring together what might be called "civilizational analysis" with a clearer grasp of the functioning of modes of production, and in particular with the historically-singular evolution of the world capitalist system, in order to construct our options for diverse potentials in the "realm of freedom." We cannot do this abstractly--academically, if you will. But we do need to think about the fact that civilization (singular noun, with adjective "capitalist") has not yet obliterated civilizations (plural noun, meaning ideologies of resistance drawing on but not based on millenial traditions) even while civilization (singular) has transformed and circumscribed civilizations (plural).

The game is far from over. And we are its players--free not to shape but to struggle.

NOTES

1. Anouar Abdel-Malek, "Marxisme et sociologie des civilisations," in *La dialectique sociale* (Paris, 1972), pp. 354-355.

2. Owen Lattimore, "La civilisation, mère de Barbarie?" *Annales E.S.C.* XVII, I (jan.-févr. 1962), p. 99.

3. *See* my two successive formulations of this position: "The Rise and Future Demise of the World Capitalist System: Concepts for Comparative Analysis," *Comparative Studies in Society and History* XVI, 4 (Sept. 1974), pp. 387-415; "The Quality of Life in Different Social Systems: The Model and the Reality," in C. K. Blong, ed., *Systems Thinking and the Quality of Life* (Washington, D. C., 1975), pp. 28-34.

4. In this respect, Marxism was a quintessential child of the Enlightenment. See this viewpoint cogently presented by Tom Nairn, "Marxism and the Modern Janus," *New Left Review* 94 (Nov.-Dec. 1975), pp. 3-29.

5. Anouar Abdel-Malek, "Esquisse d'une typologie de formations nationales dans les Trois Continents," in *La dialectique sociale,* pp. 120-122.

6. Nairn, "Modern Janus," p. 5.

7. "'National liberation' in the essentially antagonistic universe of capitalism, with its blind, competitive, and wildly uneven development, bears a contradiction within itself. It simply cannot help lapsing into nationalism in the most deleterious sense because it is a form of adaptation to this universe." Tom Nairn, "Old Nationalism and New Nationalism," in *The Red Paper on Scotland* (Edinburgh, 1975), p. 50.

8. Samir Amin, "In Praise of Socialism," *Monthly Review* XXVI, 4 (Sept. 1974), p. 16.

9. Nairn, "Modern Janus," p. 9.

CHAPTER 5

The Advanced Capitalist State and the Contemporary World Crisis

Joseph Camilleri

The role of the modern industrial state in the world system has been the subject of numerous and often conflicting interpretations. In recent years a growing number of world order theorists have highlighted the declining importance of the state by drawing attention to several contemporary trends, notably the erosion of traditional national boundaries, the blurring of the dividing line between domestic and international politics and the ineffectiveness of government in many critical areas of policy.[1] According to this perspective, world society now comprises a whole range of systems, some basically economic, others scientific, cultural or ideological, which have "little relationship to state boundaries."[2] The problem of "territorial non-coincidence," however, raises difficult questions not only about the adequacy of the state-centric model of international relations, but about the future of the state and its relationship to the world economy.

The traditional national/international dichotomy appears to have lost much of its former relevance, especially at a time when capital is outgrowing national boundaries, thereby creating new tensions between the political and economic organization of the world. Conventional wisdom has it that the nation-state enjoys or at least enjoyed in nineteenth-century Europe, a considerable degree of independence in international decision-making. However, even in the last century the alleged autonomy of diplomatic and military conduct from the operation of world market forces was more apparent than real. In the twentieth century, the internationalization of economic activity under the aegis of the transnational corporation, the deep and accelerating interpenetration of national economies, and

----

Reprinted by permission from *Science and Society* 45:2, 1981.

the increasing institutionalization of trade, monetary,
financial and technological exchanges across national
boundaries have accentuated the absurdity of sustaining
the separation of politics from economics.[3] Indeed, it
cannot be readily assumed that the state is solely or
even primarily a political actor. As I shall seek to
establish, the state has played a crucial role in the
creation of a world market and the establishment of an
international division of labor. To the extent that the
state remains central to the current functioning of the
world economy, it is bound to be one of the most
important variables in any equation which serves as an
explanation of the contemporary world system.

According to Wallerstein, the system of sovereign
states is one of the three structural constants of
international political economy which, together with the
core-periphery division of labor and the world market,
sustain capitalist commodity production.[4] The
international division of labor and the resulting
exchange between center and periphery, expressed in
productivity and wage differentials, are mediated through
the control structures provided by the state system.[5]
Thus, for example, during periods of conflict between
metropolitan states the exchange network between the
center and the periphery assumes an increasingly
multilateral character. But in addition to crystallizing
the core-periphery division of labor, the state system
also concretizes, through legal, diplomatic, and military
arrangements, the distribution of power within the core,
thereby providing the crucial mechanism for the control
of economic production in different sectors of the
capitalist world system.

In so far as the state expresses and reproduces,
both internally and externally, the process of
stratification, the formation of power blocs within
states and of alliances between states (or between power
blocs from different states) may be said to constitute
one of the essential institutional props for the
international system of unequal exchange. The division
of labor on which this system is based results in the
transfer of surpluses from the peripheral to the
metropolitan sectors of the world economy. But the
world-wide distribution of surpluses is considerably more
complex than this simple dualistic image would suggest.
Accordingly, Wallerstein has proposed a more realistic
model which postulates the existence of semi-peripheral
nations and markets which act as "intermediate" elements
in the surplus-extraction chain," and which, in periods
of international recession, may expand control of their
home market at the expense of core producers, and "expand
their access to neighboring peripheral markets, again at
the expense of core producers."[6] These shifts in
advantage are normally expressed in the pattern of
diplomatic and military alignments and in the declining

capability of metropolitan powers to engage in interventionist policies. Although this threefold division (i.e., metropolis--semi-periphery--periphery) represents a closer approximation of reality, it still does not wholly capture the complexity of the world system, for even within each of the three categories there are substantial conflicts and contradictions, with the result that some semi-peripheral states gain at the expense not only of core and peripheral states but also of other semi-peripheral states. Indeed, the large disparities in economic and military power and the diversity of roles within the semi-periphery raise serious questions as to the validity of this category. On the other hand, Wallerstein's model does illuminate the dynamics and adaptability of the international division of labor, as well as the way in which the contradictions implicit in stratification, competition and uneven development are at least moderated by the opportunity for mobility along the vertical organization of economic and political roles.[7]

But the stabilizing strategy of coopting oppositional forces within world capitalism by offering them a share in the privilege derived from the international division of labor can only be relative and temporary. It cannot resolve the fundamental contradiction inherent in a competitive and hierarchical system, and ultimately exacerbates the crisis confronting all states. The aim of this paper is to examine the systemic crisis from the perspective of the advanced (core) capitalist state, without in any way implying that states in the periphery or semi-periphery of the world economy are less deserving of attention.[8] It could be argued that the analysis of the peripheral state and of its function within the world market has been one of the most valuable contributions of dependency theory.[9]

Regrettably, it is only very recently that a comparable theoretical effort has been made to situate the metropolitan state within the contemporary international division of labor. Whether in this respect the "socialist" industrial state performs a function within the world system which is qualitatively different from that of the liberal capitalist state is not altogether clear. For even where the abolition of property relations has made possible a measure of central economic control, the planned economy is still shaped by international competition which is itself the expression of global capitalist production.[10] In so far as the satisfaction of consumer demand within the communist unified planning systems has come to depend on the import of multinational technology, capitalist penetration may be said to have become the *sine qua non* of the stability of bureaucratic socialism.[11] To a large extent the socialist state has had to operate within a framework of military competition (arms race) and economic exchange whose *modus operandi* is still very much determined by the international capitalist system. At the same time, it has to be admitted that the international linkages tying the centrally planned economies to the world market economy have yet to be subjected to close theoretical scrutiny. Such a task, however, is beyond the scope of this exposition. The aim here is simply to elucidate the increasingly complex and crisis-prone relationship between the advanced capitalist state and the world economy.

THE INTERNATIONALIZATION OF CAPITAL

Since the Second World War almost every field of economic activity has undergone rapid and accelerating internationalization. The process has been particularly evident in world trade, which has experienced an even faster rate of growth (the average annual rate in recent years has been estimated at 10 per cent) than world income. Even more impressive has been the growth of international capital flows, involving not only portfolio movements but direct investment and increasingly massive shifts of liquid balances. In 1973 business generated by multinational enterprises outside their home countries amounted to $350,000 million a year, that is, one-eighth of the gross product of the non-communist world. The internationalization of production is closely related to the extensive diffusion of capital, technology and managerial skills across national boundaries. Even labor has become internationally mobile, at least within certain regions and in certain sectors of the economy.[12]

Although reliance on external transactions by virtually all national economies has now reached unprecedented proportions, the trend has been a distinguishing feature of capitalist industrialization for more than a century.[13]. With remarkable insight into the nature of capitalist development, Marx was able to paint as early as 1848 a vivid picture of the shape of things to come:

> The need of a constantly expanding market for its products chases the bourgeoisie over the whole surface of the globe. It must nestle everywhere, settle everywhere, establish connections everywhere. The bourgeoisie has through its exploitation of the world market given a cosmopolitan character to production and consumption in every country. . . . In place of the old local and national seclusion of self-sufficiency, we have intercourse in every direction, universal interdependence of nations....[14]

Quite apart from its extraordinary prescience, the above

passage points to one of the central contradictions of contemporary capitalism namely, the tension between the territorial constraints of the state and the international expansion of capital. The very process of urbanization, of political and economic centralization, which gave rise to the nation-state, has now unleashed productive forces which cannot be contained within national boundaries.

By the turn of the century the export of capital, that is, the transfusion of capital from one national sphere to another, was widely recognized as a defining characteristic of modern economic life. Hobson's theory of imperialism (published in 1902) was explicitly premised on the expanding powers of capitalist production and the consequent endeavors of the controllers of industry to channel their surplus wealth into foreign markets and investments.[15] Bukharin, writing in 1915, maintained that the growth of productive forces had resulted in "the intertwining of national capitals or the internationalization of capital."[16] As a consequence of this process new structures were developed, mirroring the national cartels and trusts created by the growth of productive forces within the national economy. The process of international cartellization and trustification coming to the fore at the end of the nineteenth century represented in embryonic form an attempt to contain the anarchic structure of the world economy. This increase in international organization was greatly facilitated by the operations of the large world banks and the expanding interconnection between banking and industrial capital, which eventually gave rise to a new phenomenon: finance capital.[17]

Though accurate as a description of the new reality, the more valuable aspect of Bukharin's conceptual framework is his grasp of the strains and stresses arising from the internationalization of the economy, which normally found expression in sharp conflicts between national interests as defined by the ruling bourgeoisie. The growth of international commodity exchange and capital export did not necessarily enhance the degree of solidarity between the exchanging groups. On the contrary, it was often accompanied by "the most desperate competition, by a life and death struggle." The "internationalism" of capital found expression in imperialistic nationalism, while the international division of labor transformed the private national economies into parts of a rapidly integrating economic process, extending to almost every corner of the globe. As productive forces operating within the narrow limits of state boundaries broke through those limits, they inevitably collided and sought to mobilize every *national* resource in the prosecution of *international* conflict. The growth of national war machines, involving the conscription of whole nations and their economies, thus gave rise to a new phenomenon: total war. Whereas in the nineteenth century crises and depressions had sufficed to alter the conditions of production and restore capital expansion, by the turn of the century the point was reached where the restructuring of capitalist production through competition and recession was no longer sufficient to ensure adequate profitability. In Paul Mattick's words, "the business cycle became a 'cycle' of world wars."[18]

But the full implications of this revolution in international relations do not become apparent unless account is taken of the equally far-reaching and related revolution in the state structure underpinning national capitalism. The development of the world economy gave added stimulus to the process of concentration, and ultimately transformed "the entire national economy into one gigantic combined enterprise under the tutelage of the financial kings and the capitalist state."[19] But as already indicated, the progressive fusion of economic and political processes, reflected in part in the development of a central banking system, merely served to accelerate the interpenetration of national economies and to accentuate the force of national antagonisms. The First World War and the Great Depression were a dramatic expression of these two closely interacting trends. It is not surprising, therefore, to find Keynes advocating in the 1930s a return to national self-sufficiency and a retreat from international market capitalism. Expressing a view which was sharply at variance with prevailing notions of international specialization and export-oriented growth, he argued:

> We do not wish . . . to be at the mercy of world forces working out, or trying to work out, some uniform equilibrium according to the ideal principles, if they can be called such, of *laissez-faire* capitalism. . . . We wish--for the time at least and so long as the present transitional experimental phase endures--to be our own masters, and to be as free as we can make ourselves from the interferences of the outside world.[20]

But Keynes' strictures against the world market had relatively little impact on economic policies after the Second World War, which, under American leadership, ushered in a new and unprecedented period of capital expansion through the progressive integration of the world capitalist system. Taking advantage of the favorable economic and political environment created by *Pax Americana,* multinational firms initiated a program of far-reaching industrial and geographical diversification. The liberalization of international trade, the establishment of the dollar as a "vehicle currency" for international business and financial transactions, the

absence of any serious political impediments to the
export of capital and the adoption of large foreign aid
programs greatly assisted the multinational penetration
of national economies.[21]

The financial and administrative strength of the
large corporation enabled it to incorporate the advances
of the physical and social sciences and apply them to the
creation of "a new structure of international industrial
organization and a new international division of
labor."[22] As Stephen Hymer has incisively observed, what
distinguishes the transnational corporation from the
merchant firm and the large mining or plantation
enterprise of previous centuries, as well as from the
modern small-scale manufacturing firm, is the peculiar
combination of extreme specialization and differentiation
with high degrees of centralization and integration. It
is precisely the development of a highly sophisticated
"brain and nervous system" capable of connecting widely
disparate departments and geographically distant
divisions that has made possible the increasingly
cosmopolitan control over raw material requirements and
market outlets.

In the light of the above analysis, one can readily
understand why the transnational corporation should have
been described as the most powerful instrument in the
internationalization of production. According to several
writers, the international mobility of manufacturing
capital and the implicit capacity to relocate production
from one country to another have greatly enhanced
multinational leverage with respect to labor. In turn,
the existence of a relatively disciplined labor force has
been a central factor in the successful accumulation and
expansion of capital. The ability of capital to exploit
the wage differential between national economies
illustrates the international unity of the reproduction
of capital, which paradoxically thrives on and
accentuates the process of uneven development.[23]

Ironically enough, for this economic project to be
realized, it became necessary to apply the Keynesian
theory of state intervention in order to provide adequate
incentives for the private sector, create expanding
domestic and foreign markets, and devise an institutional
framework capable of underpinning the expansion of
international trade and finance. Keynes' theory of state
policy thus became a tool for the continued expansion of
private capital. both nationally and internationally.[24]
The ensuing social structure has been variously described
as the "socio-industrial order,"[25] the "new industrial
state,"[26] the "contract state,"[27] or even the "military-
industrial complex."[28] Whichever term is used to
describe the phenomenon, the inescapable fact of modern
capitalism is the progressive integration of the
productive process with the political apparatus of
society.

Enough has been said to indicate that the state has played a decisive role at each stage of the international division of labor. During the so-called competitive phase of capitalism, the theory of comparative advantage was applied to international trade, thereby producing, in Palloix's terms, the "internationalization of commodity capital." A new phase in the division of labor was ushered in by the expansion of banking capital and its interconnection with industrial capital, thereby extending the process of internationalization to "the circuit of money capital." In the current period, internationalization has spread beyond the circuits of commodity capital (trade) and money capital (finance), and entered a new stage, the internationalization of productive capital (multinational production), which necessarily overlaps with and reinforces the previous two stages.[29] Quite apart from the descriptive value of Palloix's historical conceptualization is its explanatory potential regarding the function of the state. For central to his thesis is the notion that the state has provided the structural underpinning for each of the three phases. The establishment of trading companies, the acquisition of colonies, the alternating policies of protectionism and liberalization, the development of military power, all point to the omnipresence of the state in the creation of the world economy. Applied to the contemporary period, Palloix's argument stands much of the theorizing on the obsolescence of the nation-state on its head, and stresses the critical role of the state (not only the metropolitan state, but also the peripheral and semi-peripheral state) in creating the necessary conditions for the export of capital and the internationalization of production. But in so far as it sustains the international division of labor and accentuates the process of uneven development it may be considered as both agent and victim of the contemporary world crisis.

THE FRAMEWORK OF INTERNATIONALIZATION

Although the growth of the world economy expresses the increasing interdependence of national economies, it is clear that within the world market there exists not a harmonious aggregation but a hierarchical plurality of national markets.[30] It is precisely the uneven and competitive development of the major capitalist economies that led Lenin to his distinctive theory of imperialism. In sharp contrast to Kautsky's notion of a new ultra-imperialist policy which would eliminate national rivalries and "introduce the joint exploitation of the world by internationally united finance capital," Lenin interpreted international alliances as mere truces between wars, which would eventually collapse, and cited the growth of large armament industries as evidence of the incompatibility of national capitals arising from the very internationalization of capital.[31] The Lenin-Kautsky controversy offers, then, two competing theoretical constructs for the analysis of contemporary inter-capitalist relations. On the one hand is the *ultra-imperialist model* which postulates a dominant coalition of relatively autonomous metropolitan states as providing the overarching structure needed to preserve the unity of the system. Translated into traditional phraseology, the major states assume the primary responsibility for maintaining a balance of power, thereby preventing any one among them from achieving hegemony through force. The Leninist model, on the other hand, asserts the primacy of *imperial rivalry* which periodically gives rise to inter-state violence. In other words, the state does not perform a stabilizing function for the system as a whole, but rather acts as an agent for the interests of domestic capital--hence the inevitable collision of rival national capitalisms.

There is, however, a third conceptual framework for the analysis of inter-capitalist relations which has particular relevance for the post-1945 period. This model is predicated on the tendency for economic competitive advantage to become concentrated in a single state. Although domination may not be complete and antagonisms may surface from time to time, the hegemonic state acts as the organizer of world capitalism and preserves its unity in face of internal and external threats. The restructuring of the world's trading and monetary systems at the end of the Second World War and the establishment of a network of military alliances, in so far as they ensured the strategic and economic integration of their members under undisputed American leadership, would appear to conform to this model. The monopoly position of U.S. capital made possible a new phase in capital accumulation resulting in unprecedented economic growth and the gradual absorption of the socialist economies into the world market.[32]

But inherent in this accumulation was the re-emergence of competition. A dialectical situation prevailed: the expansion of U.S. capital required the reconstruction of European and Japanese capital. The only alternative to a direct U.S. role was the creation of competitors who would eventually erode the U.S. monopoly position.[33] Predictably, with the apparent decline of American power since the 1960s, the concept of hegemony or U.S. super-imperialism as the key to an analysis of inter-capitalist relations has fallen into some disfavor--hence the revival of the other two models. Thus, for example, Mandel, who subscribes to the Leninist thesis, argues that the hegemony of the United States is being effectively challenged by the Europeans and the Japanese.[34] In his view, a series of company amalgamations in Europe and Japan, the gradual accumulation of capital, and the growing sophistication of technological know-how have sharply reduced the advantage in productivity held by American capital. To the extent that European and Japanese wages were lower than American wages, increases in productivity enable Europe and Japan to compete successfully with most American products, not only on the world market but even within the American domestic market. The rapid expansion of European and Japanese manufacturing exports as compared with America's deteriorating trade performance is cited as evidence of economic multipolarity.

For Mandel, the process of Western European economic integration is an expression of capitalist concentration on a world scale and an attempt to release European industry from the short-sighted economic nationalism of the inter-war years. The development of large financial and productive units inside the Common Market, assisted by the creation of a supranational state, is seen as dictated by competition with U.S. capitalism. To the extent that European state power is being used to assist European big capital, it acts as a "nationalist force," independent of other states, and constitutes, at least in embryonic form, an "imperialist metropolis." The relationship between capital interpenetration and political integration is described in the following terms:

> . . . the growth of capital interpenetration inside the Common Market, the appearance of large amalgamated banking and industrial units which are not mainly the property of any national capitalist class, represent the material infrastructure for the emergence of supranational state-power organs in the Common Market.[35]

European political integration, it is argued, will hasten the process of merger, rationalization and accumulation, thereby encouraging foreign investment as the most effective means of penetrating foreign markets, in the United States and elsewhere. In this sense, the forces pushing European states into closer alliance with each other are likely to exacerbate tensions between Europe and the United States. Should the European states succeed in forming a single national metropolis they would accentuate international antagonisms and reinforce the trends towards *imperial rivalry* as the dominant tendency within the international capitalist system.

Though the Mandel thesis has been supported by an impressive array of arguments, including the notion that technological superiority and financial and political leverage may be assets of limited and diminishing value,[36] several recent contributions have reasserted the applicability of the *hegemony* model. James Petras and

Robert Rhodes, for example, have argued that the
structural weaknesses of the American imperial system
have been overestimated and allowed to obscure the
reconsolidation of U.S. hegemony in global politics.[37]
In support for this proposition, they point to growing
American dominance in international finance (indicated in
part by the greatly increased assets of the foreign
branches of U.S. banks), and to the advantage which
American capital derives from it. More important, they
stress the nature of political and social relations
within the United States, especially the absence of a
well-organized labor movement, which enables the managers
of American society, unlike their counterparts in Europe
and Japan, to weather economic crises by maintaining high
rates of unemployment, low provision of social services
and large subsidies to privately controlled research and
development. A third structural feature reinforcing
American supremacy in the world economy is said to be its
much greater accessibility to world resources in
comparison with its major potential rivals. Finally, the
long reach of the American state and its continued
military preponderance are seen as enhancing the
penetration of U.S. capital, particularly in peripheral
and semi-peripheral economies. The development of an
Arab industrial complex tied to the American
multinational empire is cited as further evidence of the
overall competitive advantage of the United States within
the world economy.

   While the above assessment sounds a timely warning
to those who would prematurely pronounce the end of Pax
Americana, the argument is far too selective of
historical reality and its theoretical structure
insufficiently rigorous for it to be altogether
convincing. A somewhat more penetrating analysis is
offered by Poulantzas, for whom the decisive factor
remains the pattern of American investment in the
European Community.[38] Contrary to Mandel's argument,
Poulantzas notes that the widespread tendency for
European companies has been to merge with American
companies rather than among themselves. Even in the case
of a European amalgamation, what is normally involved is
not a real merger resulting in integrated production, but
an "understanding" or some limited form of association.
By contrast, mergers involving American corporations
almost invariably produce a substantial shift in
ownership and control in favor of American capital.
Although the consequences of the interpenetration of
capital remain ambiguous, Poulantzas undoubtedly points
to empirical evidence which must be carefully evaluated.

   In any case, Poulantzas himself recognizes that the
dependence of the metropolitan economies (Europe and
Japan) on American capital cannot be equated with the
dependence of the peripheral economies (Third World).
For the metropolises retain a certain autonomy which

leads to "significant contradictions between the internal bourgeoisie and American capital,"[39] and finds expression in the political structure of the state. In other words, the uneasy alliance between the metropolises, while reflecting American hegemony, involves considerable elements of conflict. The current internationalization of capital, far from producing the extinction of the nation-state under the aegis of the American superstate, gives rise to a system of complex and growing interactions among metropolitan states, although the dominant power (the United States) retains a decisive role both within the system as a whole and in each of its constituent units. Poulantzas concludes that American hegemony, while it has generally declined in comparison with the exceptional levels it reached soon after the Second World War, has actually gained strength by the very fact of European reconstruction. The reactivation of inter-capitalist rivalries signifies, then, a new phase but not the end of American hegemony. Clearly, Poulantzas has taken the debate a step further by shifting attention away from national economies as a whole and towards the performance of particular sectors within the national economy, notably the relationship between foreign and local capital. The other related conclusion of Poulantzas' analysis is that what is currently in crisis is not American hegemony as such, but the world economy as a whole. The crisis arises from the internationalization of capitalist relations, and is experienced *internally* within each nation-state.

Though illuminating in many respects, Poulantzas' systematic approach suffers from several defects. The first and the most obvious is the mechanistic tendency to interpret the state as a superstructure whose function is merely to represent the interests of dominant capital, whether foreign or indigenous. We shall return to this question later. Suffice it to say for the moment, the relationship between nation-states cannot be reduced to one between national capitals, nor to one between foreign and local capital within each nation-state. To this extent, the hegemony of American capital within other national economies, even if it were empirically demonstrable, need not be reflected in the hegemony of the American state. Nor can American capital be considered as a homogeneous entity either in terms of its role within the American economy or of its effects upon the European economies. Moreover, if it is true that the entire capitalist system is in crisis, then the very fact that it is internalized by each state is likely to exacerbate tensions among states, which in turn are likely to undermine the supremacy of the imperial state. Indeed, there is good reason to suggest that the crisis of world capitalism is inextricably intertwined with the decline of American power. For the American state no longer seems able to perform the stabilizing and

coordinating functions which made possible the rapid
development of capitalist interdependence. In this
sense, the crisis of the 1970s, strikingly reflected in
the decline of the dollar as the chief instrument for the
international centralization of credit and the consequent
abandonment of fixed exchange rates, is in no small
measure an expression of the destabilizing transition
from the politics of *hegemony* to the politics of *imperial
rivalry*. The crisis has become all the more acute as a
result of the Soviet-American adversary relationship and
the stalemate inherent in the balance of terror, both of
which contribute to the polycentric tendencies of the
capitalist system. Placed within this context, the
crisis of the advanced capitalist state is the internal
manifestation of the fundamental contradiction underlying
the world market as a whole, namely, the contradiction
between integration and fragmentation.

IMPACT OF INTERNATIONALIZATION ON THE STATE

Reference has already been made to the
interdependence of national economies which arises from
the international expansion of capital, but what has not
yet been sufficiently stressed is the resulting
politicization of international economic relations. The
progressive integration of the world economy drastically
increases its impact on national economic goals, while at
the same time sharply reducing the efficiency of national
policy instruments. Moreover, the process of economic
interpenetration is experienced differently not only by
different states but also by different sectors within
each state, thereby benefiting some sectors and
disadvantaging others. In so far as it encourages and
accentuates domestic conflict, international integration
threatens national disintegration.

Economic internationalization, it has been argued,
increases the vulnerability of national economies by
exposing them to unpredictable and potentially
uncontrollable external pressures. Reference is often
made to the destabilizing consequences of the enormous
and increasingly frequent capital shifts. The Eurodollar
market, for example, provides a source of credit outside
the control of national authorities, and acts as a
transmitter of changes in overseas rate structures into
the domestic money market. The global monetary policies
of multinational enterprises, implemented through a
variety of methods, including dividends, royalty payments
and transfer pricing, have often caused the movement of
short-term funds in directions contrary to domestic
policy, and have accentuated the crisis in the balance of
national payments.[40]

These monetary pressures, which are a direct
expression of economic transnationalism, have led several

writers to stress the progressive erosion of *national sovereignty*. [41] They point out that the capacity for rapid, flexible, and yet centralized decision-making which is available to the global corporation with respect to the location of personnel and capital equipment, as well as the design, marketing and distribution of goods and services, makes possible the global transfer and rearrangement of information, expertise and product components to an extent beyond the reach of a territorially restricted institution such as the nation-state. Lacking the financial, technological and managerial resources of the multinational corporation, traditional instruments of national economic management are narrowly circumscribed in their range of options and made structurally dependent on foreign capital. Although the challenge of multinational enterprise is most acutely experienced in underdeveloped economies, the phenomenon, it is claimed, is universal, and threatens to displace the state as the irreducible unit of political economy.

The preceding line of argument, with its emphasis on the obsolescence of the state, may have gained increasing support from both supporters and detractors of multinational enterprise, but it provides at best a superficial description of the historical process. To begin with, although multinational production represents a new stage in the process of internationalization, the process itself is not of recent origin. As Heilbroner has incisively observed:

> The internationalization of production undoubtedly leads to new problems, both for the economic production mechanism and the political control apparatus of capitalism. But that is a very different thing from asserting that the multinationals have transformed capitalism in such a way as to reduce its political-economic tension, much less to resolve it in favor of the hegemony of the internationalized company. [42]

The tension between business and the state is characterized as a conflict between two modes of organizing economic activity--a "vertical mode" based on the multinational corporation, and a "horizontal mode" based on the state. In Heilbroner's view, the situation of conflict is likely to persist for some time to come, and both modes of organization may enhance their power in the coming decades. However intense or protracted the contest between them, Heilbroner considers it unlikely that the corporation will ever develop "the quasi-religious appeal of identity offered by the national state," and predicts a strengthening of the political arm of capitalism as a direct consequence of the continued expansion of the international corporation and the need for increased planning and political control.

Heilbroner's conclusion undoubtedly conforms with the historically observable pattern of steadily increasing involvement by the state in economic life. Indeed, the integration of the world economy, which causes both cyclical and secular fluctuations to be transmitted more swiftly between national economies, reinforces the trend. As we have already observed, it is the very process of international accumulation and crisis which consolidates the organization of the world market into nation-states.[43] The emergence of each economic crisis drives the state further along the road of control, particularly in conditions of increasing international competition.[44] The internationalization of capitalist production, it is true, once it has advanced beyond a certain point, is not necessarily tied to the fortunes of any particular state. It is nevertheless the state rather than the individual firm which shoulders the primary responsibility for maintaining the economic and political conditions necessary for the continued viability of capitalist production. In other words, in assessing the relationship between the state and the multinational corporation, account has to be taken not so much of the independent power of the large firm *vis-à-vis* the individual nation-state considered in isolation, but rather of the relationship between the world economy and the state system as a whole, that is, between a single economic division of labor and a multiplicity of sovereign states.

Only an integrated perspective can overcome the conceptual difficulties posed by the national origins of international capital and the international functions of the nation-state. After all, the modern metropolitan state has to relate to both local and foreign capital, just as the multinational corporation has to operate in both home and host states. While home states may have traditionally exercised greater control over multinational corporations than host states, the situation may be rapidly changing, partly as a result of the new global balance of power. The hegemonic integration of the capitalist system under American leadership may have for a time suggested a declining role for the state(or at least most states) in the regulation of international economic relations. However, to the extent that the actions of a superstate may have undermined the national instruments of policy available to other metropolitan states, the shift towards polycentrism is likely to reverse the trend. In an increasingly fragmented world economy, in which the disruptive impact of competing interests is likely to outweigh the regulatory potential of existing institutions, states will find it necessary to acquire even greater powers of economic management in the defense of national interests, which may well involve supporting and extending the stake of domestic capital in economic or territorial spaces subject to the power of foreign states. The internationalization of capital, especially in times of stagflation and mounting international rivalry, will lead to the internalization of the crisis within the nation-state, which will, in turn, increase the functional importance of national economic management.

THE FUNCTIONS OF THE STATE

If one accepts the view that the interpenetration of national economies extends rather than diminishes the organizational reach of the nation-state, it becomes necessary to elucidate the function of the state and its relationship to the process of internationalization.

Much of the confusion with respect to the economic role of the state is, in fact, related to the widespread but mistaken conception of "state intervention," common to neo-classical and Keynesian economics. According to the neo-classical view, exemplified in recent years by the writings of Jacques Rueff and Milton Friedman, the state can neither foresee nor avoid economic crises. It merely encourages the development of crises by obstructing the free play of market forces.[45] Thus, for example, social measures such as employment benefits are said to destroy the mechanisms of the labor market and prevent the return to equilibrium. According to this type of argument, which finds expression in a variety of forms and provides the basis for the theoretical attack on the welfare state, the Keynesian prescription for state intervention is doubly harmful, for instead of reducing public spending to the minimum, it concentrates on fiscal and financial measures which impede the primary task of monetary control. In Friedman's view, the economic crisis of 1929-30 did not result from the drastic fall in private investment but from the failure of American monetary policy. Similarly, the crisis of the 1970s is interpreted as the outcome of a misconceived policy which transformed a transitional period between two states of long-run equilibrium into a serious recession combining high levels of unemployment with high rates of inflation.

In opposition to the neo-classical argument, Keynesian economic policy, which has held sway in most capitalist countries since the Second World War, questions the existence of a true labor market, and considers the level of employment to be dependent on the level of investment.[46] It is, therefore, the function of the state to intervene periodically in order to offset low levels of private investment with higher rates of public spending. Keynesian principles have gained widespread acceptance, especially among social-democratic parties, which have looked upon government spending as a useful instrument for maintaining full employment and redistributing income, thereby increasing total consumption and reducing social inequalities. Though the debate between Keynesians and neo-classicists points to divergent diagnoses and prescriptions, it also highlights a fundamental notion common to both schools. In each case, economic policy is conceived in terms of "intervention" by the state as a political entity entering the economic realm in order to achieve the desired state of equilibrium. Whether one views state "intervention" as disruptive of long-run equilibium (in the neo-classical perspective), or as contributing to a new and higher equilibrium (in the Keynesian perspective), in both cases economic crises are considered not intrinsic to industrial capitalism but the result of misguided intervention by the state on the one hand, or the failure of the state to intervene on the other.[47]

There is however, an altogether different perspective, shared by several Marxist theorists, which considers economic crises as integral to the process of capital accumulation.[48] A crisis does not signify simply a break in a given equilibrium or a downturn in economic activity, but "intra-class conflict over surplus value," resulting in "a failure to realize surplus value and, therefore, profit."[49] From the perspective of capitalist society, the recurrence of crisis may be considered as "a feedback loop which permits readjustment to change reproduction conditions,"[50] thereby overcoming the constraints internal to the dynamic of the capitalist economy.

According to Marx, the fundamental contradiction inherent in the capitalist mode of production does not arise so much from the lack of effective demand (underconsumption) as from the attempt to control wage costs, which undermines the possibility of a wider consumer demand and contradicts the goal of continued accumulation:

> The real barrier of capitalist production is *capital itself*. . . . The capitalist mode of production is, for this reason, a historical means of developing the material forces of production and creating an appropriate world-market and is, at the same time, a continual conflict between this, its historical task, and its own corresponding relations of social production.[51]

In other words, the crisis of capitalist accumulation can be traced to the contradictions inherent in both the processes of production and circulation. But as already indicated, the crisis reflects not only the obstacles to the self-expansion of capital (which finds expression in the tendency of the rate of profit to fall), but the various steps undertaken by the capitalist class to surmount these obstacles (i.e., to counteract the tendency of the rate of profit to fall). Understood in this sense, the crisis of capitalism should be equated not so much with economic recession and its various manifestations (e.g., rise in the rate of unemployment, acceleration in the rate of inflation, decline of production),[52] as with the fluctuation between periods of boom and periods of stagnation. The world economic crisis contains two elements: "the possibility of the recovery of capitalism and the possibility of its abolition."[53] Historically, it should be remembered, crisis, depression and world war have led not to the collapse but to the rebirth of capitalism. It is indeed, an open question whether the establishment of socialist states and centrally planned economies has entailed a clear-cut or permanent contraction of the capitalist sphere of influence.

On the other hand, it is also true that with each successive crisis, the strains operating within the system are greatly accentuated. For out of each crisis emerges the potential for the realization of a greater mass of surplus value but also for much sharper inter-class and intra-class conflict, both of which require, in the interests of the system's survival, the elimination of less efficient capitals through the process of concentration and centralization. But while this trend inevitably leads to the absorption of weaker enterprises and states by larger and more powerful ones, it proceeds under stress and is characterized by a series of political and economic conflicts and convulsions.[54] Each major crisis represents, therefore, a springboard for the reorganization of the system as a whole and the restructuring of the national barriers within which capitalism has hitherto developed. As the opportunities for the expansion of capital shift from one sector to another, from one country to another, or even from one continent to another, powerful pressures develop in the direction of the rationalization of production and the readjustment of the social and political structures of the world economy.

From this brief analysis of the concept of crisis, it emerges that the state is, on the one hand, an agent of conflict and a contributor to the crisis, since it institutionalizes and reinforces the separation of the productive capacities of society from the men whose living labor activates them. On the other hand, the state is also one of the principal instruments used to resolve the crisis and eliminate the restrictive conditions which block the reproduction of the capitalist economy.

The state may, for example, contribute to a crisis of overproduction by assisting the process of capital accumulation. But once a crash has occurred and supply has momentarily declined, the state can help to organize the political compromises which make possible the reallocation of income, thereby giving a boost to demand and allowing capital accumulation to resume its upward path. Similarly, a policy of controlled inflation can be seen as a mechanism for diffusing crises of overproduction and thereby preventing a dramatic collapse of economic activity.

Notwithstanding its conceptual elegance, this analysis has to be treated with caution, for it may end up interpreting economic crises as the conscious policy of the capitalist state, thereby endowing the state with a degree of political and economic mastery which it does not possess. On the other hand, it rightly points to the endogenous structural role of the state in the management of the economy and the reproduction of capitalist relations, a role which may in the long run exacerbate rather than relieve the crisis.

To begin with, it cannot be readily assumed that the increasing integration of political and economic functions implies that the state is the faithful and obedient servant of the capitalist class.[55] True enough, in the vast majority of advanced capitalist economies the state has assumed primary resonsibility for establishing the legal conditions for property relations, for regulating the business cycle, for reproducing the labor force and ensuring the maintenance of discipline at work, for rationalizing the land market, for supplying credit and subsidies to industry, for funding scientific and technological research, for organizing energy, transport and communications systems, for maintaining social cohesion through the provision of a wide range of welfare services, and for managing the external relations of the economy. This long list of functions and activities, however, while accurately describing the expanding economic role of the state, is nevertheless analytically deficient on two related counts: its reductionist emphasis on the instrumental character of the state, and its neglect of the contradictions to which it is subjected.[56] For capitalist state structures do not automatically represent the interests of capitalist producers; they are also the battlefield on which are fought the economic and political antagonisms in capitalist society. The state is not the expression of the capitalist general will. The administrative and political limits of the state--not the least important of which are the imperfect information on which it bases its decisions, its ideological vacillation between intervention and non-intervention, and the often conflicting functions which it is expected to perform--all tend to invalidate the notion of the state as a mere appendage of monopoly capitalism.[57] On the contrary, the growing instability of capitalism which becomes particularly acute in periods of crisis when giant financial capitals tend to eliminate their weaker brothers, compels an expanded role for the state, for it is the only institution which can act to restructure capital, rationalize competition, lessen the violence of the crisis and thereby counteract the tendency to self-destruction.

While required to provide the technocratic framework necessary for capital accumulation, the capitalist state also needs to maintain the legitimacy of this process. The accumulation and legitimation functions are translated into demands for increased state intervention, which invariably require increased state expenditures. The inability to satisfy these multi-faceted and cumulative demands is described by James O'Connor as the "fiscal crisis of the state," and is explained in terms of the contradictory relationship between the monopoly, competitive and state sectors of the economy.[58] According to Jurgen Habermas, the competing demands on fiscal policy ultimately threaten a crisis of legitimacy, for the state has the dual and unenviable task of reconciling administrative efficiency with legitimation of the process.[59] The political conflict which inevitably surrounds the task of national economic management and the shifting political coalitions to which it gives rise indicate both the relative autonomy of the state and the severe constraints within which it operates. The need to ensure legitimation through political abstinence requires that the system provide suitable private rewards, whether in terms of money, leisure time or security. But to satisfy this privatism through a welfare state program is likely to exaggerate the twin problems of inflation and government spending.[60] Resolution of the crisis at one level may tend to displace it to another and perhaps higher level.

These limitations are equally apparent in the sphere of external policy. The nation-state, it is true, does perform essential functions for the overseas operations of domestic capital as well as for foreign capital which invests within its national boundaries. It may serve their interests through a mixture of positive inducements and negative sanctions mediated through a wide range of legal and diplomatic instruments, including tariffs, monetary and aid agreements, export credits, investment guarantees, services of commercial branches of diplomatic missions, international policing, extradition treaties, military alliances, and the establishment of regional and international organizations. Indeed, the state may use force or the threat of force to alter existing state boundaries either through secession or annexation. The state thus not only reflects the prevailing international division of labor, but may interfere directly with the flow of the factors of production, thereby altering the structure of the world market.[61] However, the performance of these functions is limited not so much by the territorial reach of each state as by domestic political and economic cleavages and the competition between antagonistic national or imperial interests.

The attempt by the state to introduce a measure of order and predictability in international economic relations, by performing a regulatory function in an otherwise anarchic world economy, is at least partly undermined by the national crisis of economic management and the political polarization which it implies. The internal "disarticulation" and heterogeneity of the nation-state thus mirrors and accentuates the fragmentation of the international capitalist system, particularly in the period of imperial rivalry.

The national bankruptcies and bank failures which occurred in 1973-74 were no doubt inextricably linked with the international monetary crisis and the collapse of the Bretton Woods system. In this sense, the conflict between domestic and foreign capital, between the different sectors of capital within each national economy, and between the different political blocs which vie for control of the state apparatus, is both national and international in character. The shift towards more coercive forms of political control, reflected in the decline of parliamentary democracy and the erosion of civil liberties, together with the development of ever more sophisticated military and para-military systems of control,[62] expresses the internal and external responses of the state to the declining efficacy of its attempts to transform the crisis into recovery. This trend is also illustrated in the nuclear arms race, which contributes, through vertical and horizontal proliferation, to the pervasive international climate of hostility, suspicion and tension, thereby drastically accentuating the crisis of national security.[63] At what point the dysfunctional consequences of state action and reaction create the conditions necessary for the transformation of the system itself remains a crucial but as yet unanswered question.

SOME TENTATIVE CONCLUSIONS

The preceding pages have attempted to shed some light on the nature of advanced capitalism with particular reference to the crisis of the state, which has traditionally played a central role in the process of capital accumulation. Attention has been focused on four crucial interaction relationships--namely, those between the state and the expansion of capital; those between national economic management and international economic interdependence; those between states within varying configurations of power; and those between the different and, at times, contradictory functions of the state.

A careful examination of these processes suggests that, contrary to much fashionable theorizing, the

advanced capitalist state is not about to be superseded
by the multinational corporation as the major actor on
the world stage. Even in the periphery of the capitalist
system, where the resilience of the state is perhaps
weakest, the system of multinational enterprise gives
little indication of being able to overcome the rising
obstacles to the accumulation process. The trend applies
with even greater force in the advanced sectors of the
capitalist world, where economic crises are compelling
metropolitan states to impose new limits of manoeuvre on
the productive units within and beyond their borders.
One may, therefore safely forecast a state of continuing
tension between the state and the multinational
corporation.

In any case, the crisis of the state does not derive
from the so-called challenge of the multinational
corporation, which is the symptom rather than the source
of the problem. The crisis of the state reflects, first
and foremost, the contradiction between the declining
room for manoeuvre available to national economies and
the increasing interdependence which ties them together.
Indeed, the accelerating expansion of trade and capital
flows, characteristic of the most recent phase in the
process of internationalization , narrows the range of
national policy options, while at the same time
magnifying the need for state intervention in the
economy. Increasing economic interdependence enhances
the economic and political functions of the state while
at the same time diminishing the efficacy of its
intervention. The state's predicament has become all the
more acute in the wake of competing claims on its limited
resources and the latent conflict between the productive
and legitimizing functions. Although the state can
displace crises through various processes of bargaining
and can even shirk responsibility for certain crises,
there are limits to the viability of these options;
conflicting priorities must somehow be reconciled if the
political unity and underlying cultural cohesion of the
state are to be preserved.

An additional destabilizing factor arises from the
development of inter-capitalist rivalries. The
increasing intervention of the American state to offset
the decline of American hegemony tends to provoke actual
or threatened retaliation by other metropolitan states.
The trend towards European political integration and the
implicit mobilization of state resources on behalf of
European firms, if maintained, will assist the expansion
of European capital and intensify the conflict with
American capital. The gradual assertion of Japanese
power in the diplomatic as well as the economic arena
points in the same direction.

Paradoxically, however, polycentric tendencies
within world capitalism, precisely because they fragment
power and threaten the cohesion of the world economy,

necessitate state planning, and, by implication, a strengthening of the national capitalist state. The resulting contradiction between an integrated capitalist system, made increasingly interdependent by the international division of labor, and a capitalist system divided between rival capitals and nation-states, is crucial to an understanding of the persistence of the national state and the crisis which confronts it. The very process of internationalization helps to internalize the disruption caused by an increasingly fragmented and polarized international system and to magnify the level of domestic conflict. The resulting threat to the national cohesion of the modern industrial state finds expression not merely in the groping efforts towards regional and international organization and, less commonly, supranational integration, but also in continuing attempts to strengthen the ideological, legal, administrative and coercive levels of the state. However, the growing evidence of ethnic, cultural, generational and political conflict, coupled with the widening gap between the promise and performance of the national economy, suggests that the imposing facade of state power and authority may conceal an increasingly complex, unmanageable and fragile edifice.

NOTES

1. *See* J. W. Burton, *World Society* (Cambridge, 1972); R. Falk, *A Study of Future Worlds* (Amsterdam, 1975); Seyom Brown, *New Forces in World Politics* (Washington, D.C., 1974).

2. J. W. Burton, *Systems, States, Diplomacy and Rules* (Cambridge, 1968), p. 10.

3. The primacy of economic considerations is strikingly reflected in the foreign policy pronouncements of all major capitalist governments during the 1970s. *See* Helmut Schmidt, "The Struggle for the World Product," *Foreign Affairs,* Vol. 52, No. 3, April 1974, pp. 437-451; Walter F. Mondale, "Beyond Détente: Toward International Economic Security," *Foreign Affairs,* Vol. 53, No. 1, October 1974, pp. 1-23. *See also* J.E.S. Hayward and R. N. Berki (eds.), *State and Society in contemporary Europe* (Oxford, 1979).

4. I. Wallerstein, "Semi-Peripheral Countries and the Contemporary World Crisis," *Theory and Society,* Vol. 3, No. 4, Winter 1976, pp. 461-484.

5. Although there is considerable variation in the use of terms, for the purpose of this analysis dominant/dependent, center (core)/periphery and metropolis/satellite will be used interchangeably.

6. I. Wallerstein, "Semi-Peripheral Countries and the Contemporary World Crisis," p. 464.

7. *See* I. Wallerstein, "The Rise and Future Demise

of the World Capitalist System: Concepts for Comparative Analysis," *Comparative Studies in Society and History,* Vol. 16, 1974, pp. 387-415.

8.   For a penetrating analysis of the peripheral state in terms of its domestic functions and role within the world economy, *see* W. Ziemann and M. Lanzendorfer, "The State in Peripheral Societies," in *The Socialist Register 1977,* edited by R. Miliband and John Saville (London, 1978).

9.   For a review of the literature *see Latin American Perspectives,* Vol. 1, No. 1, Spring 1974, and J. Camilleri, "Dependence and the Politics of Disorder," *Arena,* Nos. 44-45, 1976, pp. 34-58.

10.   *See* I. Wallerstin, "Trends in World Capitalism," *Monthly Review,* May 1974, Vol. 25, No. 12, p. 16.

11.   The possible fusion of western corporate interests and communist planning systems is discussed by Irving Louis Horowitz, "Capitalism, Communism and Multinationalism," in *The New Sovereigns: Multinational Corporations as World Powers,* edited by A, Said and L. Simmons (Englewwod Cliffs, N.J., 1975).

12.   *See* C. Fred Bergsten, *Toward a New Internatonal Economic Order: Selected Papers, 1972-74* (Lexington, Mass., 1975), especially Part I.

13.   It has been argued that the world economy already existed in sixteenth-century Europe, since by that time capitalist commodity production was organized "by a world market in which both purely economic competitive advantage and political interference by states play[ed] an interactive role." (*See* Christopher Chase-Dunn and Richard Rubinson, "Toward a Structural Prospective on the World System," *Politics and Society,* Vol. 7, No. 4, 1977, p. 455.)

14.   Karl Marx and Frederick Engels, "Manifesto of the Communist Party," in Marx and Engels, *Selected Works* (New York, 1968), pp. 38-39.

15.   J. A. Hobson, *Imperialism: A Study* (Ann Arbor, Michigan, 1965), p. 85.

16.   N. Bukharin, *Imperialism and World Economy* (London, 1972), Parts I and II.

17.   *See* R. Hilferding, *Finance Capital: A Study of the Most Recent Development of Capitalism* (Vienna, 1923); also H. Feis, *Europe: The World's Banker 1870-1914: An Account of European Foreign Investment and the Connection of World Finance with Diplomacy Before the War* (New Haven, Conn., 1930).

18.   Paul Mattick, *Marx and Keynes: The Limits of the Mixed Economy* (London, 1971), p. 135.

19.   N. Bukharin, *Imperialism and the World Economy* p. 73.

20.   John Maynard Keynes, "National Self-Sufficiency," *The Yale Review,* Vol. 22, Summer 1933, pp. 761-762.

21.   For an examination of various theoretical perspectives   on   the   phenomenon   of   economic transnationalism *see* Joseph A. Camilleri, *Civilization in Crisis: Human Prospects in a Changing World* (Cambridge, 1976), pp. 92-112.

22.   Stephen Hymer, "The Multinational Corporation and the Law of Uneven Development," in J. Bhagwati (ed.), *Economics and World Order from the 1970s to the 1990s* (New York, 1972), p. 114.

23.   Christian Palloix, *Les firmes multinationales et le procès d'internationalisation* (Paris, 1973); Nicos Poulantzas,   *Classes   in   Contemporary   Capitalism,* translated from the French by David Fernbach (London, 1975).

24.   *See* Andrew Schonfeld, *Modern Capitalism: The Changing Balance of Public and Private Power* (London, 1965).

25.   Raymond Aron, *Progress and Disillusion: The Dialectics of Modern Society* (London, 1968).

26.   John Kenneth Galbraith, *The New Industrial State* (2nd ed.) (Harmondsworth, 1974).

27.   H. L. Nieburg, *In the Name of Science* (Chicago, 1966).

28.   Fred J. Cook, *The Warfare State* (New York, 1962), Sidney Lens, *The Military-Industrial Complex* (Boston, 1970).

29.   Christian Palloix, "The Self-Expansion of Capital on a World Scale," from *L'Internationalisation du capital* (Paris, 1975), *The Review of Radical Political Economics,* Vol. 9, No. 2, Summer 1977, pp. 11-12.

30.   *See* R. Murray, "The Internationalization of Capital and the Nation-State," *New Left Review,* No. 67, May-June 1971, pp. 84-109.

31.   *See* V. I. Lenin, *Imperialism: The Highest Stage of Capitalism* first published 1917 (Moscow, 1970); K. Kautsky, "Ultra-Imperialism, *Die Neue Zeit,* September 1914, translated in *New Left Review,* No. 59, January-February 1970.

32.   The hegemony model has been developed by several   writers,   including   H.   Magdoff,   *The   Age   of Imperialism*   (New   York,   1969),   and   P.   Jalee, *L'Impérialisme en 1970* (Paris, 1970).

33.   *See* John Weeks, "The Sphere of Production and the Analysis of Crisis in Capitalism," *Science & Society,* Vol. XLI, No. 3, 1977, pp. 294-295.

34.   E.   Mandel,   *Europe   versus   America? Contradictions of Imperialism* (London, 1970); *see also* E. Mandel, "The Laws of Uneven Development," *New Left Review,* No. 59, January-February 1970.

35.   E.   Mandel,   "International   Capitalism   and Supranationality," in R. Miliband and J. Saville (eds.), *The Socialist Register 1967* (London, 1967), p. 31.

36.   Bob Rowthorn, "Imperialism in the 1970s--Unity or Rivalry," *New Left Review,* No. 69, September-October

1971, p. 35.

37. James Petras and Robert Rhodes, "The Reconsolidation of U.S. Hegemony," *New Left Review*, No. 97, May-June 1976.

38. N. Poulantzas, *Classes in Contemporary Capitalism*, pp. 42-69.

39. *Ibid.*, p. 72.

40. *See* Lawrence B. Krause, "The International Economic System and the Multinational Corporation," *Annals of the American Academy of Political Sciences*, Vol. 43, September 1972; *Multinational Corporations in World Development*, published by the Department of Economic and Social Affairs, United Nations, New York, 1973.

41. This theme appears in the writings of numerous authors, many of them with sharply contrasting ideological persuasions. *See* Jean Jacques Servan-Schreiber, *The American Challenge*, translated by R. Stell (New York, 1968); Osvaldo Sunkel, "Integration capitaliste transnationale et desintegration nationale en Amerique Latine," *Politique Etrangere*, No. 6, 1970; Daniel Jay Baum, "The Global Corporation: An American Challenge to the Nation State," *Iowa Law Review*, No. 55, December 1969.

42. Robert L. Heilbroner, *Business Civilization in Decline* (Harmondsworth, 1977), pp. 75-76.

43. *See* Claudia von Braunmuhl, "On the Analysis of the Bourgeois Nation State within the World Market Context," in *State and Capital*, edited by John Holloway and Sol Picciotto (London, 1978), p. 176.

44. *See* Bill Warren, "The Internationalization of Capital and the Nation State: A Comment," *New Left Review*, No. 68, July-August 1971.

45. Milton Friedman, *Capitalism and Freedom* (Chicago, 1962); *See also* Milton Friedman and Anna Schwartz, *The Great Contraction, 1929-1933* (Princeton, 1965); Jacques Rueff, *on Le Peche monetaire de l'Occident* (Paris, 1971).

46. John Maynard Keynes, *The General Theory of Employment, Interest and Money* (London, 1965).

47. For an incisive critique of the liberal and Keynesian notions of "state intervention," *see* Suzanne de Brunhoff, "Crise capitaliste et politique economique," in *La crise de l'Etat*, sous la direction de Nicos Poulantzas (Paris, 1976).

48. Some of these theories are reviewed in D. A. Gold, C.Y.H. Lo, and E. O. Wright, "Recent Developments in Marxist Theories of the Capitalist State," *Monthly Review*, Vol. 27, Nos. 5-6, October-November 1975.

49. John Weeks, "The Sphere of Production and the Analysis of Crisis in Capitalism," p. 289.

50. Trent Schroyer, "Marx's Theory of the Crisis," *Telos*, No. 14, Winter 1972, p. 111.

51. Karl Marx, *Capital*, Vol. III (Moscow, 1968), p.

250.

52.   The   error   of   characterizing   periods   of
stability and prosperity in capitalism as temporary and
crises   as   permanent   is   incisively   argued   by   Athar
Hussain,   "Crises   and   Tendencies   of   Capitalism,"   *Economy
and Society,* Vol. 6, 1977, pp. 436-460.   This article is
essentially   a   review   of   *Late   Capitalism,*   by   E.   Mandel
(1975)   and   *Capitalism   in   Crisis,*   by   A.   Gamble   and   P.
Walton (1976).

53.   Margaret   Wirth,   "Towards   a   Critique   of   the
Theory   of   State   Monopoly   Capitalism,"   *Economy   and
Society,* Vol. 6, 1977, pp. 307-308.

54.   *See* John Weeks, "The Sphere of Production and
the Analysis of Crisis in Capitalism," pp. 281-302.

55.   *See* Boris Frankel, *Marxist   Theories   of   the
State: A Critique of Orthodoxy* (Melbourne, 1978).

56.   This pitfall is clearly recognized though not
altogether   avoided   in   Suzanne   de   Burnhoff's   masterly
analysis of the state's role in managing money and labor-
power.   *See* her book *The State, Capital and Economic
Policy,* translated by Mike Sonenscher (London, 1978).

57.   Margaret   Wirth,   "Towards   a   Critique   of   the
Theory   of   State   Monopoly   Capitalism,"   *Economy   and
Society,* Vol. 6, 1977, pp. 284-313.

58.   James O'Connor, *The Fiscal Crisis of the State*
(New York, 1973).

59.   Jurgen   Habermas,   "What   Does   a   Crisis   Mean
Today? Legitimation Problems In Late Capitalism," *Social
Research,* Vol. 41, No. 4, Winter 1973, p. 656.

60.   Habermas   analyzes   the   crisis   tendencies   in
advanced capitalism in relation to the economic system
(economic crisis), the political system (rationality and
legitimation   crisis),   and   the   socio-cultural   system
(motivation crisis).   See Jurgen Habermas, *Legitimation
Crisis* (Boston, 1975), especially Part II.

61.   *See* Immanuel Wallerstein, *The Capitalist World
Eocnomy* (Cambridge, 1979), p. 292.

62.   *See* Dominique Chavet, "Crise de la Justice,
crise de la Loi, crise de l'Etat," in *La crise de l'Etat,*
sous la direction de Nicos Poulantzas (Paris, 1976).

63.   *See* John H. Herz, *International Politics in the
Atomic Age* (New York, 1959); also Kenneth Boulding, "The
Role   of   the   War   Industry   in   International   Conflict,"
Journal of Social Issues, Vol. 23, No. 1, January 1967.

PART 3

Hegemony, Resistance, and Reassertion

CHAPTER 6

Dependence in a Unified World

Celso Furtado

INTRODUCTION

Who could fail to be aware that almost every nation
on earth is at present engaged in trying to acquire, or
not to part with, the dazzling array of technologies
developed specially since World War II? And who could
fail to realize that one group of countries holds the
lead in the accumulation process, the principal vector in
the development of these technologies? These two
questions reveal the core of a historical reality that
must be taken into account in any reflection on the
contemporary world.

Notwithstanding the diversity of world-views
produced by utopian thought in the nineteenth
century--under the impetus of the profound disruption of
social structures that took place during the first phase
of industrial civilization--the present century has
tended to be *par excellence* the age of uniformity in
relation to human needs. The Russian Revolution, at one
time regarded as the harbinger of a new project for
civilization, proved to be merely a short cut to
overcoming backwardness in the accumulation process. Its
leaders took it for granted that the quickest way to make
up for lost time was to copy the Western model of
industrialization: the more faithful the copy, the
faster the progress. Moreover, the choice of the
shortest route involved the acquisition of international
means of payment in order to acquire the necessary
techniques wherever they were available. The corollary
was to pay for them with primary products or other goods
incorporating simpler techniques and be sucked into the
system of international division of labour which operates
essentially in the interests of those in the vanguard of

Reprinted by permission from *Alternatives: A Journal of
World Policy* 8:2, 1982.

technological development. In this way, industrial civilization was able to preserve its unity, even though the processes whereby it was spread became more diversified. This situation engendered, and still engenders, a cultural dependency that affects, in varying degrees, all national economies striving to reduce the gap separating them from the economies leading the accumulation process

The structural relationships resulting from the technological unity of industrial civilization, which constitutes the basic web of dependency, should be seen against the background of developments in the countries that exercise the power of initiative in technical creativity. Progressive integration of national markets led to homogenization also of consumption patterns and to concentration of economic power on an international scale--the global market conditioning the orientation of the innovatory activity in the technology field. Potential economies of scale could be more fully achieved and the natural resource base, particularly in agriculture, could be more rationally exploited. Competition based on prices (differentiated by protective tariffs) finally gave way to competition based on innovation and vertical compartmentalization of markets backed by advertising.

It would take us too far afield if we were to give a detailed description of the complex process whereby the capitalism of the competing major national systems was transformed into this new form of capitalism, in which accumulation and innovation were essentially controlled by groups of transnationally organized enterprises. Suffice it to note that these changes are not unrelated to the two great wars of the first half of the century, which produced the enormous concentration of military power in the world. The military tutelage exercised by the United States favoured the dismantling of colonial structures and the removal of barriers to the free circulation of goods and capital, and this opened up vast new spaces for the operations of the major American enterprises, with the technical and financial capacity to structure their activities on a global scale.

THE EMERGENCE OF MULTINATIONAL CORPORATIONS

A study of the group of economies comprising the centre of the capitalist world shows that the most striking feature of their recent evolution is the strengthening of the position of the large enterprise. The large enterprise now performs far wider and more complex functions both at home and abroad. Indeed, the traditional concept of industrial enterprise no longer applies to conglomerates controlling dozens of operational units that enjoy considerable autonomy.

Their role in concentrating economic power has been intensified as a result of the opening up of new areas in the post-war period. In the United States, between 1950 and 1970, the 500 largest enterprises increased their share in employment, profits and assets of the country's manufacturing and mining activities from 40 percent to 70 percent. Even more significant, however, is the fact that the rate of concentration in the 1960s was double that of the 1950s. Transnational corporations have also rapidly increased their share of their respective home markets. Since they specialize in certain productive processes or stages, an international transaction can be transformed into a straightforward operation within the group itself. Transnational expansion of the group thus makes it possible to intensify the division of labour among its parts and to exploit economies of scale and group efforts to full advantage.

The experience of the last few decades has shown that the idea of national boundaries, which played a leading part in the earlier development of capitalism, has become an obstacle to the full employment of the technology now available. By removing constraints on the activities of enterprises at the international level, American tutelage was bound to accelerate the accumulation process. One of the consequences of the opening up of world trade was the rapid growth of productivity outside the United States, since without this development it would have been impossible to bring about the homogenization of consumption patterns in the centre. Political and economic factors were constantly interwoven in this process, whereby a constellation of powerful economic systems, occasionally in aggressive confrontation, have been transformed into a largely unified economic system in which increasingly wide-ranging innovatory and coordinating functions are being performed by techno-bureaucratic groups controlling massive financial resources.

Without the ideological confrontation between the United States and the Soviet Union, however, it would have been difficult for American tutelage to become invested with the quasi-legitimacy which it enjoys. On the other hand, the direction taken by technology in the United States has itself provided an option for the capitalist system as a whole. The style characterizing industrial civilization in the United States is not intrinsic to capitalism. Accumulation by itself may not have led to the establishment of the "American way of life" in all countries, but there is no doubt that this would probably have been the most likely outcome if all the political structures once compartmentalizing the capitalist world had not been dismantled. The political changes produced by the United States tutelage were fundamental, but the rapid development of the process can only be explained by the fact that the solution found corresponded to the use of a technological heritage of proven value.

The internal readjustments forced on the countries of the industrialized centre as a consequence of these overall changes are of great importance, since they affect social forces whose relations define the profile of capitalist society. Leaving aside the United States, which obviously constitutes a special case, we find that in the other countries of the centre there has clearly been a decline in the internal capacity to regulate the economy. Governments can always find means of injecting depressive factors into the economy, but the effects of such factors are concentrated at the level of employment and fail to have the desired effect on overall inflationary pressures. The limitations of autonomous action to expand the economy are even greater. On the other hand, national economic growth (needed to absorb unemployment) requires an ever increasing participation in the international economy. If this economy is not expanding, it requires the opening up of a new space at the expense of others. Meanwhile, however, international economic activities are becoming increasingly structured within the framework of oligopolies, whose rules of conduct are not easily affected by nation-states. The importance of international trade as an "engine of growth" has thus increased, while the initiative capacity of the state in this sector has declined.

The changes that have taken place in the process of appropriating the surplus are equally significant. In the evolution of capitalism, the emergence and consolidation of the forces controlling the distribution of income was centred on the buying and selling of the various services provided by man as a factor of production. In other words, the labour market, taken in a wide sense, constituted the historical arena in which the forces that shaped modern capitalist society emerged. The particular combination of circumstances provided the necessary conditions for workers and wage earners in general to become an autonomous social force and to struggle effectively for a share in the fruits of accumulation and technical progress. These *classic* instruments of social confrontation, which brought about the homogenization of broad sectors of society, now appear to be losing their effectiveness.

With the growing social division of labour and the greater complexity of the economic system, in which technological innovaton plays an increasingly important role in the growth of the product, the current concept of labour productivity (which is micro-economic) is becoming less and less clear, and the social nature of the phenomenon of productivity is becoming fully apparent. To understand the changes that have taken place in this area, we must take into account, not only the rationality of means, but also the rationality of ends. In other words, the influence of qualitative factors in determining the level of the social product cannot be understood in terms of the rules of conventional aggregation. In this context, it may be noted that the forms of appropriating the surplus are also changing. Holding assets, such as a piece of land located in a particular area, can provide a powerful instrument for appropriating part of the surplus generated by the collectivity at a given time. The appreciation of real estate or of works of art and many other objects, whose rarity is artificially induced, thus becomes a powerful instrument for draining the social surplus. In sum, the faster the accumulation and the more diversified the final product, the more difficult it becomes to break down the social product into components translatable in terms of the concept of physical productivity of labour. Price manipulation by groups holding the monopoly of certain forms of creativity, or simply advertising and/or the control of assets, is carrying increasing weight in the process of appropriating the surplus. In this way, the forces traditionally responsible for the distribution of income now find themselves operating in a changed situation.

The credit system tends to reinforce this trend, since it operates mainly on the basis of guarantees, even if the security provided is potential rather than real. Since inflation has become a permanent feature of the capitalist economies, access to borrowing facilities represents a privilege, which ensures that the debtor will always draw a prize in the competition for the surplus. In countries with chronic inflation, the assets-credit-increased assets mechanism has become a powerful instrument for appropriating the surplus and concentrating wealth/income. This explains why the inequities in the distribution of wealth are as high in a country like France as the distribution of income in a country like Brazil. Further, while in Brazil the intensification of accumulation has brought about an increase in income concentration, in France it has brought about an increase in wealth concentration. Finally, while in Brazil income concentration has resulted in the poorest part of the population receiving practically nothing, in France the sharp rise in national wealth has benefitted only those individuals who hold a large or medium stock of assets.

Since the last decades of the nineteenth century, the changing power relationship between groups and social classes in the national economies had acted as a kind of check on the income-concentrating tendencies of the capitalist system. But, with the changes now taking place in the process of appropriating the surplus, this relationship is no longer producing the same results. Under the influence of the groups that exercise cultural tutelage, preferences are being channelled into invisible forms of income associated with the possession of certain kinds of wealth. Manipulation of "rare" goods and services permits the introduction of price-discrimination practices that provide a powerful instrument for appropriating the surplus. The relative prices that emerge from this new constellation of forces provide the room for measuring labour productivity in the sectors producing goods and services for general use, which is where the mass of the working population is employed. The struggle for higher real wages in these sectors generates inflationary pressures if the size of the wage claim exceeds productivity increase measured in terms of relative prices. In practice, however, these prices are determined by the groups that take the initiative in innovation and are thus in a position to manipulate the rationality of ends.

The structural changes we have indicated can be narrowed down to two: (a) the loss of effectiveness of the traditional forms of struggle of the wage-earning classes; and (b) the decline of the state as the generating and regulating centre of the economic system. The workers' struggle in the framework of the labour markets no longer constitutes an effective barrier against the forces now bringing pressure towards social inequalities. Historical experience has shown that it is more important for the working class to have access to decision centres--even if only in partial form and under the cover of class alliances--than to exploit the possibilities of class confrontation and organized pressure on the labour market. The path of social democracy, as practised in Sweden and England, has proved more effective in reducing social inequalities than the Leninist line of systematic ideological confrontation followed in France. Control of the state, even when that state continues to be essentially a reflection of the social structures engendered by the bourgeois hegemony, is a necessary condition for carrying the struggle into other arenas and effectively confronting the new wealth-concentrating forces that manifest themselves at a more advanced stage of accumulation. What has come to be called Euro-communism is, in fact, no more than a recognition of the need to break down the narrow limits to which the organized masses of certain countries have been confined.

The struggle to control the state, which has actively engaged the wage-earning masses in the national economies of the centre over the last few decades, has come to a head at a time when the state's own field of action is narrowing. The unprecedented expansion of the state's activities in the area of infrastructural and welfare services has been accompanied by a reduction in its capacity to generate economic growth and regulate economic activities. The hypertrophy of the international finance market is no more than an indicaton of the large enterprises keeping a high proportion of their liquid assets outside the control of the nation-states; and their indebtedness to this market reveals their concern to conceal from the governments of their home countries a large part of the investments they make abroad. Since the overseas activities of the multinational are coordinated with its domestic operations to form a coherent whole, its greater freedom of action abroad enables it to expand its room for manoeuvre on the home front. The British experience provides an excellent illustration of this. The growing influence which the wage-earning class managed to wield over the state produced an advanced fiscal legislation that should have checked the trend of concentration of wealth and provided the mass of the population with an invisible wage in the form of national insurance and other social security benefits. What in fact happened, however, was that the weakening of the state's capacity to stimulate and regulate the economic system tended to neutralize much of the effect of this policy. The major British firms gave priority to overseas investment and handed over control of a growing share of their domestic market to groups managed from abroad. The rate of accumulation in Britain slowed down in comparison with that in competing countries, and this engendered a marked propensity for balance-of-payments difficulties. The development of North Sea oil has temporarily interrupted this process, but the basic features of the problem remain unchanged.

The new antinomies that are emerging may possibly account for the fact that the capitalist countries of the centre now constitute one of the world's most politically active areas. In these countries the trend towards internationalization of a great number of high-level economic decisions is generally recognized as inevitable. Nonetheless, it remains to be seen whether the broadening of the representative basis of the nation-states--their effective control by the wage-earning masses--will be achieved in time to influence this process. If so, the new supranational structures will undoubtedly have a political and social connotation, and one of their main functions will probably be to control the transnational enterprises. If not, the new coordinating and decision-making centres will be essentially technocratic in nature and will merely serve to reinforce the present structures that tend to increase social inequalities.

In the capitalist countries leading the industrial civilization, technical creativity takes two main directions: (a) elimination of obstacles to the reproduction of internal social structures; and (b) military confrontation with countries with centrally planned economies, particularly the Soviet Union. The growing importance of the impetus to technical invention provided by this latter development has introduced an element of irrationality in relation to ends which is penetrating every sphere of industrial civilization. Quite apart from this overriding problem, the subordination of technical creativity to the competition for world political hegemony has far-reaching consequences.

The Arms Race

The arms race has spurred the United States to spend enormous sums on research and development and thus acquire effective technological leadership of the capitalist centre. In the process, military spending has become a vital element of the U.S. economic system.

The arms race entails a tremendous drain on resources, including some of the scarcest. All the same, in the case of the United States the arms race has produced two positive features in the economic system: (a) it has brought an element of stability to one of the most sensitive segments of demand; and (b) it has cut the costs of technical innovation for the enterprises, increasing their competitive capacity abroad. The situation is different in the Soviet Union, which has no instability problem deriving from lack of effective demand and which is not in a position to take advantage of technological leadership at the international level, other than by means of direct sales of arms. In fact, the acceleration of technical advance under the impetus of the arms race in the Soviet Union has led to a distorted development of the productive forces, which manifests itself in the technological dependence of a large number of sectors and hastens subordination to the logic of the capitalist system.

Production Towards Expansion

The tensions created in the process of maintaining inegalitarian social structures, combined with the effects of the arms race on technology, engender pressures on the central economies to open up new spaces, particularly in the peripheral areas. External expansion in this case has two main purposes: (a) to gain access to sources of non-renewable resources; and (b) to incorporate cheap labour into the system indirectly. Pressure on the domestic ecological system, aggravated by intense accumulation, brings about a rise in production costs and thus increases the obstacles to the process of renewal of social structures. The easiest way to relieve this pressure is to extend the available space by integrating foreign sources of natural resources into the system and, in particular, those resources which are non-renewable. However, the effects of this indirect incorporation of natural resources are limited. At a given point, domestic accumulation created pressures which affect the efficiency of the system; and these pressures do not always yield to technical solutions. Bringing in foreign workers has been one of the means used to cope with this problem, even though it is not very reliable. There can be little doubt, however, that in the long term the reproduction of social structures in the central countries will be dependent on the indirect incorporation of cheap labour. This is already being achieved through the spatial organization of production on a transnational basis. In the final analysis, this is what makes expansion towards the peripheral areas a necessary condition for ensuring social stability in the central countries.

The behaviour of the Swiss economy in this respect provides a perfect example. Given the inelasticity of the labour supply (Switzerland's capacity to absorb foreign workers is considered to have reached saturation point), growth of the productive units of the enterprises is taking place abroad. In fact, at least three-quarters of the total sales earnings of the country's large enterprises are derived from their foreign operations. Irrespective of the actual location of their industrial activities, production costs have to provide for the expenditures on research and development so as to enable the Swiss enterprises to remain in the technological vanguard. Research and development activities are, of course, concentrated in the Confederation, but even when such activities are conducted abroad they are capitalized by the parent company. Control of technical know-how permits indirect incorporation into the Swiss economy of an abundant and cheap supply of labour located abroad and thus averts the social tensions that would undoubtedly arise if conventional accumulation within the country were to be intensified.

Decolonization

If there can be little doubt that the social repercussions of the rapid accumulation that has taken place in the central countries over the last few decades have been a major factor in intensifying the spread of industrial civilization across the globe, the part played by other factors in this process should not be underestimated. One such factor is the dismantling of colonial domination structures associated with such factors as the rise of the United States as a tutelary power, the growing integration of the domestic markets of the central countries, the determination of transnational enterprises to evade control by nation-states—in short, the need to abolish the outdated systems of social domination that had survived under the colonial regimes.

In the most significant case--the decolonization of India--endogenous factors were by far the most important. The demonstration effect of the Indian example accelerated an historical process which unfolded in a number of different ways. The need to create modern infrastructures to facilitate exploitation of natural resources required international financial support--under the supervision of specialized agencies such as the World Bank. This was incompatible with the narrow preference systems that had enabled the industries of the colonial powers to survive. Faced with both external and internal pressures--the former more or less extant and the latter, in many cases, still potential--the colonial powers speeded up the decolonization process--to convert colonies into spheres of influence and to avert major disruptions in the local social domination systems. By and large, the more rapid the withdrawal of the colonial power, the fewer were the changes made in the internal domination structures.

Once the basis of the new nation-state had been laid in the former colonies, conflicts turned on the means to be used for accelerating industrial civilization. This raised the crucial issue of choosing foreign allies and or protectors to provide the necessary help in speeding up accumulation. Both in countries where the structures of social domination forged under colonial rule were preserved and in those where they were dismantled and replaced by techno-bureaucratic power structures (nearly always of a corporate-military nature), the new state's functions evolved in the same direction: the creation of a society equipped with the material and psychological requisites for accelerating accumulation and so paving the way for rapid access to the forms of life created by industrial civilization.

North Korea exemplifies this development. Everything has been placed at the service of modernization based on industrialization. The population has been successfully trained to perform as a kind of vast symphony orchestra, each individual being assigned a part in a minutely orchestrated score. The results, in purely material terms, have undoubtedly been spectacular. But, since the technique incorporated in the more complex sectors is acquired abroad, and since the possibilities of gaining entry into international markets (other than through the export of primary products) are not only limited but also subject to conditions dictated by multinationals, the economic system is under constant threat of obsolescence. The difficulties this country has been experiencing for a number of years in meeting payments for external credits have confirmed that, in order to eliminate technological dependence, it is not enough for the state to impose strict social discipline and elaborate central planning.

The current problem takes a different form:

intensification of accumulation and modernization are based on direct cooperation with transnational enterprises, whether through the export of non-renewable resources or the exploitation of local manpower. This does not prevent the state from basing its legitimacy on a doctrine of "national interest" by attacks on the foreign enterprises (which are at once the mentors and collaborators in the process of modernizing the country). The climate of hostility (apparent rather than real) in which this cooperation takes place reinforces the position of the techno-bureaucracies in their negotiations with the enterprises and helps to sharpen national consciousness in areas where the horizon of political awareness is mainly local or tribal. The activities of the techno-bureaucracies are mediated by other power structures with a tribal, religious or paternalistic basis. However, the rapid modernization of military corporate groups, which, lacking in tradition, are all the more ready and willing to act to further general modernization, and the growth of higher bureaucratic status groups composed of elements trained abroad have given increasing autonomy to the techno-bureaucratic structures (often the only cohesive force for national unity). The new state thus plays a crucial role in the formation of national consciousness; the greater the success in spreading the values of industrial civilization, the more effective this role is.

It would be a mistake to underestimate the scope for manoeuvre of the techno-bureaucracies controlling many of the new peripheral states. We are not dealing with the classic type of Weberian bureaucracy; the techno-bureaucracy of the new state, even when linked to traditional status groups, plays a hegemonic role by virtue of its functions in the sphere of external relations, particularly in the confrontation with the transnationals. Since they have access to certain sources of information and have mastered certain communication techniques, the elements comprising the techno-bureaucracy find opportunities for external cooperation. This they use to change power relations to their own advantage in their confrontation with the multinationals. In many cases, confrontation centres upon the appropriation of the local surplus generated by the exploitation of local resources. Since it has considerable autonomy, techno-bureaucracy has, in some cases, taken the path of structural reform--almost always with a view to speeding up the modernization process. The Nasserism of the 1950s and the Valascism of the 1960s are notable instances of social reconstruction processes carried out by leaders who manipulated techno-bureaucracies. But this reconstruction of society from the top hardly penetrates the consciousness of the populations. Hence the passive social climate in which many of these reforms are carried out, and the ease with which they are repealed or neutralized. If the reforms lead to the breakdown of traditional forms of social domination, they considerably increase the power of the techno-bureaucracy, which proceeds to take over direct control of the population.

China: A Special Case

The revolutionary experience of the People's Republic of China cannot, of course, be taken as typical, since this vast nation is in many respects unique. But whatever the direction China may eventually take, the social reconstruction process now in progress in that country cannot fail to have global repercussions. For the first time, the entire system of values that emerged from the bourgeois revolution has been subjected to criticism in depth, and an attempt has been made to put into social practice a comprehensive alternative to industrial civilization.

In the seventeenth century, when the bourgeois revolution launched a frontal attack on the medieval hierarchical world-view, its most progressive thinkers bypassed the literate class of clerks and university scholars, addressing themselves in the vernacular to the common man, who may have lacked *culture* but was, in their view, endowed with *reason*. In China, three centuries later, the universities were closed down for a number of years, and the clerks of the bureaucratic structure were silenced. The common people--conceived mainly as a stable group in which there is direct communication between individuals--were encouraged to take the initiative in criticism and action. The only stable parameters were the teachings of Mao: to explore contradictions to the full and to accept only those solutions that emerged from the deeper knowledge gained from exhausting and resolving such contradictions; to trust the creative genius of the people; to denounce all forms of class structure.

The Chinese Cultural Revolution was inspired by a principle diametrically opposed to the Soviet brand of Marxism. In Mao's view, the systematic destruction of the superstructure and its reconstruction must precede the construction of a new material infrastructure. In fact, the concepts of "infra" and "super" structures, the pillars of orthodox Marxism, were overturned. Mao thought that, although ownership of the means of production was important, no less important was the framework within which economic life was organized. He unleashed the Cultural Revolution to uproot and destroy the traditional habits of thought and modes of behaviour and social organization, as well as such remnants of these as had infiltrated into, among others, the communist party itself--e.g., the sharp dividing line between intellectual and physical labour, the vast disparity between the town and the village; the privileged position of the techno-bureaucrat (in the party no less than in the government and industry); and the tendency towards consumerism--and lay the foundation of a genuinely collective society.

China in Mao's time seemed to be the only country able and willing to pursue an independent course and so escape the process of cultural homogenization to which all Third World societies are succumbing. There are also reasons to believe that if this attempt fails, China will run the risk of taking the path of dependency and the consequent crises of instability. Modernizing the urban areas would further accentuate the disparities in living standards between the town and the countryside, which would be reflected in growing regional inequalities.

It takes little insight to realize that the excessive reliance on non-renewable resources, a characteristic of the industrial civilization, makes this civilization a non-viable proposition for a country seeking to achieve social equality, which is China's present aim. The systematic adoption of centralized planning, with its inevitable concentration of decision-making process in the bureaucracy, must entail even higher social costs than it does in the Soviet Union. The elitism essential to industrial civilization (even in the richest countries it has engendered sharp social inequalities) will become even more pronounced in China. It is understandable, therefore, that many Chinese leaders should have declared their intention to open up a new path, which, though utopian in inspiration, is not devoid of practical sense. The abandonment of these policies will put the country back on the narrow path of accumulation to serve the transplant of industrial civilization.

The revolutionary experience of China cannot really be isolated from the context of the country's history and complex culture. Nevertheless, four main currents may be identified. The first is the influence of Marx. This influence (essentially philosophical) is manifested in the dialectical perception of social reality leading to the constant search for " "contradictions" as the basis for social creativity. Whereas in the Soviet Union, the reading of Marx focused essentially on his critique of the capitalist system and led to a positivist view of the social process, in China greater prominence was given to the more genuinely holistic side of Marx's thought.

The second current coincides with the Soviet practice of social control and management of economic activities: a one-party political system and central planning of the economy by the state. The combination of these two vectors leads to "democratic centralism," with a hierarchical structure that reproduces in all its dimensions the rigidity of the economic system. These

principles rapidly took hold in a culture deeply imbued
with the traditions of state centralism and mandarinic
social code. This explains why the struggle to replace
traditional cultural structures finally became confused
with the denunciation of the Soviet model of socialism.
But one cannot ignore the fact that such practices
provided the basis for the rapid reconstruction of the
Chinese state and for the comprehensive reach of the
centralized system of social control.

The third current stems from what is conventionally
referred to as "the thought of Mao Zedong," which
provided the rationality of ends in the revolutionary
process. In contrast with the thought of Lenin, which is
essentially action oriented and is expressed in an
analytic discourse--and is consequently open to argument
on its own premises--Mao's thought is synthetic and is
expressed in a poetic discourse. In a profound sense, it
is of the same genre as the thought of Confucius or of
any other great thinker with a totalizing vision of man
and history. Whereas utopian socialist thought in the
West has its roots in humanism--placing the individual at
the centre of history and taking its starting point from
the idea of Reason as the inalienable attribute of the
individual with an autonomous destiny--in Mao's thought
the concept of the individual has no place; it posits
social creativity with which each member of the
collectivity can identify as the only way in which the
individual's potentialities can be fully realized. The
feature it shares with Western utopianism--and in this
sense it can be said that Mao was one of the heirs of the
eighteenth-century Enlightenment--is the highly
optimistic message communicated in the idea of
development for the potentialities of the social whole.

The fourth current is voluntarism--fed by the
charisma surrounding Mao. In the service of Mao's
thought, this voluntarism provides a sporadic challenge
to the hidebound structures of control that tend to
suffocate society and engender social stratification.
With the death of the "Great Helmsman," the problem of
transmitting his charisma has become vital, since without
it the voluntarism ensuring coherent management of the
system may lose a good deal of its effectiveness.
However, there is little likelihood that Mao's thought
will be transformed into positivist evolutionism (to use
Althusser's phrase) as Marxist-Leninist thought was in
the Soviet Union. In all probability, the history of
collectivist China will continue to be marked by pendular
movements, and new social upheavals in that country will
undoubtedly make themselves felt in other parts of the
world. Breaking with orthodox Marxist tradition, Mao
stated that "the struggle of opposites is present in all
processes of development: it is unconditional and
absolute." Thus, this struggle will continue to
determine history, whatever form the society may take.

THE CENTRALITY OF THE ACCUMULATION PROCESS

Leaving aside China, no other country has the necessary combination of circumstances to escape the gravitational pull of industrial civilization. They are all, by definition, *peripheral*: they identify themselves with either the centre of the capitalist system or the centre of the socialist system, or aspire to keep an equal distance from these two poles of attraction. Those that seek to isolate themselves under the illusion that they have found an "autonomous path" find it extremely difficult to attain the minimum levels of economic efficiency required for survival, and their economies are corroded by contraband activities and multiple forms of parallel markets. The most telling instance of this is Burma, where, since the *coup d'état* of 1962, a techno-bureaucratic structure supported by the military has proclaimed autonomy as its goal, basing its legitimacy on the struggle against tribalism and regionalism. Others, which are successfully applying Soviet techniques of social control and central planning--such as North Korea--must face technological dependence, with the inevitable political consequences. Still others, where the application of such techniques has met with less success--such as Cuba--have compounded their technological dependence with financial dependence, since they would otherwise find it difficult to preserve the gains made in the domestic arena of social reconstruction.

In sum, under present historical circumstances, a country lagging behind in accumulation cannot open up an "autonomous path" of development simply by breaking its external bonds and/or opting for centralized planning of economic activities, whatever the ideology of those controlling the state may be. The structural changes achieved under the banner of socialism in peripheral countries have undoubtedly made it possible to reduce social inequalities, but these changes have not always had a positive impact on the accumulation process. To the extent that the aim pursued is the reproduction of the material values of industrial civilization, dependency will persist and will have to take new forms if the external relations are confined to countries where financial transfers and technology are strictly controlled by the state.

Since the technology of industrial civilization is constantly developing, and since accumulation provides the vector for this progress, any relative backwardness in accumulation will be translated into the higher cost of imported techniques, measured in terms of the unit cost of labour in the importing country. Dependency should be understood, first of all, as a set of structural features that are determined by historical circumstances: the entry into the international division of labour system will engender a relative backwardness in the development of productive forces; industrialization promoted by modernization programmes will reinforce trends towards the concentration of income; the need to import certain techniques will facilitate control of economic activities by the transnational enterprises. Only secondarily should dependency be seen as a weak or subordinate position in the confrontations that lead to international price fixing and ultimately determine the appropriation of the surplus generated by the international division of labour.

Accumulation, which makes it possible to raise a country's technical level, is, as a rule, a necessary condition for reducing dependency, but it is far from sufficient in itself. If this accumulation takes place within the framework of industrialization, it will introduce new constricting elements typical of a situation of dependence. It is not difficult to see how this can arise. Control over the management of these industries will prove an insufficient means of eliminating dependency, since such control is necessarily limited to the activities of the industries in the country concerned. To control a copper-producing enterprise is one thing, but to be able to influence the pricing of copper on the international market is quite another. Even when the industry produces solely for the home market, the room for manoeuvre will be narrow if the required technology is obtained abroad. Access to technology through licensing offers no escape, either, if the licenser retains ownership of technology. Control of local industries dependent for their survival on the commercial networks and technology of other enterprises, on which little or no pressure can be brought to bear, will not in itself change the situation of dependency.

If we consider industrial civilization as a process based on accumulation, we realize that all the sub-systems comprising it--such as regional units with varying degrees of political autonomy--identify themselves with one another. The relative position of each reflects, in one way or another, the level of accumulation and the degree of technological autonomy. There is generally a high correlation between these two variables, but not in countries engaged in the intensive exploitation of non-renewable resources, where accumulation can sometimes reach high levels even in the context of total technological dependence. Territorial and population size--China is the outstanding example--can also alter the correlation: technological autonomy, albeit limited, can be achieved at a low level of accumulation. Disparities in accumulation levels--countries with a relatively low level of accumulation generally regard this as an indication of backwardness--reflect the global configuration of the system. In other words, the level of accumulation (in

the productive forces) in a given sub-system is not
independent of its position in the whole. A country (or
region) specializing in extensive livestock farming or
coffee production will continue to have a low level of
accumulation (in the productive forces) irrespective of
the income level of its population. In such cases,
accumulation outside the productive forces (in housing,
durable goods, urban infrastructure and the like) may
reach relatively significant levels.

The exploitation of a non-renewable resource with
high economic value, when controlled, even in part, by
the producing country, opens up a new horizon of options
in the struggle against dependency. But it cannot ensure
that dependency will be overcome. Take the case of an
oil-exporting country like Iran, for example. Let us
assume that this country will make use of the money it
currently earns from its oil exports to finance
industrialization and that within the next 20 years it
will have managed to establish an industrial base with
international competitive capacity. (Its competitive
edge may, of course, be limited to certain sectors in
which it has an additional relative advantage, such as
petrochemicals, chemical fertilizers, etc.) Once the
manna supplied by its oil export earnings is exhausted,
however, the country will find itself facing the problem
of ensuring the reproduction of the new industrial system
so as to maintain its international competitive position.
This means that it will have to keep its relative
position in the face of competition from those holding
the technological lead in the sectors concerned. If it
is by then in a position to ensure the required
reproduction by using its own technology or techniques
acquired in exchange for the export of other techniques,
Iran will have succeeded in making the leap from
dependence to interdependence. If not, association with
transnational enterprises which can ensure access to
technology (and markets) will be inevitable. The price
of the imported techniques will tend to increase relative
to that of local labour, and the country will continue to
remain in the framework of dependency.

STRUGGLE AGAINST DEPENDENCE--NOT ISOLATION

The extreme case outlined above--a peripheral
country with the combination of circumstances necessary
to overcome backwardness in accumulation and establish an
internationally competitive industrial base under local
control--helps us to understand that the struggle against
dependence lies in advancing along the path of
international relations (and managing to effect a
qualitative change in this area) rather than in retreat
and isolation. For almost all the peripheral countries
there is no longer any chance of escaping from the

gravitational pull of industrial civilization; consequently it is in this framework that the struggle against dependence will take place. The Chinese Cultural Revolution--the only historically significant attempt to escape this gravitational pull--constitutes a separate chapter of contemporary history. Anyone bold enough to affirm that this chapter is now closed would run the risk of proving a poor prophet. But if this should turn out to be the case, and if China comes to stabilize its orbit within the gravitational field of industrial civilization, it will inevitably lose much of its significance. Its international economic relations are limited and will be dominated for some time to come by the need to gain access to the technology available to the central capitalist countries.

If we accept that isolationism is not a solution, the strategic aim should be to minimize the cost of dependence and to explore all paths leading to interdependence. This involves changing the power relationships underlying the international economic order. The struggle against dependence thus requires an effort to change the global configuration of the system. The fact that this problem is now being raised--or, to be more precise, that the global configuration of the system has been questioned--is a clear indication that power relations are changing in favour of the dependent countries. True, in most peripheral countries external relations of dependence are embodied in the structures of social domination. But, as we have seen, this does not prevent the emergence of techno-bureaucratic power structures capable of exploiting the new situation that is beginning to emerge. Furthermore, developments will initially seem to be external to the individual countries considered in isolation, and will be exploited mainly by countries having the necessary combination of domestic circumstances to do so. But the initiative taken by these countries in concrete situations will stimulate global change and will strengthen the hands of other peripheral countries.

Power Resources: The Key Element

The underlying forces in international economic relations have become so complex a fabric that it is no longer easy to distinguish what is important from what is secondary in this area. International prices have become extraordinarily sensitive because of the information revolution. Thanks to their global reach, the large multinationals (and particularly the major financial groups) can coordinate their activities over large areas and monopolize the power of initiative. To cope with this situation, the peripheral states have set up banking systems and marketing boards in an attempt to organize supplies of certain products and thus exert pressure on markets. Nevertheless, behind all these "games," which the new managers and techno-bureaucrats handle expertly, lie the real power resources on which long-term action is based. It is on these that we should concentrate if we wish to assess the possibilities of change in the power relations governing the international economy.

Amongst the various power resources on which the so-called international economic order is based, particular importance attaches to: (a) control of technology; (b) control of financial resources; (c) control of markets; (d) control of non-renewable resources; and (e) control of access to cheap labur. Used in varying combinations, these resources determine the bargaining strength of the state, or major economic groups, in the struggle for the appropriation of the surplus generated by the international economy. These tend to become *organized,* producing a structure. The struggle against dependency is no more than the struggle of the peripheral countries to change this structure. Conditions among these countries occasionally make it possible to obtain the critical mass required to control a particular resource, or combination of resources, which may prove to be a highly effective means of generating power. Controlling the supply of a product is undoubtedly important, but it is even more important to have the financial resources to extend this control. The availability of oil resources provides a weapon, but the effectiveness of this weapon can be considerably increased if the oil-producing countries manage to achieve the global organization of petroleum supplies on the international market.

Control of Technology. Of the power resources mentioned above, control of technology constitutes the cornerstone of the international power structure at the present time. In the final analysis, the struggle against dependence becomes an effort to neutralize the effects of the technological monopoly held by the central countries. Technology is potentially capable of replacing, in one form or another, all the other power resources. It may be worth recalling that in industrial civilization technology has become the ultimate expression of human creativity; all other forms of creativity have been progressively placed at its service. The vector for the fruits of this creativity is accumulation: through the instruments of labour, through the infrastructures (which produce aggregate effects), and through human knowledge (which increases man's capacity to act and also to produce new knowledge). What we have called industrial civilization is nothing but the outcome of a given orientation of human creativity, an orientation that favours accumulation and leads to the reproduction of given social structures. The product of this particular orientation of creativity is modern technology, the key ingredient of the accumulation process. Those who control technology hold dominant positions in the struggle for the surplus. To challenge these positions in the international sphere, by using suitable combinations of other resources, or by obtaining the critical mass necessary to control some of them, is the essence of the struggle against dependence.

There can be little doubt that technological dominance tends to increase as the network of interests of the transnational enterprises becomes more tight-knit. In the final analysis, these enterprises are determined to retain their hold over technology at a time when industrial activity is spreading across the globe. To cede technology by means of a licensing contract is of little or no interest to an enterprise that has the option of exploiting this technology directly, using it to create the capital to establish affiliates or subsidiaries, to mobilize local financial resources and to extend its sphere of action. This is why industrialization, such as it is, of the peripheral countries has failed to create an international "technological market." In fact, the effective transfer of advanced techniques has been confined to the groups which are in a position to provide mutual guarantees of technological compensation.

Control of Financial Resources. Nevertheless, the evolution of the peripheral countries on other fronts is in many ways favourable. The pattern of control over financial resources has changed considerably in the last few decades. What with the development of banking networks, the direct state action to channel finances, and direct access to the international finance market, many peripheral states enjoy a freedom of manoeuvre unheard of during the years of strict tutelage by the International Monetary Fund. Transnational enterprises operating in the peripheral countries raise a large part of their finances locally (profits from import-export transactions, association with local groups, government subsidies, etc.), and the finances obtained from the international finance market frequently have the guarantees of the local financial institutions, state-owned or private. The investments in infrastructures that make it viable for the transnationals to establish local subsidiaries are financed from compulsory local savings and external resources guaranteed by the state. In sum, this potential of financial resources could be used by the peripheral states to increase their capacity for initiative in international relations.

The emergence, after 1973, of a substantial balance-of-payments surplus in a small group of peripheral countries--exporters of crude petroleum--is the second significant development in the area of financial resources. For the first time, peripheral countries have found it possible to promote major projects of common interest to them, without submitting to the tutelage of the central countries or the international finance institutions under their control. Capital transfers between peripheral countries have begun to reach significant levels, and it is now possible for peripheral countries to find the finances for maintaining buffer stocks of certain primary products (in order to regulate their prices) on less unfavourable terms. The periphery has become an important source of credit on the international finance market--a market which supplies the transnational enterprises and strengthens their hand in using their technological power to control the peripheral economies. On the whole, this new element has brought increasing awareness within the dependent countries of the real nature of international economic relations.

Control of Domestic Market. Control of access to the domestic market is another source of power in international realtions. Tariff barriers have been used everywhere and at all times as an instrument of attack or defence in confrontations with outside interests. At the present stage in the race between the transnational enterprises to gain control of strategic positions across the entire surface of the globe, the control over markets exercised by the state has become increasingly important. Establishing themselves in these markets is easier for enterprises which already have a marketing network at their disposal, controlling a section of the market through imports or establishing connections with the local finance system. By capitalizing on these "invisibles" (with the prestige of trademarks and the security of fully amortized plant and equipment), an enterprise can establish itself without straining its own resources.

The small investment generally required for a transnational to establish a subsidiary in a peripheral country lowers the barrier to the entry of competitors. As a result, the market that emerges tends to be more hospitable to what is called monopolistic competition in economic theory than to oligopolistic structures prevailing in the central countries. Monopolistic competition leads to a fragmentation of the market through intensive product-differentiation and advertising. Its inherent features are underutilization of productive capacity and high social costs. An alternative to this wasteful use of resources is to grant to one or two enterprises favourable concessions which enable them to enjoy considerable privileges. The perpheral states will then find it easier to exercise greater control over the transnational enterprises and, in some cases, to demand a share in their management.

The limited size of the home market in many peripheral countries has led to the establishment of free trade zones, customs unions, "common markets" and other forms of association, all of which are designed to enlarge the space within which the enterprises organize their activities. Therefore, the need to coordinate local policies in dealing with the transnationals becomes even more pressing, if these enterprises are to be prevented from taking advantage of possible rivalries between various countries. Coordination of economic policies and joint financing of projects of common interest thus serve to strengthen the position of small states in their dealings with the transnationals.

It was in this context of the narrowness of their home markets that the outlines of a policy designed to safeguard control over such markets in the face of the offensive launched by the transnationals began clearly to emerge. This policy has been directed mainly towards limiting the transnational's control over a segment of the market to a specified period of time, since such control is generally unavoidable, at least in the initial stage, to overcome difficulties in gaining access to technology. Concessions to exploit the market for an unlimited period are now being replaced by fixed-time contracts. Control of the enterprise--not merely of its share capital, but of its production, finance and marketing departments--must be progressively transferred to the host country's own decision-centres. Access to local finance capital should be made conditional on this transfer of control. The aim is to ensure that the enterprises become an integral part of the local economic system--or regional system in the case of an association of countries--establishing their internal rationality in terms of this system; their interaction with the transnational groups that supply them with technology or services must be a secondary consideration. If local control is extended to a sufficient number of sectors, the peripheral countries will obtain the critical mass necessary to pressure the transnationals into making their technology available on less burdensome terms. It will also become possible to orientate technology to clearly defined objectives and to create a market for locally developed technology. The aims of this policy may be completely frustrated if the required critical mass is not obtained. The bigger the domestic market, the easier it will be to achieve positive results. Hence, for the small countries, association is the *sine qua non* for the success of a policy of this type.

<u>Control</u> <u>of</u> <u>Non-renewable</u> <u>Resources</u>. Control of access to non-renewable resources has always been regarded as one of the main sources of power in international relations. The explanation for the division of a large part of the globe between a small group of industrial nations in the second half of the nineteenth century lies in this fact rather than in the need to open up new markets or to invest "surplus" capital. What is new today is the world-wide spread of the industrialization process that has accompanied the considerable intensification of accumulation in the

central countries. For a long time, technical advance in
a world that was only beginning to be explored fostered
the illusion that the supply of such resources would
remain elastic for an indefinite period. The possibility
that some day many of the resources which man extracts
from nature, particularly metals, would be recycled and
so become in some form partly renewable was not excluded.
But this was not the direction taken by technological
development in industrial civilization. The logic of the
present accumulation system, with its relatively short-
time horizon, tends to create growing pressures on non-
renewable resources. Inasmuch as these are located in
peripheral countries, which now have the opportunity to
use them directly, an entirely new set of problems is
beginning to take shape. True, there are powerful
interests in the central countries determined to prevent
awareness of these problems and to maintain the illusion
that technology itself will solve all the problems it
creates. These interests are responsible for keeping up
the present scale of waste, sacrificing, in the first
instance, the reserves held by many of the central
countries. The United States, Canada and Australia
continue to exploit their reserves of non-renewable
resources on the basis of criteria derived from private
appropriation of such resources. They therefore block
all attempts to organize supplies of these resources on a
global scale. In these circumstances, an increase in the
relative prices of most non-renewable resources is
necessary to bring about an immediate reduction in their
wanton waste.

The suicidal policies of certain central countries
in relation to their own resources cannot fail to
strengthen the position of the periphery in the medium
and long term. In this sector, more than in any other,
what is required is concerted action by associations of
countries, but such action will depend on the financial
capacity to affect the market. The financial weakness of
the peripheral copper-producing countries is undoubtedly
the main cause of their inability to make their weight
felt on the international copper market. Nevertheless,
it cannot be denied that the basic trend is towards a
strengthening of the bargaining power of countries
controlling the supply of non-renewable resources.

Control of Access to Labour. The vast reserve of
manpower in many peripheral countries has been a major
source of their weakness in international relations. It
is worth recalling that this massive labour force, with
no choice of employment outside a subsistence economy, is
the underlying cause of the low supply prices of many of
the agricultural products exported by the peripheral
countries. Organizing the markets for these products was
the first step in the struggle against dependency. This
same work force has now begun to play a part in the
international market through the embodiment of its labour

in the manufactured goods produced by the affiliates and subsidiaries of transnational enterprises located in the periphery. Given the tendency towards the decentralization of industrial activities (through the transnationals), control of access to this labour reserve may well become a source of power in international relations. At present, all countries with an abundant labour supply are encouraging the transnationals to exploit this labour on favourable terms. The terms offered for investment in industrial activities geared to the export market are, throughout the periphery, the most generous. If there is any obstacle to the expansion of the transnationals in this direction, it originates in the central countries themselves. For instance, trade unions, particularly in the United States, worried by the direct and indirect effects of the "export" of employment by certain enterprises, oppose such expansion. Nevertheless, there are many indications that the transnationals will continue to pursue a policy of decentralizing their activities, establishing production units in countries with an abundant labour supply whenever they are provided with suitable conditions.

If the trends noted above continue, and if the manpower channelled in the form of manufactured goods for the international market becomes sufficiently important to the transnationals, the peripheral countries will be in a position to transform a traditional weakness into a new source of power. Even if there is a substantial increase in the cost of this labour (measured in terms of what it produces for the international market), it will still be cheap for the transnationals which have access to the markets of the central countries where wage rates for the same work are currently five to ten times higher. Countries with the cheapest labour to sell could introduce an export tax on manufactured goods to cover all or part of the difference between the local wage rate and that of the other peripheral countries competing in the same markets. It would not be surprising if the periphery were to make moves towards establishing a coordinated fiscal policy designed to retain part of the surplus derived by the transnationals from the exploitation of cheap labour. At present, the transnationals can pick and choose from among many countries. By playing one country off against another, they can ensure that wage levels are kept low and that export subsidies are granted. However, in the new structures now emerging, the work force of the periphery is playing an increasingly important role in the reproduction of social forms in the central countries. Traditional international relations, mediated by the commodity markets in which the financial power of certain groups carried considerable weight, are being replaced by a new model in which it is political action that has the decisive influence.

The power resources we have been considering should not all be treated on the same level. In varying degrees, nearly all have been used by many of the peripheral countries for some time. Only recently, however, have they been used in a deliberate way with the explicit aim of changing international relationships to the advantage of countries with dependent economies. Since technology is the key resource, and since it is monopolized by the central countries, *dependence* can be said to be first and foremost *technological*. Thus, combining other power resources in order to counter the burden of technological dependence has become the esence of the effort now being made by the peripheral countries to advance along the road of *development*.

CONCLUSION

The struggle against dependence generally begins when a dependent country demands control over its sources of non-renewable resources. The next step is to establish positions that will enable the country to gain control, even if only in part, of access to its home market. Victories on these two fronts will create the critical mass of financial resources needed to consolidate the positions already won and to extend the active front. The struggle on the technological front will have a chance of success only when control of major segments of the domestic market has been ensured and the critical mass of financial resources obtained.

At all stages in the effort to change international relations, coalitions and alliances among peripheral countries have played and will play a strategic role. This is true both of regionally based associations--among countries in the same area--and of associations of a functional nature--among countries exporting the same product or involved in a joint project of common interest. These associations have made it possible to bring together a cluster of power resources capable of making an impact with irreversible effects.

The struggle against dependence has been taking the form of *confrontation,* although the aims of the peripheral countries at each stage are apparently modest. This possibly reflects the gap between the power resources potentially at their disposal and the tiny fraction of these resources they have effectively managed to mobilize. The immediate aim is to create bonds of genuine interdependence despite lack of technological autonomy and to try to change the orientation of technology despite the lack of control over it. Only from a more advanced and solid position will it be possible to envisage more ambitious aims, such as instilling a new logic of ends into the accumulation process and freeing creativity from the straitjacket of instrumental rationality in which it finds itself at present.

The central issue will continue to be that of creating forms of collective will in the periphery, since only in this way will it be possible to activate its potential power resources. In this respect, nothing could be more counter-productive than regional rivalries that spark arms races. The sophisticated arms supplied by the central countries are a terrible drain on the financial resources of peripheral countries, and they open the door to new forms of dependence whose consequences are unimaginable. The final madness in this senseless game, which may wipe out all the gains already made in the struggle against dependence, would be to embark on a nuclear arms race. That a peripheral country should acquire nuclear weapons is of no relevance whatsoever to the strategic balance on a global scale. But it would have profoundly negative consequences on relations between countries of the periphery, especially those in the same region. Such solidarity as now exists among dependent countries would be destroyed. Many of the peripheral countries would react to this situation by seeking protection that the superpowers would not hesitate to offer. If we add to this the tremendous drain on resources for any country unwise enough to embark on this dangerous course, we will have a rough idea of the negative effects such a step would entail for the struggle against dependence.

If these frightful possibilities are eliminated, we may affirm that the advances already made have opened up options for the peripheral countries to establish new forms of coalition and to take new initiatives in the struggle to reorder international relations. Nonetheless, we must not lose sight of the fact that the struggle against dependency is simply one aspect of the development process and that development does not exist unless the creative capacity of a people is liberated. The most negative aspect of the tutelage of the transnationals over production systems in the periphery is their role as a mere transmitter of cultural values generated abroad so that the dependent system loses the capacity to determine its own ends. This is why political authoritarianism fits it like a glove. Economic dependence, cultural tutelage and political authoritarianism complement and reinforce one another.

But it must be recognized that the periphery is now a vital part of the machinery of industrial civilization. True, it does not carry the weight that political unity gives China, and it does not occupy a position in the vanguard of military technology like the Soviet Union; nor can it claim the level of accumulation and social advance of the central capitalist countries. But history can no longer be made without bringing this new actor onto the stage.

CHAPTER 7

The Occultation of Egypt

Anouar Abdel-Malek

Raise your head, Brother!

Gamal Abdul Nasser, July 23, 1952

Ramses: For powerful is the Lord of Egypt, too powerful to allow those Barbarians to approach his path. I call you, [oh] my father Amon, I am amongst innumerable Barbarians whom I do not know. All countries have rallied in league against me, and I am absolutely lonely, nobody with me. . . . Here am I, therefore, praying thee from the depths of barbarian lands. . . .
Amon: Forward, forward, I am with thee, thine father. My hand is with thee, and I shall stand thee more efficiently than hundreds of thousands. For here am I, the Lord of Victory, and I love courage.
Ramses: My courage surges again. My heart rejoices. Everything succeeds which I attempt. Here am I, like Montu. I throw arrows at my right, take prisoners at my left. I am now facing them, like Baal, when his hour comes. . . .

From the prayer of Ramses II at the
Battle of Qadesh, ca. 1270 B.C.

March 26, 1979 constitutes, first and foremost, the "second foundation of the State of Israel," the end of "the Arab refusal"; these are the words, now finally understood, of two leading liberal progressive Zionist

----

Reprinted by permission from *Arab Studies Quarterly* 1:3, 1979.

thinkers. March 26, 1979 gives legitimacy to the racialist State, and sanctifies its military domination over the land of Palestine and several Arab countries. It is the negation of the whole course of the modern and contemporary history of the Arab nation.

March 26, 1979 constitutes, in the second instance, the creation of a new military alliance, under the formal domination of U.S. imperialism and the effective hegemonic leadership of Zionist racialist imperialism. This has occurred at the time of the crumbling of CENTO (crushed by the Iranian national revolution) and SEATO (dismantled by the victory of socialism in China and Vietnam).

It in no way constitues a fact of "peace" in the Arab nation. More than ever before, Palestinians are deprived of their fatherland, Syria and Jordan of large portions of their national territories. The Arab nation is ruptured geographically, its League of States rendered ineffective, and its very center marginalized. The Sinai and Egypt's northeastern frontiers are dismantled and the historic route of invasions is opened wide. The whole front of Afro-Asian peoples' solidarity, the Tricontinental front, the group of nonaligned States, stand severely weakened. The African mainland is offered as a prey in the midst of the mounting struggles between superpowers, and Asia--57 percent of mankind--waits just beyond. A process of disruption has struck the immediate Arab national circle, and menaces the two outer circles of Africa and Islam, while antagonizing the system of European socialist countries around the second, socialist, superpower, the U.S.S.R.

Nobody chooses his time in history.

Our time in history, the present phase of our generation's time in history,[1] is verily the time of the occultation of Egypt.

I

Geopolitics fell into disrepute in the West in the 1929-1945 era. It has also fallen into disrepute among two generations of Arab intellectuals and policymakers--with the single exceptions of Gamal Abdul Nasser and Gamal Hamdan.[2] Yet, geopolitics alone provides the clue to answer out question: Why did it happen? Why here? Why now?

An aura of ideologism pervades the most recent wave of Arab intellectual thinking. It has produced questions like: What is the relevance of Vietnam to our national liberation struggle, and could we, in a way, start along this path? Other questions which include dimensions like "guevarism" and ongoing illusions of subjective internationalism are still operating to a degree among some activist, radical progressive sectors of our

intelligentsia.[3] To invoke the primacy of the political,
the central influence of geopolitics as determined by the
"depth of (our) historical field," would be tantamount to
renouncing subjectivism, i.e., the primacy of the
ideological approach to the problem of power. It is felt
that little would then be left for the intelligentsia.
But they forget that the royal road charted by Plato, Ibn
Khaldun, Mao Tse-tung and others provides the linkage
between culture and power, thought and action, the realm
of ideas and the hard road of realpolitik.

Ideologism, of all brands, has converged in our
recent history to vitiate and falsify the very position
of our national problem. It is the first element that
bears analysis in examining the outer circle of the
social dialectics of our Arab nation. Till Yalta and its
aftermath, and since the latter part of the ninth
century, the problem of the Arabs in history has always
been seen in terms of the dialectics between the
different civilizations of the Orient and Occident. Such
was the meaning of the civilizational counteroffensive,
the ten-centuries-long Crusades of the Kingdom of
Jerusalem, erected in the very heart of the Arab Orient
to break any potential unification of its territories
around the Egypt of Salah al-Din. Such was and remains
the meaning of colonialism, traditional imperialism in
the eighteenth and nineteenth centuries, and hegemonic
U.S. imperialism in our times. Such is, above all, the
significance of the racialist , expansionist and military
Zionist imperialism in our area, through our times and
lives. It will be asserted by some that "imperialism,"
as a conceptual category, also relates to the life-
experiences of societies and nations like Vietnam,
Mozambique, Chile and Brazil. It does, no doubt, in many
ways, but only conceptually and not in an equal manner.
The history of the transformation of the world from the
rise of the West to hegemony in the fifteenth century
until our times must be read in macro-dimensions. Then
it would become easier to understand the significance of
the Arab-Islamic civilizational area in the dialectics of
civilizations, as an ongoing dialectical process of
historic, all-encompassing dimensions--perhaps the
strongest formative influence in the structuring of the
balance of power throughout modern times.

The position of the problem, the position of the
Arab problem in our times, is therefore exactly as
visualized by Muhammad 'Ali at the beginning of the
nineteenth century: How to put an end to decadence? How
to promote renaissance? His answer to these challenges
was: by uniting the territories of the Arabs and Islam
around one modern, powerful, progressive nation-state,
i.e., Egypt, under his reign, thus seizing the keys to
historical legitimacy (Islamic historical legitimacy at
that time).

Only then would the Arab-Islamic national-cultural

area be able to promote renaissance in the face of the onslaught and penetrating impact of the West, due to the combined effects of the industrial revolution, the bourgeois democratic revolutions and the flawless coalition of modern European nation-states. Facing the challenge of Muhammad 'Ali's Egypt, all the European powers, without a single exception, entered into a strategic coalition to corner this nascent center of world power after the breakup of Napoleon. The Treaty of London in 1840, the destruction of the Egyptian fleet at Navarino, the ultimatum to the Egyptian Armies at Konieh and Nacibin, the doorsteps of Istanbul--these were the immediate steps which broke Egypt around 1840 and easily disposed of Arab and Islamic territories, then linked with the fragile framework of a decaying Ottoman Empire.

"The beginning of the contemporary phases of international history" was therefore directed against the rising power of the Arab nation, sixty years before the collective intervention of European powers against the Boxer Rebellion in China in 1900.

A little more than a century afterwards, Egypt, once again, broke the bonds of dependency. The national revolution under Nasser from July 23, 1952 until September 28, 1970 became the focus for the uprooting of imperialism in Egypt and most Arab countries, the initiation of the first Arab unity, and the reorientation of the Arab national movement toward socialism. All this within the framework of Nasser's great international project, i.e., the rerouting of Egypt's and the Arab nation's international course toward the Orient, thus the three circles of identity (Arabic, African, Islamic) and the Afro-Asian solidarity movement launched in Bandung with Chou En-lai, Nehru and Sukarno in 1954, toward the Tricontinental front. This immensely contradictory and potent upsurge of Egypt and the Arab nation took place during the dangerous days of the Cold War, and continued until the beginning of the second phase of post-Yalta international relations between the two superpowers, the phase of "peaceful coexistence." Little sympathy could be expected from international quarters, and, on the contrary, protracted aggressive onslaught. The wars of 1948 and 1956 and, more so, that of 1967, were to play the same role as the military-political operations between 1832 and 1840 against Muhammad 'Ali. And it was in fact thanks to the recycling of Arab national dynamic potentials, and thanks above all to the Algerian Revolution, seconded by the aftermath of the war in Yemen and the rise of the Palestinian Resistance, that the cornering and uprooting of Nasser's Egypt did not occur during the black days of June 1967--when the people of Egypt stood, as a nation, as a "House of flesh" (Yusuf Idris) to preserve the Ra'is.

This psychological environment led important sectors of the intelligentsia and public opinion to accept the explanation of the problematic of the Arab national movement in vitiated terms. Instead of understanding that our times were the contemporary phase of the civilizational confrontation between the Orient and Occident--now in the form of the Arab nation and the Zionist State--they went along with the ideological explanation of the problem. The Arab-Zionist conflict was labelled "the Middle East problem" or "the Middle East conflict," similarly the mythical centering of this regional conflict around one factor labelled the Palestinian "Revolution"--revolution, and not national liberation or resistance, as was the case in, say, Algeria and Vietnam. From then on, the way was cleared to turn against the negativity of the Egyptian experiment,[4] to disregard the central character of the contemporary Arab national movement around Egypt, to comprehend the conflict as a diplomatic-cum-guerillaist problem which should be approached via the more promising paths of diplomacy, subjective internationalism and genuine emotional ideologism. Thus a large sector of the Arab political class allowed itself to be preempted by the ideological position.

Thus began the process of the occultation of Egypt. The implementation of this occultation could proceed once the objective premises were laid in our very midst. When Kissinger said, "We are trying to get a Middle East settlement in such a way that the moderate regimes are strengthened and not the radical regimes," this was interpreted, through the ideological approach, as an invitation for Arab analysts to compute how "moderate" or "radical" the various Arab regimes were. The heyday of epistemology (What does the concept of "progressivism" mean? What is a "nation"?) and quantitative functionalist analysis (combining GNP and the "mode of production" keynote approaches, etc.) had arrived. It was as if we were living in a no-man's-land and could visualize our historic process only through the combined prisms of ideologism and Zionism. Ideological discussions focused on the degree of moderation versus radicalism in Nasser's Egypt, its historic significance being computed on the basis of the "percentage" of progressive or conservative variables.

This aura of ideologism is the first dimension of the outer circle of the social dialectics of our Arab nation. The second dimension lies in the structure and complex evolution of the world system since Yalta.

II

The historical view of large sections of the modernizing, mainly Westernized sectors of our Arab intelligentsia and political elites was influenced during World War II and immediately afterwards by the image of

the U.S.S.R. as the major anti-fascist power and the more
progressive element of the Allied coalition against
German Hitlerism and its accomplices. This image
supported the belief that the Leninist strategy--the
world alliance between working class movements in the
West and the national liberation movements in the
Orient--remained in full force.

Few noticed and cared to assess the fact that the
partition of Palestine was engineered through a joint
proposal put before the U.N. General Assembly by the
Soviet Union and Great Britain in December 1947. Large
sectors of the progressive left in the Arab world--a
majority of Communist parties, leading to the division of
the Communist movement in Egypt--ingeniously contrived
justifications along the lines of "objective realities of
the internationalist struggle." Few realized that this
simplistic adequation of Arab national progressive
political movements with the State policy of the U.S.S.R.
encapsuled two phenomena: (1) the loss of momentum for
communism at the helm of both the Arab national
liberation and national unity movements, and (2) the now
acknowledged processes whereby several leading members of
the Arab left, in Egypt notably after 1967, became
negotiators with the Zionist State, via well-known
mediators in Western Europe.[5] Few attempted to reassess
their analyses of world politics at this juncture.

Yet, from 1946 on, the rising tides of conflict and
war, coupled with national and social revolutions, were
beginning to sweep over the Arab and Western Asian
Islamic regions. A grand saga began to unfold--one of
unexpected achievement, lost momentum, powerful
resurgence, and the emergence of a combination of
political Islam and national radical activist trends that
was to become the cradle of Nasserism at the very heart
of contemporary Arab destinies.

The world system establishing the climax of Western
hegemony over the world at Yalta in 1945 was rapidly
entering a phase of crucial reassessment. In the face of
Soviet military might and the advanced realpolitik of
Stalin in the de facto partitioning of Europe and the
creation of a system of socialist States around Moscow,
the United States chose to rebuild Western Europe through
the Marshall Plan, and thus to solidify the front of ex-
colonial imperialist capitalist States of Western Europe
under its leadership through the Atlantic Pact, its
political and military organizations. This opened the
first phase after Yalta, the phase of the Cold War, from
1947 to the time of Suez in 1956. That period
encompassed the emergence of the great revolution in
China under Mao Tse-tung and national communism, the
difficult war in Korea, the first Vietnam war, the rise
of national revolutions in Egypt, Syria and Iraq,
parallel to the national liberation revolution in
Algeria, as well as Cuba's rejection of U.S. hegemony.

The transition from the Cold War to "peaceful coexistence" was interpreted, in the West, as a result of the political strategy devised by Khrushchev and Brezhnev, to catch up to the U.S. level of production and consumerism and, at the same time, to recover from the terrible hemorrhage of the great patriotic war of liberation. A central factor, no doubt. Yet, a more important factor in this strategy, so it is now felt, was the emergence of the hitherto hidden continents of Asia and Africa--the Orient--and, later on, of Latin America, i.e., the reemergence of the civilizational Orient, coupling national liberation with socialist revolution, in many patterns, toward civilizational renaissance. This immensely potent impetus--around its two core areas of China and Egypt--was gradually compelling both sectors of the West to adjust to realities, to lower the level of military and political confrontation , for fear that the proliferation of conflicts and mounting tensions--due to the rise of the Orient--would unexpectedly, or objectively, lead to a confrontation between the two superpowers.

Thus, "peaceful coexistence" as a step toward political rationality, owes more to the impact of national liberation movements--to the rise of the Orient--than to a mere political analysis to avoid nuclear confrontation and readjust the two superpowers adverse positions within the framework of nuclear deterrence.

Gradually, analysts began to perceive that the major challenge to the Yalta bipolar Western hegemonic systems came from China. The decision of the U.S.S.R. to bring Mao Tse-tung and the Chinese leadership to heel, to compel China to follow the Soviet path of development, led directly to the series of policies which were to break the last links of objective imitation and bondage. Such is the meaning of the "Great Leap Forward," the "Hundred Flowers" period and the first phase of the "Cultural Revolution." Such is the meaning of Chou En-lai's "Four Modernizations." For to make China a powerful, modern , socialist country by the end of this century can only mean to change the structure of the world power system for the first time since the fifteenth century, with the dynamic help of Japan, the second most advanced industrial and technological State in the capitalist system, a step lying at the very heart of the August 1978 epoch-making Sino-Japanese treaty of peace and friendship.

Much earlier, the growing power and momentum of the Arab national unity movement came dangerously near to achieving the dream of Salah al-Din, Muhammad 'Ali and Nasser, not only during the short period of life of the United Arab Republic, but perhaps more so in the aftermath of the terrible days of the 1967 June War. For it was then that President Nasser began to reformulate his Arab unitary policies in confederal, populist and realistic terms, thus making them immensely more acceptable to the wide variety of interests, political inclinations and forces in the Arab world at large. We now know the true story of the relations between the U.S.S.R. and both Nasser and the leadership of the Arab unitary movements at that time, through extremely well-documented sources, from the period of the tentative first Arab unity to the crucial days of the 1973 October War. They show, in an implacable manner, that the State policy of the U.S.S.R. could not reconcile itself, in any visible way, to the emergence of a modern, unified, powerful, advanced Arab State under the leadership of Egypt, in an area which it considered crucial to its own national security. For such an Arab State, around its capital, Cairo, could command the emotional and political loyalties of the whole of Afro-Asia: the Islamic area ranging from Morocco to the Philippines, lying at the very frontiers of the U.S.S.R., India and China, and including the uniquely rich oil region of Arabia and Iran. This emerging superpower could disrupt the fragile equilibrium of the bipolar détente. [6]

Everything, therefore, was to be done to circumvent this process, albeit in totally different terms from those of U.S. imperialism. To circumvent--not to destroy. To circumvent, i.e., to neutralize, limit the actual efficacy of its immense potentials, always remaining in alliance with the Arab radical sectors, while never giving them, at any time, and under any pretext, the means to take central action to change the balance of power in this area. Their policy also included taking action everywhere around this core area, in order to neutralize the Arab-Iranian oil region, after Nasser, as happened in Afghanistan, Ethiopia, Angola, Mozambique and the ongoing process in Rhodesia and other sectors. A masterful, forward, advanced strategic global offensive, objectively helping, in many cases, progressive causes, and often creating terrible tensions between fraternal countries to the point of deeply harming the national interests of some of them (Eritrea, the Somalis in Ogaden). A process of world magnitude, sustained and made possible by the control of the oceans through the mighty Soviet fleet, led and engineered by Admiral Gorchkov, with the help and inspiration of the whole of the Soviet leadership, from Stalin to Brezhnev. [7]

For the Arab nation, the situation was ripe with danger, particularly with the post-Watergate rise of the new Cold War and the Zionist apparatus, the U.S. presidency around the Trilateral Commission and Brzezinski, which meant that the days of détente would be waning little by little, even if the signature of SALT II appeared unavoidable for strategic reasons. A new period of confrontations, political for the time being, was rapidly emerging. Perhaps a new phase in the post-Yalta period? The situation became extremely dangerous for the Arab national movement everywhere. And it soon was to become intolerable because of the explosion and the cataclysm brought about by the Iranian revolution, the dismantlng of the glass menagerie, the showpiece of artificial Westernized compradore modernization, and the rise to power of political Islam[8] in the second major oil country, which also happens to be one of the three oldest nations in history, hand in hand with Egypt and China. Conditions were ripe to achieve the ideal situation through which the Zionist

racialist imperialist State could strike and assert its hegemony over the Arab nation. On the one hand, we see a Western global strategic counteroffensive against the rise of the Arab-Islamic oil area after the October war. On the other hand, the Soviet Union decides to gain time, to avoid confrontation in that crucible, and at the same time to pursue an advanced policy of encirclement, containment, giving the U.S.S.R. a strategic advantage in the long run, while creating a host of new problems of heretofore unprogrammed dimensions.

The world is now on the move. The key to war and peace does not lie--as the ideological approach would have it--in armed clashes in Southeast Asia, or in the intrusion of Cuba in Africa, or in the discovery of oil in Mexico or elsewhere. It lies, and will lie for a very long historical period indeed, where it always lay at those times when the dialectics of civilizations rose to the level of confrontation: in the Arab-Islamic area, the linkage between Orient and Occident, the turning point between the three continents of Europe, Asia and Africa, the locus of decisions between the major powers and weltanschauungs in history.

The analytic elements sketchily discussed thus far can help answer basic questions revolving around our central interrogative: Why did it happen? Why did March 26, 1979 happen? Why did Egypt acquiesce to isolate itself, for a time, from its own wider framework, the Arab Nation?[9] How could the occultation of Egypt, removed from the very center of decision at the heart of the Arab nation, take place?

III

Central to our analysis is an understanding of the forced division imposed upon State and society in Egypt after 1970. A sequential comparative study of different modes of production and modes of State power in Egyptian society, from its inception to the death of President Nasser, shows a remarkable continuity in the specificity of the interrelationship between the State and society. Egypt, that most compact of hydraulic societies, gave birth to the oldest centralized State in the history of humanity, with a continuous history of about seventy centuries, to say nothing of the preceding centuries now gradually coming to be perceived. The combined unity of the control of water, the control of power through the national army, and the contol of the ideological-theological Pantheon gave the Egyptian State its unique weight in societal processes, thus imposing upon Egyptian analysts a permanent interrogation about whether their own history is to be viewed as a curse or as a promise.

Throughout its history, the State, at the helm of Egyptian society, based its power on the surplus value extracted from the control and use of the Nile waters, in irrigation, draining, dam-building, and allocation of the lifeline of food production, human reproduction and well-being. This specific structuring of the objective source of power of the Egyptian State gave it a near-unique continuous character as a national State, as the State of the nation, albeit under the hegemony of the leading classes and power groups--the triad of landowners-army command-religious and ideological leaders. For good and bad, more often it must be recognized for the very preservation of Egypt as a nation, the State of Egypt identified the restrictive class interests of its leadership with those of the national existence at large. Such is the history of the Egyptian army from Seknen Ra' to 'Abd al-Mon 'em Riyad and Sa 'd Eddin al-Shazli, of the Egyptian State (at the center of its circle of influence) from Ramses and Thoutmes to Nasser, of the hydraulic engineers and mathematicians and the great tradition of medicine, from the time of the pyramids to Qasr al-'Aini, of the importance of religious leaders and leading intellectuals in national political life to this day.

As long as this integrated pyramid maintained its cohesion, on the basis of a unified national economy, little, or nothing, could really be done from within. The strategic counteroffensive of imperialism and Zionism aimed at disrupting this monolithic unity by a combined thrust along two main lines:

1. Oil revenues, petrodollars, were used massively and objectively to create a parallel sector to the traditional national economy of Egypt. A new sector of considerable means and affluence (a bilingual secretary would earn the salary of a Cabinet Minister) gradually led to the creation of a *parallel compradore economy,* from bottom to top, an inverted pyramid. The parallel economy was used to weaken the national economy, to debauch its cadres attracted by incredible privileges on their doorsteps, to demoralize the millenary Egyptian bureaucracy, so genuinely concerned with the maintenance of Egypt, its independence and sovereignty (as witnessed by their resistance to the politics of so-called *infitah*), in brief, to provoke a hemorrhage from within

that was to prove particularly dangerous at that juncture.

2. This parallel sector contributed to the impoverishment of Egypt, especially after the four wars and the immense strains put on the one economy in the Arab world with no oil resources. This led to the mass immigration of hundreds of thousands of the best cadres of Egyptian society--from top engineers and physical scientists to the best craftsmen--eager to seek adequate means to overcome the deadly inflation at home, to be able, after years of work aboad, to secure a modest apartment for their family and children.

The aim was implacable: never, ever again to permit another October war, never again to allow the reconstitution of the sacred unity of the United National Front around the popular masses and the national army. Day after day, the existential problems of men and women in Egypt became gradually more intolerable. Transport, communications, telephones, the sewage system, often coupled with difficulties in food supply (which remain available to the poor sections only thanks to massive Government subsidies), converged to make life intolerable for the immense majority of the Egyptian society, with the sole exception of the compradore parallel society. Day after day, the dual hemorrhage led to the disaffection of wide sectors of the public. A skillful propaganda campaign about the abuses by Arab millionaires of their oil resources was begun, negating the parallel massive help handed to Egypt by its Arab brethren from rich oil countries.

Thus the basis was laid to launch policies seeking a separate arrangement with the Zionist State, the dream of the compradore leadership in Egypt, who did understand--better than the national bourgeoisies and the popular forces, both Islamic and socialist--the implications of détente. If the U.S.S.R. was ever to receive advanced computer technology from the United States, it could only do so by overcoming the veto of the controlling Zionist apparatus, at the very heart of the U.S. Congress. It logically followed that no direct intervention was to be expected from the U.S.S.R. at this stage of history, as the only way to reach for the American miracle was by submitting to Zionist imperialism, not as the agent and means of U.S. imperialism, but as the rising contending force within the world front of Western imperialism, toward central leadership, for its own sake. A separate peace could bring respite to the harassed Egyptian masses, lulled into believing that they would soon have "chicken for breakfast," be widely applauded in Western public opinion, and allow for an access to joint compradorism for the affluent groups, full partnership in the club of the "haves"--at the expense of the isolation of Egypt in its own national mold.

IV

The experience of the first attempt to provide a unified framework for the Arab nation has played, and is still playing a powerful role in ongoing processes and reactions. The call for Arab unity was not specifically, i.e., formally, Egyptian. It was no doubt the Wafd which launched the League of Arab States in 1945. But the call for Arab unity remained the privilege of Arab national leaderships in the Arab East, essentially the Ba 'th party.

Nasser's approach to Arab unity was, from the beginning, civilizational and strategic, rather than immediately institutional. He defined the Arab circle as the first among the three circles of Egyptian identity and Egypt's national project in his "Philosophy of the Revolution." He lent direct powerful support to anti-imperialist forces at work in several parts of the Arab world, especially in Algeria and Yemen, at a very high cost indeed. The 1956 Suez war was a retaliation against Nasser's Algerian policy. In Yemen, twenty-six thousand Egyptians lost their lives in vicious battles at the entrance of Bab el-Mandeb, the destruction of feudalism in Yemen guaranteed the security and accessibility of the Red Sea at the time of the October war. In 1958, the Syrian Arab national leadership prevailed, and Nasser, with massive support in Egypt, accepted the creation of the United Arab Republic, in which Egypt, for the first time in its history, lost its very name to become the "Southern province" of the U.A.R. Though the initiative was not his, no unified State, according to the Egyptian specific political tradition, could or would function in the loose regionalist style of ideological regimes. The autocratic State apparatus of Egypt operated in Syria exactly as it did, at that time, in Egypt, creating inevitable difficulties and oppositions from different factions. The striking characteristic of this period, the first Arab united State in modern history, is that nearly all factions of the Arab political spectrum rallied against the centralized State led by Egypt--while appealing forcefully for Egyptian leadership of this first united Arab State.

With the collapse of the U.A.R. Nasser understood that his first realistic, pragmatic, approach was much more adequate to the political realities of our times, as noted in the analyses of Egyptian Communists. His self-criticism of October 1961 meant that Egypt had opted for a more supple form of Arab unity, perhaps a confederation-to-be, taking into account regional specificities, yet maintaining a powerful centralized control of internal and external political matters as well as of the armed forces.

It was obvious, at this juncture, that the reticence and, at times, the opposition of minority political trends in Egypt against the crescendo of Arab unity would rally against the problematic of Arab unity per se. In doing so, these minority groups could plead the sacrifices of Egypt and its President, the undisputed leader of the Arab nation and a towering figure of this century, in the face of the dissensions, plots and counterplots, ideological manipulations, and regional distinctions, alien to the very concept of a unified Arab State. After all, neither modern Germany nor Italy achieved unity through a series of compromises between warring ideological factions, regions and sub-regions. Nor, for that matter, did France and England at a much earlier time. Unity meant a powerful unifying political leadership. And Egypt was called upon to provide such leadership. It was immensely difficult for wide sectors of its population to accept the onslaught of mounting criticism against Egyptian hegemony. Why not, therefore, take stock of reality, and dig in the Egyptian mainland: Egypt, the crucible?

More than they would think, Arab ideological factions and regional centrifugal forces paved the way for the emerging and growing distance between Egypt and the immediate circle of the Arab nation. No doubt, the 1973 October War played a powerful role in reviving the ethos and spirit of unity. During the war itself, and in its aftermath, the oil-rich Arab States rallied to the support of Egypt and Syria and exerted oil pressure against Western hegemony. Yet all wounds were soon to bleed again--from the very first hours of October 6, 1976, imprecations, criticisms, defiance and accusations were thrown at Egypt as if the whole process was but an organized plot. Once again, centrifugal forces could only comfort the more prudent, conservative diffident trends in Egypt toward a new isolationism.

The significance of this counterproductive process was not self-evident at first glance. Yet, observers could detect exactly the parallel process at work at the time of Ibn Khaldun. For then, during the fateful fourteenth century, political power passed from the hands of the rugged mounted military dynast of Morocco to the more open, divisive weakened peripheral groups in the Eastern part of the Maghreb, in Tunisia, facing Europe. In Ibn Khaldun's view, such was the historic setting for the weakening of national unity (the famed 'Asabiyyah) which rendered the very existence of a powerful State leadership unobtainable at that time. He, therefore, decided to migrate to Egypt, where he spent twenty-six years writing the towering work on the Philosophy of History that made him the founding father of history and social science. Centuries later, and for the second time--after Muhammad 'Ali in 1840--State power and its mainstay Egypt were denied their role in the foundation of a united Arab nation by peripheral, centrifugal forces, taking the image of immensely rich bedouinic and

sedentary groupings around the Gulf area. How could
State power obtain if such forces could be arrayed to
allow for the creation of the parallel compradore sector
in the Egyptian economy and society, via the
manipulations of the West? No Arab unity could obtain at
this point, inasmuch as the only center toward
unification was denied the objective means to achieve its
historic legitimacy, claimed in the first place by Arab
countries around Egypt. The scene was set for
retraction.

A central factor would have been the emergence of an
Egyptian leadership willing and capable of defining ways
and means toward new patterns of Arab unity, combining
Egyptian central might and potentials with the new-found
oil resources and the overall dynamics of the Arab
national liberation movement, after October 1973, and the
Palestinian Resistance. This did not happen because of
the overall setting of the détente, and also because of
the subjective characteristics of the post-Nasser
political leadership in Egypt, fully and deep at heart
reconciled with the imperatives of becoming a minor
partner in the modernized dependent world.

Ibn Khaldun revisited--during the period of détente
and the changing patterns of world power. A situation
fraught with danger. A historic challenge which could
only be met by statesmen of the mold which gave Muhammad
'Ali and Gamal Abdul Nasser to the world.

It is fashionable, among liberal-oriented
Westernized intellectuals, to criticize Nasser's
leadership along the lines of autocracy-cum-human rights.
Yet, history has shown and will show that the weaknesses
in Nasser's Egypt were precisely of a contrary nature.

During the last phase of his very short eighteen-
year leadership, the Egyptian Revolution, having adopted
scientific socialism in 1962 and put an end to the "war
in darkness" which had separated the central national
core from its Left allies, in 1964 launched a more
radical socialist-oriented State policy. The creation of
the political organization at the heart of the Arab
Socialist Union brought together radical officers,
national progressives, Communists, trade-unionists and
patriots for the first time since the Wafd's secret
organization of 1919-1923, and echoing Ahman 'Arabi's
coalition with the National party in 1881-82. State
policy soon included a radical transformation of agrarian
reform, to be remodelled along the lines of the agrarian
cooperative organization, both in matters of property and
exploitation of the immensely limited agricultural lands.
It was then, and at this precise point, i.e., in 1966,
that the Zionist State decided to launch the 1967 June
War to destroy the emerging national progressive State in
Egypt, which international Zionism saw as deadly to its
racialist expansionist policy in the Arab region.

Time was short, immensely short. Not even a year.

No time to build structures, let alone to deploy. And, once the global strategic counteroffensive was launched, the institutions and traditions of Nasserism in Egypt could not withstand the storms of the time and had to revert to either internal exile, impotent opposition, or even rally, here and there, to the acceptance of inevitable compromises. It was then, more than on any other occasion, that the achievements of the process of radicalization of the Egyptian National Revolution took a very heavy toll.

Other important factors and forces were also at work: The inward-looking policies of several Arab States, both radical and conservative. The repeated attempts to pour ridicule on Egyptian initiatives, to corner Egypt in order to snatch an evasive leadership. The misuse, to a large extent, and for a considerable time, of oil potentials--between 1952 and 1973--in spite of the existence of a powerful centripetal Arab leadership in Egypt. These were major factors and forces that inevitably weakened the pro-Arab stance of large sectors of Egyptian public opinion and leadership. The last point was particularly perplexing: the very organization of the Egyptian national project under Nasser was to bring peripheral oil into close interaction with the powerful State machine at the center with a view to promote a united Arab renaissance. Yet, repeatedly, wave after wave, this was dismissed as hegemonism, over-centralization, imposed autocracy etc., as shown by the writings of Mohamad Hassanein Heykal and Ahmed Baha`'Eddin.[10] It became apparent that the aim of some quarters was to reestablish the Holy Alliance, the Middle East Defence Pact, the hegemony of the Fertile Crescent, at the time of the Baghdad Pact and its transformation into CENTO.

All of the factors presented thus far were conducive to March 26, 1979, to the breakup of Arab unity, and to the occultation of Egypt.

V

This period of the transformation of the world demands a meaningful Arab prospective, an Arab civilizational strategy. Strategic planning must be of a fundamentally different nature than the usual short- or mid-term political planning, of a tactical or strategic nature. We need to develop an Arab vision of history, derived from our historically defined national-cultural specificities, and from a novel understanding of the dialectical dynamics of the transformation of the world in our times.

This is a totally and altogether different matter from the paraphrase of different sets of analysis presented by Western thinkers and epigones.[11] The aim of this Arab civilizational strategy would be to give the Arab nation a forward depth of historical field, a middle- and long-range perspective, a comprehension of the geopolitical space in which it could operate fruitfully, an understanding of the timing at which such potentials--objectively understood--could deploy. And, as a result, a vision of the future in which the Arab nation would verily set itself to achieve the tasks of the unfinished nineteenth-century *Nahdah,* by contributing its own civilizational project to the world, at the time of the in-depth crisis of the civilizational model of productivism and consumerism, the self-destructive ethos of the acquisitive advanced industrial societies of the West.

Fundamental factors for analysis toward this Arab prospective are:

1. The differentiation between the world economic crisis of 1929-1932 and the present slowing of economic growth, the so-called "recession." And the latter's relevance to the altogether different societal groupings and structures of power in Western Europe and North America, and in different nation-states of Western Europe itself.

2. The dialectical evolution of Soviet society and power at the end of this century, and its different prospective paths: The structural transformation of demography in favor of the Asian-Islamic central Asian and Siberian Republics. The rise to power and influence of the new generation of highly-trained cadres at the time of Soviet global policy and détente. The interaction between the basic contradiction of strategic advantage and a persistently lesser tempo of economic growth as compared with the United States. The way to analyse, comprehend and tackle the basic challenges posited by the creation of a third center of world power and influence in China. The attitude and relations with political Islam in Afro-Asia, inter alia.

3. The prospective course of the crystallization of a third center of world power and influence in China, essentially in alliance with Japan, with the converging and the differentiating factors of Korea, Vietnam, India and Southeast Asia. Particularly important would be the interrelation between Arab-Iranian oil and the vital need of Japan (as the chief modernizing agent of China) for this oil, a factor still little used by the Arab and Islamic areas.

4. The evolution of Europe--both Western and Eastern--and particularly the prospect of a not too distant German reunification, in the form of a German confederation, creating a formidable center of economic power, closely linked with the U.S.S.R. via the Ostpolitik. Prospective scenarios should be studied as they relate to the possible future courses of Great Britain, France, Germany, Italy and other regions.

5. The emergence of sub-Saharan Africa, either in liaison with Arab oil, technology and political alliances, or (through the creation of situations of imbalance and racialism in Southern Africa) in a strategic military alliance with the Zionist State--a most dangerous situation for world peace, let alone the Arab nation and Islamic areas.

6. The rising potentials of Latin America, particularly Brazil, as well as the oil affluence in Mexico. The latter is amenable to U.S. encirclement and therefore potentially less usable politically. The Brazilian dimension represents a significant linkage with the African continent, and can thus process advanced potentials in the industrial, scientific-technological and atomic fields. These factors, coupled with its geographic depth, make Brazil a sizable contender for the position of major world power in the coming ten years, and therefore an importnt new influence in the Arab-Zionist conflict.

7. The problem of control of the seas and oceans, as well as the gigantic reserves of food resources. Sea power can either open up or strangle marine communications, linkages, the transportation of oil, etc. to and from the pivotal Arab geopolitical area.

The last three items (5-7) directly link with the Arab nation's role at the heart of the anti-imperialist struggles of our century, through the Afro-Asian and the Tricontinental solidarity movements, in the great tradition of Bandung, now taking the form of the group of nonaligned countries. It does, however, in many regions, take a much more activist stance exactly as in the times of the positive neutralism of Nasser's Egypt.

The central instrument toward achieving an Arab civilizational strategy is the United National Front, the optimum combination of the national potentials of each nation-state within the broader framework of the Arab nation. To quote from our 1977 formulation:

A. THE STRUCTURATION OF THE UNITED FRONT: THE TWO DIMENSIONS

1. The problem of the structuration of the United Front would [thus] appear to be significantly different from the hitherto prevailing practice or practices. And this difference would lie in two areas:

a) the area of the structuration of the United Front itself;

b) the area of the durability of the United Front, i.e., whether it is a problem for political tactics, political strategy or a wider problem.

We will here first attempt to deal with the first dimension, i.e., the structuration of the United Front.

It is our view that the optimal inner structuration
of the United Front consists in combining two different
component groups, or levels, of constitutive factors, in
the manner described hereunder.

2.   The   first,   more   traditional,   group   of
constituent   factors   of   which   the   first   level   of   the
United Front can be said to be made, is the one which
obtains in all political fronts put forth by forces of
transformation and socialism, as well as indeed by all
political forces.   It starts from the fact that the body
politic,   which   expresses   the   differentiation   of   any
societal formation, of any nation, is made of different
groups: social classes, social groups, sub-groups and
sectors, professional and political groups, etc.   This is
the   place   for   political   parties,   trade-union
organizations, professional organizations, cooperatives,
popular and mass mobilization organizations, etc.   There
is   here   no   problem   of   particular   relevance   to   our
analysis   at   the   level   of   structuration   itself.   The
problems will obtain when we discuss the durability of
the   United   Front   itself,   that   is   whether   it   is   a
tactical,   political   or--as   we   here   submit   a   historical
strategy.

3.   The   second   group   of   structuring   factors,   of
which the second level of the structuration of the United
Front is made, is of a far more subtle nature, more
hidden as it were in the hidden part of the iceberg.   For
this is the group of factors which lie beyond the more
immediately apparent political surface of activism, but
is fixed in the historical roots of societal continuity
at work in the unit which we mentioned as being the only
meaningful unit for the social dialectics, once we enter
the era of globalization of the world, i.e., the nations
and national-cultural regions of the world.   We have
explained, hereabove, the way in which the factors of
societal maintenance at work in nations and national-
cultural areas are intimately bound around the couple of
political power-cum-national culture as the axis for
societal maintenance throughout centuries, through the
succession   of   different   modes   of   production,
sociopolitical and ideological systems.   It is a fact of
life, as it is a fact of politics, and history, that we
observe in the meaningful nations and national-cultural
areas of the world, major trends of thought and action,
"les grandes familles spirituelles," as the French so
excellently   put   it,   which   are   the   constitutive
structuring   basic   visions   of   thought   and   national
sensibility, continuously expressed in the realm of
political   action,   in   which   the   different   human
groups--social and ethnic groups--which have come to make
a specific nation, have accepted to link their destiny,
join hands and elaborate this highly complex societal
unit which has come to be known under the name of
"nation."

This second group, level, of the structuration of
the United Front will therefore be made of the
representative formations and epigones of these major
intellectual trends of the national-cultural tradition.
For example, if we consider closely the socialist
movements of a great number of nations in the Orient,
yesterday and today alike, we shall find that they can be
divided certainly along more conservative and more
radical, more compromise-oriented and more revolution-
oriented sectors. But we shall also find, deep at work
within all these divisions, a central division between
groups which belongs to different national-cultural
traditions: some groups will be linked with the
modernizing, Western-oriented, sectors of the
intellectual trends of the national-cultural life of a
given country; while other groups will be more deeply
rooted in the autochthonous national tradition of this
given country. Thus, we would have modernizers on the
left, and also traditionalists on the left. And we shall
also find the same type of division among the right,
reactionary forces. We shall have to accept that, in
countries of the Christian tradition, there would be
major groups among the forces of socialism which are and
will be, for a very long time indeed, inspired by the
Christian philosophy, theology and social ethics, as we
can witness in countries like Italy, Spain, France,
Germany, Latin America, etc. At the same time, we find
the same phenomena in countries of the Islamic
civilizational mold, in Asia and Africa. The same also
goes for Buddhism in the Asian continent.
Traditionalists and modernizers of all faiths and credos,
inasmuch as they are *genuinely rooted and constitutive of
the national-cultural tradition,* have their say at that
second, formative, level of the structuration of the
United Front.

Once again, let us stress that this second level or
group of structuring factors has been put forth as a
central consideration in our analysis by the very moment,
the objective reality, of social dialectics in our
times--and not through epistemological analysis. That
is, through the analysis of the actual functioning of
sociopolitical systems, and not through an exegesis of
19th century teachings on socialism, in the West.

4. It is important, in that respect, to understand
that the combination of these two sets of structuring
factors, of these two levels of structuration, will show
a highly complex interplay of forces, influences and
reciprocal interactions between the different units of
each one of these two factors and levels. That type of
dialectical interaction is the one with which we must
understand to live. For here, *dialectical contradiction
is by nature a non-antagonistic contradiction, not
leading to manichean, centrifugal, divisiveness, but to
dialectical complementarity in thought and actions alike.*

As we go through this highly complex network of social dialectics in the United Front, we shall recognize that in the so-called "Left" as well as in the so-called "Right," we are confronted with two major forces that go to make the central difference and contradiction in each one of these two camps:

a) The first force can and must be labelled the force of conservatism, whether *conservatism* flies under the reductionist flag of modernization and conformity with the so-called scientific and technological revolution, or whether it purports simply to maintain old traditions.

b) On another hand, we find the radical forces, the forces of *radicalization,* which always seek to dig to the roots of social dialectics and provide radical policies capable of restructuring the impact of these very roots in political life.

To be sure, there is no royal road: there is no recipe, no golden methodology, no political theology capable of distinguishing abruptly and in a definite manner these two groups. There is however one major rule of political praxis and that is the *mass line:* the way and extent in which policies promoted by each major trend can be, more or less, a mobilizing force in the concrete transformation of the life and destiny of the majority of the working population, in a way which does not distort national character as determined by history, the genetic structuration of national specificity, but, on the contrary helps toward its development and fruition.

5. At the nexus of these two dialectically converging formative groups of factors stands the army--conspicuously so, in both the old established nations, and the new national States. While the broad majority of the officers corps reflects quite naturally the equilibrium of sociopolitical power in any given society, concerned principally with maintaining both the order of society and its independence facing external hegemonies, it becomes increasingly clear that the armed forces are gradually acquiring, at one and the same time, a much greater economic and scientific-technological role, and an increasing political autonomy, to the point of functioning sometimes as the formative "political class" of a whole nation--especially when confronted with direct and repetitive foreign menaces and invasions, such as has been, and still is, the case in areas of maximal tensions (the Western Asian-Middle Eastern area, sub-Saharan Africa, the Indian Ocean area, notably). In any case, the extension of conscription to the whole population, including its majority of workers, peasants and clerical employees and petty bourgeois, raises the problem of the extent to which armed forces, though basically led by the hegemonic sociopolitical groups, can develop into the army of the nation. Such, in any case, is the legacy of Nasserism to our joint theoretical and

political interrogation. But one would recall the
examples of Bonapart(ism), of the Long March, of the
young Turks under Ataturk, of the armed resistance
against fascism in Europe, of Peron, the Algerian F.L.N.;
and the negative effects of doggedly refusing to readjust
to reality, in Chile, Portugal, inter alia.

Volens nolens, the armed forces stand at the center
in the new developing patterns of united front strategies
in Asia, Africa and Latin America, in a highly
diversified array of ways and paths yet not integrated to
(normalized) social and political theory.

B. ON THE HISTORICAL AND CIVILIZATIONAL CHALLENGES

1. We are now dealing with the second factor, the
second set of the problematic of the United Front, i.e.,
the question of its durability. Till now, the United
Front, in the Western socialist tradition, has been
conceived of as a tactical, or, at best, strategic
expedient, to achieve some form of maximal resistance or
national durability to the hegemony of socialist
leadership within the political process.

However, in Asia, Africa and Latin America, and in
all instances in which the forces of socialism have not
been able to assert their hegemony and leadership in the
liberation fronts, we are witnesses to the fact that
United National Fronts are either a de facto or a formal
long-term continuing institution. For here, there is a
feeling that the only front of cohesiveness—both for
resistance and national buildup and social
transformation—is indeed the one provided by the United
Front, by the unification process, by the unitary
tendency, by bringing in short the basic forces of the
nation, along with and in spite of class groups and
struggles, to converge in the same broad camp facing
imperialism, hegemony and the compradores.

This is the tonality of the present-day United
National Front as political strategy. Could there be
another dimension?

2. Here we have to revert, once more, to the
globalization of the world and the challenges which it is
putting today to all national units, to all political
movements, to all initiatives in thought and action to
change the situation of mankind toward a more equable,
more humane, more free, richer life which has come to be
known by the name of socialism. It is a question for
political thought and action alike to ponder the
following: if the United Fronts are conceived of, not as
a political tactical expedient, but as a long-term
political strategy, will it not be that the different
units which make the two levels of these new United
Fronts, linked in action, in combat, in perpetual
interaction and exchange, in non-antagonistic dialectical

opposition, in de facto complementarity, will they not come to consider that, in fact, the promises and programme of socialism can be better realized through a much wider front of forces than the mere hegemony of the working-class, at best allied with groups of the peasantry and lower petty bourgeoisie? Will they not come to consider that the mobilization of the widest sectors of the population, across class lines, through national culture and ideologies, through religions and philosophies--all belonging, let us stress this again, to the formative national-cultural tradition of the nation, to its "grandes familles spirituelles," will be a tremendously powerful asset capable of minimizing the difficulties, of minimizing the pains and sufferings, entailed by major processes of social transformation? In short, would not the United Front, conceived and accepted as long-term political strategy, lead the way to consider that such United Fronts are in fact within the mainstream of the very logic of history? And, if so, would it not be proper for us to consider that the United Front is not a political strategy--a "historical compromise" within its perforce limited limits--but, more audaciously along the line of this thinking, a historical strategy?

For the choice here is, really, between two attitudes. Either to choose the shortcut of political conspiracy, of minority activism and hegemony--but then the proponents of such an attitude must understand that they are running counter to the massive traditions of popular movements in history, and also against the iron ring of geopolitics and the globalization of the world. Whenever such attitudes have been attempted, they have only helped the enemy of the people, as witness some recent tragic experiences, notably in Chile. Or--and this is here and now our plea as it has always been--to choose the wider avenue for lessening human sufferings and shortcutting the maximization of sufferings, tensions, difficulties, in the broad direction of social progress, public happiness, and the ascent of the peoples to the role of the direction of their own destinies. This could be the way, and such the promises, of the United Front as historical strategy.[12]

The United National Front, thus understood, is at variance with the class-against-class approach of centrifugal social dialectics specific of the Western political tradition and ideology. It does, on the other hand, relate directly to parallel forms of societal mass mobilization at the very heart of the renascent nations of the Orient: the Long march of Chinese Revolution, the Islamic concept of *Ummah,* the *'urwah al-wuthqa* of Afghani and 'Abdoh--the United National Front of our contemporary Arab political tradition.

It, and it alone, will enable the Arab nation to draw upon its immense wealth of intellectual, human and voluntary resources in order to launch the cultural revolution at the very heart of the process of devision and implementing our Arab civilizational strategy. It, and it alone, will enable us to revive the 'Asabiyyah, vital to overcoming the occultation of Egypt and the resumption of our joint Arab national course.

Our Arab nation lies at the very center of the Islamic Afro-Asian civilizational area, from Morocco to the China Seas. The occultation of Egypt deprives the Arab nation of its center of efficient power and unity.

Facing the rising tide of the Three Continents--and principally of the Orient, Asia and Africa--the combined civilizational counteroffensive of imperialism, led by Zionist racialist imperialism, is penetrating, not only political structures, but political will in depth, at long last at the very center. The two major socialist powers, as we have seen, are now distantiated from effective action in the Arab area. The danger of protracted decadence therefore looms large on the immediate horizon.

Yet, a close scrutiny of the geopolitical and the geocultural map shows promise. Throughout the range of the Islamic Afro-Asian civilizational area, a massive wave of national revolutions, sometimes coupled with social revolutions, is taking place, and is now capable of availing itself, for the first time since the golden age of Islam and the Orient, of the most important source of wealth in the contemporary world. This area does not seem to be in a situation that would enable superpowers to create vassal dependent States for a long time, in a durable manner. Deep in the hearts of men, deep at work at the roots of national movements in this area, lie the will to independence, liberation, the desire for renaissance, the potentials for a meaningful upsurge through national unity, the combination of temporal and spiritual power, between the popular masses and the army, an urge toward spirituality, toward charting new paths of inter-human and inter-societal relations--in brief all the elements of a civilizational renaissance of immense magnitude.

In a more narrow way, the greatest proportion of the Islamic masses lies at the juncture between the U.S.S.R., China, India and the Arab-Iranian oil regions. More than ever before, our Arab nation could be the mediating link, the intercessor between different national cultures, States and socioeconomic formations which appeared to lie separate.

More than ever before, our Arab nation could chart the path toward the bringing together of other forces of national liberation and social progress in the Orient, essentially in Asia and Africa, coupled with an organic linkage with the bulk of the populations of the

continental mass of Euro-Asia, now living under the
banner of socialism.

More than any "historical compromise," the unfolding
of the Arab renaissance--as of liquidation of the
occultation of Egypt--could chart the path toward a
global transformation of world power in our times, and
therefore of the very destiny of humanity.

Nobody chooses his time in history

To meet the vital challenge of our time in history,
let all patriots join hands and take action to save our
beloved land, "Egypt, mother of the world."

NOTES

1. On "That generation which has a date with
history," cf. our *Egypte, Société militaire* (Paris,
1962); better, its second authoritative version, *Al-
Mogtama' al-Micri wa'l-Gaysh, 1952-1970* (Beirut, 1975);
on the longer range, *Idéologie et Renaissance Nationale:
l'Egypte moderne* (Paris, 1969). The best scholarly
authoritative history of Egypt's wars is being researched
and published by maj.-Gen. Hassan al-Badri: *Al Harb fi
Ard al-Salam-al-Gawlah al-'Arabiyyah al-Isra 'illiyyah
al-Ula* (Cairo, 1976), and, with Maj.-Gen. Taha al-Magdub
and Brig.-Gen. Dia 'Eddin Zuhdi, *Harb Ramadan-al-Gawlah
al 'Arabiyyah al-Isra'illiyyah al-Rabi'ah* (Cairo, 1975).

2. See the towering seminal work of Gamal Hamdan,
Shakhciyyat Micr-dirasah fi 'abqariyyat al-Makan (Cairo,
1965) and *6 Oktober fi'l-Stratijiyyah al-'Alamiyyah*
(Cairo, 1975). Cf. our "Geopolitics and National
Movements: An Essay on the Dialectics of Imperialism,"
Antipode 9, no. 1, p. 28-36; and "The Civilizational
Significance of the Arab National Liberation War," in
Middle East Crucible, ed. Naseer H. Aruri (Wilmette,
Ill.: Medina University Press, 1975), pp. 389-407, and
Journal of the Middle East, no. 3 (1976).

3. Notably in the works of the late Yasin al-Hafez.
See the perceptive analysis by Ahmad Baha 'Eddin in his
editorials in *Al-Mustaqbal,* 1979.

4. A perusal of the Ba'thist press, of all trends,
from 1952 until, say, 1973, will prove instructive.
Algeria, on the one hand, and Tunisia and Kuwait, on the
other, do provide a healthy climate to assess the period.

5. Cf. repeated sequences in *Le Nouvel Observateur,*
and the left Zionist press, now confirmed by a recent
publication, and the venomous a posteriori
disqualification of Joseph Kraft, "A divided opposition
to Sadat," *International Herald Tribune,* 11 April 1979.
A good socio-historical perspective is provided by Ahmad
Mohamad Ghoneim and Ahmad Abu Kaff, *Al-Yahud wa'l-Harakah
al-Cahyuniyyah fi Micr 1897-1947* (Cairo, 1969); while
'Abd al-Wahab al-Mesiri presents a sophisticated detailed
Egyptian-Arab vision of the civilizational thrust in his

148

remarkable *Mawsu'at   al Mafahim'wa'l-Mustalahat   al-Cahyuniyyah - ru'yah naqdiyyah* (Cairo, 1975).
Ironically, there is now even an Arab-Zionist version of
the history of the Egyptian left, by Rif'at Al-Sa'id,
Tarikh al-Munazzamat al-Yasariyyah al-Micriyyah 1940-1950
(Cairo, 1976).

6. The full story is told with detailed, minutely
researched documentation in *Qiccat al-Khilaf fi'l-Hizb
al-Shuyu'i al-Souri* (Beirut, 1974). *See also* the memoirs
of President Nasser's secretary, 'Abd al-Magid Farid, in
Al-Dustur of 1978-1979; Mohamed Hassanein Heikal, *Sphinx
and Commissar--The Rise and Fall of Soviet Influence in
the Middle East* (London, 1978); Lt.-Gen. Sa'd Eddin al-
Shazli's memoirs, *Harb Oktober 73,* chap. 5, sec. 4, "Ayna
akhta'at Moscow wa ayna acabat?," *Al-Watan al-Arabi,* 6
April 1979.

7. Cf. the crucial work by Admiral Sergei Gorchkov,
The World-Ocean (London, 1978), at a par with Clausewitz.

8. We have attempted to develop this notion, from
our "Introduction à la Pensée Arabe Contemporaine" in
Anthologie de la Litterature Arabe Contemporaine (Paris,
1965) [the edited version of our 1964 doctoral
dissertation in sociology], via *La Pensée Politique Arabe
Contemporaine* (Paris, 1970) onwards, notably in "Islam et
Marxisme," *I Problemi di Ulisse:* L'Islam 14 (July 1977):
114-122; "Political Islam--Positions," Third Round Table
on Socialism in the World, Cavtat, 1978; "Al Madd al-
Islami houwa al-Radd al'Arabi," *Al-Nahar Arabe et
International,* 15 February 1979.

9. Of particular importance, in this respect, is
our definition of "the twin-levelled nation" (la nation a
double palier), in "Introduction à la Pensée Arabe
Contemporaine," *La Pensee Politique Arabe Contemporaine,*
pp. 23-25; *Dirasat fi'l-Thaqafah al-Wataniyyah* (Beirut,
1967); *Al-Fikr al-'Arabi fi Ma'rakat al-Nahdah* (Beirut,
1975).

10. Cf. key texts from that period in our *La Pensee
Politique Arabe Contemporaine.* A recent lucid expostion
is found in Maj.-Gen. 'Adli Hassan Sa'id, *Al-Amm al-Qawmi
al-Arabi wa Stratijiyyat Tahqiqihi* (Cairo, 1977) facing
Yeshoshafat Harkabi's *Arab Strategies and Israel's
Response* (New York, 1977).

11. Cf., inter alia, Edward Mortimer's "Making
Zionism Acceptable to the Arabs" (on M. Rodinson's
credentials for being granted the 1974 Isaac Deutscher
Memorial Prize), *The Times,* 2 January 1975. On the true
nature of the neo-orientalistic "scientific" political
offensive, cf. the rich body of critical literature from
our essay, "L'Orientalisme en crise," *Diogene,* no. 44
(1963): 109-142, to the major work by Edward W. Said,
Orientalism (New York & London, 1978).

12. "The United Front as Historical
Strategy--Positions," *Socialism in the World* , no. 7, pp.
59-74.

CHAPTER 8

Oppression and Human Liberation: Toward a Third World Utopia

Ashis Nandy

> Alas, having defeated the enemy, we have ourselves been defeated. . . . The . . . defeated have become victorious. . . . Misery appears like prosperity, and prosperity looks like misery. Thus our victory is turned into defeat.
>
> *The Mahabharata*[1]

I

All utopias and all visions of the future are a language. However majestic in their architectonics or tame in their earthiness, they are an attempt to communicate with the present in terms of the myths and allegories of the future. When they are fiercely vindictive, they are a warning to us; when they are benign or forgiving toward the present, they can be an encouragement. Like history, which exists ultimately in the mind of the historian and his believing readers and is thus a means of communication, utopian or futurist thinking is another aspect of--and a comment upon--the here and now, another means of making peace with or challenging man-made suffering in the present, another ethics apportioning responsibility for this suffering and guiding the struggle against it on the plane of contemporary consciousness.[2]

No utopia can be without an implicit or explicit theory of suffering. This is particularly so in what is euphemistically called the Third World. The concept of the Third World is not a cultural category; it is a political and economic category born of poverty, exploitation, indignity, and self contempt. The concept is inextricably linked with the efforts of a large number of people trying over generations to survive quasi-extreme situations.[3] A Third World utopia--the South's concept of a decent society, as Barrington Moore might call it-- must recognize this basic reality.[4] To have a meaningful life in the minds of men, such a utopia must start with the issue of man-made suffering, which has given the Third World both its name and its uniqueness.

This essay presents an intercivilizational perspective on oppression, with a less articulate psychology of survival and salvation as its appendage. It is guided by the belief that the only way the Third World can transcend the sloganeering of its well-wishers is (1) by becoming a collective representation of the victims of man-made suffering everywhere in the world and in all past times (2) by internalizing the outside forces of oppression and then coping with them as inner vectors, and (3) by recognizing the oppressed or marginalized selves of the First and the Second Worlds as civilizational allies in the battle against institutionalized suffering.[5]

The perspective is based on three assumptions. First, as far as the core values are concerned, goodness and right ethics are not the monopoly of any civilization. All civilizations share some basic values and such cultural traditions as derive from man's biological self and social experience. The distinctiveness of a complex civilization lies not in the uniqueness of its values but in the gestalt that it imposes on these values and in the weights it assigns to its different traditions or values and subtraditions. So, certain traditions or cultural strains may, at a certain point of time, be recessive or dominant in a civilization, but they are never uniquely absent or exclusively present. What looks like a human potentiality that ought to be actualized in some distant future is often only a cornered cultural strain waiting to be renewed or rediscovered.

Second, human civilization is constantly trying to alter or expand its awareness of exploitation and oppression. Oppressions that were once outside the span of awareness are no longer so, and it is quite likely that the present awareness of suffering, too, would be found wanting and would change in the future. Who, before the socialists, had thought of class as a unit of repression? How many, before Freud, had sensed that children needed to be protected against their own parents? How many believed, before Gandhi's rebirth after the environmental crisis in the West, that modern technology, the supposed liberator of man, had become his most powerful oppressor? Our limited ethical sensitivity is not a proof of human hypocrisy; it is mostly a product of our limited cognition of the human situation. Oppression is ultimately a matter of definition, and its perception is the product of a world view. Change the world view, and what once seemed natural and legitimate becomes an instance of cruelty and sadism.

Third, imperfect societies produce imperfect remedies of their imperfections. Theories of salvation

are always soiled by the spatial and temporal roots of
the theorist. Since the solutions are products of the
same social experiences that produce the problems, they
cannot but be informed by the same consciousness and, if
you allow a psychologism, unconsciousness. Marx wrote
about the process of declassing oneself and about
breaking the barriers of one's "ideology" and false
consciousness; Freud, about the possibility of working
through one's personal history or, rather, the defenses
against such history. I like to believe that these
intellectual folk heroes of our times were only
reflecting an analytic attitude that allows a human
organism to work through its own history, and to
critically accept or reject it, or, if necessary, use it
as a part of its living tradition. They were reflecting
a continuity with the tradition of exegesis-as-criticism
that was associated with some mythopoeic traditions as
well as with some forms of classical scholasticism. It
is perhaps in human nature to try to design--even if with
only limited success--a future unfettered by the past and
yet, paradoxically, informed with the past.

II

What resistance does a culture face in working
through its remembered past and through the limits that
past sets on its cognition? What are the psychological
techniques through which the future is controlled or
preempted by an unjust system or by the experience of
injustice? What are the inner checks that a society or
civilization erects against minimizing man-made
suffering? What can liberation from oppression in the
most utopian sense mean?
We cannot even begin to answer these questions
without recognizing three processes that give structured
oppression its resilience.
1. The first of these processes is a certain anti-
psychologism which oppression breeds and from which it
seeks legitimacy. The fear of soft answers to hard
questions is a fear of cultures that refuse to give an
absolute value to hardness itself. Many years ago
Theodor Adorno and his associates found a link between
authoritarian predisposition and anti-psychologism (which
they, following Henry Murray, called anti-
intraceptiveness).[6] Implicit in that early empirical
study of authoritarianism was the recognition that one of
the ways an oppressive social system can be given some
permanence is by promoting a tough-mindedness that
considers all attempts to look within to the sources of
one's consciousness, and all attempts to examine one's
authenticity, as something compromising, soft-headed, and
emasculating. Twenty-five years afterwards Adorno recast
that argument in broader cultural terms:

Among the motifs of cultural criticism one of the most long-established and central is that of the lie: that culture creates the illusion of a society worthy of man which does not exist; that it concedes the material conditions upon which all human works rise, and that, comforting and lulling, it serves to keep alive the bad economic determination of existence. This is the notion of culture as ideology. . . . But precisely this notion, like all expostulation about lies, has a suspicious tendency to become itself ideology. . . . Inexorably, the thought of money and all its attendant conflicts extend into the most tender erotic, the most sublime spiritual relationships. With the logic of coherence and the pathos of truth, cultural criticism could therefore demand that relationships be entirely reduced to their material origin. . . . But to act radically in accordance with this principle would be to extirpate, with the false, all that was true also, all that however impotently strives to escape the confines of universal practice, every chimerical anticipation of a nobler condition, and so to bring about directly the barbarism that culture is reproached for furthering indirectly. . . . apart from this, emphasis on the material element, as against the spirit as a lie, has given rise to a kind of dubious affinity with that political economy which is subjected to an immanent criticism, comparable with the complicity between police and underworld. Since Utopia was set aside and the unity of theory and practice demanded, we have become all too practical. . . . today there is growing resemblence between the business mentality and sober critical judgement.[7]

Thus, in a peculiar reversal of roles, the vulgar materialism Adorno describes is now an ally of the global structure of oppression. It colludes with ethnocide because culture to it is only an epiphenomenon. In the name of shifting the debate to the real world, it reduces all choice to those available within a single culture, the culture affiliated to the dominant global system. In such a world, ruled by a structure that has coopted its manifest critics, the search for freedom may have to begin in the minds of men, with a defiance of the cultural themes that endorse oppression. Oppression to be oppressive must be felt to be so, if not by the oppressors and the oppressed, at least by some social analyst somewhere.

There is a second issue involved here. Theories of liberation built on ultramaterialism invariably inherit a certain extraversion. The various perspectives upon the future emerging from the women's liberation movement, from the ongoing debates on the heritability of IQ and from the North-South differences, all provide instances of how certain forms of anti-psychologism are used to avoid the analysis of deeper and long-term results of cruelty, exploitation, and authoritarianism. The idea that the problem is exclusively with the political position of women and not with the politics of femininity as a cultural trait, the idea that racial discrimination begins and ends with the racial differences in IQ and does not involve the definition of intelligence as only productive intelligence and as a substitute for intellect, the belief that North-South differences involve only unequal exchange of material goods and not unequal exchange in theories of salvation themselves--these are all significant tributes to a global culture that is constantly seeking new and more legitimate means of shortchanging the peripheries of the world. Yet, most debates around these issues assume that the impact of political and economic inequality are skin-deep and short term. Remove the inequality and oppression, they say in effect, and you will have healthy individuals and healthy societies all around.

This anti-psychologism, partly a reaction to the overpsychologization of the age of the psychological man, is another means of belittling the long-term cultural and psychological effects of violence, poverty, and injustice--effects that persist even when what is usually called political and economic oppression is removed. Continuous suffering inflicted by fellow human beings, centuries of inequity and deprivation of basic human dignity, generations of poverty, long experience of authoritarian political rule or imperialism--these distort the cultures and minds, especially the values and the self-concepts, of the sufferers and those involved in the manufacturing of suffering. Long-term suffering also generally means the establishment of powerful justifications for the suffering in the minds of both the oppressors and the oppressed. All the useful modes of social adaptation, creative dissent, techniques of survival, and conceptions of the future transmitted from generation to generation are deeply influenced by the way in which large groups of human beings have lived and died, and have been forced to live and forced to die. It is thus that institutionalized suffering acquires its self-perpetuating quality.

In sum, no vision of the future can ignore the way that institutional suffering touches the deepest core of human beings, and that societies must work through the culture and psychology of such suffering, in addition to its politics and economics. This awareness comes painfully, and each society in each period of history builds powerful inner defenses against it. Perhaps it is in human nature to try to vest responsibility for unexplained suffering in outside forces--in fate, in history, or, for that matter, in an objective science of nature or society. When successful, such an effort concretizes and exteriorizes evil and makes it psychologically more manageable. When unsuccessful, it at least keeps questions open. Predictably, every other decade we have a new controversy on nature versus nurture, a new incarnation of what is presently called sociobiology, and a new biological interpretation of schizophrenia. Biology and genetics exteriorize; psychology owns up.

  2. The second process is a certain continuity between the victors and the victims. Though some awareness of this continuity has been a part of our consciousness for many centuries, it is in this century--thanks primarily to the political technology developed by Gandhi and the cultural criticisms ventured by at least some socialist thinkers and some interpreters of Freud--that this awareness has become something more than a pious slogan. Though all religions stress the cultural and moral degradation of the oppressor and the dangers of privilege and dominance, it is on the basis of these three eponymic strands of consciousness that a major part of our awareness of the subtler and more invidious forms of oppression (that make the victims willing participants and supporters of an oppressive system) has been built. The most detailed treatment of the theme can be found in Freudian metapsychology. It presumes a faulty society that perpetuates its repression through a repressive system of socialization at an early age. Its prototypical victim is one who, while trying to live an ordinary "normal" life, gives meaning and value to his victimhood in terms of the norms of an unjust culture. Almost unwillingly, Freud develops a philosophy of the person which sees the victim as willingly carrying within him his oppressors.

  In other words, Freud took repression seriously. He did not consider the human nature a fully open system that could easily wipe out the scars of suffering and could, thus, effortlessly transcend its past. Like all history, the history of oppression has to be worked through. This piercing of collective defenses is necessary, Freud could be made to say, because human groups can develop exploitative systems within which the psychologically deformed oppressors and their psychologically deformed victims find a meaningful life-style and mutually potentiating cross-motivations. Such cross-motivations explain the frequent human inability to be free even when unfettered, a tendency that Erich Fromm, as early as the 1940s, called the fear of freedom.

  That is the warning contained in Bruno Bettelheim's and Victor Frankl's chilling accounts of the Nazi extermination camps, based on their personal experiences.[8] Both these gifted and courageous psychoanalysts describe how some of the victims internalized the norms of the camps and became the exaggerated, pathetic, but dangerous versions of their oppressors. Losing touch with reality out of the fear of inescapable death and trying to hold together a collapsing world, they internalized the norms and the world view of the SS and willingly collaborated with their oppressors, thus giving some semblance of meaning to their meaningless victimhood, suffering, and death, and to the degradation and monstrosity of their tormentors. (Elsewhere Bettelheim affirms that this was, everything said, an instance of the death drive wiping out the victim's will to live.[9] It is possible to view it also as a part of a dialectic that offsets the ego defense called "identification with the aggressor" against the moral majesty of the human spirit, which, when faced with the very worst in organized oppression, would rather give up the last vestiges of self-esteem and see itself as an object of deserved suffering than believe that another social group could deliberately inflict suffering without any perceivable concern for injustice.[10]) The killers in this case skillfully built upon this resilience of the victim's social self, particularly the persistence of his moral universe, and used it as a vital element in their industry of suffering.[11] The Nazis, one is constrained to admit, knew a thing or two about organized violence.

    3. The third process that limits man's vision of the future is his refusal to take full measure of the violence that an opppressive system does to the humanity and to the quality of life of the oppressors. Aimé Césaire says about colonialism that it "works to *decivilize* the colonizer, to *brutalize* him in the true sense of the word. . . ."[12] And, that decivilization and that brutalization one day come home to roost: ". . . no one colonizes innocently, . . . no one colonizes with impunity either."[13] If this sounds like the voice of a Black Cassandra speaking of cruelties that take place only outside the civilized world, there is the final lesson Bettelheim derives from his study of the European holocaust--"So it happened as it must: those beholden to the death drive destroy also themselves."[14] Admittedly we are close to the palliatives promoted by organized religions, but even in their vulgarized forms, religions do maintain a certain touch with the eternal verities of human nature. At least some of the major faiths of the world have not failed to affirm that oppressors are the ultimate victims of their own systems of oppression; that they are the ones whose dehumanization goes farthest, even by the conventional standards of everyday religion. We have probably come full circle here in post-modern, post-evolutionary social consciousness. It again seems obvious that no theory of liberation can be morally acceptable unless it admits that, in addition to the violence done to the obvious victims, there is the exploitation by imperfect societies of their instruments

of oppression.

This general continuity between slaves and masters apart, there is the more easily identifiable penumbra of the oppressed in any organized system of oppression. In addition to the millions of direct victims, there are also millions of secondary victims of the oppressive systems. Their brutalization is planned and institutionalized,[15] as is the hostility these "legitimately" violent groups often attract to protect those more central to the oppressive system. The ranks of the army and the police in all countries come from the relatively poor, powerless, or low-status sectors of society. Almost invariably, imperfect societies arrive at a system of mobility under which the lower rungs of the army and the police are some of the few channels of mobility open to the plebians. That is, the prize of a better life is dangled before the socioeconomically deprived groups to encourage them to willingly socialize themselves into a violent, empty life-style. In the process, a machine of oppression is built; it has not only its open targets but also its dehumanized cogs. These cogs only seemingly opt for what Herbert Marcuse calls "voluntary servitude"; actually they have no escape.

Though I belong to a society that was once colonized and ruled with the help of its indigenous population, where the number of white men rarely exceeded 50,000 in about 400 million, I shall give an example of this other oppression from another society in more recent times. The American experience with the Vietnam war shows that even anti-militarism, in the form of draft dodging or avoidance of military service, can become a matter of social discrimination. Pacifism can be classy. The better-placed dodge better and avoid the dirty world of military violence more skillfully. In the case of Vietnam, this doubly ensured that most of those who went to fight were the socially underprivileged, men who were already hurt, bitter, and cynical. As is well known, a disproportionately large number of them were Blacks who had no respite from the system or from their progressive and privileged fellow citizens protesting the war and feeling self-righteous. They were people who had seen and known violence and discrimination--manifest as well as latent, direct as well as institutional, pseudo-legitimate as well as openly illegitimate. Small wonder, then, that in Vietnam many of them tried to give meaning to possible death and mutilation by developing a pathological overconcern with avenging the suffering of their compatriots or "buddies," by stereotyping the Vietnamese and the communists, or by being aggressive nationalists. The Vietnam war was, in the ultimate analysis, a story of one set of victims setting upon another set of victims on behalf of a reified, impersonal system.[16]

III

An insight into such processes helps us visualize utopias of the Third World different from the ones that a straight interpretation of some of the major civilizations can be made to yield. This does not mean that cultural themes or cosmologies are unimportant. It means that the experience of exploitation and suffering is a great teacher. Those who maintain, or try to maintain, their humanity in the face of such experience perhaps develop the skill to give special meaning to the fundamental contradictions and schisms in the human condition--such as the sanctity of life in the omnipresence of death; the legitimate biological differences (between the male and the female, and between the adult, the child, and the elderly) that become stratificatory principles through the pseudo-legitimate emphases on productivity, performance, and "substance"; and the search for spirituality and religious sentiment, for human values in general, in a world where such a search is almost always a new sanctification of unnecessary suffering and status quo. Like Marx's "hideous heathen god who refused to drink nectar except from the skulls of murdered men," human consciousness has sometimes used oppression to sharpen its sensitivities and see meanings that would have been otherwise lost in the limbo of oversocialized thinking.

One important element in their vision that many major civilizations in the Third World have protected with care is a certain refusal to think in terms of opposed, exclusive, clear, Cartesian dichotomies. For long, this refusal has been seen as an intellectual stigmata, the final proof of the cognitive inferiority of the nonwhite races. Today, it triggers debates on race and IQ and on the metaphors of primitivism and infantility. Arguments against such accounts of the non-West have ranged all the way from the empirical-statistical to the philosophical. (Césaire, for example, has mentioned the "barbaric repudiation" by Europe implied in Descartes' charter of universalism: "reason . . . is found whole and entire in each man."[17]) Perhaps the time has come to work through this memory of intellectual racism, to admit that Descartes is not the last word on the intellectual potentials of humankind, and to acknowledge that what was once an embarrassment may some day become a hope.

Many have lamented the "genetic" gap between man's intellectual and moral development. Arthur Koestler is only the last in a long line of thinkers to feel that in this matter nature, particularly human evolution, has "let us down."[18] Perhaps what looks like a failure of nature is after all one civilization's death wish, restricted in time as well as in space. Let us not forget that Freud had a purely psychological--and by implication, time and space-bound--account and a name for this Cartesian pathology; he called it the ego defense of isolation[19] a process that isolated reason from feelings. And there is also an implied cultural context when Adorno quotes Holderlin: "If you have understanding and a heart, show only one. Both they will damn, if both you show together."[20] In such a world, it is remarkable that in spite of all the indignities and exploitation they have suffered, many of the Eastern civilizations have not drawn a clear line between the victor and the defeated, the oppressor and the oppressed, and the rulers and the ruled.[21] Unwillingly they have recognized that the gap between cognition and affect tend to get bridged outside the Cartesian world, whether the gap is conceived as an evolutionary trap or as a battle between two halves of the human brain. Often drawing inspiration from the monistic traditions of their religions, from the myths and folkways that have set some vague half-effective limits on intergroup violence and on the objectification of living beings, some civilizations have carefully protected the faith--now mostly lost to the modern world--that the borderlines of evil can never be clearly defined, and there is always a continuity between the aggressor and his victim, and that liberation is not merely the freedom from an oppressive agency outside, but also ultimately a liberation from a part of one's self.[22] This can be seen as wishy-washy collaboration with the powerful and the victorious; it can be also seen as a more humane strain in political and social awareness.

Frantz Fanon's concept of the cleansing role of violence--and the implicit ideology of the drive to "annihilate class enemies" in some Third World societies--sounds alien and Western to many sensitive Afro-Asians mainly because of this awareness.[23] Fanon admits the presence of the oppressor within the oppressed, but calls for an exorcism, where the ghost outside has to be finally confronted in violence and annihilated because it carries the burden of the ghost inside. The outer violence, Fanon suggests , is only an attempt to make a painful break with a part of one's self. He fails to sense that such a vision ties the oppressed more deeply to the oppressor and to the culture of oppression than any collaboration can. Continuous use of the major technique on which an oppressive system is based, namely, the cultural acceptance of violence, gradually socializes the peoples fighting oppression to some of the basic values of the systems that oppress them. Violence converts the battle between two visions of the human society into a fight between two groups sharing some of the same values, for spoils within a permanently power-scarce and resource-scarce system. The groupings may change; the system does not. If Fanon had lived longer, he might have come to admit that in this process of internalization lies a partial answer to two vital questions about the search for liberation in our times, namely, why dictatorships of the proletariat never end and why revolutions always devour their children. Hatred, as Alan Watts reminds us at the cost of being trite, is a form of bondage, too.

In contemporary times, no one understood better than Gandhi this stranglehold of the history of oppression on the future of man. That is why his theory of conflict resolution is something more than a simpleminded emphasis on nonviolence. It recognizes that the meek are blessed only if they are, in Rolo May's terms,[24] authentically innocent and not pseudo-innocents accepting the values of an oppressive system for secondary psychological gains. Gandhi acted as if he was aware that nonsynergic systems, driven by zero-sum competition and search for power, control, and masculinity, force the victims of oppression to internalize the norms of the system, so that when they displace their exploiters, they build a system in which the older norms covertly prevail. So his concept of noncooperation set a different goal for the victims; he stressed that the aim of the oppressed should be, not to become a first-class citizen in the world of oppression instead of a second- or third-class one, but to become the citizen of an alternative world where he can hope to win back his human authenticity. He thus becomes a nonplayer for the oppressors--one who plays a different game, refusing a role in the oppressors game. Perhaps this is what a Western biographer of Gandhi means when he suggests that Gandhi's theory of conflict resolution imputes an irreducible minimum humanity to the oppressors and militantly promotes the belief that this humanity could be actualized.[25]

The basic assumption here is that the oppressor in his state of dehumanization is as much a victim of the exploitative system as the oppressed; he has to be liberated, too. The Gandhian stress on austerity and pacifism does not come so much from the traditional Indian principles of renunciation and monism as from a deep-seated, early Christian belief in the superiority of the culture of the victims of oppression, and from an effort to identify with the more humane cultural strain within an oppressive system. All his life, Gandhi sought to free the British as much as the Indians from the clutches of imperialism and the Brahmins as much as the Untouchables from the caste system. Such a position bears some similarity to certain forms of Marxism and Christianity. Father G. Gutierrez represents both these ideological strains when he says:

> One loves the oppressors by liberating them from their inhuman condition as oppressors, by liberating them from themselves. But this cannot be achieved except by resolutely opting for the

oppressed, i.e., by combating the oppressive classes. It must be real and effective combat, not hate.[26]

This other identification, which Gandhi so successfully made, is difficult for even those identifying with the victims. The temptation is to use a psychological mechanism more congruent with the basic rules of the exploitative system, so as to have a better scope to express one's aggressive drives. The temptation is to equal one's tormentors in violence and to regain one's self-esteem as a competitor within the same system. Thus, identification with the oppressed has often meant identification with their world view, not in its original form but as adapted to the needs of legitimizing an oppressive machine. Through this two-step identification, even the interpreters of oppression begin to internalize the norms of one exploitative system or another. As a result, the fantasy of the superiority of the oppressor gets even more deeply embedded in contemporary consciousness. We may openly attack the exploiters of the world, we may even speak of their loneliness, mental illness, or decadence, but we are unable to sympathize with them--as if a corner of our mind continued to believe that the privileged were superior to the underdogs we supported; that they were more powerful economically, politically, or socially and, as powerful counterplayers, at least deserved to invite jealousy or hatred from us.[27]

I have tried to convey some idea of how Gandhi's future began in the present , why he constantly sought to convert the struggle against oppression from an intergroup conflict to a within-person conflict, and why his utopia was, to use Abraham Maslow's word, a eupsychia.[28] For better or for worse, this is the age of false consciousness; it is the awareness of the predicament of self-awareness that has shaped much of this century's social thinking and helped the emergence of the psychological man. In this sense, Gandhi's concept of self-realization is the ultimate product of an age that has been striving for the means of locating *within the individual* and *in action* the subject-object dichotomy (man as the maker of history versus man as the product of history; man as a product of biological evolution versus man as a self-aware aspect of nature; the ego or reality principle versus the id or pleasure principle; praxis versus dialectic or process).[29] Such a concept of self-realization is a "primitive" corrective to the post-Enlightenment split in the vision of the liberated man. During the last two and a half centuries--starting probably with Giambattista Vico--the Western sciences of man have worked with a basic contradiction. They have sought to make man the maker of his own fate--or history--by making him an object of the modern incarnations of fate--of natural sciences, social history, evolutionary stages, and cumulative reason. This overcorrection can only be remedied by world views that reemphasize man's stature as a subject, seeking a more humble participation in nature and society. There are world views in which man is a subject by virtue of being a master of nature and society *within*. He acknowledges the continuities between the suffering outside and the suffering within and defines the self as consisting of both the sufferings of the self and of the nonself.[30]

Here lies the import of someone like Gandhi who, probably more than anyone else in this century, tried to actualize in practice what the more sensitive social thinkers and litterateurs had already rediscovered for the contemporary awareness, namely, that any oppressive system is only overtly a triad of the oppressor, the victim and the interpreter. Covertly the three roles merge. A complex set of identifications and cross-identifications makes each actor in the triad represent and incorporate the other two. This view--probably expressed in its grandest form in the ancient Indian epic on greed, violence, and self-realization, the *Mahabharata* --is the flip side of Marx's belief that even the cultural products thrown up by the struggle against capitalism and created by the victim and enemies of capitalism were flawed by their historical roots in an imperfect society.[31] In fact, one may say that Gandhian praxis is the natural and logical development of radical social criticism, because it insists that the continuity between the victim, the oppressor, and the observer must be realized *in action,* and one must refuse to act *as if* some constituents in an oppressive system were morally pure or uncontaminated.

To sum up, a violent and oppressive society produces its own special brands of victimhood and privilege and ensures a certain continuity between the victor and the defeated, the instrument and the target, and the interpreter and the interpreted. As a result, none of these categories remain pure. So even when such a culture collapses, the psychology of victimhood and privilege continues and produces a second culture that is only manifestly not violent or oppressive. Not to recognize this is to collaborate with violence and oppression in their subtler forms, which in effect is what most social activism and analysis begin to do once the intellectual climate becomes hostile to manifest cruelty and exploitation.

IV

A second example of this consciousness of nonduality can well be the refusal of many cultures to translate the

principles of biopsychological continuities such as sex
and age into principles of social stratification. Many
of the major Eastern civilizations, in spite of all their
patriarchal elements, have continued to see a certain
continuity between the masculine and the feminine, and
between infancy, adulthood, and old age. Perhaps this is
not all a matter of traditional wisdom. At least in some
cases it is a reaction to the colonial experience that
assumed clear breaks between the male and the female, the
adult and the child, and the adult and the elderly, and
then used these biological differences as the homologues
of the secular political stratifications. In the
colonial ideology, the colonizer became the tough,
courageous, openly aggressive, hyper-masculine ruler and
the colonized became the sly, cowardly, passive-
aggressive, womanly subject. Or, alternatively, the
colonizer became the prototype of a mature, complete,
adult civilization while the colonized became the mirror
of a more simple, primitive, childlike cultural state.
In some cases, faced with their own ability to subjugate
complex ancient civilizations, the colonial cultures
defined the colonized as the homologue of the senile and
the decrepit who deservedly fell under their suzreignty
to become the responsibility of more vigorous
civilizations.

Once again I shall invoke Gandhi, who built an
articulate model of political action to counter the
models of manhood and womanhood implicit in the colonial
situation in India.

It is an indication of how systems of oppression
draw their strength from certain aspects of the "mother
culture" that British colonialism in India made an
explicit order out of what they felt was the major
strength of the Western civilization vis-à-vis the
Indian. It went:

Masculinity > Femininity > Femininity in man

In other words, masculinity is superior to femininity,
which in turn is superior to effeminacy. (One major
pillar of this cultural stratarchy was the British
emphasis on the differences between the so-called martial
and nonmartial races of India. The other was--and this I
venture as another instance of the continuity between the
oppressors and the oppressed--the presence of a similar
stratarchy in some Indian subtraditions, which acquired a
new cultural ascendency in British India.)

As against this, Gandhi posited two alternative sets
of relationships. In one, masculinity was seen to be at
par with femininity and the two had to be transcended or
synthesized for attaining a higher level of public
functioning. Such "bisexuality" or "trans-sexuality" was
seen as not merely spiritually superior both to
masculinity and to femininity as it was in Indian

(particularly Indian ascetic) traditions, but also politically so. Gandhi's second model saw masculinity as inferior to femininity which, in turn, was seen as inferior to femininity in man. I have discussed the psychological and cultural contexts of these concepts in some detail elsewhere.[32] All I want to add is that the formal equality that is often sought by the various movements fighting for the cause of woman is qualitatively different from the synergy Gandhi sought. For the former, power, achievement, productivity, work, and control over social and natural resources are seen as fixed quantities over which men have held a near-monopoly and which they must now share equally with women. In the Gandhian model, these values are indicators of a system dominated by the masculinity principle, and the system and its values must both be jettisoned for the sake of building a new world, unfettered by its history of sexual oppression. To fight for mechanical equality, Gandhi seems to suggest, is to accept or internalize the norms of the existing system, and pay homage to the masculine values under the guise of pseudo-equality.

Similarly with age. Whereas societies that have built upon the traditions of hyper-masculinity have conceived of adulthood as the ultimate in the human life cycle because of its productive possibilities, many of the older cultures of the world, left out of the experience of the industrial and technological revolutions, have refused to see childhood as merely a preparation for, or an inferior version of, adulthood. Nor have they seen old age as a decline from full manhood or womanhood. On the contrary, each stage of life in these cultures is seen as valuable and meaningful in itself. No stage is required to derive its legitimacy from some other stage of life, nor need it be evaluated in terms of categories entirely alien to it. It has been said in recent times that alternative visions of the human future must derive their ideas of spontaneity and play from the child.[33] Implied in this very proposal is the tragedy of Western adulthood, which has banished spontaneity and play to a small reservation called childhood, protecting the adult world from contamination. Spontaneity, play, directness of experience, and tolerance of disorder are for the children or their homologues, the primitives in their own world.[34] Power, productive work, and even revolutions are for the mature adults and their homologues, the advanced historical societies with their ripened revolutionary consciousness and their experience with modern urban-industrialism.

Concurrently, the dominance of the productivity principle in Western modernity, and the unending search for the new or the novel, do not allow age to be seen as giving a touch of wisdom to social consciousness or transmitting to the next generation valued elements of culture--elements that cannot be precisely articulated or transmitted in the form of packaged products but must be transmitted in the form of shared experiences. Old age is seen primarily as creating a problem of management of less productive or nonproductive human lives. With the decline in physical prowess in men and sexual attractiveness in women, the self-image of the Western man or woman becomes something less than that of a complete human being. The pathetic worship of youth and the even more pathetic attempts to defend oneself against the inner fears of losing youthfulness and social utility--with the help of pseudo-respectful expressions such as "senior citizens"--is produced not merely by rampant consumerism and limitless industrialism but also by a world view associated with complex systems of oppression trying to deny the reflective or contemplative strains of the civilization. Gerontocracy may be a noncreative alternative to such a world view, but it nevertheless provides a better baseline for envisioning an alternative cosmology where age and sex do not serve as principles of social ordering, and where it is recognized that respect for the qualities of old age gives completeness to youth and young adulthood, too.

V

This brings me to my third example of a nondual vision of "positive freedom," namely, the cultural refusal in many parts of the savage world to see work and play as clearly demarcated modalities of human life. Once again I shall refer to modern colonialism not merely because it is a shared legacy of the Third World but because it did much better than many other exploitative systems of the modern world in terms of having an articulate ideology, a culturally rooted legitimacy, and, sometimes, a tendency to avoid counterproductive violence. That colonialism is, for this very reason, one of the most dangerous forms of institutionalized violence is part of the same argument. It is not accidental that the British empire lasted two centuries, the Third Reich for little more than a decade. Successful institutionalization of a large-scale oppressive system is not an easy attainment. It needs something more than martial skills and nihilistic passions; it needs some awareness of human limits.

One of the first things the colonial cultures invariably did was to promote the belief that the subject communities had a contempt for honest work, that they consisted of indolent shirkers who could not match the hard work or single-minded pursuit of productive labor of the colonizers. This was a belief sincerely held by the rulers. But sincerity in such matters, one knows, is only a defense against recongizing one's deeper need to justify a political economy that expects the subject community to work without human dignity, without an awareness of being economically exploited, and without a meaningful concept or goal of work.

The oppressed, I have argued, are never pure victims. Within them one part collaborates, compromises, and adjusts; another part defies, "noncooperates," subverts, or destroys, often in the name of collaboration and under the garb of obsequiousness. (It is the second part of the story that creates problems for the social sciences. The modern tradition of social criticism is unidirectional. It can demystify some forms of dissent and show them to be nondissent. It has no means of demystifying some forms of collaboration so as to discover underneath secret defiance. The reason is that such social criticism equates interpretation with debunking and such debunking always has to reveal the base of evil beneath the superstructure of the "good." An underlying philosophy of man guides this tradition of interpretation.) The colonized subjects, too, soon learned through the subtle communication that goes on between the rulers and the ruled, to react to and cope with the obsessive, driven concept of productive work brought into the colonies by the European and Christian subtraditions that dominated the colonial cultures and had already cornered other subtraditions within Western Christianity.[35] At one level of awareness, the subjects knew they could retaliate, tease, and defy their oppressors--"fools attached to action," as the Bhagavad Gītā might have called them--by refusing to share the imposed concepts of the sanctity of work and such work-values as productivity, control, predictability, manipulation, and utility. The differences between work and play, stressed by a repressive conscience that had to idealize colonialism as a civilizational mission, could only be resisted through an unconscious noncooperation that included "malingering," "shirking," and "indiscipline." (If this vaguely reminds the reader of the folk response of American Blacks to slavery,[36] it only once again shows that there is something sharable in the experience of man-made suffering, which cuts across cultures. And this shared experience cuts across the folk and the classical. In India at least there was the more classical Gītā, waiting to be "misused" by those on the wrong side of history:

Who dares to see action in inaction,
and inaction in action
he is wise, he is yogi,
he is the man who knows what is work.[37]

This may not be the scholar's idea of the true meaning of the *śloka*, but what are religious texts for if they cannot occasionally provide folksy guides to survival?)

If colonialism took away the human dignity of its

subjects, the subjects unconsciously tried, in attempts to minimize suffering and protect their self-esteem, to take away the dignity of their oppressors by requiring them to use ugly force to make the subjects work, produce, and be useful. This is perhaps the way helpless victims are often driven to affect and monitor their tormentors and maintain an "internal locus of control." In their near-total impotency, they strip their authorities of the pretences to civilized authority, humane governance, and, ultimately, self-respect. This is the unnoticed magic of subjugation. It ensures that if the victims are sometimes pseudo-innocent part-victims, the victors are often no more than pseudo-profiteering part-victors.

In rejecting the principle of productivity and work, many subjugated Third World societies have also rejected the concept of workability. They have preserved with some care the banished consciousness of the First and Second Worlds that knowledge and ideas are valuable, not only in terms of applicability, usefulness, or testability, but also in terms of aesthetics, relatedness to man and nature, self-transcendence, and self-realization, and in terms of forms that are not subservient to so-called substances. Certain intuitive and speculative modes of perception have come naturally to these peoples, giving rise, on the one hand, to an institutionalized dependence on music, literature, fine arts, and other creative media for the expression of social thought and scientific analysis; and, on the other hand, to a dependence upon highly speculative, deductive, mathematical, and, even quantitative-empirical modes of thinking as vehicles of normative passions and as expressions of religious or mystical sentiments. I have in mind here not the feeling man that Leopold Senghor offsets against the Cartesian man of the West, but cultures that refuse to partition cognition and affect, both as a matter of conviction and as a technique of survival.[38]

This blurring of the boundaries between science, religion, and arts is also of course a defiance of the modern concept of classification of knowledge and education.[39] At one plane it represents an obstreperous refusal to be converted to the modern world view that is seen, from before such perceptions became fashionable among some social scientists, as a legitimation of new forms of structural and cultural imperialism. At another plane, it is a recognition that the megamachines of the technocratic societies--as Lewis Mumford would describe them--have coopted mainstream science to their purpose and, since about the seventeenth century, have consistently contributed to the blurring of the difference between science and technology. It is a recognition that technology now legitimates science in many societies, so that the spirit of demonstrative technology, not the spirit of scientific enquiry, is the dominant consciousness of the modern world. You need technological marvels not only for acquiring a sense of personal potency and self-esteem but also for acquiring a sense of national power and self-fulfillment. Along with development, technology has become a new reason of state. As technology has grown in power, it has begun to confer status, to perform a pace-setting role within science, and to use a scientific knowledge for increasing productivity and control. Only technology can now provide absolute legitimation within the estate of science.

As opposed to this culture of instrumentality, which works with a concept of a universal, perfectly objective, cumulative science and admits at best only the existence of peripheral folk-sciences from which modern science may occassionally pick up scraps of information, the subjugated and marginalized sections of the world--the third-class citizens of the world inhabiting the Third World--have sought to maintain their dignity by conceptualizing the world of science as a number of competing or coexisting universal ethnosciences, one of which has become dominant and usurped the status of the *only* universal and modern science.[40] Various traditional systems of medicine, artisan skills that retain the individuality of the producers and refuse to draw a line between art and craft, certain agricultural practices that have resisted modern agronomy--these are not only aspects of a resilient cultural self-affirmation: they are indicators of a spirit that defies the power of a way of life that seeks to cannibalize all other ways of life. The Third World has vested interest in refusing to grant sanctity to a science that sees human beings and nature as the raw material for vivisectional and scientific experimentation. What seems an irrational resistance to the products of modern science and technology in the peripheries of the world is often a deeply rooted and perfectly legitimate suspicion of sectors that live off these peripheries, and a desperate attempt to preserve an alternative concept of knowledge and technique in the interstices of the savage world.

VI

Fourth, the experience of suffering of some Third World societies has contributed a new theme to utopianism by sensing and resisting the oppression that comes as "history." By this I mean not only the limits that our past always seem to impose on our visions of the future, but also the use of a linear, progressive, cumulative, deterministic concept of history--often carved out of humanistic ideologies--to suppress alternative world views, alternative utopias, and even alternative self-concepts. The peripheries of the world often feel that they are constrained not merely by partial, biased, or ethnocentric history, but by the idea of history itself.

One can give a psychopathological interpretation of such skepticism toward history, often inextricably linked with painful, fearsome memories of man-made suffering. Defiance of history may look like a primitive denial of history and, to the extent that the present is fully shaped by history in the modern eyes, denial of contemporary realities. But, even from a strict clinical point of view, there can be reasons for and creative uses of ahistoricity. What Alexander and Margarete Mitscherlich say about those with a history of inflicting suffering also applies to those who have been their victims:

> A very considerable expenditure of psychic energy is necessary to maintain this separation of acceptable and unacceptable memories; and what is used in the defence of a self anxious to protect itself against bitter qualms of conscience and doubts about its worth is unavailable for mastering the present.[41]

The burden of history is the burden of such memories and anti-memories. Some cultures prefer to live with the burden and painfully excavate the anti-memories and integrate them as part of the present consciousness. Some cultures prefer to handle the same problem at the mythopoeic level. Instead of excavating for the so-called real past, they excavate for other meanings of the present, as revealed in traditions and myths about an ever-present but open past. The anti-memories at that level become less passionate and they allow greater play and lesser defensive rigidity.

What seems an ahistorical and even anti-historical attitude in many nonmodern cultures is often only an attempt, on the part of these cultures, to incorporate their historical experiences into their shared traditions as categories of thinking rather than as objective chronicles of the past.[42] In these cultures, the mystical and consciousness-expanding modes are alternative pathways to experiences that in other societies are sought through a linear concept of a "real" history. In the modern context these modes can sometimes become what Robert J. Lifton calls "romantic totalism"--a post-Cartesian absolutism that seeks to replace history with experience.[43] But that is not a fate written into the origins of these modes. If the predicament is the totalism and not the romance, the *history* of civilizations after Christopher Columbus and Vasco da Gama also shows that the totalism can come from a history that seeks to replace experience--especially so when after the advent of the idea of *scientific* history,

history has begun to share in the near-monopoly that
science has already established in the area of human
certitude. Albert Camus, it seems, once drew a line
between the makers of history and the victims of history.
The job of the writer, he reportedly said, was to write
about the victims. For the silent majority of the world,
the makers of history also live in history, and the
defiance of history begins not so much with an altenative
history as with the denial of history as an acreage of
human certitude.

In their skepticism toward history, the oppressed
cultures have an ally in certain recessive orientations
to the past in the Western culture, manifested in the
ways of thinking that have been formalized in recent
decades by structural anthropology and psychoanalysis,
which see history either as a language with its own
semiotics or as a "screen memory" with its own rules of
psychological defenses. Both these disciplines see the
construction of history as an important clue to the
principles of the human mind, on the one hand, and the
experiences of the here and now, on the other. The
dynamics of history, according to such a point of view,
is not in an unalterable past moving toward an inexorable
future; it is in the ways of thinking and in the choices
of present times.[44]

There is a fit between this hostility to history and
the need to protect self-esteem and ensure survival in
many Third World societies. History, as it is commonly
defined, has never been fair to these societies. Nor
could history do otherwise, given the structure of
cognition that it presumes. The more scientific a
history, the more dangerous a kitbag of ideas it is for
the inhabitants of the experimental laboratory called the
Third World. History has frequently allowed ideas of
social intervention to be swallowed up by ideals of
social engineering in modern times. In the dominant
cultures of the West, history has always been the
unfolding of a theory of progress, a serialized
expression of a *telos* that, by definition, cannot be
shared by the communities placed on the lower rungs of
the ladder of history or even outside the scope of
history. Even the histories of oppression and the
historical theories of liberation include stages of
growth that, instead of widening the options of the
victims, reduce them. In fact, one of the main functions
of these theories is to ensure the centrality of cultural
and intellectual paradigms within which not only the
experiences of a few societies are dominant but models of
dissent from these experiences can be accommodated.
Following an old Bengali saying, such paradigms first
bite as snakes and then offer a cure in the incarnation
of witch doctors.

The ethnocentrism of the anthropologist can be
corrected; he is segregated from his subjects only

spatially and, some day, his subjects can talk back. But the ethnocentrism toward the past often goes unchallenged. The dead do not rebel, nor can they speak out. In this sense, the subjecthood of the subjects of history is absolute, and to admit the existence of a real or scientific history is to admit a continuity between subjecthood in history and subjection in the present.

The refusal to acknowledge the primacy of history is therefore also the refusal to chain the future to the past. This itself is a special attitude toward human potentialities, an alternative form of utopianism that has survived till now as a language alien to, and subversive of, every theory that in the name of liberation circumscribes and makes predictable the spirit of human rebelliousness.

VII

As my final example, I shall briefly discuss the controversial dependency syndrome in some Third World cultures. When offset against Occidental man's unending search for autonomy or independence, this syndrome in the non-Western personality allegedly explains the origins, meaning, and resiliences of colonial rule as well as subjugation.

Such explanations have been savagely attacked, by both Césaire and Fanon, as parts of a racist psychoanalysis. Césaire quotes the following words of Manoni as virtually the final proof of the Western psychologist's prejudice against the oppressed cultures:

It is the destiny of the Occidental to face the obligation laid down by the commandment *Thou shalt leave thy father and thy mother*. This obligation is incomprehensible to the Madagascan.

At a given time in his development, every European discovers in himself the desire . . . to break the bonds of dependency, to become the equal of his father. The Madagascan, never! He does not experience rivalry with the paternal authority, "manly protest," or Adlarian inferiority--ordeals through which the European must pass and which are civilized forms ... of the initiation rites by which one achieves manhood . . .[45]

I have not been able to locate this passage in Manoni's *Prospero and Caliban* and do not know in which context it occurs.[46] Nor do I know Manoni's politics, which presumably can provide the other context of these lines. Thus, I have to accept at face value Césaire's and Fanon's plaint that Manoni vends " down-at-heel cliches" to justify "absurd prejudices" and "dresses up" the old stereotype of the Negro as an overgrown child.

However, there cannot but be a nagging suspicion
that a third view on the subject is possible. That view
would recognize that the modern West has not only
institutionalized a concept of childhood that legitimizes
oppression in terms of an ideology of masculine
nondependent adulthood, but it has also popularized a
devastatingly sterile concept of autonomy and
individualism that has now totally atomized the
individual. Many non-Western observers of the culture of
the modern West--its life-style, literature, arts, and
social sciences--have been struck by the extent to which
contractual, competitive individualism--and the utter
loneliness that flows from it--now dominates the Western
consciousness. From Frederich Nietzsche to Sigmund Freud
and from Karl Marx to Franz Kafka, much of Western social
analysis, too, has stood witness to this cultural
pathology. And what once looked like independence from
one's parental authorities and defiance of the larger
aggregates they represented now looks more and more like
aspects of a Hobbesian world view gone rabid. It has
manifestly reduced the Western individual to a
consumption unit to which impersonal "machines" sell
consumables and from which other machines get work in
order to produce more consumables. To the extent Manoni
imputes to the Madagascan some degree of anti-
individualism, to the extent the Madagascan is not a
well-demarcated person, Manoni unwittingly underscores
the point that the Western version of individualism--and
the insane search for unlimited autonomy it has
unleashed--cannot be truly separated from the thirst for
colonies *lebensraum,* and for dominance over one's fellow
humans. In an interrelated world, total autonomy for one
means reducing the autonomy of others.
    Thus, although the much maligned dependency complex
may not be the best possible cultural arrangement when
facing the juggernaut of modern oppression, it could be
seen as a more promising baseline for mounting a search
for genuine social relatedness and, for that matter, for
maturer forms of individuality than the individualism
that now dominates the world. It may not meet the
exacting standards of the Westernized critics of the West
in the Third World, and its origins may be in racism.
Even those whose ancestors for centuries have lived with
only the extremes of relatedness and dependency will
never guess that, in a world taken over by the autonomy
principle and by the extremes of individualism,
dependency and fears of abandonment could represent a
hope and a potentiality. The pathology of relatedness
has already become less dangerous than the pathology of
unrelatedness. What looks like an ego "wanting in
strength" in the Malagasy or a straightforward instance
of a weak ego in the Indian, can be viewed as another
class of ego strength; what looks like insufficient
independence training in the nonachieving societies and

"willing subservience" and self-castration" in the Hindu may be read also as an affirmation of basic relatedness and of the need for some degree of reverence in human relations.[47] At one place in his *Discourse on Colonialism,* Césaire relates Nazism to Europe's bloodstained record in the colonies.[48] He seems unaware that some scholars have already traced Nazi satanism to the unrestrained spread in Europe, over the previous century, of the doctrines of amoral *realpolitik* and *sacro egoismo* and of the "morals of a struggle that no longer allows for respect."[49] All that remains to be done is to relate the colonial impulse, too, to the search for nonreverential autonomy and total individualism, even if the latter are now a part of many anti-colonial ideologies.

VIII

I have chosen these examples to depict what I have described above as the indissoluble bond between the future of the peripheries of the world and that of the apparently powerful, prosperous, imperial cultures. This is necessarily an essay on the continuity between the winners and the losers, seen from the losers' point of view. The reader must have noticed that each of the examples I have given also happens to be a live problem in exactly those parts of the world that are commonly considered privileged. The various forms of neo-Marxism, the various versions of the women's liberation movement, the numerous attempts to build alternative philosophies of science and technology by giving up the insane search for total control and predictability are but a recognition that the gaps between the so-called privileged and underprivileged of the world are mostly notional. As the peripheries of the world have been subjected to economic degradation and political impotency and robbed of their human dignity with the help of dionysian theorems of progress, the First and the Second Worlds too have sunk deeper into intellectual provincialism, cultural decadence, and moral degradation. If you grant me the right to my version of an old cliché, no victor can be a victor without being a victim. In the case of nation-states as much as in the case of two-person situations, there is an indivisibility of ethical and cognitive choices. If the Third World's vision of the future is handicapped and enriched by its history of man-made suffering, the First World's future, too, is shaped by the same experience.

The reader might also have noticed that I have tried to give moral and cultural content to some of the common ways in which the savage world has tried to cope with modern oppression, and that I have projected these common ways as possibilities or opportunities. How far is this

justified? After all, as one popular argument goes,
history is made through the dirty process of political
economy; it has no place for any defensive moralizing
about human frailties and for attempts to make a virtue
out of necessity. Perhaps, in line with my comments
above on the traditions of interpretation, I could be
allowed to argue that the so-called ultimate realities of
political economy too could be further demystified to
obtain clues to new visions of the human future. The
frailties of human nature produced by a given social
arrangement, in the context of a given political economy,
can begin to look like the baseline of a new society,
once another social arrangement is envisioned. The
frailty of human frailties, too, is an open question. A
brain researcher has recently said, summing up
comparative zoological work on evolution, that there also
is a "survival of the weak," and the weak do inherit the
world.[50]

For instance, what looks like an incapacity to build
proper nation-states in large parts of the world can
surely be read as a political or cultural failure to
enter the modern world. Moreover, such a failure can
then be read as a further endorsement of the rule of a
few chosen nation-states in the global arena. However,
by only slightly straining one's primitive credulity, the
failure could also be read as a refusal in some cultures
to believe that when the reasons of state under a nation-
state system do not coincide with the needs of personal
or collective morality, it is the reasons of state that
should get priority. The latter reading is not negated
by the blood-drenched history and the coups and
countercoups in the Third World--I am speaking of
possibilities and opportunities, not offering a prognosis
of the future based on a trend analysis. Likewise, what
looks like superstitious pantheism or crass
anthropomorphism may be celebrated as a defiance of
totalist monotheism and of modern anthropocentrism and
their arrogant ecocidal world conception. Once again,
the second interpretation is not disproved by the poor
conservationist record of much of the Third World. I am
speaking of what could be, in the future, a new cultural
self-expression of an ancient man-nature symbiosis; I am
not projecting statistically the past or the present into
the future.

I hope all this will not be seen as an elaborate
attempt to project the sensitivities of the Third World
as the future consciousness of the globe, or a plea to
the First World to wallow in a comforting sense of guilt.
Nor does it, I hope, sound like the standard doomsday
"propheteering" that often prefaces fiery calls to a
millenial revolution. All I am trying to do is to affirm
that ultimately it is not a matter of synthesizing or
aggregating different civilizational visions of the
future. Rather, it is a matter of admitting that whereas

each civilization must find its own authentic vision of the future and its own authenticity in future, neither is conceivable without admitting the *experience of cosuffering* that has now brought some of the major civilizations of the world close to each other. It is this cosuffering that makes the idea of cultural closeness something more than the chilling concept of One World, which nineteenth-century European optimism popularized and promoted to the status of a dogma.[51]

The intercultural communion I am speaking about is defined by two intellectual coordinates. The first of them is the recognition that the "true" values of different civilizations are not in need of synthesis. They are, in terms of man's biological needs, already in reasonable harmony and capable of transcending the barriers of particularist consciousness. In other words, the principle of cultural relativism--the fact that I write on the possibilities of a distinct eupsychia for the Third World is a partial admission of such relativism--is acceptably only to the extent that *it* accepts the universalism of some core values of humankind. Anthropologism is no cure for ethnocentrism; it merely pluralizes the latter. Absolute relativism can also become an absolute justification of oppression in the name of scholarly commitment, as it often becomes in the apolitical treatise called the anthropologist's field report.

The second coordinate is the acknowledgment that the search for authenticity of a civilization is always a search for the other face of the civilization, either as a hope or as a warning. The search for a civilization's utopia, too, is part of this larger quest. This utopia needs not merely the ability to interpret and reinterpret one's own traditions, but also the ability to involve the dominant or recessive aspects of other civilizations as allies in one's struggle for cultural self-discovery, the willingness to become allies to other civilizations trying to discover their other faces, and the skills to give more centrality to these new readings of civilizations and civilizational concerns. This is the only form of dialogue of cultures that can transcend the flourishing intercultural barters of our times.

NOTES

1. *The Mahabharata,* Sauptik Parva 10, Slokas 9, 12, 13. Translated by Manmatha Nath Dutt (Calcutta: Elysium, 1962), p. 20.

A paper such as this cannot but try to grow over its various versions. It was originally presented at the first meeting of the group on Alternative Visions of Desirable Societies at Mexico City in April 1978. The meeting was organized by Centro de Estudies Economicas y

Sociales del Tercier Mundo and the project on the Goals, Processes and Indicators of Development of the United Nations University. Earlier incarnations of the paper have been published in *Alternatives* 4 (3), 1978-1979, and in Eleonora Masini and Johan Galtung, eds., *Visions of Desirable Societies,* vol. 1 (London: Pergamon, in press). The present version has gained much from the suggestions and criticisms by the participants in the Mexico meeting and by M. P. Sinha, R.A.P. Shastri, Rajni Kothari, and Giri Deshingkar.

2. Such a utopianism is of course very different from the ones discussed by Karl Popper ("Utopia and Violence," in *Conjectures and Refutations, The Growth of Scientific Knowledge* (London: Routledge and Kegan Paul, 1978, pp. 355-363) or Robert Nozick *(Anarchy, State and Utopia,* Oxford: Basil Blackwell, 1974, Part III).

3. I have in mind the extremes Bruno Bettelheim describes in his "Individual and Mass Behaviour in Extreme Situations" (1943), in *Surviving and Other Essays* (New York: Alfred A. Knopf, 1979), pp. 48-83.

4. Barrington Moore, Jr., "The Society Nobody Wants: A Look Beyond Marxism and Liberalism," in Kurt H. Wolff and Barrington Moore, Jr., eds., *The Critical Spirit: Essays in Honour of Herbert Marcuse* (Boston: Beacon Press, 1967), pp. 401-418.

5. Though this is not relevant to the issues I discuss in this essay, the three processes seem to hint at the cultural-anthropological, the depth-psychological, and the Christian-theological concerns with oppression, respectively.

6. T. W. Adorno, Else Frenkel-Brunswik, Daniel J. Levinson, and R. Nevitt Sanford, *The Authoritarian Personality* (New York: Harper, 1950).

7. T. W. Adorno, *Minima Moralia,* translated by E.F.N. Jephcott (London: New Left Books, 1977), pp. 43-44.

8. Bettelheim, "Individual and Mass Behaviour in Extreme Situations," in *Surviving and Other Essays;* and Victor E. Frankl, *Man's Search for Meaning,* (New York: Pocket Books, 1959). *See also* the excellent summary of related studies by Barrington Moore, Jr., *Injustice: The Social Bases of Obedience and Revolt* (New York: Macmillan, 1978), pp. 64-77. Moore also covers the Untouchables of India from this point of view; see pp. 55-64.

9. Bettelheim, "The Holocaust--One Generation Later," *Surviving and Other Essays,* pp. 84-104.

10. That this is not merely wishful thinking is partly evidenced by Helen Fein, *Accounting for Genocide: National Responses and Jewish Victimization During the Holocaust* (New York: Free Press, 1979), Chapter 12. Gerda Klein says so movingly, "Why? Why did we walk like meek sheep to the slaughter house? Why did we not fight back? . . . I know why. Because we had faith in

humanity. Because we did not really think that human beings were capable of committing such crimes." *All But My Life* (New York: Hill and Wang, 1957), p. 89, quoted in Terence Des Pres, *The Survivor* (New York: Oxford University Press, 1976), p. 83.

11. Adorno, *Minima Moralia,* p. 108.

12. Aimé Césaire, *Discourse on Colonialism,* translated by Joan Pinkham (New York and London: Monthly Review Press, 1972), p. 11. Italics in the original.

13. Ibid., p. 170.

14. Bettelheim, "The Holocaust--One Generation Later," in *Surviving and Other Essays,* p. 101.

15. *See,* for example, Chaim F. Shatan, "Bogus Manhood, Bogus Honor: Surrender and Transfiguration in the United States Marine Corps," *Psychoanalytic Review* 66 (1977):585-610.

16. This issue has been approached from a slightly different perspective in Maurice Zeitlin, Kenneth Lutterman, and James Russell, "Death in Vietnam: Class, Poverty and Risks of War," in Ira Katznelson, Gordon Adams, Philip Brenner, and Alan Wolfe, eds., *The Politics and Society Reader* (New York: David McKay, 1974), pp. 53-68.

17. Césaire, *Discourse on Colonialism,* pp. 35, 51-52.

18. Arthur Koestler, *The Ghost in the Machine* (London: Picador, 1976), Chapter 18.

19. For a fuller discussion of this subject, *see* Ashis Nandy, "Science, Authoritarianism and Culture: On the Scope and Limits of Isolation Outside the Clinic," M. N. Roy Memorial Lecture, 1980, published in *Seminar* 261 (May 1981):25-33.

20. Adorno, *Minima Moralia,* p. 197.

21. The post-Renaissance Western preoccupation with clean divisions or oppositions of this kind is of course a part of the central dichotomy between the subject and the object, what Ludvig Binswanger reportedly calls "the cancer of all psychology up to now," in Charles Hampden-Turner, *Radical Man* (New York: Doubleday Anchor, 1971), p. 33. For "psychology" in the Binswanger quotation, one must of course read "modern Western psychology."

22. *See,* for example, an interesting cultural criticism of Hinduism by even a person as humane and sensitive as Albert Schweitzer *(Hindu Thought and Its Development,* New York: Beacon Press, 1959) for not having a hard, concrete concept of evil. For discussions of the debate around this issue, *see* W. F. Goodwin, "Mysticism and Ethics: An Examination of Radhakrishna's Reply to Schweitzer's critique of Indian Thought," *Ethics* 67 (1957):25-41; and T.M.P. Mahadeven, "Indian Ethics and Social Practice," in C. A. Moore, ed., *Philosophy and Culture: East and West* (Honolulu: University of Hawaii, 1962), pp. 579-493.

23. Frantz Fanon, *The Wretched of the Earth*

(Harmondsworth: Penguin, 1967) and *Black Skin, White Masks* (New York: Grove Press, 1967).

24. Rollo May, *Power and Innocence: A Search for the Sources of Violence* (New York: Delta, 1972).

25. Erik H. Erikson, *Gandhi's Truth: On the Origins of Militant Nonviolence* (New York: Norton, 1969).

26. G. Gutierrez, *A Theology of Liberation* (Maryknoll, New York: Orbis Books, 1973), p. 276.

27. The obverse of this is of course the oppressors' search for the "proper" worthy opponent among the oppressed. For an analysis of such a set of categories in an oppressive culture, *see* my "The Psychology of Colonialism: Sex, Age and Ideology in British India," in Ashis Nandy, *The Intimate Enemy: Loss and Recovery of Self Under Colonialism* (New Delhi: Oxford University Press, 1983). *See* an earlier and briefer version in *Psychiatry* 45 (1982):197-218.

28. As it happened, he was clearly influenced by important strands of Indian traditions that did stress such interiorization and working through. Being a critical traditionalist, he therefore had to do the reverse, too, namely exteriorize the inner attempts to cope with evil as only an internal state. His work as a political activist came from the exteriorization.

29. I have derived this formulation from a set of somewhat casual comments made by Neil Warren in his "Freudians and Laingians," *Encounter*, March 1978, pp. 56-63. *See also* Philip Reiff, *The Triumph of the Therapeutic* (New York: Harper, 1966).

30. Though some Western scholars like Alan Watts would like to see such location of others in the self as a typically Eastern enterprise (Alan Watts, *Psychotherapy East and West,* New York: Ballantine, 1961), this has been occasionally a part of Western philosophical concerns, too. *See,* for instance, Jose Ortega y Gasset, *Meditations on Quixote* (New York: Norton, 1967). Within the Marxist tradition Georg Lukacs has argued that in the area of cognition and in the case of the proletariat at least, the subject-object dichotomy is eliminated to the extent self-knowledge includes molar knowledge of the entire society (Georg Lukacs, *History and Class-Consciousness,* London: Merlin, 1971).

31. It is one of the minor tragedies of our age that many of Marx's disciples sought to place Marx outside history and culture. He himself knew better. In another essay ("Evaluating Utopias," paper presented at the Second Meeting on Alternative Visions of Desirable Societies, Mexico City, May 1979; briefer version in *Mazinqira* 12, 1980), I have briefly discussed how far any theory of salvation, secular or otherwise, can shirk the responsibility for whatever is done in its name.

32. Ashis Nandy, "Woman Versus Womanliness: An Essay in Social and Political Psychology," in *At the Edge*

of Psychology: Essays in Politics and Culture (New
Delhi: Oxford University Press, 1980), pp. 32-46; and
"The Psychology of Colonialism."
    33.   See an articulate plea for this in Johan
Galtung, "Visions of Desirable Societies," in Masini and
Galtung, eds., Visions of Desirable Societies.   This of
course is complementary to the ideas of "graceful
playfulness" in Ivan Illich; see his Tools for
Conviviality (Glasgow: Fontana/Collins, 1973).   For the
same awareness within "proper" Marxism, see Evgeny Bogat,
"The Great Lesson of Childhood," in Eternal Man:
Reflections, Dialogues, Portraits (Moscow: Progress
Publishers, 1976), pp.   288-293.   The somewhat prim
psychoanalytic idea of "regression at the service of the
ego" can also be viewed as an indirect plea for the
acceptance of the same principle.   It is possible to
hazard the guess that these are all influenced in
different ways by the association Christ made between
childhood and the Kingdom of God.   That association
survives within Christianity in spite of what Lloyd de
Mause ("The Evolution of Childhood," in History of
Childhood, New York: Harper Torchbook, 1975, pp. 1-74)
considers to be the faith's overall thrust.
    34.   See Ashis Nandy, "Reconstructing Childhood: A
Critique of the ideology of Adulthood," to be published
in my The Politics of Awareness.   Earlier and briefer
versions appeared in The Times of India, February 2, 3,
and 4, 1982, and in Resurgence, May 1982.
    35.   On activity and work as the first postulates of
a Faustian civilization, see a brief statement by Roger
Garaudy, "Christian Faith and Liberation," in Masini and
Galtung, Visions of Desirable Societies.
    36.   Cf. E. D. Genovese, Roll, Jordan Roll: The
World the Slaves Made (New York: Pantheon, 1974).   See
also Moore , Injustice , pp. 465-466.
    37.   The Bhāgavad Gītā, IV: 18, translated by P. Lal
(New Delhi: Orient Paperback, 1965), p. 33.
    38.   For a fuller treatment of the psychology of
partitioning cognition and affect, see my "Science,
Authoritarianism and Culture."
    39.   See J.P.S. Uberoi, Science and Culture (New
Delhi: Oxford University Press, 1979).
    40.   Ashis Nandy, "Dialogue on the Traditions of
Technology," Development 3 (4) (1981):98-105.
    41.   Alexander and Margarete Mitscherlich, "The
Inability to Mourn," in Robert J. Lifton and Eric Olson,
eds., Explorations in Psychohistory, The Wellfleet Papers
(New York: Simon and Schuster, 1974), pp. 257-270.   The
quotation is on p. 262.
    42.   See a fuller discussion of these themes with
reference to Gandhi's world view in my "The Psychology of
Colonialism."
    43.   Robert J. Lifton, Boundaries: Psychological
Man in Revolution (New York: Simon and Schuster, 1969),

pp. 105-106.

44. I need hardly add that within the modern idea of history, too, this view has survived as a strain. From Karl Marx to Benedetto Croce and from R. G. Collingwood to Michael Oakeshott, students of philosophy of history have moved close to an approach to history that is compatible with traditional orientations to past times.

45. Césaire, *Discourse on Colonialism,* p. 40. Italics in the original.

46. O. Manoni, *Prospero and Caliban, The Psychology of Colonization,* translated by Pamela Powesland, 2nd ed. (New York: Frederick A. Praeger, 1964).

47. For instance, Manoni, Ibid., p. 41; G. Morris Carstairs, *The Twice Born: A Study of a Community of High-Caste Hindus* (Bombay: Allied, 1971), p. 160. I have of course in mind a galaxy of other well-motivated academics and writers, such as, to give random examples, David C McClelland and David G. Winter, *Motivating Economic Achievement* (New York: Basic Books, 1969); Alex Inkeles and Donald H. Smith, *Becoming Modern* (London: Heinesmanner, 1974); Nirad C. Chaudhuri, *The Continent of Circa* (London: Chatto and Windus, 1965); V. S. Naipaul, *India: A Wounded Civilization* (London: Andre Deutsche, 1977); and *Among the Believers: An Islamic Journey* (London: Andre Deutsch, 1981).

48. Césaire, *Discourse on Colonialism,* passim.

49. Frederick Meinecke and Gerherd Ritter, quoted in Renzo de Felice, *Interpretations of Fascism,* translated by Brenda H. Everett (Cambridge, Mass.: Harvard University, 1977), pp. 17-18.

50. Paul D. MacLean, "The Imitative-Creative Interplay of our Three Mentalities," in Harold Harris, ed., *Astride the Two Cultures: Arther Koestler at 70* (New York: Random House, 1976), pp. 187-213.

51. As Fouad Ajami recognizes, "The faith of those in the core in global solutions came up against the suspicions of those located elsewhere that in schemes of this kind the mighty would prevail, that they would blow away the cobwebs behind which weak societies lived. . . . in a world where cultural boundaries are dismantled, we suspect we know who would come out on the top." *See* Ajami's "The Dialectics of Local and Global Culture: Islam and other Cases," (paper written for the meeting of the group on Culture, Power and Global Transformation, World Order Models Project, 1980), mimeographed. Ajami rightly advises us to walk an intellectual and political tight rope, avoiding both the "pit of cultural hegemony" and "undiluted cultural relativism."

PART 4

Ideology and
World Order Discourse

World Politics and Western Reason: Universalism, Pluralism, Hegemony

R.B.J. Walker

I. INTRODUCTION

The study of world order--or world politics, international relations, or any other differentiation of this discourse--is part of a pervasive metatheoretical contradiction. As an essentially European or Western tradition of thought, with particular historical, geographical, economic and ideological interests, it seeks to understand, explain and guide events which have long ceased to be only European or even Western in their scope. While grasping at a global or universal phenomenon, it does so almost entirely within one culturally and intellectually circumscribed perspective.

This general dilemma has increasingly been noted in several areas of modern social and political thought. It has perhaps become most familiar in the context of critiques of imperialism, colonialism and neocolonialism. Considerable controversy has arisen recently out of Edward Said's study of the relationship between political dominance and the traditions of Orientalism that have produced systematically distorted accounts of the Middle East.[1] Anthony Smith's analysis of the "geopolitics of information" raises the same issue in terms of the way in which the mass media in the developed states have misrepresented the affairs of developing societies.[2] These specific diagnoses of some of the cultural contradictions of modern world politics have emerged out of a more wide ranging critique of the use of Western conceptions of political and economic development as an appropriate guide for the rest of humankind. The terms "development" and "modernity," for example, have come to be indicted as key elements in an elaborate rhetoric which serves to both justify and disguise the prevailing

----

Reprinted by permission with minor revisions from *Alternatives: A Journal of World Policy* 7:2, 1981.

patterns of global hegemony.[3]

A number of Western intellectual disciplines have also developed a long-standing sensitivity to this general problem, although more often on philosophical than on political or economic grounds. Anthropology, for example, although far from being free from complex forms of culture-bound presuppositions in its analysis of other cultures, has at least generated some concern about the dilemmas of ethnocentrism which necessarily arise in its analysis.[4] Whether in terms of cultural and epistemological relativism or of the ideological accompaniment to patterns of exploitation in the modern world system, the confrontation of Western traditions of thought with a variety of challenges to the natural superiority of the West seems likely to provide a bundle of problems at least as difficult and important as the disputes about the nature and appropriateness of science which have characterized so much of modern social and political thought.

International political theory appears to be particularly susceptible to this general problem. And yet, of all the areas of modern social and political thought, it is the study of world politics which seems to have most stubbornly resisted any examination of the central contradiction inherent in its subject. This lack of any sustained interest in the issue, of course, is not surprising. It accurately reflects and supports the prevailing dominance of the West in the modern world. The European states system has in fact spread globally. Consumerism has effectively penetrated most of the urban areas of the world. The Western way of life, or modernity, has become the West's gift to all humankind—a gift with many tangled strings attached. For most students of international politics this process seems to be inevitable and/or desirable, and the contradiction is thereby resolved. We have a universalization of modernity which may then be understood in terms of the logic of system-dominant relations between modernized states, or of the logic of modernity and industrialization itself.

On the other hand, much of the substance of recent international politics has centred on the often violent rejection of this process. Resistance to the all-pervasive forces of modernization along Western lines, like the process of modernization itself, has become a major characteristic of the twentieth century. Concepts of autonomy, nationalism and pluralism have come to challenge the assumed universality of progress towards the "civilization" of the West. It is in fact far from clear that an assumption of the inevitability of the universalization of modernity provides a very secure base from which to understand the dynamics of modern world politics, let alone from which to contemplate normative questions or future possibilities.

Although the literature on modern world politics has
been singularly reticent about the broad implications of
its culturally circumscribed heritage, it has been almost
hypersensitive to the suggestion that the transformations
of the modern world have begun to undermine the language
and concepts in which international affairs have usually
been understood. This has in turn generated a number of
attempts to pose alternative conceptual schemes and
methodological strategies, as well as strong
counterassertions of orthodoxy. As I have argued
elsewhere,[5] most of this activity occurs well within the
bounds of conventional Western liberal categories.
Occasionally, however, the difficulties involved in
attempting to understand a global political system within
the categories of a dominant but parochial tradition
emerge quite forcefully. Indeed, it is not surprising
that one of the few attempts to study world politics from
a position which is rather more open than usual to
metatheoretical, and particularly to normative or ethical
issues--world order studies--has come to present its own
formulation of this problem.[6]

The clue to this particular development is perhaps
given in the misbegotten term "world order" itself: the
aspiration towards one united world in the face of
increasing vulnerability arising from "irrational"
fragmentation, a vision of the cosmopolitan unity of
humankind and the transcendence of artificial boundaries
and national interests. Yet it is the order and the
authenticity of the implied universals that come under
suspicion. For universals and order imply a potential
for domination and homogenization, for maintaining the
status quo in the interest of the stronger, and for the
suffocation of autonomy, self-determination, and self-
reliance. It is in any case a suspicion more than
adequately supported by the various notions of global
management, Trilateralism and the co-optation of emerging
elites which have characterized much of the strategy and
rhetoric of recent world politics.

This study has been generated out of simultaneous
sympathies both for universalist aspirations and for the
current pluralist critique of Western hegemony. The
expression of precisely this tension seems to me to be
one of the more important contributions of the recent
literature on world order. Yet the issues raised are far
from easy to resolve. At the very least, they point to
the need for a more sustained consideration of
metatheoretical and philosophical issues than in usual in
the analysis of world politics. This study is thus a
preliminary exercise, one which aims to underline the
importance of the tensions emerging out of the pluralist
challenge to the universalist aspirations of conventional
world order thinking, and to unravel some of their
complexity. It is structured as an examination of
certain legacies from Western traditions of social and

political thought in order to create some epistemological space in which more detailed analysis may be pursued. More specifically, it seeks to draw attention to the extent to which even our discourse about and understanding of this issue, both on the part of those who search for universals and those who resist the reified universals of Western modernity, may be colonized by the historical-philosophical categories of the currently dominant powers. It begins from the assumption that social and political change is both reflected in and constituted by language. We remember Machiavelli and Hobbes, for example, for the way in which they created a new universe of (liberal) discourse; if the movement towards some kind of global sociopolitical order is judged to involve a transformation on something like that scale, then we may expect the study of world order to be deeply implicated in a similar series of conflicts constituted in developing linguistic and conceptual structures. And language, meta-theory, and knowledge in general are, of course, not unconnected with power. Thus while it may be necessary to support the emerging critique of cultural and ideological aspects of imperialism in the modern world, it is also necessary to go even further. For it is quite possible, even while talking about culture or ideology, to end up doing so in a way which merely perpetuates the particular culture and ideology under critique.

This study focuses on three elements of Western sociopolitical thought as they have developed in the context of the universalist-pluralist antinomy: the classical liberal theory of international relations, in both its traditional ontological and more recent epistemological forms; the historical development of the concept of culture as a response to the universalizing tendencies of the European Enlightenment; and the way in which the few attempts that have been made within the study of world politics to take the issue of cultural pluralism seriously tell us more about the character of Western culture and assumptions than they do about other traditions. Analysis of each of these three themes underlines the way in which current analysis of world politics, as well as the critique of that analysis, hinges upon a culturally and historically specific account of the relation between subject and object--an account which poses many of the most difficult problems in modern social and political thought.

II. THE DILEMMAS OF INTERNATIONAL POLITICAL THEORY

A tension between universalism and pluralism may be traced throughout the development of Westen political theory. It was evident in the debate between "realists" and "nominalists," between those who assigned reality to

the universal, treating individual instances as a mere
shadow, and those for whom the universal was merely
nominal and the individual instance the only reality. It
can also be examined as a response to specific
historical-geopolitical developments. Classical Greek
thought asserted the priority of the small unit, the
importance of the perfect internal ordering of the polis,
an assertion accompanied by a sharp distinction between
Greek and barbarian. With the expansions of the Hellenic
period, the speculations of the Cynics, Stoics and early
Christians began to adopt a more cosmopolitan tone. With
later Christianity, the distinction between temporal and
spiritual realms tempted political thought with two
competing versions of universalism. But with the rise of
the European state, particularism reasserted itself. It
resulted both in a long-standing conflict between the
emerging values of the secular state and the remnants of
a universalist natural law, and, as with Hobbes, the
conversion of natural law itself into a principle of the
liberal theory of the state. It is the classical
(liberal) tradition of international political theory,
however, which provides what is now perhaps the clearest
expression of this tension in modern social and political
theory. Despite repeated assertions of the irrelevance
of this tradition today, it continues to provide a clear
guide to the way in which the contradictions between
universalism and pluralism have been worked out in
Western political theory, and of how they now confront
rapidly changing circumstances. For, although it may be
true that students of modern world politics have shown
little concern with the metatheoretical critique of the
implications of applying European or Western concepts to
global phenomena, the general contradiction between
universalism and pluralism has in fact been the central
feature of the prevailing account of modern world
politics.

Any analysis of world politics made in terms of the
traditional liberal model begins with the assumption that
a sharp dichotomy can and must be made between the nature
of life within sovereign states and the interactions that
occur between such states. It has been this assumption,
more than any other, that has guided judgement on the
value and legitimacy of competing theoretical positions.
The dichotomy has been expressed in a number of different
ways. International "anarchy" is frequently contrasted
with domestic "community." International relations is
similarly distinguished from foreign policy. The
popularity of mechanistic images among those who seek to
explain the international system contrasts with the
greater influence of organic metaphors in a domestic
context. Martin Wight, one of the major historians of
this tradition, has argued that where domestic politics
is concerned with "progress" and the "good life,"
international politics is a realm of "recurrence and

repetition," one where the highest value is "survival."[7] E. H. Carr, in a formulation which has provided a paradigmatic text for traditionalists for the past 40 years, addresses the issue as a conflict between "realism" and idealism."[8] Carr continues a theme familiar to Friedrich Meinecke[9] and others in the tradition of German historicist thought, who were torn between the imperatives of ethics and those of power in the context of nationalism. International law is usually distinguished from municipal law--a distinction which reflects both Kant's observation that the international realm differs from the domestic mainly in its absence of publicly legal coercion, and the long historical dispute between natural law and positivism.

Perhaps most significantly, the classical tradition of international relations theory reflects the fateful distinction between public and private virtue, between raison d'etat and ultimate ends, by which Machiavelli undermined the medieval assumption of the universal principle of divine creation and natural harmony. With the emergence of the modern state system in fifteenth-century Italy, the notion of just wars, judged according to the rightness of the cause and waged for total victory, began to give way to that of wars of political expediency between secular states among which none could claim to hold a monopoly of right. With the development of the state as a moral force came a conception of order attained by the pursuit of interest, recognition of the interests of others, and by the connivances, intrigue and compromise of traditional diplomacy. Thus for a defender of the classical tradition, the irreducible conflict between international "order" and domestic "justice" in the modern world is merely a recurrence and repetition of dilemmas identified by Machiavelli at the dawn of the modern state system.

If this distinction is valid, then international political theory can only be what many traditionalists assert that it has always been: concerned with crude power, pragmatic custom and unstable cooperation. From this point of view, it is possible to justify the intellectual and moral poverty of international political theory, the oft-noted tendency for statesmen to be radical in domestic affairs and conservative in foreign policy, and the limitation of democratic principles in the affairs of state as a consequence of the need to defend the "national interest." The cardinal sin for the analyst of international politics is to transfer assumptions, images, or values from the domestic to the international context. This is a sin which has been said to beset both the (idealistic) aspiration for global harmony in human affairs (most notably as it has influenced American foreign policy or provided the justification for supranational institutions) and the (subversive) indiscretion of those who would judge international events by the standards of domestic morality.

Even among traditionalists, however, this initial distinction between domestic and international politics is rarely pushed to its most extreme conclusions. Some influential writers have ignored it altogether, merely asserting, like Hans J. Morgenthau, that all politics, international or otherwise, is power politics. Most others express some hope that the antinomies which are central to the classical tradition can eventually be shown to be resolvable. A Carr or a Meinecke may fail to reconcile "power" and "morality," or "realism" and "utopianism," but their analyses retain their importance, and even poignance, by virtue of their struggle to achieve some kind of reconciliation. In fact, it the uneasy tension which is drawn between the pluralist values of international political theory and the universals of domestic theory which distinguishes the serious theorist from the cruder polemicists of power politics and militarism.

Moreover, within the classical tradition, this tension emerges in the form of contrasting subtraditions, some evoking a Hobbesian account of the state of war, others emphasizing elements of community, society, legitimacy and so on. Thus for Wight, international political theory still reflects universalist themes from both Christian natural law (Grotius) and the Enlightenment (Kant) as well as the pluralist realism of Machiavelli. Hedley Bull's use of the term "anarchical society" points in the same direction, as do earlier accounts of the systemic or cultural ("European") coherence of international politics. Similarly, Fritz Kratochwil has argued that Hume's critique of Hobbes' account of social order leads to a better understanding of the norms and conventions of international order than the Hobbesian world portrayed by the cruder realists.[10] Rather than a simple "anarchy" as opposed to "society," traditional international political theory has sought some understanding of how states can in fact enter into "relations" at all, how some form of order arises and is maintained. Thus the "society of states" has come to be explained variously in terms of the craft of statesmen or the automatic operation of the system itself, with both versions paying particular attention to conceptions of the "balance of power." By the nineteenth century, international relations had come to be viewed in terms of the proper maintenance of the balance of power, a matter which could by then be reduced by Gentz to a number of rules and maxims, and provide for von Ranke a basis for explaining the history of the great powers. The idea of the society of states as involving a moral community of some kind had also come to play an important role, one mainly considered in terms of international law.

Nevertheless, no matter how much the basic domestic-international dichotomy has been tempered by emphasizing the cohesion of international systems, or admitting the importance of conceptions of justice or legitimacy in their operation, the dichotomy itself has been tenaciously defended. From Machiavelli through to the present century, the dilemma of international politics has been said to have remained essentially the same. It is a dilemma that is expressed, as Stanley Hoffmann once noted, as "a kind of permanent dialogue between Rousseau and Kant."[11] In Rousseau's gloomy scenario, nations have only the choice of opting out of relations altogether or attempting to survive the inevitable conflict between them through the use of fragile mitigating devices like the balance of power. Kant, beginning with essentially the same pessimistic view of the state, argued that the very evils inherent in the system will compel men to discover means against them, to develop a "united power" which would enable a universal peace among nations.

According to the traditionalist or classical liberal account, then, the essence of world politics is its pluralism, war being the ultimate arbiter in the conflict between plural values and interests. Domestic political theory, by contrast, is usually said to be characterized by universalist values. For the traditionalist, therefore, the transfer of domestic theory to an international context can lead only to naivety and wishful thinking; even Kant, unlike some of his nineteenth-century liberal followers, was forced to recognize that pluralistic conflict could only be ended with a long-term radical transformation of the international system itself. Kant's speculations remain the most influential guide for those who, for one reason or another,[12] find the traditionalist account to be superficial. For the convinced traditionalist, however, even Kant's highly qualified universalism remains entirely utopian, a proper understanding of international politics being provided instead by those who recognize the preeminence of pluralism--Carr, Meinecke and Machiavelli.

In a world in which we have become ever more conscious of our shared fate, this dilemma has become increasingly intolerable. Indeed, the classical approach has come to be assailed from all sides, even while the modern world continues to provide traditionalist theorists with ample evidence to support their gloomy prognosis of our fate. In fact, however, there is a recurring suspicion that the classical model, championed by traditionalists as "realism," may well mark a theoretical and political naivety of a most obtuse and dangerous kind.

If the domestic-international distinction is the primary starting point for the classical liberal tradition, much of the recent debate begins with a questioning of its relevance, both historically and in terms of current developments. Historically, it can be pointed out that domestic and international political theory portray two complementary aspects of the liberal theory of the state and that therefore their underlying unity is of far greater significance than conventional discussions allow. Furthermore, this unity can be located as a manifestation of a broader dialectic between the state and an increasingly global system of capitalism which has been identified by currently fashionable exponents of world system analysis, international political economy, and so on. Whether or not the traditional account is useful historically, hardly any account of modern world politics, with the significant but even then only partial exception of those concerned exclusively with the so-called "security dilemma," is complete without some prefatory condemnation of the inadequacy of the traditional model and a call for conceptual reorientation. Modern empirical analysis of world politics in fact now seems to coalesce around three major models: the classical Machiavellian account modified by the requirements of twentieth-century technology and great power configurations; a liberal functionalism which seeks to portray the modern world not as a fragmented plurality of competing units but as a pluralism of community interests much like a recently familiar account of domestic American politics, and an updated brand of Marxist structuralism. Each approach presents a number of rather obvious difficulties. The classical state-centric approach persists in its stubborn blindness to anything but diplomatic and military relationships, or "high politics." The liberal-pluralist or functional approach, while emphasizing other kinds of relationships--most notably economic interdependence--persists in its adherence to concepts or ideologies of progress, modernity and the benign influence of economics on political affairs, characteristic of nineteenth-century liberalism. And, the economic structuralists, while pointing to significant patterns of domination in the modern world, usually persist in an economic reductionism which reproduces crucial flaws in the account of capitalism developed either by Marx or his followers, or both.

While defenders of each of these positions assert their superiority as guides to the empirical developments of the modern world, it is possible to see that they are all perched somewhat precariously on a number of epistemological assumptions about the legitimacy of empirical knowledge. In short, they all confront the problem of the underdetermination of theory by data. Appeals to scientific method, for example, are as unlikely to arbitrate between rival theoretical positions here as in any other area of social and political enquiry. Thus the study of world politics has become thoroughly embroiled in the melange of disputes about

appropriate method which have been the life blood of
social and political theory for much of the twentieth
century.   In fact, a brief glance at the nature of
research on modern world politics quickly reveals the way
in which the classical tradition of international
political theory is now most commonly denied. For we now
find not so much an insistence on the radical schism of
international and domestic theory as a radical reduction
of all human action to the same common denominators
required by a positivist conception of knowledge.   The
study of international relations, which has been very
much an American enterprise, has largely absorbed the
premises of professionalism and scientific method which
swept American social science in the middle decades of
this century.
    Positivistic social science has taken a number of
different forms.   Sometimes, it is treated as an
extension of the purely epistemological arguments derived
from the tradition of British empiricism as modified by
the Vienna Circle in the 1920s. At others, it appears as
a broader political or metaphysical vision in the
tradition of Comte.   But whether in its narrower or
broader form, the so-called behavioral revolution clearly
inherited the valued of the European Enlightenment.   And
these values are preeminently universalist. They provide
the proper antithesis of the pluralism which emerges from
Machiavelli.   As such, they were certain to antagonize
the upholders of the classical tradition; and, indeed,
the most important debate in recent international
relations theory reflects this underlying conflict.[13]
    Essentially, the traditionalists once again argued
that, while the universalizing values of the
Enlightenment might be appropriate within the secure
confines of the state, international relations (the realm
par excellence of the conflict of values) cannot escape
from the pluralist dilemmas of Machiavelli.   This must
apply as much to questions of epistemology as to anything
else.   Thus, from the traditionalist point of view, what
now passes for mainstream international relations theory
violates the central assumption on which the subject
depends.   For all that Bull's polemic against the
"scientific" approach was formulated in epistemological
terms, the root of the issue was primarily ontological
and ethical in nature. From the "scientific" viewpoint,
espoused with some confusion by Morton Kaplan, the only
important issue was epistemological. The conception of
science which then prevailed involved all the
myths--about objectivity, the separation of facts and
values, and so on--that were engendered by Enlightenment
reason. The real importance of this debate lies mainly
in its translation of the major metatheoretical problem
of international political theory--the conflict between
international anarchy and domestic community, and with it
the conflict of pluralism and universalism--into an

epistemological form.

As a debate about epistemology, the polemics of the 1960s left much to be desired. For just as it may be argued that the traditional distinction between domestic and international politics must be considered in terms of a broader complementarity, so also the protagonists in this debate had much in common. Epistemologically at least, they participated in the same fundamental tradition: empiricism. Certainly there were important methodological differences between the largely deductive positivism of the "scientists" and the ideographic empiricism which emerges from diplomatic history and other writings of the traditionalists. Some traditionalists have also learnt something from the critiques of empiricism offered by English idealism (notably R. G. Collingwood) or German historicism (as in Raymond Aron's debt to the more pessimistic side of Max Weber). In practice, the products of both schools of thought share more epistemological similarities than the polemics between them might indicate. The real problem is one that they both share. For it is precisely the tradition of empiricism which they have in common that has come into question in almost all forms of modern philosophy.

For a brief period recently, it seemed as if Western social and political theory might be banished completely from legitimate discourse. For many it had become a variety of dodo, made irrelevant to the modern age by the proper use of scientific method. Inevitably it soon became clear that, far from replacing social and political theory, the scientific method had become, and not for the first time, a major issue within it. The history of the philosophy of science, critiques of positivism, explications of alternative logics of explanation and understanding, the relationship between knowledge and human interests, and so on--all have come to the forefront of discussions about the nature of modern social and political life. The spirit of positivism undoubtedly still prevails as a guide to research methodology; whenever it has been closely examined it has collapsed into dust at the first touch.

Interpretations of the implications of this debate vary considerably. For some, it seems to have implied little more than a slight change of emphasis--possibly a turning towards immediately pressing policy issues, or the cultivation of a skeptical attitude towards the more notoriously naive conceptions of "value free" research. For many of those concerned with more general metatheoretical problems, however, such an interpretation appears to be, at best, myopic. For them, it obscures the severity of the problems evident in the positivist conception of knowledge, and it is blind to the variety of recent attempts to understand social and political life in less narrowly constrained epistemological categories. In this interpretation, recent changes in social and political theory reflect a convergence of many streams of thought in a joint condemnation of positivist conceptions of science and knowledge, and, more significantly, of the longer philosophical traditions from which positivism has grown. It is this position, which is reflected in, for example, Richard Bernstein's popular account of the "restructuring" of social and political theory.[14] For Bernstein, in fact, the collapse of the positivist mainstream has been the most important feature of recent sociopolitical thought. This collapse is said to have resulted from influential criticisms of the positivist account of the logic of explanation and prediction, and its accompanying conceptions of both objectivity and the relationship between facts and values. This general critique is in turn seen as one aspect of a substantial revolution in modern thought. In Bernstein's account, the most important contributions have been made by phenomenologists like Edmund Husserl and Alfred Schutz, by American pragmatists, and by those who have followed Marx in stressing the role of *praxis* and human interests in all forms of knowledge. Other accounts may be found which make parallel claims for recent developments in hermeneutics and structuralism, and for the interest in traditional political and moral theory which has recently revived despite positivistic insistence on its permanent demise.

It is not necessary to accept Bernstein's more specific conclusions ("all roads lead to Jurgen Habermas") in order to accept his more general claim that important changes have occurred in discussions about appropriate social science method, and that these reflect far more than simple antiscientism. But if we turn more critically towards the sources from which Bernstein is able to see a convergence in modern thought, they seem to present not so much a convergence towards any form of solution to philosophical puzzles as one towards a general agreement on the nature of the problem which confronts Western philosophy in the twentieth century. For they all point to the need to transcend the epistemological dilemmas which found their mature formulation with the Enlightenment: most specifically the dilemma of self-consciousness; the opposition between knowing subject and object known; the theme of the simultaneous freedom and alienation of man from the world; the oscillation from objectivity to subjectivity, from universal truth to pluralistic skepticism and relativism.

There are, however, several serious problems confronting any attempt to speak of a transformation in thought of the kind attempted by Bernstein. Most significantly, any claim about a radical break with tradition must rest upon some historical understanding of the tradition itself. Yet the very identity of a tradition of thought is constantly at issue, not least because of the difficulties of defending an internalist-objectivist account of the growth of knowledge from an externalist-historicist critique. Conceptions of science which view it as an autonomous development, in ever closer a approximation to some universal truth, tend to support a more sanguine attitude towards its role as a model for all forms of knowledge than those which view it as merely a product of a particular time, place or class interest. Thus, if Bernstein is correct in speaking of the transformation of social and political theory in terms of a deeper transformation in philosophy, then it becomes important to examine the conception of the history of philosophy in terms of which this transformation is judged to be occurring. This is particularly so given that the history of philosophy, like any history of thought, tends to consist of a set of conventions, an account of what philosophy is or should be. More specifically, modern histories of philosophy usually appear as the captive of the antinomies of the Kantian critical philosophy. The categories of Kant, the highest achievement of Enlightenment reason, have come to provide the framework in which all philosophy can be located. The history of philosophy in its conventional form has thus "enshrined the idea that past philosophers, in constituting their rival systems had been constantly disagreeing concerning a repertoire of Kantian questions."[15] It provides an account in which the values of the Enlightenment are elevated into greater prominence, while those not sharing such values become relegated to the periphery of philosophy--to "literature" perhaps. Such has been the fate in particular of writers who constitute what has come to be called the Counter-Enlightenment, and who have increasingly been canvassed as sources of inspiration for social and political theory in its postpositivistic phase.[16] Vico comes to appear as an alternative father figure to Descartes. Herder once again challenges Kant in a latter-day era of post-Enlightenment thought. The emergence of meaning in historical context challenges the search for truth through universal reason. And once some such alternative history of philosophy is resurrected, its major theme quickly emerges as a celebration of particularity and a denial of the necessary harmony of values in a rational universe. The counterpoint to the cosmopolitanism of the *Aufklarung* is the pluralist and relativist sensibility of Romanticism, nationalism and historicism--the darker side of Western thought against which the white knights of science and objectivity are regularly sent forth.

Much of the recent critique of science in modern social and political theory has reflected this Counter-Enlightenment tradition. T. S. Kuhn and Paul Feyerabend[17] are lauded or condemned for their reluctant or enthusiastic portrayal of science as an inherently relativistic enterprise; Enlightenment objectivism collapses into Romantic subjectivism. If the retreat from positivism involves nothing more than this, then it would be more accurate to speak of a "realignment" of social and political theory, a movement within existing categories, than of a "restructuring" with its implication of a radical alteration in the categories themselves. Many of the philosophical currents to which Bernstein refers attempt to cut deeper, and most have done so on the basis of a critical reassessment of the Western philosophical tradition as it has come to be formalized. Heidegger believed the real mistakes were already made in the pre-Socratic period, and attempted to overcome the dominance of epistemology over ontology of which Renaissance and Enlightenment dualism was but a necessary consequence. Many others--Husserl, Merleau-Ponty, Peirce, Mead, Dewey, Whitehead, Collingwwod, and so on--all articulated their positive philosophy in terms of a critique of the "huge outbreak of dualisms" (Collingwood's phrase) which followed Descartes and Galileo. Wittgenstein and the analytic movement generally adopted the precarious strategy of ignoring the tradition altogether. Whether or not any of these writers provides a very secure ladder by which to transcend the problem that they define is clearly another matter. Certainly some have contributed to the development of important research traditions that emphasize the reflexivity of self and society, mutual participation in linguistic structures, and so on. But whatever one makes of these alternative traditions, it is clear that any restructuring of social and political theory must involve a judgement that it has moved beyond yet another oscillation from universal reason to particularist relativism, from untainted objectivity to unfettered subjectivity.

Social and political theory of civil society, then, has been dominated by Enlightenment sensibilities. The vision of universal reason and progress, of science and freedom, has come to permeate all our values. Yet the celebration of self-consciousness which makes this possible simultaneously creates the problem of man's alienation from nature. It allows for the possible reduction of man to a mere part of the natural world (thus making him subsumable under the "laws of nature") or for the dissolution of man into mere subjectivity. The Romantic or expressivist critique of this dualistic mode of thought sought to rescue man from this dilemma by denying man's alienation from nature. These universalist and pluralist themes have thus been complementary. Some have suggested that the complementarity is structured in terms of a division between public and private life. Others view it in terms of a collapse of optimism into pessimism. But the universalist theme has been dominant:

That is why those thinkers who stand in a Romantic or expressivist tradition of whatever kind, disciples of Rousseau, or of de Tocqueville, or Marx, whether they be socialist, anarchists, partisans of "participatory democracy" or admirers of the ancient polis like Hannah Arendt, are all estranged from modern Western society. And those who feel at home in it are the heirs of the Enlightenment mainstream, who proclaimed recently (and somewhat prematurely) the "end of ideology."[18]

It is in this context that the tradition of international political theory is most fundamentally different from domestic politics. For here pluralism reigns, and it is the universal values of the Enlightenment that provide the source for those who attempt to mitigate the resort to violence implicit in the pluralist position. The "radical" in international politics is precisely the one who cherishes the values which the radical in a domestic context seeks to escape. Whereas in a domestic context, we look to Kant for the classical formulations of the problems of modern philoosphy, in the international context Kant provides the inspiration for solutions.

It is precisely this paradox within the liberal tradition of social and political theory, I would suggest, that emerges once again in recent discussions about world order. That part of the liberal tradition which is prepared to accept the possibility of universal values has developed in the specific historical context of the domestic European state. It leads one to reify that context into the universal experience of humankind. And this is then challenged by those who object that such values are really quite parochial, whether in their conception of human rights or in their account of the appropriate development of modernity. On the other hand, that part of the tradition which is prepared to take seriously the diversity of peoples and aspirations in the world is precisely that part that denies the very possibility of a community of humankind. In extreme form, it insists instead on a perpetual conflict of values arbitrated only by configurations of power and violence. In a less extreme form, it accounts for the rationality of nationalism in the modern world, a rationality which is simultaneously a form of collective idiocy.

III. THE CONCEPT OF CULTURE AND ITS CONTRADICTIONS

To the extent that the study of world politics has escaped from the "realism" of state-centric conceptions, and thus from the impasse of the classical liberal antinomy of universalism and pluralism, it has done so mainly in economic terms. On the one hand, there has been an optimism that capitalist economic relations will eventually smother the aggressive tendencies of nations with functional arrangements of some kind. On the other, it has been argued that the primary dynamic of the modern world involves a system of economic relations through which the industrial powers maintain a position of dominance and exploitation in the world as a whole. In both cases, the forces of universalism are assumed to be in the ascendent, although evaluations of the desirability of this process vary considerably.

All three of the major accounts of modern world politics--the liberal realists, the liberal functionalists/technocrats/utopians, and the neo-Marxian structuralists--however, seem to some observers to be excessively reductionist and determinist. They appeal to certain basic underlying forces at work: the pursuit of power in equilibrium systems or the dynamics of economic structures. Thus, quite apart from the adequacy of each on its own terms, it is possible to question the narrow assumptions about human action on which they all depend. One may particularly question the lack of concern about those aspects of human action which are usually subsumed under the term "culture"--values, aspirations, creativity, language, and ideology.

The recent focus on culture in discussions of world order seems to emerge from both of these considerations. It is a term which is used to communicate at least two primary theses. First, that any account of an emerging global order must recognize the plurality of cultures in the world, together with the structural processes which presently assert the "hegemony" of the culture of Western modernity. Second, that any account of an emerging global order must recognize the importance of the "superstructural" sphere of ideas, values and so on. Together these two theses converge on a set of concerns about "cultural imperialism."

One need not look very far into the literature, however, to discover that the term culture is one of the most complex entities in the modern lexicon. Like other key concepts of modern social and political theory, it has been thoroughly implicated in, indeed constituted by, the development of Western industrial society. The possibility is therefore raised that not only will the search for universals in an emerging world order be predicated on the reified universals of a dominant tendency in a dominant but parochial culture, but also that the critique of that process as cultural imperialism will be co-opted into the linguistic categories of that imperialist culture. Thus, like Raymond Williams, in his recent discussion of the concept of culture from within the Marxist tradition, I would emphasize the importance of understanding the way in which this term retains the residues of social processes and philosophical debates peculiar to one particular culture:

At the very centre of a major area of modern thought and practice, which it is habitually used to describe, is a concept, "culture," which in itself, through variation and complication, embodies not only the issues but the contradictions through which it has developed. The concept at once fuses and confuses the radically different experiences and tendencies of its formation. It is then impossible to carry through any serious cultural analysis without reaching towards a consciousness of the concept itself: a consciousness that must be . . . historical. . . . When the most basic concepts—the concepts, as it is said, from which we begin—are suddenly seen to be not concepts but problems, not analytic problems either but historical movements that are still unresolved, there is no sense in listening to their sonorous summons or their resounding clashes. We have only, if we can, to recover the substance from which their forms were cast.[19]

The problem arises most clearly once we begin to examine the way in which different schools of thought conceive of the relationship between culture and other aspects of human life. Thus, on the one side, we find various forms of reductionism or materialism, in which culture is in some way dependent on or determined by something else, an epiphenomenon of more fundamental forms. The biological version insists that culture is merely a mask for innate biological drives like territoriality, differences between the sexes, aggression, reproduction, species survival, and so on. The economic version treats culture as a by-product of primary economic formations, particularly, in the present age, of capitalism. The concept of culture thus becomes entangled with the concept of ideology, and the analysis of culture becomes concerned with the attempt to "demystify" the conceptions of "reality" which are favored by the dominant class in society and reified by the dominant cultural forms. On the other side are those who view culture as a more or less autonomous realm, one uncontaminated by more mundane social or biological processes. Some forms of this are merely naive, though they have inspired libraries full of the "history of art" portrayed as nothing more than a sequence of ideas outside of history. Others are generated from a more engaged critique of the pessimistic conclusions required by a determinist position. In this view, the realm of culture is seen to be at least potentially (in some areas, or in some kinds of society) the realm of freedom and creativity. Thus as a captive of the broader battle between materialism and idealism, the concept of culture betrays its very culturally specific lineage. It is in this sense that "culture" is not so much a concept as an unresolved historical movement.

Like all other major categories of modern social and political thought, culture has changed its meaning quite radically both in response to the transformations from feudal to industrial society and in response to changes in the meaning of other analytic categories. As we know it now, it is largely a product of the late eighteenth century, before which it merely implied the culture *of* something, notably crops, animals and minds. Williams emphasizes the way in which the term reacted to changes in the terms "society," "economy" and, particularly "civilization." For it developed essentially as part of a complex critique of the kind of society that had in the sixteenth and seventeenth centuries come to be understood through these concepts. "Civilization" in particular encompassed all kinds of notions which we now see as characterizing the development of a new kind of society, particularly the rise of the bourgeoisie and the acceleration of capitalism. The most familiar of these are the conception of progress, the distinction between civilization and barbarism, secular rationalism, and individualism: the world enshrined in the Universal Histories of the Enlightenment. "Culture," in short, came to be associated with the critique of Enlightenment values. The relationship was far from straightforward, although two main lines of thought can be distinguished.

On the one hand, there is the view, associated with Rousseau and the Romantics, that the "civilized" values of the Enlightenment were in fact "artificial" rather than "natural": Blake's "single vision and Newton's sleep." From this direction, the term culture absorbed a series of meanings relating to art and imagination, and to family and personal life--to subjectivity. Between the Enlightenment and the Romantics a gap opened between the objective sciences and subjective arts, between positive knowledge and literature, between public and private.

On the other hand, there is the view, particularly associated with Vico and Herder, which reacted against the assumption that it is the natural sciences which provide the essential foundation of reason by which the enlightened understanding of humankind could contribute to the building of a higher social order. The first step was taken by Vico with the idea that man made his own history, a line later taken up by Marx. Herder's contribution was the rejection of a unilinear view of this vision and the emphasis on plural ways of life; from culture to cultures.

The essential point to be made is that in both of these forms, the concept of "culture" was part of a retreat into the particular--the individual on the one hand, the group or nation on the other--as a reaction to the universalist values of the Enlightenment. Both affirmed the particular and "meaning" as an attack on the materialist and mechanistic values of the ascendent scientific rationalism. In retreating into the particular, the concept of "culture" was absorbed into the specific cultural forms of European capitalism. For culture had now come to be viewed as a realm of ideas, located within the individual or group, and opposed to other aspects of society. The analysis of particular "cultural" forms reflected the same kind of schism; some of them still pose the most intractable problems in modern social and political thought. The study of language, for example, has for the most part been conducted in a more or less objectivist or scientific fashion. It has resulted in a vast knowledge of "other" languages--not unrelated, of course, to the dynamics of European conquest--and of formal linguistic structures, most notably typified by Saussure. But language in this tradition appears as something alien to man. The alternative and diametrically opposing line, rooted explicitly in Herder, emphasizes the expressive and subjective nature of language. Thus the study of the cultural form reflects the categorization by which the term "culture" itself has been alienated from the material world.

The concept of "culture," the analysis of particular forms like language, and traditions of thought which attempt to examine culture in the context of broader social formations, have all participated in a common conceptual transformation. They have all in some way been moulded by the assumption of a radical split between ideas and the physical world. "Culture" has become one of a barrage of terms which now reside in the idealist and subjectivist pole of an idealist-materialist/subjectivist-objectivist polarity. The study of language struggles to escape from the Cartesian divorce of "language" and "reality." The analysis of the relationship between culture and society remains mired in similar problems. In short, they participate in, reflect, and indeed constitute central features of what is generally called the culture of modernity.

The term "culture" thus leaves us with a fundamentally ambiguous legacy. As part of a legitimate critique of the kind of mechanistic and reductive scientism of the Enlightenment tradition, it guides us towards the importance of ideas, consciousness, human meaning, values and so on. As part of a legitimate critique of the reified universals of Enlightenment reason, it guides us towards the diversity of human experience. But as a particular historical-philosophical formation which responds to a false antithesis of subjective and objective by a retreat into the subjective, it is at once a partial solution and a reaffirmation of the original problem. It becomes one of a series of partial solutions. The subjectivist or relativist philosophy of science à la Kuhn or Feyerabend goes some way towards restoring some balance in our conception of knowledge in a world which has more or less completely succumbed to the objectivist illusion. The retreat into privacy and family life becomes a reasonable response to a public realm increasingly governed by bureaucratic or instrumental reason. The search for deep subjectivity is defensible in a world where the pressures of work and commerce require merely a cog in the machine, the homogenized individual of the modern consumer culture. But as partial solutions, they also ensure the continuity of the problem to which they are a response; the ongoing conflict between the values of Enlightenment reason and its expressivist, subjectivist or Romantic critique, which are at the heart of Western social and political values. Like these other major themes of dissent in modern industrial societies, discussions of culture are eminently susceptible to co-optation:

> The major theoretical problem, with immediate effect on methods of analysis, is to distinguish between alternative and oppositional initiatives and contributions which are made within or against a specific hegemony (which then sets certain limits to them or which can succeed in neutralizing , changing or actually incorportaing them) and other kinds of initiative and contribution which are irreducible to the terms of the original or the adaptive hegemony, and are in that sense independent. It can be persuasively argued that all or nearly all initiatives and contributions, even when they take on manifestly alternative or oppositional forms, are in practice tied to the hegemonic: that the dominant culture, so to say, at once produces and limits its own form of counter-culture.[20]

This does not, of course, dismiss the possibility of "authentic" critique and transformation:

> It would be wrong to overlook the importance of works and ideas which, while clearly affected by hegemonic limits and pressures, are at least in part significant breaks beyond them, which may again in part be neutralized, reduced, or incorporated, but which in their most active elements nevertheless come through as independent and original.[22]

It is merely difficult--but immeasurably important--to separate the life-sustaining wheat from the co-optable chaff.

This problem has been particularly important for those who, like Williams, draw on the various traditions of Marxism. Despite Marx's own sensitivity to the need to transcend the strict separation of subjective and objective, idealism and materialism, and of the need to

explain the historical forces which generated these forms
of discourse in the first place, much Marxist discussion
of culture has degenerated into crude determinism.
Culture became merely superstructural, something
determined by the base. With the resurgence of the more
Hegelian tendencies of "Western Marxism," there has again
been an attempt to transcend those categories. Antonio
Gramsci's conception of "hegemony," for example, goes a
considerable way towards restoring the integrity of
cultural and other aspects of life in a constitutive
rather than a determinist manner.[22] And the vitality of
recent discussions of the concept of ideology clearly
stems in large part from a recognition of the need to
overcome a wide range of philosophical assumptions
associated with the Cartesian divorce between
consciousness and world.[23] Moreover, the most important
controversies in the analysis of ideology--those which
occur between historicists and structuralists[24]--return
us to precisely the same dilemmas posed by the tension
between relativistic pluralism and objectivistic
universalism, which I have suggested lies at the heart of
international political theory.

IV. ORIENTALISM AND INTERNATIONAL POLITICAL THEORY

Modern Western social and political thought is far
from bereft of attempts to transcend the kinds of
problems outlined so far, despite the institutionalized
prevalence of naive empiricism, positivism, reductive
materialism and other similarly dubious tales. Nor are
the more creative lines of thinking restricted to the
reassertion of subjectivity in the face of an
increasingly instrumental objectivism in modern society.
Much of the debate on language, meaning, dialectic,
structure, *praxis,* and so on is explicitly intended to
transcend the horizons of the liberal dualist heritage.
From within this tradition, the problem appears to
involve three main dimensions: the (critical)
demystification of the way in which the consciousness of
modernity has been guided by certain powerful but
simplifying assumptions about the nature of
knowledge--those which we have largely inherited from the
Renaissance and Enlightenment and which have become
reified within capitalism; the (potentially reactionary)
recovery of alternative traditions which have come to be
buried in this historical development; and the
(potentially emancipatory) construction of new forms of
knowledge and "authenticity." The balance between these
tendencies varies from discourse to discourse, but they
all play an important role in the political and
intellectual life of modern industrial societies.
In addition to this internal debate within Western
social and political thought, however, there has

developed a suspicion that the parochialism of the Western tradition itself may provide intrinsic limitations to the emancipatory project. Hence a concern with non-Western traditions at many different levels: from "primitive art" and exotic mysticisms to identification with the creation of a new socialist paradise a la Mao, perhaps in some more fragile part of the Third World. Whether as a mirror to reflect upon the shortcomings (or superiority) of Western "civilization," or as a source of regeneration for alienated bourgeois life, an interest in non-Western thought and culture has become something of a growth industry in the West. While the mainstream traditions of international relations encourage obliviousness of, rather than sensitivity to this kind of thinking, it will clearly become an issue as the hegemony of modernity comes under increasing challenge.

Even with an emphasis on the importance, indeed necessity, of an openness to other cultural traditions in the analysis of world politics, the difficulties of the enterprise should not be underestimated. After all, imported cultural forms have had a long history of subtle and not so subtle translation and co-optation by Western industrialism and consumerism. Many oriental spiritual disciplines, for example, have been easily adapted to the requirements of post-Romantic subjectivity.

Similarly, disciplines like anthropology which have been forced to take the issue seriously have constantly run into interpretive problems at the level of epistemology. Moreover, always in the background is a set of implicitly racist assumptions inherited from nineteenth-century social Darwinism. As Ernest Gellner has emphasized, modern anthropological research can itself be viewed against the background of its own Age of Darkness in which non-Western thought came to be explained either in terms of a "primitive mentality" theory, according to which "savages" get things wrong and confused so systematically that their thought must be categorized as "Pre-logical," or according to a "Jacob's Ladder" or evolutionary theory, by which such savages are seen as being on the same ladder, though on a lower rung; that is, that they are simply unskilled at the same logical principles.[25] Much of the modern philosphical discussion ofthis problem has developed as a direct response to the issues as raised within the Socio-Darwinian context of debate, in the early decades of this century, by Lucien Levy-Bruhl, Emile Durkheim and Marcel Mauss. More recently this problem has developed as a direct response to the issues as raised within a variety of pluralist perspectives, notably that of Ludwig Wittgenstein--"the unitary vision that all unitary visions were mistaken and the source of all error."[26]

Most of the discussion of this issue in anthropology, however, focuses on the problem of explanation, on the difficulty of "understanding a primitive society." In this sense, its primary interest is in elaborating on the concept of "rationality" and its implications both for the problem of developing appropriate research procedures, and for our understanding of the nature of science. Thus, even here there has been some reluctance to consider that while explanations and theories may not be *verifiable* (to allude to the positivist context of most discussions of explanation) they are *realizable*. [27] The real problem concerns not merely whether in understanding a society one has to understand its concepts, or if, in understanding the concepts, one has understood the society. It concerns also the equally complex problem of reification and the sociopolitical context in which reification occurs.

While in anthropology the hegemonic universals of social Darwinism may have been vanquished by a radical pluralism, a rather different set of attitudes prevails in the analysis of international relations. It is possible to find a few isolated critiques of the reification of Western universals into legal and institutional entities like the United Nations. Adda Bozeman's analysis of "politics and culture in international history," for example, is a thorough-going formulation of the pluralist position. She contends that many Occidental instruments of government, notably written constitutions, parliamentary procedures and the concept of state, are "fundamentally uncongenial to those people who have inherited non- or semi-literate forms for the expression of their political destinies and disposition."[28] Thus, Bozeman's own work is taken up with a series of histories of the cultural traditions of the ancient Near East, of Greece, of Alexander's Empire, of Rome, Mediaeval Europe, Byzantium, and of the Muslim Empire, culminating in an analysis of the establishment of the modern European state system.

Bozeman's analysis is open to a variety of criticisms. Quite apart from the fact that it is fairly simple-minded history, it is highly culturally deterministic and tends to exaggerate the differences between cultures at the expense of commonalities. More significantly, and in sharp contrast to the anthropological literature, she does not really attempt to consider any of the wider implications of cultural relativism. The basic position, however, is important. It parallels the earlier critique, by Rousseau, of the liberal presuppositions underlying the concept of a universal community. A forthright defence of orthodoxy can be found in Werner Levi's critique of Bozeman.[29] Levi takes her to task for her heavy reliance on the philosophy and theory of various legal systems while underplaying their "reality," and also for her under-estimation of the impact of the international system on the behavior of states. He suggests instead that "cultural differences have minor influence upon the existence of universal international law and, *a fortiori,* upon the existence of particular international law." As evidence for this, he argues that "every state in the world, regardless of its culture, acknowledges the existence of international law by its actions, either explicitly or implicitly." Furthermore, because all states subscribe to the basic features of the international system in practice, the systemic influences on their behavior are inescapable, and cannot be very much affected by cultural peculiarities. "Universal nationalism and system membership," he says, "shape the behavior of states toward basic uniformity." In addition to this somewhat extreme systemic determinism, Levi presents a functionalist account of a developing world culture--"supermarkets from Afghanistan to Zanzibar." Again, "insofar as culture--when broadly defined--is relevant at all, international culture has more relevance than any national culture."

This is a typical if extreme response by theorists of international politics to the issues raised by Bozeman. It makes explicit a set of assumptions found implicitly in much of the recent analysis of international relations. And as a response to the superficiality and rather uncritical nature of Bozeman's position, it does have some merit. Beyond that, it no more addresses the major issues involved than does the opposite school of thought. It resembles more the affirmation of a party platform than a serious analysis. To begin with, we may object to the viability of Levi's self-styled empirical analysis. It is in fact not so much empirical as an articulation of two major theoretical premises--the state-centric national interest image of international interaction, and a functionalist model of international law and institutions--neither of which is subjected to any particular justification.

Quite apart from this, it fails to address three main issues. First, whether an empirical tendency towards systemic and functionalist determinism can be treated simply as a given concrete reality, or as a particular manifestation of a culturally specific view of the world which has, historically, managed to develop a hegemonic grasp over the whole. That the rest of the world has been increasingly "Westernized" does not make it any less "Western" or more "Universal." It merely raises the question of the relationship between Western assumptions and the dominant mode of global socioeconomic and political organization. Second, whether this supposedly "realist" view of international behavior justifies a similarly "realist," positivist, or instrumentalist view of international law. Third, whether this view of international politics is sufficient to brush aside the wide range of epistemological problems

which are raised by the pluralist critique. In fact, it
may be countered that this supposedly "realist" position
is a classic example of a nonverifiable theory which
seeks to mould the world in its own image. In which
case, this kind of analysis is open to the charge that it
is, at best, a naive realism, and at worst, a variety of
intellectual and cultural imperialism: might makes
right. In this sense, it may be seen as a parallel to
that Socio-Darwinian attitude which views Western science
and its associated concepts of rationality as the supreme
value which other supposedly primitive superstitions will
naturally wish to emulate.

There has been, however, another way of cutting into
this problem, one which I think is rather more
instructive. It is an approach which is usefully
examined through the writings of the philosopher F.S.C.
Northrop. Northrop's work has now largely been forgotten
in international political theory, although it once
enjoyed a minor popularity. Much of his more specific
analysis is now obviously dated, and his general attempt
to relate cultural gestalts to "practical politics" has
not been easily reconcilable with the more fashionable
modes of socio-scientific analysis. More seriously,
however, if we move beyond some of the superficialities
of his writings, we find that it is an almost classical
epistemological dualism adopted from the mainstream of
Western scientific philosophy which underlies and thereby
restricts the value of his approach.[30]

Northrop's early work was in the philosophy of
science, particularly in an examination of the
philosophical implications of the theoretical upheavals
of twentieth-century physics. Influenced by Ernst
Cassirer, A.N. Whitehead and Albert Einstein, among
others, the dualism of subject and object, as formulated
most notably in the positivist and neo-Kantian traditions
of the early twentieth century, quickly became the
central thread of his later "philosophical anthropology."
In its simplest formulation, his approach is predicated
upon a basic distinction between two modes of knowledge.
The first is characterized in terms of "concepts by
intuition," one of which "denotes, and the complete
meaning of which is given by something which is
immediately apprehended." The second is characterized by
"concepts by postulation"--"one the meaning of which in
whole or part is designated by the postulates of some
specific, deductively formulated theory in which it
occurs." In his philosophy of science, these represent
successive stages of scientific enquiry, both of them
indispensable in any coherent account of scientific
knowledge. The gap between the two is bridged by a
technical epistemological operation which he calls an
"epistemic correlation . . . a relation joining an
unobserved component of anything designated by a concept
by postulation to its directly inspected component

denoted by a concept by intuition."[31]

It is not necessary here to assess the limitations of this basically Kantian starting point; it is merely one variation of a theme made familiar by Rudolph Carnap and Carl Hempel, and it has been thoroughly demolished by the post-positivistic philosophy of science over the last three decades. What is important is that it forms the basis of Northrop's philosophy of culture. For his analysis, again reduced to its most elementary formulation, is that a common tendency to emphasize either one or the other of these two modes of knowledge at the expense of the other has been a primary factor in two major divisions in the modern world, one between the Occident and the Orient, another between the sciences and the humanities.

To take the first of these, Northrop argues that there is a tendency in the East to emphasize concepts by intuition ("the aesthetic continuum"), while the West places greater emphasis on concepts by postulation. Thus, where for Plato, for example, the world of forms is fundamental, and the ever-changing reality a mere reflection, for Chinese philosophy it is the bright vividness of the concrete world which is said to be fundamental and the general concepts which are the pale reflection.

This analysis is extended to a comparison of legal systems. Western law, he suggests, is characterized by abstract contractual law which recognizes ethical norms other than those of the *status quo,* thereby allowing for progressive dynamism and universal application. The Orient, by contrast, is said to rely upon an "intuitive mediational" type of law. It tends to push legal codes into the background, preferably dispensing with them altogether. and to bring the disputants into a warm give-and-take relationship, usually by way of a mediator, so that the previously made demands can be modified gracefully, and a unique solution taking all of the exceptional circumstances of the case into account is spontaneously accepted by both disputants.[32]

Thus, for Northrop, it is the heavy emphasis on the theoretic component of knowledge, epitomized by the physical sciences, which is the hallmark of Western thought, and which, when contrasted with Oriental traditions, may be seen as a fundamental aspect of its ethnocentrism. Culture is seen in terms of the articulation of certain philosophical principles in a variety of different aspects. Moreover, these philosophical presuppositions are said to be rooted ultimately in "science." As a consequence, given that all the main cultural systems and social institutions are based on their respective philosophies, which in turn are grounded in their respective "sciences," the most effective way of solving conflicts is to eliminate contradictions between the sciences of various cultures.

When the conflict between the true foundations of antagonistic culture systems is removed, the cultures upon which they are based will be harmonious

There are clearly a number of enormous difficulties with this analysis, particularly in the conception of culture as being rooted in scientific epistemology, and also in the conception of the underlying sources of conflict in human societies. It may well be that there are aspects of validity in both assertions; physical science, for example, has been of immense importance in the development of Western civilization. Northrop's detailed analysis, however, quickly attracted critical appraisal. It was criticized for playing down important theoretic elements in Chinese culture.[33] Similarly, his characterization of science, and Western thought in general, in terms of the Platonic-Galilean tradition of rationalism, belies the complementary stereotype of science as Baconian induction. It is in fact precisely this schism between two opposing traditions, faithfully reproduced in the presuppositions from which Northrop begins, which has been the major characteristic of Western thought, particularly since the Renaissance. One does not have to dig very far into comparative philosophy to discover that it is just this dualism which becomes the central focus of mutual reference and contradistinction. Thus, in his classic history of Chinese philosophy, Fung Yu-Lan seeks to differentiate it in a general way from the Western tradition and comments on the minor role played by epistemology in China. Epistemology, he says, has "not formed an important part of Chinese philosophy, not only because Chinese philosophy has not cared to pursue knowledge for its own sake, but also because it does not demarcate clearly the distinction between the individual and the universe."

> A very important feature of modern western history has been the consciousness by the ego of itself. Once it has consciousness of itself, the world immediately becomes separated into two: the ego and the non-ego,or what is subjective and what is objective. From this division arises the problem of how the subjective ego can have knowledge of the objective non-ego, and from this arises the great emphasis which Western philosophy has laid upon epistemology. In Chinese thought, however, there has been no clear consciousness by the ego of itself, and so there has been equally little attention paid to the division between the ego and the non-ego; therefore epistemology has likewise not become a major problem.[34]

Similarly, Joseph Needham has offered his opinion that Northrop is "deeply mistaken" and points to the proper context in which the undoubted difference between Chinese and European thought has to be considered:

> There is no good reason for denying to the theories of the Yin and Yang, or the Five Elements, the same status of proto-scientific hypotheses as can be claimed by the systems of the pre-Socratic and other Greek schools. What went wrong with Chinese science was its ultimate failure to develop out of these theories forms more adequate to the growth of practical knowledge, and in particular its failure to apply mathematics to the formulation of regularities in natural phenomena. This is equivalent to saying that no Renaissance awoke it from its "empirical slumbers." But for that situation the specific nature of the social and economic system must be held responsible, and differences in the apprehension of Nature as such cannot, as we see it, explain the differences between Chinese and European conceptions of law.[35]

What is really of interest in analyses like that offered by Northrop, therefore, is the way in which a well-intentioned attempt to take the differentiation of cultures as a serious issue in the study of world politics ends up as an imposition of distinctly Western categories on other cultures. In terms of the devasting polemic offered by Edward Said,[36] it can be seen as part of a long historical project of Orientalizing the Orient. And far from encouraging a headlong leap into an assessment of the possible contributions of non-Western cultures for the construction of alternative world orders--desirable as this is--it provides a warning that the analysis of social and political life is beset with philosophical and methodological difficulties which are merely magnified by a recognition of the historical, economic and political contexts in which our prevailing images of other cultures have been developed.

V. CONCLUSION

Recent thinking about international politics and world order reflects a number of challenges to the global hegemony of Western modernity at the level of both theory and praxis. It draws upon critiques of the processes of underdevelopment, of the exploitation of labor and resources in the Third World by multinational conglomerates, and of the more subtle processes of cultural domination which accompany the blunter forms of political and economic control. It thus depends upon the identification of the central contradictions of the modern world as those which involve North/South, developed/underdeveloped, white/colored relations.

Consequently, it converges upon a major challenge to the universalist aspirations for one united world which have emerged from the utopian or idealist traditions of world order thinking.

Three elements of this challenge seem to be of particular importance: the reassertion of the value of nationalism and autonomy in the face of a tradition of thought which has usually viewed the state as the major problem to be overcome; the emphasis on the importance of "culture" as the central focus of analysis; and the attempt to canvas non-Western cultural traditions as a necessary part of the search for a "just" world order. Each of these elements raise a wide range of questions of the greatest significance for any analysis of modern world politics. And at the level of critique, they each point to limitations in the conventional wisdom of international political theory.

Beyond the level of critique, however, we move quickly to the realm of dilemmas which have come to exercise a large part of modern social and political thought. Modern philosophy, together with those who ruminate on the epistemology of the social sciences, still struggles with the revolt against dualism, or else relapses into yet another return to Kant. Those who attempt to make sense of the empirical transformations of modern world politics can still easily be categorized as Machiavellian realists or Kantian utopians. The most penetrating discussions of culture and ideas are those which attempt to transcend the twin demons of reductionism and idealism, the objectivist illusion and the relativist abyss. And the dialogue of civilizations, perhaps the primary inspiration for those reluctant to equate world politics with Western reason, is increasingly being charged with becoming less of a process of mutual comprehension that a systematic objectification of the Other. An even greater difficulty involves the retreat to nationalism. It is a retreat which can be defended in much the same way as the Romantic and pluralist critique; it is simultaneously an escape from, and a perpetuation of, the problem. For the antinomy of universalism and particularism is no longer one usefully structured on the classically dualist lines of Enlightenment thought. Nor is it one that can be dissolved by the universalization of a parochial pluralism, unless we are to opt for authoritarian modes of global politics. Within the liberal tradition, the antinomy has been resolved by assigning each part to separate spheres: domestic and international, public and private--a resolution which is deeply implicated in the crisis of the modern age.

The foregoing analysis has been concerned to delineate the way in which each of these issues appear if examined in the context of recent critiques of conventional categories in modern social and political theory. At the broadest level, it has suggested that the external challenge to Western hegemonic discourse impinges directly upon a knot of difficulties within this discourse itself. It is the convergence that is important.

To begin with, the possibility is raised that the critique of Western hegemonic discourse inevitably becomes co-opted into the categorial scheme of that discourse. Enlightenment reason, the universalization of interest as the essence of political life, is challenged once again by a pluralist defence of the passions in the form of "authentic" traditional cultures. Like the assertion of authentic subjectivity in the face of an alienating objectivism, the challenge expresses the dilemmas of an epoch. For, while the patronizing assumption that all traditions will become modern may now be fading, the retreat to traditions still appears to be the most obvious means of defence against the internationalization of modernizing values. And such a retreat does not often seem to be a credible defence, if only because the traditions themselves have become frozen in their own inertia or irreparably damaged through rapid confrontations with modern life. Culture as hegemony becomes challenged by culture as mystification. And culture as mystification, as justification for repression in the name of authenticity and autonomy, merely feeds a defence of a universalized modernity based now not on some elevated vision of progress but on a resigned acquiesence in the least undesirable alternative. The new "realism" recalls Max Weber's ambivalence towards the disenchantment of the world, the universalization of instrumental rationality, far more than the ethical dilemmas of Machiavelli or the reductionist imperatives of Hobbes.

More seriously, however, the convergence of the anti-hegemonic critique with the dilemmas of modern social and political theory opens up alternative perspectives on both issues. We move from anti-hegemonic critiques, from a reversed we/they opposition, to recognition of dilemmas confronting the world as a whole. We move from attempts to transcend Western reason merely from within Western reason to recognition that there are other ways of thinking than those enshrined in the reified categories of Western epistemology. Without such convergence, we seem doomed to merely reproduce the contradictions which we seek to escape.

In attempting to situate an important recent tendency within international political theory and world order studies into a broader compass of metatheoretical controversies, this study has inevitably stressed the realm of abstract dilemmas rather than the historical circumstances in which these dilemmas have been generated. It has also sought to point to resolutions of these dilemmas which do not seem to be fruitful rather than those which might be. In a broader context, neither limitation can be justified, and as such the study can be little more than a preliminary exercise. It should be clear, however, that the theme which I regard as being central to all these issues is the imperative to dichotomize, whether in its epistemological subject-object or its imperially useful we/they form. It should also be clear that dichotomies only persist in a static universe: the classical dualisms of Western reason took their most intractable form in the context of the Parmenidean Permanence of mechanics from Galileo to Newton, a context which can also be understood as sociopolitical. But it is at the very least a good wager that we do not live in a static universe.

NOTES

1. Edward W. Said, *Orientalism* (New York: Pantheon, 1978). For a variety of perspectives on this theme, *see* Albert Hourani, *Europe and the Middle East* (London: Macmillan, 1980); V.G. Kiernan, *The Lords of Human Kind: European Attitudes to the Outside World in the Imperial Age* (London: Wiedenfeld and Nicolson, 1969); Ashis Nandy, *The Intimate Enemy: Loss and Recovery of Self Under Colonialism* (New Delhi: Oxford University Press, 1983); Bryan S. Turner, *Marx and the End of Orientalism* (London: George, Allen and Unwin, 1978); and Anouar Abdel-Malek, *Civilizations and Social Theory,* M. Gonzalez, trans., (Albany, N.Y.: State University of New York Press, 1981).

2. Anthony Smith, *The Geopolitics of Information: How Western Culture Dominates the World* (London: Faber and Faber, 1980); *see also,* for example, Herbert I Schiller, *Mass Communications and American Empire* (New York: Augustus M. Kelley, 1969); Schiller, *Communication and Cultural Domination* (White Plains, N.Y.: International Arts and Science Press, 1976); Rita Cruise O'Brien and G. K. Helleiner, "The Political Economy of Information in a Changing International Economic Order," *International Organization* 34:4 (Autumn 1980); Robert Stam and Louise Spence, "Colonialism, Racism and Representation--An Introduction," *Screen* 24:2 (March-April 1983):2-20; and A. Mattelart, *Multinational Corporations and the Control of Culture* (Brighton, Sussex: Harvester Press, 1979).

3. This theme has, of course, become commonplace in the literature on development economics and the political economy of imperialism and dependence. Useful general discussions include S. K. Arora, "Preempted Future? Notes on Theories of Political Development," *Behavioural Sciences and Community Development* 2:2 (September 1968):85-120; Reinhard Bendix, "Tradition and Modernity Reconsidered," *Comparative Studies in Society and History*

9:3 (1967):292-346; Howard J. Wiarda, "The Ethnocentricism of the Social Sciences: Implications for Research and Policy," *Review of Politics* 43:2 (April 1981):163-197; and Carl E. Pletsch, "The Three Worlds, or the Division of Social Scientific Labour, Circa 1950-1975," *Comparative Studies in Society and History,* 23:4 (October 1981):565-590.

4. *See* , for example, Eric R. Wolf, *Europe and the People Without History* (Berkeley: University of California Press, 1982); Talal Asad, ed., *Anthropology and the Colonial Encounter* (London: Ithica Press, 1973); and Asad, "Anthropology and the Analysis of Ideology," *Man* 14:4 (December 1979):607-627. For important recent philosophical discussions of the general problem of cultural relativism in socio-political theory, *see* John Skorupski, *Symbol and Theory* (Cambridge: Cambridge University Press, 1976); Bryan R. Wilson, ed., *Rationality* (Oxford: Basil Blackwell, 1970); Ruth Finnegan and Robin Horton, eds., *Modes of Thought* (London: Faber and Faber, 1973); Ernest Gellner, *Legitimation of Belief* (Cambridge: Cambridge University Press, 1974); and Martin Hollis and Steven Lukes, eds., *Rationality and Relativism* (Oxford: Basil Blackwell, 1982).

5. R.B.J. Walker, *Political Theory and the Transformation of World Politics,* World Order Studies Program, Occasional Paper No. 8 (Princeton, N.J.: Princeton University, Center of International Studies, 1980).

6. I have in mind most particularly Rajni Kothari, "Towards a Just World," *Alternatives* V:1 (June 1979):1-42.

7. Martin Wight, "Why Is There No International Theory?," in Herbert Butterfield and Martin Wight, eds., *Diplomatic Investigations: Essays in the Theory of International Politics* (London: George, Allen and Unwin, 1966), pp. 17-34.

8. E. H. Carr, *The Twenty Years Crisis, 1919-1939,* 2nd ed. (London: Macmillan, 1946).

9. Friedrich Meinecke, *Machiavellianism: The Doctrine of Raison d'Etat and its Place in Modern History* (1924), D. Scott, trans. (London: Routledge & Kegan Paul, 1957); and *Historicism: The Rise of a New Historical Outlook,* J. E. Anderson, trans. (London: Routledge & Kegan Paul, 1972).

10. *See* Hedley Bull, *The Anarchical Society: A Study of Order in World Politics* (London: Macmillan, 1977); Fritz Kratochwil, *International Order and Foreign Policy* (Boulder, Colo.: Westview Press, 1978); and Raymond Cohen *International Politics: Rules of the Game* (London: Longmans, 1981).

11. Stanley Hoffmann, *The State of War* (New York: Praeger, 1965), p. 86. The continuing importance of this dilemma has recently been stressed by Ian Clark, *Reform*

and Resistance in the International Order (Cambridge: Cambridge University Press, 1980).

12. For comments on the contemporary importance of Kant in the analysis of world politics see W. B. Gallie, "Wanted: A Philosophy of International Relations," *Political Studies* 27:3 (September 1979):484-492; and Ian Clark (Note 11), *Reform and Resistance,* pp. 31-54. The real importance of Kant for contemporary thinking in this area lies, I would suggest, precisely in the unresolved tension between universalism and pluralism which is at the heart of the critical philosophy; for useful discussion, *see,* for example, Hans Saner, *Kant's Political Thought,* E. G. Ashton, trans. (Chicago: University of Chicago Press, 1973).

13. Hedley Bull, "International Theory: The Case for a Classical Approach," *World Politics,* (April, 1966); and Morton A. Kaplan, "The New Great Debate: Traditionalism vs Science in International Relations," *World Politics,* (October 1966); both reprinted in Klauss Knorr and James N. Rosenau, eds., *Contending Approaches to International Politics* (Princeton, N.J.: Princeton University press, 1969), pp. 20-38 and pp. 39-61, respectively.

14. Richard J. Bernstein, *The Restructuring of Social and Political Theory* (Philadelphia: University of Pennsylvania Press, 1976). *See also* Richard Rorty, *Philosophy and the Mirror of Nature* (Princeton, N.J.: Princeton University Press, 1979); and Rorty, *Consequences of Pragmatism* (Minneapolis: University of Minnesota Press, 1982).

15. Jonathan Rée, "Philosophy and the History of Philosophy," in Ree et al., eds., *Philosophy and Its Past* (Hassocks, Sussex: Harvester Press, 1978); pp. 3-39. *See also* John Passmore, "The Idea of a History of Philosophy," *History and Theory,* 4 (1965):1-32.

16. For useful discussions of this general theme *see* Patrick Gardiner, "German Philosophy and the Rise of Relativism," *The Monist* 64:2 (April 1981):138-154; Isaiah Berlin, *Vico and Herder* (New York: Viking Press, 1976); Berlin, *Against the Current: Essays in the History of ideas* (New York: Viking Press, 1979); and Albert O. Hirschman, *The Passions and the Interests: Political Arguments for Capitalism Before Its Triumph* (Princeton, N.J.: Princeton University Press, 1977).

17. T. S. Kuhn, *The Structure of Scientific Revolutions* (Chicago: University of Chicago Press, 1962); and Paul Feyerabend, *Against Method: Outline of an Anarchistic Theory of Knowledge* (London: New Left Books, 1975).

18. Charles Taylor, *Hegel* (Cambridge: Cambridge University Press, 1975), p. 542.

19. Raymond Williams, *Marxism and Literature* (Oxford: Oxford University Press, 1977), p. 11. *See also* Williams, *Culture* (London: Fontana, 1981).

Williams, *Marxism and Literature,* p. 114.

21.   *Ibid.*   Cf. Stanley Diamond, "Subversive Art," *Social Research* 49:4 (Winter 1982):854-877.

22.   Antonio Gramsci, *Selections from the Prison Notebooks,* Quintin Hoare and Geoffrey Nowell-Smith, trans. (London: Lawrence and Wishart, 1971).   *See also* Chantal Mouffe, *Gramsci and Marxist Theory* (London: Routledge & Kegan Paul, 1979);   Walter L. Adamson, *Hegemony and Revolution: Antonio Gramsci's Political and Cultural Theory* (Berkeley: University of California Press, 1980); Joseph Femia, *Gramsci's Political Thought: Hegemony, Consciousness and Revolution* (Oxford: Clarendon Press, 1981); and Robert W. Cox, "Gramsci, Hegemony and International Relations: An Essay in Method," *Millenium: Journal of International Studies* 12:2 (Summer 1983):162-175.

23.   Recent contributions to what is becoming a very large literature include Jorge Larrain, *The Concept of Ideology* (London: Hutchinson, 1979); Larrain, *Marxism and Ideology* (London: Macmillan 1983), Rosalind Coward and John Ellis, *Language and Materialism* (London: Routledge & Kegan Paul, 1977); Bhikhu Parekh, *Marx's Theory of Ideology* (London: Croom Helm, 1982); Centre for Contemporary Cultural Studies, *On Ideology* (London: Hutchinson, 1978); and Sakari Hänninen and Leena Paldàn, eds., *Rethinking Ideology* (New York: International General, 1983).

24.   *See* for example, Alfred Schmidt, *History and Structure: An Essay on Hegelian-Marxist and Structuralist Theories of History,* Jeffrey Herf, trans., (Cambridge, Mass.:   M.I.T. Press, 1981); and Anthony Giddens, *Central Problems in Social Theory* (Berkeley and Los Angeles: University of California Press, 1979).

25.   Ernest Gellner, "Concepts and Society," in Wilson, ed., *Rationality,* pp. 28-29.

26.   Gellner, *Legitimation of Belief,* p. 133.

27.   This particular formulation of the issue is borrowed from Chang Tung-Sun, "A Chinese Philosopher's Theory of Knowledge," *Yenching Journal of Social Studies* 1:2 (1939) (Peking), reprinted in Gregory P. Stone and Harvey A. Faberman, eds., *Social Psychology Through Symbolic Interactionism* (Waltham, Mass.:   Ginn-Blaisdell, 1970), pp. 121-140.

28.   Adda B. Bozeman, *Politics and Culture in International History* (Princeton, N.J.:   Princeton University Press, 1960); *see also,* Bozeman, *The Future of Law in a Multi-cultural World* (Princeton, N.J.: Princeton University Press, 1971); and Robert S. Wood, "History, Thought and Images: The Development of International Law and Organization," *Virginia Journal of International Law* 12:1 (December 1971).

29.   Werner Levi, "International law in a Multicultural World," *International Studies Quarterly* 18:4 (December 1974).   More sensitive versions of a

similar position are developed by Hedley Bull, "The Third World and International Society," *Yearbook of World Affairs,* 1979, pp. 15-31, and James Mayall, "International Society and International Theory," in Michael Donelan, ed., *The Reason of States* (London: George, Allen and Unwin, 1978).

30. *See,* for Northrop's philosophy of science, *Science and First Principles* (New York: Macmillan, 1931); for his general theory of knowledge, *The Logic of the Sciences and Humanities* (New York: Macmillan, 1947) and "The Relation Between Naturalistic Scientific Knowledge and Humanistic Intrinsic Values in Western Culture," John E. Smith, ed., *Contemporary American Philosophy,* 2nd series (London: George, Allen and Unwin, 1970), pp. 107-151; and for his philosophical anthropology, *Philosophical Anthropology and Practical Politics* (New York: Macmillan, 1960); *The Meeting of East and West: An Inquiry Concerning World Understanding* (New York: Macmillan, 1952); *The Complexity of Legal and Ethical Experience: Studies in the Methodology of Normative Science* (Boston: Little Brown, 1959); "The Relation Between Eastern and Western Philosophy," in *Radhakrishnan: Comparative Studies in Philosophy Presented in Honour of His Sixtieth Birthday* (London: George, Allen and Unwin, 1951), pp. 352-378; and Northrop and H. H. Livingston, eds., *Cross-Cultural Understanding: Epistemology in Anthropology* (New York: Harper & Row, 1964).

31. Northrop, *The Logic of the Sciences and Humanities,* pp. 32, 62, 119.

32. Northrop, *The Complexity of Legal and Ethical Experience,* pp. 84-85.

33. *See,* for example, Hu Shih, "The Scientific Spirit and Method in Chinese Philosophy," and E. R. Hughes, "Epistemological Methods in Chinese Philosophy," in Charles A. Moore, *The Chinese Mind: Essentials of Chinese Philosophy and Culture* (Honolulu: East-West Center Press, 1967); and Arthur F. Wright "Northrop on the Traditional Culture of the Orient," *Journal of the History of Ideas* 10 (1949):143-149.

Fung Yu-Lan, *A History of Chinese Philosophy,* Derk Bodde, trans. (London: George, Allen and Unwin, 2nd ed., 1952), vol. 1, 3.

35. Joseph Needham, *Science and Civilization in China* (Cambridge: Cambridge University Press, 1954 ff.) vol. 2, 579. For a recent discussion of this issue, which has resulted in an enormous literature, and which involves important alternative traditions generated by Marx and Weber *see,* for example, Bryan S. Turner, *Marx and the End of Orientalism.*

36. Said, *Orientalism.*

CHAPTER 10

On Marxian Thought
and the Problem
of International Relations

R. N. Berki

My argument is that the very existence of
international relations poses a serious, and perhaps
intractable, *problem* for Marxism. This is easy enough to
see on the level of empirical politics, and even on the
level of ideological controversy, but it is a still too
little appreciated issue in the context of a
thoroughgoing theoretical analysis of Marxian thought. I
would like to offer some tentative remarks on this latter
plane. My suggestions are not as conclusive as I would
like them to be, but they may at least raise some
important and topical questions. Briefly, it is my
intention to show that since international relations
presuppose the horizontal division of mankind into
nations or states, and since Marxian thought postulates
the absolute unity of mankind as its ideal, problems
relating to horizontal group diversity are much more
centrally relevant to the Marxian doctrine than it is
usually thought. Not only is there a clear moral
argument in Marxian thought against group diversity as
such, but the very central tenets of Marxism have a
direct, though implicit, reference to the relations
between horizontal groups such as nations. I believe,
further, that these aspects of Marxian thought have been
lost sight of and confused or underemphasized over the
years, partly by Marx and Engels themselves at the very
start, and partly by their political followers, and
(later) academic critics. There are fairly obvious
historical reasons for this gradual process of dilution,
and it is not my intention to play down the importance of
living, political Marxism, the system of thought and
concrete guide to action into which Marx's original ideas
have turned. Nevertheless, it may be of some value to
attempt an analysis of Marxism and international

Reprinted by permission from *World Politics* 24:1, 1971;
copyright © Princeton University Press, 1971.

relations from the standpoint of the original vision, or insight--especially as this has become, in the last few decades, the major preoccupation of commentators on Marx who are tackling other aspects of his thought.

I

To make clear the distinction between the central, though covert, message of Marxian thought, and its one-sided, conventional understanding, I shall begin by referring to an important theoretical work on international relations, K. R. Waltz's *Man, the State and War*.[1] Professor Waltz addresses himself to one of the most pressing problems of international relations, the phenomenon of war. He distinguishes between three sorts of answers that have been given to questions inquiring into the causes of war. The first answer is in terms of human nature; the second is in terms of the internal structure of states; the third focuses on the existence of an international "system" characterized by the absence of legal and political unity and an overriding community of interest. It is the second "image" that interests us here. This postulates, according to Waltz, "that the internal structure of states determines not only the form and use of military force but external behavior generally."[2] He argues further that "Marx and the Marxists represent the fullest development of the second image."[3] The evidence he adduces to show this consists of the well-known and well-worn propositions of historical materialism, supplemented by a consideration of the attitude of some notable Socialists to war and international relations in the period preceding the first World War. On the face of it, on this particular level of abstraction, the pronouncements of Marx, Engels and other prominent theoreticians certainly appear to confirm Waltz's thesis.

The status that overt, conventional Marxism affords to war and international relations is clearly secondary and derivative. The theory starts out from the concept of production which is seen as the basis, and the overall determinant, of social forms and the forms of human consciousness at any time and any place. The historical dynamic of human societies is supplied by contradictions between the smooth development of productive forces and the uneven, angular changes in productive relations. Within the latter, the underlying contradiction appears as a struggle between social groups, classes, which are defined in terms of their relationship to the means of production, ultimately reducible to the division of labor. Classes then, and not nations or states, are the basic units in history, and the struggle between classes, instead of inter-state conflict, occupies the center of attention. In more concrete terms, the Marxian theory

conceives of a definite historical sequence leading
through successive stages of society thus determined by
conflict: Asiatic, ancient, feudal, capitalist, and
finally to socialism (non-antagonistic society still
based on production) and communism (society of plenty).
The "present" for Marx and Engels is capitalist society,
the last historical form of the antagonism between groups
in the productive process. Its basic features are
private property of the means of production in the hands
of the bourgeois class, universal market relations, the
development of machine industry, the vast expansion of
world trade, and the presence of a formally "free"
propertyless group, the proletariat, who maintain
themselves under conditions of exploitation by the sale
of their labor-power. This capitalist society is
historically condemned to a more or less violent death,
occasioned on one level by the secular development of the
forces of production for which at one point its
anarchistic, necessarily expansionist, and profit-based
productive relations appear as "fetters," and on another
level by the conscious political actions of the
proletariat who put an end to the "exploitation of man by
man" and inaugurate socialism.

It already emerges from this rather crude and
simplified summary that, for Marxism, international
relations and conflict inhabit a world at a second remove
from relations and conflicts that are really significant.
Domestic politics itself, together with the political
forms of the class struggle, and all types of ideological
consciousness such as religious beliefs and national
identities, belong to the "superstructure." The modern
sovereign state, the supreme politico-legal authority
over a certain part of the earth's territory and a
certain number of the world's population, is itself the
emanation of the class struggle in its capitalist phase.
Internally, the state's function as the "managing
committee of the ruling class" is to maintain the system
of exploitation; externally, its main preoccupation is to
facilitate the economic expansionism of its own
bourgeoisie. The ceaseless endeavor to expand is itself
made necessary by the position of the bourgeois class in
its own territory, as a class whose power vis-a-vis the
proletariat is maintained, inter alia, by its ability to
enhance its productive potential through the acquisition
of ever larger "markets." This competition for markets
by a self-divided bourgeois class turns from time to time
into open, violent conflict, i.e. war. Thus the whole
paraphernalia of horizontal diversity derive from the one
basic vertical conflict between classes. As Marx puts
the question rhetorically: "Is the whole inner
organization of nations, are all their international
relations anything else than the expression of a
particular division of labour? And must not these change
when the division of labour changes?"[4] Again, "The

relations of different nations among themselves depend upon the extent to which each has developed its productive forces, the division of labour and internal intercourse.[5]

Nations themselves, in Marxian theory, are not absolute, but historical, and hence ephemeral, units. The emergence of nations in Europe is explained as being cotemporaneous with, and engendered by, the appearance of the bourgeoisie as the dominant class. With the further development of the capitalist mode of production, national diversity itself is gradually eroded. Industry destroys "the peculiar individuality of the various nationalities."[6] Also, "the intellectual creations of individual nations become common property. National one-sidedness and narrow-mindedness become more and more impossible, and from the numerous national and local literatures, there arises a world literature."[7] Thus, while on the one hand capitalism retains horizontal divisions (a reflection of the character of the bourgeois class itself on the domestic level) and perpetually engenders international conflict that is liable to turn into armed clashes, on the other hand its expansionist, economically progressive character prepares the world for the final overcoming of national and state divisions, and the establishment of socialism which is necessarily internationalist in character. The proletariat--at any rate as seen by Marx and Engels in the heady atmosphere accompanying the mid-nineteenth century social upheavals--is the first truly international, truly human class, without national ties and allegiances. The *Communist Manifesto* declares optimistically: "The working men have no country. We cannot take from them what they have not got."[8] And so, after the overthrow of capitalism, the victorious proletariat sets about to replace the antagonistic relations of the market with the "conscious organization of production" to the benefit of the producers. The ending of conflict between classes inevitably brings about its elimination in the wider area of international relations. The toil, strife, division, and enmity of today give rise to tomorrow's peace and brotherhood of all the toilers.

II

At this point, however, we encounter a stumbling block, and I again refer to Waltz by way of illustration. Marx and Engels, Waltz contends, are ambiguous as to what they precisely mean by the absolute dependence of international antagonism on domestic strife. The equations and logic at first appear straightforward: war is conflict between states; states are coeval with capitalism; socialism is the negation of capitalism; *ergo,* socialism has no room for the state; *ergo,* socialism knows no war. But the point is that Marx and Engels fail to show, in the first place, that there is an absolute coincidence between capitalism and the state, and second, they fail to demonstrate that the *capitalist* state (with its *internally* antagonistic character) is the only possible form of political authority that still allows *external* diversity; hence the possibility of international conflict even in a hypothetical post-capitalist world. Thus Waltz's question is legitimate: "is it capitalism or states that must be destroyed in order to get peace, or must both be abolished?"[9] The distinction between these two phases, or tasks, is certainly warranted in point of theory. And in the realm of empirical politics it acquires a special relevance as soon as the tasks cease to be remote ones but appear more imminent. Waltz sees the question as assuming special importance later in connection with Marxist revisionism: the attempt to square certain parts of the dogma with a sluggish and recalcitrant political reality. "For Marx the international political problem will wither away only as states disappear. For the revisionists the problem will wither away not as states disappear, but as the separate states become internally more perfect."[10] I do not intend to go into detail on this particular point beyond noting that in my opinion the Marxian ambiguity regarding the disappearance of states is even more impenetrable than Waltz makes allowances for. It seems, further, that the belief that the "internal perfection of states" (that is, their transformation into Socialist communities) is itself a guarantee for the nonrecurrence of international conflict, has not been confined to "revisionists," but is shared by the most radical groups among Marx's followers. I shall have more to say about the latter point below.

As regards Marx's ambiguity, it is essential to see that in orthodox, conventional Marxism, in the mature writings of Marx and Engels, the point is not resolved in an explicit form at all. The problem, to repeat, is whether the disappearance of the "state" after the overthrow of capitalism refers only to its internal character as an agency maintaining oppression and exploitation of one class by another (to expect this, by Marxian standards, is surely most reasonable), or also to its external function, which can be defined as organizing and promoting the interests of a group of people distinguished by their permanent occupation of a certain geographical area. It does not matter, of course, whether now one calls it "state," or "nation," or "community," or the "administration of things" (Engels' renowned phrase from *Anti-Dühring*), as long as what is meant is a plurality of these units. In other words, are socialism and communism envisaged as the completely unified society of the human race or a society where group diversity continues to exist, albeit in a non-antagonistic form?

The Marxian corpus, particularly in Marx's early writings, contains a few references, some explicit, some oblique, especially with application to the ultimate goal of communism, that postulate a complete unity of mankind. But elsewhere Marx and Engels seem to recognize the existence of "nations" as distinguished from "states," and although nations appear in their theory as historical categories, Marx and Engels are aware of their enduring character. Consider, for example the sentence following directly the statement quoted above from the *Manifesto:* "Since the proletariat must first of all acquire political supremacy, must raise itself to be the leading class of the nation, must constitute itself *the* nation, it is, so far, itself national, though not in the bourgeois sense of the word."[11] To begin with, that is, the forces that are supposed to create unity in the future are to become confirmed in their diversity. Engels remarks in a letter to Bebel in 1875: ". . . as soon as it becomes possible to speak of freedom the state as such ceases to exist. We would therefore propose to replace *state* everywhere by 'community' *(Gemeinwesen)."* [12] Note the adverb "everywhere" which indicates a multiplicity of "communities." Or consider the highly significant (and amusing) story related by Marx to Engels about a meeting of Socialists in France, where some radicals were arguing that nations were "antiquated prejudices," to be abolished forthwith. Marx contemptuously calls this "Proudhonized Stirnerism" (anarchistic individualism) and records his rejoinder: "I suggested that by the negation of nationalities he (Lafargue) appeared, quite unconsciously, to understand their absorption into the model French nation."[13] As we shall see, Marx's insight here casts an ominous shadow over the whole career of Marxian thought. The point is that whether or not the ultimate goal is the complete unity of mankind, the separateness of nations is *given,* and as long as this separateness lasts, for instance, in the form of linguistic diversity and separate identities, a demand for unification is tantamount to a demand that small nations be absorbed into, and ruled over by, big ones. Hence, in part, Marx's and Engels' later insistence on "national" self-determination as a goal that is not only compatible with, but essential to, the realization of socialism. Incidentally, the belief in the eventual eclipse of the political state and in the future harmony of "liberated" nations was shared by most representative liberal thinkers of the nineteenth century, including John Bright and Mazzini.

The recognition of national diversity is based on sober, realistic considerations, and it is held not only by Marx and Engels, but by practically all the leading exponents of Marxism. In their attitudes as reflected in their writings and policies, this leads, if not always to

contradictions, to an unresolved tension, a constant
vacillation between two positions. These are a final
goal and ideal in terms of a complete unity of human
society, and an intermediate goal (sometimes turning into
an ideal itself) postulating non-antagonistic diversity
along national lines. This vacillation, as I have said,
is a necessary corollary of the doctrine's coming to
terms with reality, and for this reason it ought to be
viewed with sympathetic understanding. However, the
interesting question is: can Marxiam *afford* this
compromise? Does it make sense, in terms of Marxian
thought, to talk about non-antagonistic diversity? Can
Marxism at all entertain the idea of liberated but
separate nations living peacefully side by side, without
thereby losing its coherence as a philosophy of man and
society? Although conventional interpretations, of which
Waltz's "internal structure of states" model is an
example, usually assume that such an eventuality is in
full accord with the meaning and intention of Marxian
thought, it is at least arguable that the separate
existence of nations, in principle, negates the very
essence of Marx's original ideas. Before plunging into
analysis, however, I propose to survey, very briefly, the
subsequent history of Marxism in relation to the problem
of national diversity.

III

    The rather complicated story of Marxist attitudes to
this question in the intervening hundred-odd years can be
approached by noting two important factors that have
succeeded in modifying its original import. The first is
the intrusion of strategic considerations, by which I
mean the adoption of certain positions as means to an
end, as goals which derive their value from what they are
seen to be promoting. The second is the appearance of
political realism in the wake of success--as a result, in
a sense, of the successful employment of the strategic
considerations themselves. Realism here means the
identification of the original ideals with the viewpoint
and interests of particular countries. The two factors,
of course, the extension and the modification of the
Marxian doctrine, can very rarely be disentangled in
practice. Both have tended to reinforce an attitude that
is increasingly sympathetic to diversity. Although the
ideal of complete unity was never entirely lost, there
has been a growing feeling of pessimism regarding its
realization.
    As a strategic weapon, national self-determination
was considered indispensable by Marx and Engels. They
were living in a Europe dominated objectively by the
repressive regimes of multinational empires, such as
England, Austria, and Russia, and subjectively by the

growing feeling of national identity and, hence, demands for national self-determination. Even though national feelings were thought by Marx and Engels to stem (at least in part) from false consciousness, they were acknowledged to be there and to be giving rise to demands more pressing and more immediate than any desire to overthrow capitalist society. These national feelings had, therefore, to be harnessed to the chariot of socialism. As Engels put it in his 1892 preface to the *Manifesto:* "Without restoring autonomy and unity to each nation it will be impossible to achieve the international union of the proletariat, or the peaceful and intelligent cooperation of these nations toward common aims."[14] Two oppressed nations especially engaged the attention of Marx and Engels: Ireland, on account of its proximity to Marx's and Engels' working locality, England; and Poland, chiefly because of the fact that it was being oppressed by Tsarist Russia, the country they believed (to some extent erroneously) to be the central bastion of European reaction. Irish independence, Marx thought, was necessary to enable not only the Irish, but also the English working class--which itself was participating in the oppression of Ireland through false consciousness--to start on the road towards liberating itself from the capitalist yoke. For the English workers "the *national emancipation of Ireland* is no question of abstract injustice or human sympathy but the first condition of *their own emancipation.*"[15] Engels, in the strategic vein, regards national independence as the means to social revolution. It is the first task to be achieved: "to fight, one must first have the ground, air, light and elbowroom."[16] And, "two nations in Europe have not merely the right but the *duty* to be national before becoming international: the Irish and the Poles."[17]

Even though the character and position of Marxism have changed, the purely strategic aim of using nationalism and national self-determination as weapons with which to fight capitalism again looms conspicuously in our own age. Now it is the United States that is regarded (and this time with more justification) as the mainstay of capitalism in a worldwide context; accordingly, all aspirations to national independence and freedom from the domination of international finance capital receive both verbal and material encouragement from Marxist countries. The process of decolonization as a means to weaken Western capitalism in its dependencies in Asia, Africa, and Latin America has been utilized by Communists to further their own ends ever since the 1920s--not always with success, it should be added. It is also of some interest to note that whereas the Communist espousal of anti-Western nationalism might sometimes ring hollow, as in the case of the Middle East, Communist hostility to nationalism in the service of reaction is both genuine and logically fully consistent with Marxism. Here the most conspicuous examples are Pan-Slavism in the nineteenth century, and Zionism today. At the present age the anti-colonialist slogan is only the major theme in this context. Less noticeable but scarcely less important is the Marxist attempt to use nationalistic feelings, and in particular the fairly widespread anti-American sentiment, to drive wedges between the advanced capitalist countries themselves. Thus the nationalist aspect of Gaullism has been embraced by the French Communist Party, and arguments and slogans couched in patriotic terms now belong to the essential armory of Marxists in Britain, Italy, the Scandinavian countries, and Japan.

It would, however, be a gross mistake to reduce all Marxian arguments favoring national diversity to conscious Machiavellian ruses. The strategic considerations are there at every turn, but policies, at first of Marxist parties and later of Marxist states, have also been modified by what I have called political realism, the gradual process of coming to terms with the given reality of the separate identity of nations. Here the focus is not so much on the masses yet to be redeemed and converted, as on the feelings and consciousness of those who are already members of the Marxist community—either in the spiritual sense, as adherents or sympathizers of Marxist parties, or in the political sense, as inhabitants of Marxist states. Consequently, the dilution of Marxian thought by arguments that accept national diversity tends to become more important the better and the more securely and extensively Marxism is established in the world of politics and power. One can, it seems, put one's finger on this growth of heterogeneity in Marxian thought by reference to five significant landmarks, amounting to traumatic changes in the Marxist consciousness that punctuate the history of Marxism.

The first is the European war of 1914-1918 which effectively shattered the naive illusion of Marxists that the workingmen in capitalist states really "have no country." European social democracy, as is well known, became deeply divided over the issue of patriotism, and the breach, of course, has not been healed by the subsequent theoretical concessions of radical, "internationalist" Marxists to national feelings. The second landmark is the establishment in the 1920s, of "Socialism in one country" by the isolated and bitter Bolsheviks whose earlier expectations of a worldwide proletarian revolution had come to nought.

The third is the conscious resuscitation of Great Russian nationalism by Stalin in the late 1930s, partly as a means of consolidating his own Party, and partly as a weapon to be used in the conflict with Germany in the second World War.[18] Obviously, national feeling is not the kind of skeleton that one can put in and out of a

closet, and postwar European communism, the revolution
exported by the Russian army, was for a considerable time
colored by the ruthlessly russifying nationalistic
policies of the Soviet Union (for instance, the
imposition of "Socialist realism" in the Zhdanov era,
prescribing, as it did, classical Russian literature as
the model for socialist writers). The fourth landmark,
national communism and polycentrism, begins with
Yugoslavia's "own road" in 1948, moves through the
dislocations accompanying de-Stalinization in the fifties
to the virtual independence of Marxist parties in
opposition, with their own separate national roads to
socialism, and on to a schism and bipolarity within the
ruling Marxist camp itself, with the involvement of
national feelings on all sides (Chinese xenophobia being
only the most obvious example). The fifth and most
recent landmark is the dramatic reappearance of romantic
radicalism on the left flank of conventional Marxism,
lurking in the background ever since the rediscovery of
the young Marx, but making its power-political debut only
with the abortive French revolution of 1968. The impact
of this trend on the Marxist attitude to national
diversity would, of course, be as yet well-nigh
impossible to gauge, though the prominence given to anti-
colonial heroes like Guevara and Fanon, and the near-
anarchistic stress on "self-governing communities" would
indicate that this influence again is in favor of
accepting and even idealizing diversity.

Regarding the substantive issues--world unity as a
goal, the nation, self-determination, national feeling,
and so forth--a quick glance through some of the more
interesting pronouncements of Marxists should be
instructive. It reinforces our expectation of an
unresolved tension extant in Marxism since Marx's time.
Uncompromising internationalists, such as Rosa Luxemburg,
might declare: "Speaking of the right of nations to
self-determination, we dispense with the idea of a nation
as a whole."[19] But attitudes of this kind have been the
exception rather than the rule. Lenin, whose position is
sophisticated and who fully grasps the implications of
the "givenness" of national diversity,[20] upholds the
ultimate goal of "the eventual amalgamation of all
nations,"[21] at the same time declaring his support for
"the absolutely direct, unambiguous recognition of the
full right of all the nations to self-determination,"[22]
as well as his belief in the "complete equality of all
nations."[23] Stalin, the original Bolshevik "expert" on
nationality, is even more categorical, both on diversity
and unity: "the right of self-determination means that
only the nation itself has the right to determine its
destiny, that no one has the right *forcibly* to interfere
in the life of the nation."[24] But then, "the question of
the rights of nations is not an isolated, self-sufficient
question; it is a part of the general problem of the

proletarian revolution, subordinate to the whole."[25] He defines his goal as a "single world economic system."[26] For Bukharin, "all peoples constitute a great, single-minded family of work,"[27] and he and Preobrazhensky call for the eradication of national enmities and "for the organization of a single world-wide economic system." They go on to say, "if national prejudice and national greed oppose the internationalization of industry and agriculture, away with them, wherever they may show themselves and under whatever colour they may sail."[28] But again, the 1919 Bolshevik Party Program declares: ". . . it is necessary to abolish all privileges of any national group, to proclaim the fullest equality of all nationalities."[29]

The most recent manifestations of Marxist thinking on these issues show no important changes in outlook, except, perhaps, to the extent that unity now tends to be presented as a goal only dimly visible in a distant, misty future. For example, the new Party Program adopted by the Twenty-second Congress of the CPSU in 1961 (a most significant document in other respects) still sees the eventual establishment of a "world Communist economy regulated by the victorious working people according to one single plan."[30] This, however, is a distant "tendency." In the meantime, the "Socialist world system" is a community consisting of separate, diverse units. "The distinctive features of the relations existing between the countries of the Socialist community are complete equality, mutual respect for independence, and sovereignty and fraternal mutual assistance and co-operation."[31] Amongst them, "a new type of international division of labor is taking shape."[32] But, ". . . the obliteration of national distinctions and especially of language distinctions, is a considerably longer process than the obliteration of class distinctions."[33] The pessimism is echoed in other sources. A *Pravda* editorial in 1963, for example, refers to Lenin's teaching that "national and state differences among peoples and countries would continue for a very long time even after the establishment of proletarian dictatorship on a world-scale."[34] It reaffirms, further, the curious double commitment to unity and diversity: "We are obligated to inculcate in the people a love not only for their own country but for the other Socialist countries as well, so that each person will feel that he is a patriot both of his own country and of the entire world Socialist commonwealth."[35] Mao Tse-Tung, not surprisingly, says: "Can a Communist, who is an internationalist, be at the same time a patriot? We hold that he not only can but must also be one."[36] And, "The principle of integrating internationalism with patriotism is practised in the relations between [the Socialist] countries."[37] Finally, we should note that, even if the Warsaw Pact intervention in Czechoslovakia in August, 1968, is deemed to have been a clear manifestation of "great power imperialism," the point is that it has not been justified in terms of "unity." The significance from our point of view of even the infamous "Brezhnev doctrine" is that it still upholds the principle of national "sovereignty." Brezhnev, in his Warsaw speech of November 12, 1968, is adamant in asserting the "strict respect" for sovereignty held by the Socialist countries, and his tone becomes almost apologetic when he declares: "Naturally an action such as military assistance to a fraternal country designed to avert the threat to the social system is an extraordinary step, dictated by necessity."

IV

Now to return to analysis. The above illustrations from Marxist texts have been cited to demonstrate the continuing vacillation in Marxian thought between world unity and national diversity. The tendency is to afford more and more implicit recognition to the ideal of a non-antagonistic world community consisting of separate national units. It has to be emphasized that this ideal is not fully accepted by orthodox, institutionalized Marxism, and one cannot say with any degree of certainty whether or not it ever will be. My concern in the following is to indicate why I think that the question should receive more attention than it has up to now. First, a case against diversity as such seems to be contained in Marx's early works. Second, I believe that the concepts with which Marx criticized capitalist society can be profitably utilized in a criticism of an international society consisting of separate units, whatever their "internal structure."

The first point to grasp about Marx's thought is that the Marxian analysis of class society, in particular the arguments about the contradictions of capitalism and the exploitative, inherently antagonistic character of the institution of private property, does not originate in a conceptual vacuum, and is not formulated in abstraction from deeper-lying philosophical conceptions. Although Marx--to a large extent correctly--claimed to have demonstrated the further fate and necessary demise of capitalism scientifically in his mature works on economics, his scientific empirical premises rest firmly on his fundamental assumptions about man, human society and human destiny. Questions such as why, after all, private property, or the division of labor, or the extraction of "surplus-value" from the worker are *antagonistic,* do not get a reply in terms of scientific propositions about the law of the falling rate of profit and the like. Those propositions, however, assume this basic antagonism from the very start. The meaning, let alone the validity, of this major basic premise, in turn, is by no means self-evident. If we are interested in knowing the ultimate rationale for asserting this antagonism, we are led on to the *fons et origo* of the Marxian system, Marx's concept of man. A world in which the means of production are owned by one group of people, to the exclusion of another group who belong to the community only negatively, producing its wealth by their labor-power but not sharing its enjoyment, and whose labor-power is therefore sold on the market as though it were a product ("commodity" in Marxian terminology) is an antagonistic world *per se*. The Marxian argument, basically, has nothing to do with living standards, though obviously the palpable misery of the industrial working class in Marx's time served to corroborate and visibly underline Marx's thesis.

A society of this kind is antagonistic, because in it the laboring human being is *alienated*. Marx's early concern wth "alienation" is not only logically compatible with his later doctrine of historical materialism, but it bestows on the latter its ultimate philosophical meaning. Alienation is the basic condition, and from it follow the more directly empirical manifestations of antagonism in society.

To take the more immediately relevant dimension first, alienation is man's severance from other men, his becoming a mere "individual," an impoverished, one-sided being, with his private worries and concerns, private vices and virtues, isolated sorrows and inwardly perceived happiness. Marx pours a lot of scorn over the "solitary" and "calculating" individual, the hero of early liberal philosophy. Now Marx's point is that the self-regarding individual, the inhabitant of capitalist, private-property oriented society, is "alienated," "estranged"; that is, as he sometimes puts it, "not at home." The question is therefore, where, or what, is man's true "home"? Marx's answer, on this plane, is that man's home is the "species." The restricted individual appears "alienated" to Marx only because he conceives of man as essentially a "species-being." Man's true home, his true world is the whole of mankind: alienation makes him something less than he truly is. Ideally, "man is a species-being . . . because he treats himself as the actual living species; because he treats himself as a *universal* and therefore a free being," ". . . a being that treats the species as its own essential being."[38] But conditions in actual society negate this. Here "estranged labour estranges the *species* from man. It turns for him the *life of the species* into a means of individual life."[39] The estrangement from nature thus means "the estrangement of man from man."[40] Man in this society is not merely severed from his essence, not merely a piece apart, but *fragmented,* broken up, crumbled, lost in a chaotic hostile world of antagonistic productive relations. In this world he is no longer a "universal" being, but an "individual" (self-centered) and also "particular" being, with sectional, restricted group-loyalties and allegiances. Marx's vision of communism is the total, final "negation of the negation," the cancellation of man's existence in the capitalist, individualist wilderness. Communism is "the complete return of man to himself as a *social* (i.e. human) being"; ". . . the true resolution of the strife between existence and essence, between objectification and self-confirmation, between freedom and necessity, between the individual and the species." It is "the positive transcendence of all estrangement—that is to say, the return of man from religion, family, state, etc., to his *human*, i.e. *social* mode of existence."[41]

Now, disregarding the philosophical terminology (copied from Feuerback), which Marx undoubtedly shed and even ridiculed in his later development—without, however, moving an inch from the underlying assumptions—the relevant point of all this for our purposes is Marx's dialectic of "universal" and "individual," the single human being and the species. His assertion, translated into simpler language, is that man's ultimate satisfaction is found only in a union with his fellow human beings. What we must concentrate on here, of course, is not the over-debated, trite problematic of "individualism versus collectivism." I think it can be safely assumed that Marx is a certain kind of collectivist—not, of course, in the sense of "subordinating" the individual to society, but on the grounds of believing (rightly or wrongly) that the individual is a *social* being, i.e., a social being in and for a genuinely human, that is, unalienated, society. Our concern is with the *extent* of the collective unit—with the precise limits, for Marx, of this ideal "society." In this respect Marx's emphatic assertion of the essential "oneness" of man and his species, and his corresponding total silence (in this context) on lesser, intervening collectives such as the nation, the region, the race, and so forth, are instructive—though not, of course, conclusive. Marx's attention is obviously centered on vertical fragmentation and not on horizontal diversity. His condemnation of vertical divisions and group-loyalties in society is total and unambiguous. (The oft-quoted Marxian call for a "proletarian class-consciousness" might mislead us here. In truth it is, as it were, a strategic device intended to bring about the abolition of all classes in society). Does Marx, however, feel equally strongly about national and state divisions? Or, alternatively, can anything be inferred from his earlier theoretical conceptions in this respect?

On the first count, evidence is only indirect. Marx and Engels, like everybody else, were aware of existing differences between nations and races, and freely employed these differential notions in their correspondence and other writings in a lighter vein--speaking, for example, about the difference between English and French materialism,[42] the undesirable qualities of Jews and Slavs, and the superiority of German philosophy. I think, however, that it is easy to show that insofar as these criticisms are meant seriously by Marx and Engels, they derive their force from an association of ideas, i.e., Jews are identified with the spirit of capitalism, Slavs with political reaction, and German philosophy with the dawn of proletarian consciousness. On the whole, Marx and Engels are emphatic in holding that "national narrow-mindedness is everywhere repellent."[43] Further, Marx holds that "the egotism of the nation is the natural egotism of the general state system. . . . The supreme being is the higher confirmation of the general state system, that is, again the nation. Nevertheless, the supreme being is supposed to curb the egotism of the nation, that is, of the general state system."[44] Statements of this kind (others occur in Marx's early writings devoted to a critique of Hegel) can, with some legitimate attempts at projection, be construed to suggest that Marx, in truth, is in possession of a higher, more refined conception regarding international society than the view Waltz attributes to him. Marx's connecting of the "nation" with the "state system" in this way indicates that his thought in reality approximates Waltz's "third image." At the least, his pronouncements show a strong dislike of national diversity *per se*.

On a deeper level, the Marxian critique of the capitalist state, put forward most forcefully in his early polemics with Bauer over Jewish emancipation, is revealing. The overt context--political society in the bourgeois era--is of course a restricted one, but this restriction is not such as to make it impossible for Marx's arguments to be extended. On the contrary, an extension to cover the whole world of bourgeois political societies is demanded by the thrust of the Marxian critique. Marx's point here concerns Bauer's confusion of "political emancipation and universal human emancipation."[45] Political emancipation, of course, is the great achievement of the bourgeoisie, and in the bourgeois state all are "citizens," free and equal before the law. "*Political* emancipation certainly represents a great progress. It is not, indeed, the final form of human emancipation, but it is the final form of human emancipation *within* the framework of the prevailing social order."[46] What is the nature of bourgeois freedom? It is, in the first place, the freedom of the impoverished restricted individual. This "liberty as a right of man is not founded upon the relations between man and man, but rather upon the separation of man from man."[47] Also, this freedom is the freedom of reified entities, such as religion, property, and the state, these being opposed to the interest of man as a species-being. The bourgeois state provides freedom of religion, but Marx wishes for freedom from religion. The fact that in the modern secular state political emancipation could go side by side with the continuing practice of Judaism, with continuing particular group-loyalties within the community shows that "*political emancipation* itself is not *human* emancipation."[48]

I want to suggest that here we should pay attention to the wider implications of Marx's onslaught on bourgeois society. The Marxian distinction between "political" and "human emancipation" has an all-important horizontal dimension. The "state" represents not merely class divisions, but also national divisions; the bourgeois "citizen" is separated not merely from his fellow-citizens, but also, and even more, from the citizens of other states; the "prevailing social order" refers not merely to capitalism, but, over and above that, to the all-round separation and division between the peoples that alone make capitalism possible. Horizontal separation is not a sufficient, but certainly a necessary condition of the bourgeois order of society, the latter being, in a sense, a minute replica of the former. Moreover, I would like to suggest that the Marxian vision of man as a species-being is so advanced and so radical that in comparison even such modern ideals as "internationalism" and "cosmopolitanism" appear timid and inadequate. For the internationalist, nations still count as real entities. The cosmopolitan, though rising above national distinctions, is still a "citizen," a separate individual, and thus alienated. For Marx, however, in the last analysis all group-identities issue from reifications. All these lesser entities--the state, the nation, the tribe, the family, and even the class--stand between "man" and the "species." Patriotism of any kind, therefore, will appear as a particular form of alienation.

V

These considerations, of course, only show that in Marx there is a strong suspicion attached to any kind of diversity, and that, for Marx's original humanism, separation and, *a fortiori*, political or national separation, appear abhorrent. However, the aforementioned early Marxian position still leaves open the question whether horizontal diversities are necessarily antagonistic--in theoretical terms, as opposed to moral ones. Now I do not think that such a universal necessity is postulated in Marx's doctrine, early or mature. It is, however, possible to show that the necessity of horizontal antagonism *in certain circumstances* can be inferred from the main propositions of Marxism. To see this we have to go back to "alienation."

The more important sense of alienation is that it is the severance of laboring man from nature. It means that man is no longer living in harmony with nature, his own "essence," but is leading a falsified, distorted, estranged "animal existence," prostituting his creative energy in working for a price, a wage, a mere shadow of his full potentialities. This aspect of alienation signifies the exclusion of the worker from what ought to be his inalienable possession, namely inanimate nature which is the necessary milieu of his life activity, labor. Nature is indispensable to labor's fulfilment. The worker's exclusion from nature does not mean that nature is now independent or rules over the worker --though sometimes Marx's words suggest that this is the case. In truth, the alienation of the worker from nature means that nature is now owned by another man, in this case the capitalist. "The relationship of the worker to labour engenders the relation to it of the capitalist. . . . *Private property* is thus the product, the result, the necessary consequence, of *alienated labour,* of the external relation of the worker to nature and to himself."[49]

Private property thus is something more than the capitalist's basis of domination over the worker, although it is this latter dimension that receives special emphasis in Marx's later works. It reflects, as we have seen, man's dehumanization, his severance from his genuine environment. The point, however, should be grasped concretely, not in relation to any abstract transcendental notion of "man." Marx does not base his denunciation of alienation and private property on any conception of "natural right," in terms of which man, as man, would be seen to have a categorical claim to nature. In the first place, man lives in a community, and thus deprivation and exclusion are measured in terms of the community's aggregate potentialities. The ideal is human equality towards nature, a community where nature's random distribution of resources is cancelled out by the conscious organization of production. Second, with reference to more advanced societies, the Marxian emphasis is on the *worker* who produces for his society, and who, most importantly, does this in association with his fellows. Thus the social aspect of private property appears as usurpation, the exclusion of precisely those who are indispensable for the creation of property in the first place. In other words, private property expresses the fundamental *asymmetry* of social relations in societies where it is found: wealth is created by the "associated producers," the whole of the productive community, and yet it is the effective possession of a restricted group who constitute merely a part of that society. For our purposes it is immaterial whether this

restricted group of property owners dominate through the
ownership of land, or capital, or military power; what is
crucial is that they are always merely a part of the
whole. The basic contradiction of such a society,
therefore, is not between two classes appearing side by
side, but between a totality (society organized for
production) and an abstracted, elevated section of that
same totality (i.e., the owners of the means of
production). In Marx's economic theory all this is
expounded in detail, with the employment of sophisticated
tools of analysis, like the Labor Theory of Value. I
cannot, of course, go into this, but I can try to analyze
the notion of private property further, in a direction
relevant to our concerns.

It seems evident to me that although Marx's emphasis
is on domestic societies where the antagonism of private
property appears in the form of enmity between classes,
there are compelling reasons why his analysis ought to be
extended to cover a wider area where, in certain
circumstances, it will be seen that the *same* antagonism
that results in vertical conflict within a society now
appears as a horizontal conflict among societies. Only
two shifts in the theory are needed, and these are merely
clarifications of doctrine and not alterations of
substance. In the first place, the basic unit should now
be the "whole," meaning not a particular "nation," or
"community," or "society," but a *whole world* of
societies, where these lesser groups live side by side
and are aware of the existence of one another. This
"world" is still not necessarily coterminous with the
objective category, the human race, though in the modern
age the two would be seen to coincide--indeed, this is
one of the essential traits of modernity.

The second and more important clarification concerns
the concept "private," especially as understood in the
term "private property." I think this term, in its
Marxian usage, should be understood to mean "part of a
whole." It refers not to an entity, but to a *position* in
society. "Private property" thus may mean property owned
by an individual, but it may also mean property owned by
a group--as long as this group is less extensive than the
community where the property owned by it has its effect.
Capitalism does not cease to be capitalism when the
individual entrepreneur is replaced by the joint stock
company. "Private," to put it another way, refers not so
much to the nature of the entity that owns, but to the
fact that it is an entity, a unit whose ownership of
nature (in the form of resources or the product of labor)
signifies the exclusion of others from this ownership.
The "internal structure" of this ownership is not only
immaterial from the point of view of an analysis of its
wider, social significance, but, as Marx insists, it is
the social position of this owner, as owner, that
determines its internal characteristics. A capitalist

might be a "good man" in some vague psychological sense; to the extent that he is a capitalist, an owner of property, he is necessarily an exploiter. In principle, the same applies in the case of any other owner, of whatever size or other superficial characteristics.

VI

Thus it is possible to erect models, in strict adherence to the substantive tenets of Marxism, where we have a "world" of several horizontal groups, where the internal composition of these groups shows no trace of private property and consequently no antagonism between owners and workers, but where there is antagonism nevertheless among the groups themselves, and where this horizontal antagonism can be shown to derive from the existence of "private property" in our extended sense. Such a simple model, as a matter of fact, is contained in an embryonic form in one of the seminal works of Marxism, Engels' *Origin of the Family, Private Property and the State*.[50] In this work it is interesting to see how the basic contradiction is played out between an ideal seen exclusively in terms of a domestic situation and an analysis in terms of a total world community. Engels' concern is with putting a Marxian gloss on the anthropological theories of Lewis Morgan, whose *Ancient Society* was published in 1877. We can disregard here the more problematic aspects of the original theory of Morgan as well as Engels' interpretation. The significant point is this. Engels stresses the fact that, in prehistoric society, property was held in common by the "gentes," matriarchal tribal groups. The absence of private property there meant, indeed, the absence of antagonism within these groups. Engels' tone in describing the quality of life in the gentes is bordering on plain adulation.[51] "And this gentile constitution is wonderful in all its childlike simplicity. Everything runs smoothly without soldiers, gendarmes or police: without nobles, kings, governors, prefects or judges; without prisons; without trials. All quarrels and disputes are settled by the whole body of those concerned." "There can be no poor and needy--the communistic household and the gens know their obligations towards the aged, the sick and those disabled in war. All are free and equal--including the women."[52]

A blueprint for the Marxian future? Perhaps, *mutatis mutandis*. It is, at any rate, instructive to see how this idealized picture of the happy, peaceful character of human relations in the "communistic" gentile world is dealt a fatal blow as soon as attention is focused on the nature of *intergroup* relations found in this world. Engels, having devoted a few pages to unqualified praise for the gentes, now admits that "this is one side of the picture." "Where no treaty of peace existed, war raged between tribe and tribe; and war was waged with the cruelty that distinguished man from all animals."[53] ". . . war was as old as the simultaneous existence alongside each other of several groups of communities."[54] And what was the cause of warfare? None other than the same old Marxian explanation used to account for all kinds of antagonism: "The wealth of their neighbours excited the greed of the peoples who began to regard the acquisition of wealth as one of the main purposes in life."[55]

Obviously, such a simple model cannot be directly applied to modern society, and certainly not in terms of the Marxian doctrine for which the unilinear development of human history is a fundamental truth. On a more concrete level, it would be absurd to attempt to transfer the ignorance, barbarity, and primitive living conditions of the prehistoric world to the civilized human community of the capitalist and post-capitalist stages of development. However, it is by no means the case that all the secular differences between a gentile world and a world of separate nations point in the same direction. Certain changes, such as the growth of culture and the emergence of a common human consciousness, might indicate that, in the latter case, "greed" will not invariably lead to the cruelty of "perpetual warfare."[56] But these, we could say, are changes involving merely the subjective side of human life, and, in terms of Marxism, what should count is the objective basis. And on this level the changes might show the presence of factors leading to the increase of antagonism, not its abatement. In the gentile world the gentes lived "side by side." In the modern world nations live not only side by side, but in an *integrated* community, where the requirements of livelihood of the separate units have created universal economic interdependence. Here it is essential to see that Marx unequivocally welcomes this interdependence, and his ideal of socialism is the very opposite of the romantic-anarchistic vision of autarchic "self-governing communities" replacing the world economy of capitalism. In such an integrated world the random distribution of natural resources does not merely lead to the development of differentials in living standards, wealth, armed strength, and, in turn, to warfare and ultimately relations of domination among the separate units--as was the case, *ex hypothesi,* in the primitive prehistoric world. Economic interdependence means that in such a world the differentials are augmented and aggravated by relations of *production.* Here, therefore, these relations of domination also reflect the exploitation, by the owners of the means of production, of those who have, in the last resort, nothing but their labor-power to sell. The conclusion appears unavoidable: an economically disintegrated world still consisting of separate nations is, whatever the internal structure of these nations, a *capitalist world*.

How, then, should a consistent Marxist look upon "nations"? While analogical reasoning has its rather obvious dangers, and while the Marxian analysis of capitalism can obviously not be extended indefinitely, there are certain phenomena, especially in modern images of the nation, that ought to be taken into account. Here I am referring again to some of the concepts used conspicuously in present-day Marxist utterances on the subject of international relations. On closer analysis these concepts, e.g., "sovereignty," "equality of nations," "fraternal assistance," "international division of labor," reveal themselves to be notions uncannily reminiscent of the terms well known from Marx's critique of capitalism.

Take "sovereignty." In modern useage, this concept has come to signify the nation's absolute supremacy to conduct its relations, external and internal, according to its own will and without any obligation to a higher, more comprehensive community. Most significantly, it refers also to the nation's unlimited right to use and dispose of its material wealth, natural resources, scientific know-how, skill, manpower, and so forth. It confirms, in other words, the position of the nation as *owner*--owner of property which, in the context of a community of nations, appears as "private property" pure and simple. In Marx's words, "the right of property is . . . the right to enjoy one's fortune and to dispose of it as one will; without regard for other men and independently of society. It is the right of self-interest."[57] Does not the "fortune" of nations, in the shape of fertile soil, mineral wealth, access to the seas, as well as a higher state of productive development, belong essentially to the same category? Then, take the supposed "equality" of nations. Nations, whichever way one looks at them, are much less "equal" than individuals, and Marx, for one, certainly did not commit the fallacy of taking unequal individuals to be equals. He accepted human inequality as a fact (naming the division of labor as the cause),[58] and his ideal was the progressive equalization of human beings. But whereas it makes sense to envisage the equalization of individuals, nations cannot be subjected to the same process. Individuals can be defined in terms of their potentialities and it can be held that they are all inherently equal in respect of these potentialities, but nations, as inert, immobile, earth-bound entities, can only be defined in terms of their assets, their existing possessions.[59] There may be a thoroughly egalitarian ideal of "man." Such an ideal applied to the "nation" would be a palpable absurdity.

Capitalist society, for Marx, is a society inhabited by "sovereign" property owners and formally "equal" partners in the exchange relationship, where the owner's capital is exchanged for the worker's labor-power. The situation is essentially the same in a "Socialist" community where nations are sovereign and assumed equal, and where their economic relations are conducted with a "strict respect" for their sovereignty. I am not denying that "Socialist cooperation" and the "new Socialist division of labor" might not be accepted as higher and more humane than the purely competitive, anarchistic relations among capitalist states. But, again, the relevant comparison here is not between two types of international relations, but between relations within a confined group, and relations among the groups themselves. It appears to me that the "fraternal assistance" and "mutual aid" allegedly informing the relations among Socialist states do not essentially change the character of these relations, but leave them, in Marxian terms, fairly and squarely at the level of typical capitalist relations. After all, capitalism for Marx is not literally the law of the jungle, but an "orderly" society with universal laws, rules for conduct, a more or less genuine regard for the (alienated) "person," and even organized welfare services, either by the state or by private charity. Such features of a capitalist society, of course, do not fundamentally alter its essence, the raison d'etre for the antagonism contained in it, viz., the institution of private property. Likewise, genuinely friendly understanding among Socialist countries, treaties like the COMECON agreement, can certainly mollify (like progressive taxation in capitalist countries) the antagonism created by the differences of existing and potential wealth, but they cannot eradicate it--short of the abolition of its mainstay, the sovereignty of nations. It makes no difference that Socialist nations are all "fraternal" and concerned "with the vital interests and tasks of the harmonious and all-round development of all Socialist states."[60] The point is that nations *cannot help but be* self-regarding, as long s their position is that of owners of property in a wider community characterized by economic interdependence.

VII

In this light, then, it affords some amusement to consider a few of the more explicit pronouncements of heretical or reformist Marxists on this vital issue. The unresolved tension between "sovereignty" and a "world economic system," between "patriotism" and "internationalism," is apparent even in the case of such mainstream figures of Marxism as Lenin, Stalin, Mao, and Brezhnev. There are, however, also new departures, and while we may with good reason regard these as desirable, in accordance with the requirements of peace and stability, and based upon a better recognition of the nature of human society, it would be sophistical to regard them as "Marxist" departures, whatever sense of Marxism we have in mind. Edvard Kardelj, for example, realistically perceives that there are contradictions specific to socialism, one of these being "the necessity for relationships between one Socialist country and another to be founded on interstate relationships, which makes possible tendencies towards a desire to dominate others, to national egoism and like phenomena."[61] If what Kardelj says is true, I submit socialism should be redefined as the "highest stage of capitalism." (This redefinition would, as a matter of fact, also be warranted on the basis of other features of "socialism," irrelevant in the present context. And such a redefinition, of course, does not imply a pejorative view of socialism.) Alexander Dubcek, in the ill-fated 1968 Action Program of the Czechoslovak Communist Party, declares that his country's foreign policy "will continue, on the basis of mutual respect, to intensify sovereignty and equality, and international solidarity."[62] The intensification of sovereignty, one may say, certainly does not lead to the original Marxian goal, whatever else it may lead to. Finally, Milovan Djilas, talking about Yugoslavia, states: "There is no equality among nationalities without human freedom, or without the genuine right of each national community to secesssion, the right to a *self-contained economy*."[63] In emphasizing the need for a "self-contained economy," Djilas might be said to be drawing a logical conclusion from given facts. But this ideal, of course, is directly opposed to the vision of Marx.

Now let me address myself to the vital question: is the problem presented by the separate existence of nations such that Marxism, as a *theory* of man and society, can extricate itself from it in the foreseeable future? I would tend to answer in the negative. The dilemma certainly appears inescapable. In practice and in propaganda it might be obscured with greater or lesser temporary success, but it is bound to reassert itself continually for a long time to come. One horn of the dilemma is provided by the necessarily capitalistic, antagonistic character of a world community that consists of separate units. The centripetal pull of radically centralist Marxist aspirations, therefore, certainly appears legitimate in terms of the ultimate ideal postulated by the Marxian doctrine. But is centralization the right answer? Would the abolition of national sovereignty, the replacement of, say, COMECON by centralized, fully supranational planning by a socialist community really achieve complete unity? And would this unity be desirable, in terms of the very same Marxian ideal? Here we again meet a stubborn obstacle that was noticed a long time ago by Marx himself, viz., the *given fact* of separate nations. This is the other horn of the dilemma. As long as separate national identities exist, unity inevitably means hegemony. As is being recognized with increasing openness by Soviet spokesmen, national differences are more enduring than class distinctions (and can we really see the end of class distinctions yet?). My conclusion, then, must be presented in this disjunctive form: the Marxian ideal of socialism appears either in the shape of hegemony, as the domination of strong nations over weak ones; in this case it is no longer tinged with the features of capitalism, but neither is it the realization of a higher human freedom. Or, it appears in the shape of a community of independent nations, in which case it may come to represent freedom and progress over capitalism proper, but remains a system still visibly bearing the birthmarks of capitalism.

NOTES

1.   Kenneth R. Waltz, *Man, the State and War* (New York, 1954).
2.   *Ibid.,* p. 63.
3.   *Ibid.*
4.   Letter to P. V. Annenkov, December 28, 1846. Reprinted in Karl Marx, *The Poverty of Philosophy* (Moscow n.d.), 174.
5.   *Ibid.,* Karl Marx and Friedrich Engels, *The German Ideology,* trans. by R. Pascal (New York 1947), 8.
6.   *Ibid.,* 57.
7.   Marx and Engels, *Communist Manifesto* (Moscow n.d.), 49.
8.   *Ibid.,* 76.
9.   Waltz (n. 1), 127.
10.   *Ibid.,* 155.
11.   *Communist Manifesto* (n. 7), 76; emphasis in original.
12.   Reprinted in Marx, *Critique of the Gotha Programme* (Moscow n.d.), 42; emphasis in original.
13.   Marx to Engels, June 20, 1866, in Marx and Engels, *Correspondence 1846-1895* (London 1934), 208. Parts of the letter are quoted with approval by Lenin, who also supplies his own paraphrasis. *See* V. I. Lenin, "On the Right of Nations to Self-determination," *Selected Works* (Moscow 1935), IV, 275.
14.   *Communist Manifesto* (n. 7), 39.
15.   *Correspondence* (n. 13), 290; emphasis in original.
16.   Karl Kautsky, *Aus der Fruhzeit des Marxismus. Engels Briefwechsel mit Kautsky* (Prague 1935), 68.
17.   *Ibid.,* 69; emphasis in original.
18.   The extent of the change from internationalism to nationalism has really been striking. Stalin, who in

1905 rejoiced in the defeat of the Tsarist armies in the Russo-Japanese War, in 1945 claimed that Soviet victory over Japan wiped out the "dark stain" of defeat by Tsarist Russia. *See* E. R. Goodman, *The Soviet Design for a World State* (New York 1960), 92. For further interesting details *see* a recent study of changes in Soviet historiography, Lowell Tillet, *The Great Friendship* (Chapel Hill 1969), esp. chap. 4.

19. In her untranslated Polish article, "The question of nationality and autonomy," quoted in J. P. Nettl, *Rosa Luxemburg,* abridged edition (London 1969), 507.

20. Cf. Marx and Engels, *Correspondence* (n. 13).

21. Lenin, *Marx, Engels, Marxism* (Moscow 1965), 284.

22. "On the Right of Nations to Self-determination" (n. 13), 271.

23. *Ibid.,* 293.

24. Iosif V. Stalin, *Marxism and the National and Colonial Question* (Moscow 1935), 18; emphasis in original.

25. Stalin, *Problems of Leninism* (Moscow 1943), 52.

26. *Ibid.,* 56.

27. Quoted from Nikolay Bukharin, *Das Programm der Kommunisten,* in Theodore Denno, *The Communist Millennium: the Soviet View* (The Hague 1964), 66.

28. N. Bukharin and E. Preobrazhensky, *The ABC of Communism* (London 1969; first ed. 1921), 244.

29. *See* Jan F. Triska, ed., *Soviet Communism: Programs and Rules* (San Francisco 1962), 138.

30. *The New Soviet Society. Final Text of the Program of the CPSU, July 1961. Adopted by the 22nd Congress* (New York 1962), 238.

31. *Ibid.,* 49.

32. *Ibid.,* 52.

33. *Ibid.,* 193.

34. *See* Alexander Dallin, ed., *Diversity in International Communism; A Documentary Record 1961-1963* (New York 1963), 770.

35. *Ibid.,* 779.

36. Mao Tse-Tung, *Selected Works* (London 1958), II, 201.

37. Speech, November 1957. In *Quotations from Chairman Mao Tse-Tung* (Peking 1966), 178.

38. Marx, *Economic-Philosophic Manuscripts 1844* (Moscow 1961), 74, 75; emphasis in original.

39. *Ibid.,* 77; emphasis in original.

40. *Ibid.*

41. *Ibid.,* 192-193; emphasis in original.

42. Cf., ". . . the difference between French and English materialism follows from the difference between the two nations. The French imparted to English materialism wit, flesh and blood eloquence. They gave it the temperament and grace that it lacked. They civilized

it." Marx and Engels, *The Holy Family* (Moscow n.d.), 174.

43. *German Ideology* (n. 5), 99.

44. *Holy Family* (n. 42), 161.

45. "On the Jewish Question," reprinted in Marx, *Early Writings,* trans. and ed. by T. B. Bottomore (London 1963), 8.

46. *Ibid.,* 15; emphasis in original.

47. *Ibid.,* 25.

48. *Ibid.,* 21; emphasis in original

49. *Economic-Philosophic Manuscripts* (n. 38), 80; emphasis in original.

50. Engels, *The Origin of the Family, Private Property and the State* (Moscow n.d.)

51. It is true that Marx's own pronouncements on primitive society are not tinged with the same kind of idealization. Indeed, Marx seems to maintain, in his scarce references to the subject (e.g., in *Grundrisse der Kritik der politischen Okonomie),* that "Asiatic" society was also antagonistic. However, I don't think that there is evidence to show that "until his death Marx upheld the Asiatic concept" [K. A. Wittfogel, *Oriental Depotism* (New Haven 1957), 373]. Marx's remarks were written in the 1860s whereas Morgan's *Ancient Society* appeared in 1877. Engels claims in the preface to *Origin of the Family* that he is executing Marx's "behest."

52. *Origin of the Family* (n. 50), 159.

53. *Ibid.,* 161.

54. *Ibid.,* 249.

55. *Ibid.,* 270.

56. *Ibid.,* 154.

57. "On the Jewish Question" (n. 45), 25.

58. Cf., "In principle, a porter differs less from a philosopher than a mastiff from a greyhound. It is the division of labour which has set a gulf between them." *Poverty of Philosophy* (n. 4), 123.

59. I am adapting here C. B. Macpherson's insightful comparison of the individualist and marxist conceptions of human nature. *See* his "The Maximization of Democracy," in Peter Laslett and W. G. Runciman, eds., *Philosophy, Politics and Society,* Third Series (Oxford 1967).

60. The words of the Polish Prime Minister, Jaroszewicz, expounding the "Fundamental Principles of International Socialist Division of Labour," in the course of the meeting of COMECON, Warsaw, June 1961.

61. Edvard Kardelj, *Socialism and War: A Survey of Chinese Criticism of the Policy of Co-existence* (London 1961), 189.

62. Reprinted in H. Lunghi and P. Ello, *Dubcek's Blueprint for Freedom* (London 1969), 207.

63. Milovan Djilas, *The Unperfect Society* (London 1969), 153; emphasis in original.

CHAPTER 11

The Discourse
of World Order

Mark Blasius

In spite of a rhetorical resurgence of statism in the recent literature on world politics, the theme of "world order" has become an important descriptive and prescriptive category of contemporary political life. It has been introduced into the rubric of laws and institutions, into the programs of political movements, and into the more reflective literature of political theory. By analysing how issues of daily life--of identity and solidarity, of techniques of governance, of the status of knowledge, of historical "consciousness"--became identified as "world order issues," we are able to see *how* a politics is constituted. This is not to address the abstract and transhistorical question of "what is politics," but to look for what actually happens in politics, what happens when something becomes identified as political and, in this case, as something that is constitutive of world order politics.

This paper is concerned to develop a preliminary sketch of what it is we speak about when we speak of world order, and of how this issue is introduced into the realm of politics, thereby effecting what politics is as both discourse and practice--in Michel Foucault's terminology, a discursive practice.[1]

The sense of discourse that I have in mind here hinges on a theoretical assumption about the importance of language in social life. Hans-Georg Gadamer once drew attention to it when discussing the crucial role that language would play in relation to the concept of world order. For Gadamer, language creates a world and reproduces it from one generation to the next. "As a language is learned, it creates a view of the world which conforms to the character of the speech conventions that

----

Written under the auspices of the Center of International Studies, Princeton University.

have been established in the language. A thing is defined by the words one uses."[2] Furthermore, while admitting that "it is not certain that occidental civilization will proceed without resistance to displace and suffocate all other forms of order," he goes on to discuss the potential development of a universal language in relation to the scientific mastering of the problems of a global order:

> The creation of a technically uniform civilized man, who acquires the use of a correspondingly uniform language . . . would certainly simplify the ideal of a scientific administration. But the relevant question is precisely whether such an ideal is desirable. Perhaps developments in linguistics can provide us with an insight into how the leveling process will work itself out in our civilization. The system of sign notation, which both requires the services of a technical apparatus and makes it possible, develops a dialectic all its own. It ceases to be simply a means for the attainment of technical ends, since it excludes the data which the apparatus does not transmit. The perfect functioning of an international language of discourse is subject to the limitations imposed by the information to be communicated.

He also suggests that the development of the language of science, and especially the human sciences as they pertain to a science of administration, circumvents the need to "invent" a future world language (presumably like Esperanto), and that this development would incorporate all living languages like a translation machine and would guarantee uniform intelligibility, thereby eliminating "all imprecision and ambiguity in inter-human understanding." He continues:

> This is all possible and perhaps quite near. But here again it might be unavoidable that the universal means would become universal ends. Therefore, we would not have acquired a means to say and communicate everything imaginable; we would, however, have obtained a means--and we are on the way to achieving it--which would ensure that only the data assimilated in the programming [of the metaphoric translation machine] would be communicated or even thought.

Language, therefore, exercises its own controls on cognition and even experience. A universal language, like the discourse of social administration in its relation to a global administrative order, would act as a system of exclusion, defining what constitutes objects for cognition and experience and how their "truth" is to be obtained and by whom, who may speak, under what conditions, and so on. Finally, Gadamer warns prophetically of the manipulation of language:

> The forbidding possibility of speech control, which has evolved with the growth of modern mass media, expresses clearly how the dialectic of such means and ends operates. In our own day this dilemma is reflected in the confrontation of the cold war antagonists: What in one part of the world is called democracy and freedom appears only as a convention of speech which in the other part of the world is interpreted as a device for mass manipulation and domestication. But that demonstrates only the incompleteness of the system. The manipulation of language has permeated everything and has become an end in itself. In the process it has concealed itself and passes unnoticed.

Here Gadamer hints at the historical evolution of a discurse of world order, albeit narrowly conceived as the discourse of social administration in a world that has become ideologically unified. However, one does not have to presuppose an end to a certain kind of ideological conflict to comprehend the possibility of a seemingly "trans-ideological" discourse. Therefore, the sense of discourse that is employed in this paper with respect to world order is somewhat broader in its character *as discourse*, (i.e., it is not merely verbal language). It is also qualitatively different, in that it is not merely "scientific" discourse (although it employs science, especially the human or social sciences) in its operation. The discourse that I think is most relevant to the concept of world order can be described more as a language of political experience. It not only organizes our understanding of daily life, that is, our understanding of the human condition and its relation to the way in which our society is ordered, but sets definite limits upon what we can do, because it is discourse itself that defines subjective experience and ensures that only a certain kind of communication can take place between individuals and groups.

Discourse, like language, is a mode of human communication and, also like language, it can have verbal and nonverbal components. What distinguishes discourse, however (and this, I think, describes more precisely what Gadamer means when he speaks of the power of language), is that it is a second-order language rooted not merely in a set of linguistic conventions (grammatical, phonological, etc.), but in a set of inter-subjective common meanings that correspond to a set of common social practices. The existence of a discourse implies, to use Charles Taylor's phrase, a "common reference world" of meanings, institutions, and practices of which discourse is constitutive.[3]   Indeed, as recent French theorists Michel Foucault, Jacques Donzelot, Jacques Lacan, and others have suggested, discourse exercises a kind of "disciplining" function with respect to cognition and experience.   Human communication produces discourses "about" objects that are integrally related to the structure of the society (its child-rearing practices, sexual behavior, the distinction between the normal and the pathological, and so on); the discourse specifies the "true" nature of these objects, which, in turn, cannot be thought about or spoken about extra-discursively, save through a related, critical, or complementary discourse.

Consequently, discourse is, in a fundamental sense, a colonization of our understanding by the society in which we live and, because of its constitutive relation to social practices, implies a uniformization of our lives.   Every discourse exists as a means by which social power and human cognition are consolidated through communicational conventions.   In Michel Foucault's terms,

> . . . we should abandon a whole tradition that allows us to imagine that knowledge [translation of *savoir*: in French it connotes formal knowledge although Foucault later acknowledges the organization of human cognition through discourse] can exist only where the power relations are suspended and that knowledge can develop only outside its injunctions, its demands, its interests. . . . We should admit rather that power produces knowledge (and not simply by encouraging it because it serves power or by applying it because it is useful); that power and knowledge directly imply one another; that there is no power relation without the correlative constitution of a field of knowledge, nor any knowledge that does not presuppose and constitute at the same time power relations.[4]

Indeed, "it is in discourse that power and knowledge are joined together."[5]   The study of discourses, their character as more formal (disciplines of knowledge, rules of diplomatic intercourses, etc.) or less formal (any other organized modes of communicating common social meanings, as with the set of verbally and nonverbally articulated meanings communicated in a television news broadcast), and their historical transformations is, I would suggest, central to studying world order.

Language clearly plays an important role in political life.   Sheldon Wolin, for example, has drawn attention to the significance of the etymology of *communicare,* meaning to share and to participate in, and thus of the way in which communication "organizes the uses [of language] and initiates them into a form of 'taking part.'"[6]   Further, the use of language to effect a form of communication in which sharing (as distinct from, say, exchange) is the crucial element is a means by which its users gain a collective identity. They do so by creating and naming (as in a constitution) a form of association that both provides a response to the most fundamental questions of collective existence and generates sufficient power to preserve and extend its existence. Thus political discourse has a dual character in form and substance. It is a language of collective being. It is a distinctive form of communication in that it implies a certain structure to the communicative process (in legislative assemblies, courts and tribunals, committees, etc.), as well as, perhaps, to itself as a *discourse*--a semiological system with a distinctive "grammar." It is also substantively the collectivity's self-understanding of its own nature: it rests upon a "claim to the truth about the nature of the reality in which collective existence should be grounded and thereby constituted."

Unlike the concept of ideology, which has most commonly been employed to describe an individual or group's false consciousness about collective existence, thereby implying the possibility of the eventual emergence of a true consciousness, that of discourse or discursive practice implies no distinction between "consciousness" and "real conditions of existence." Rather it suggests that we look at the way in which social practices and beliefs about those practices are inextricably woven together. "The world is not a play which simply masks a truer reality that exists behind the scenes. It is as it appears."[7] The task is to examine how discursive practice "works" in constituting "the real." This does not, however, abolish the possibility of criticism.

In order to undertake this task it seems useful to outline what I believe to be the principal dimensions of the discourse constitutive of world order and to suggest why these are its principal dimensions. I will refer to them individually as discourses, but always with respect to their interaction in forming the discourse of world order as a whole. Following Sheldon Wolin again,[8] three discourses, which together constitute a discursive practice of world order, can be distinguished: theoretical, strategic, and rhetorical.

The *theoretical* is the fulcrum of this triangulation of discourse. It is a constitutive knowledge that makes a claim to the truth about the nature of the reality in which world order is or should be grounded. Historically, it is found in the passing references of political philosophers, but it was always a subordinate discourse, one that existed as a projection of the inherently political nature of the state, its "other." This conception having been increasingly perceived as inadequate, a realm of enquiry was constituted (that of international relations and law) that strove to establish those enduring truths and practical maxims pertaining to the "society," "system," or "environment" that was created *among* states.

In theoretical discourse, three principal understandings of this ordering of the world of states have developed, resulting in a corresponding ordering of theoretical discourse about world order. These understandings are the "statist" (exemplified recently in the work of Hedley Bull and Robert Gilpin); the "liberal internationalist" (which draws upon various functionalist and neo-functionalist accounts of interdependence and transnational relations; the World Order Models Project may be understood as a "critical" discourse within this field of understanding); and finally the "neo-Marxian" (represented in the works of Immanuel Wallerstein and the theorists of *dependencia*).[9] *These three understandings, in addition to their status as theoretical texts* themselves, provide an orientation to other texts (not necessarily theoretical), through which the extant theoretical discourse constitutive of world order may be subjected to interpretation. They do so in the sense that they address, respectively, three dimensions of the object of theoretical discourse of world order: (1) the nature of the state and the order that it creates in relation to other states and for itself, internally; (2) the relation between "the political" and "the economic" in the discourse of world order (in other words, the political and what is not distinctively so in understanding the nature of world order); and (3) the character of the historical transformation both of world order and the theoretical discourse constitutive of it.

I say "respectively" not because I believe, for example, that there is no Marxian theory of the state or liberal-internationalist understanding of historical change, which there obviously is, in both cases. I make this assertion as a methodological one, because it appears that their formulation of a theoretical conception of world order, one pertaining to the nature of the reality in which world order is or should be grounded, is primarily addressed to (and most revealing about) the dimensions of understanding that I have indicated, i.e., the state and state system, the question of what is political, and the historical character of the extant world order through the development of a global economy.

It would be misleading to conceive of *strategic discourse* as constitutive of the larger discourse of world order (and therefore constitutive of world order itself), or as mainly concerned with the instrumentalities of diplomacy or of explicit state coercion, as in war and geopolitics. It has a much broader, even historical significance. Historically, strategic discourse is related to the discourse of *counsel,* of advising the Prince (Machiavelli and More are principal early exponents); and later, in nonmonarchical bureaucratized states, to the language of "policymaking." It is increasingly the language of administrators and others who are in the position of having to make decisions by choosing more or less narrowly defined alternatives. This kind of discourse is concerned not directly with constitutive principles, as is theoretical discourse, but rather with the instrumentalities by which these principles may be made operational. Strategic discourse thus presupposes a theoretical understanding of the nature of world order. Although such a theoretical understanding is the fulcrum of all discourse of world order--setting its basic terms of reference in "reality"--strategic discourse has increasingly exercised a hegemony over all the modes of discourse of world order.

The French philosopher André Glucksmann has emphasized the historical significance of strategic discourse in relation to world order, and its philosophical significance in relation to the nature of political discourse in the modern world. He comments upon the role of the political thinker with respect to the exercise of power in a world that, he believes, has been strongly influenced by a Hegelian conception of the historical mission of the state.

> Contemplating in silence, reluctantly, the political thinker does not reflect upon his own nature like the classical philosopher; in the depths of his solitude he discovers not his own freedom but that of history, he constructs conceptually the context within which history decides everything for itself. Whether the object is the Prince, the nation, or the revolution, the "decision" remains the first concern, all politics is strategy.[10]

Thus there was established "a term for term correspondence between political 'logic' and its expression, strategic grammar."[11]

Glucksmann argues (employing the writings of Machiavelli, Clausewitz, Lenin, and contemporary strategic and "decision" theorists to support his thesis) that the discourse of war and its conceptual framework, which are "about" (discours *sur* la guerre) the exercise of collective power through a unified command (or social will) through a calculus of action (or rationale for decision based upon the polarization of agents and the primacy of defense), is increasingly what political thinking has come to mean. The thermonuclear age, in which the notion of decisive victory over a state's external enemy is incoherent, results in an indefinite international truce. Such a truce, in strategic discourse, requires the sublimation of state power in two ways. First, there is an increasing imperative to maintain a defensive position that will maintain the truce, which operates according to a logic of *dissuasion:* the state is forced to escalate its corporeal power to dissuade others from attacking it. This, in turn, generates continual international (e.g., geopolitical) crises instead of wars. Second, and perhaps more significant, the state's defense in the context of such a truce requires unity of will within: strategic discourse "domesticates" a population by turning the dissuasive strategy inward. Survival, in a world of nuclear truce, depends on a powerful state externally; internally, the state's power over its own population works most efficaciously to the extent that it "masks" its corporeal nature. It does so through the hegemony of strategic discourse in relation to what politics is conceived to be about, and in correspondence with a social economy of discourses that act as a means of social control.

Glucksmann's thought here merges with that of critics of the "administrative economy" of the welfare state and contemporary theorists of the "disciplining" function of discourse in relation to specific domains of social life. Strategic discourse operates according to two intrinsic characteristics. First, as the grammar of governance, it has the unique capacity for resolving any human conflict without recourse to a "rationality" other than its own (i.e., to constitutive or theoretical knowledge), and this is effected through "negotiation" among parties to reach a "reasonable" solution (the best they can get or hope for under the circumstances). Second, the dissuasive character of strategy means that a domestic social "order" is created through discourses about its "nature" (the family, mental and physical health or disease, deviancy, "standards" of well-being and the system of social insurance that promotes them, etc.); the discourses act both to normalize all social relations and to accumulate power over the means of domestic survival, the institutional manifestations of which are monitored and regulated by the state. This new "coding of power," that of supporting life or disallowing it, is quite modern and, in Foucault's words, its "operation is not ensured by right but by technique, not by law but by normalization, not by punishment but by control, methods that are employed on all levels and in forms that go beyond the state and its apparatus."[12]

The role of strategic discourse is constitutive in relation to the creation of an "order" that goes beyond the individual state: the progressive "modernization" of the world economy through a global division of labor; the consolidation of the Western state system monitored by superpowers and administered by regional overlords; the combination of a globally coordinated intelligence and communications network (both state and corporate) with the techniques of the social sciences, which together

control subjective perceptions and aspirations as well as
keep them under surveillance. All this points, I think,
to a world order in which the state becomes mainly a
"register" for this new coding of power and, only in the
case of crisis, its enforcer. The new "enemies" in the
calculus of strategic discourse are no longer other
states, but those who pose a challenge to the ordering of
normalization itself, that is, to the constituting
activity of discourse.

Rhetoric, in its classical definition given by
Aristotle, is "the faculty of observing in any given case
the available means of persuasion."[13] As a form of
political discourse, it is characterized not only by its
use of logical demonstration (Aristotle called it the
counterpart of dialectic, which is the art of logical
discussion, and contrasted it with that form of
persuasion based upon the arousal of the emotions), but
also by its subject matter, that "public business" that
is the concern of the entire political community.
However, like strategic discourse, it is not directly
concerned with constitutive knowledge about the nature of
the reality in which collective life is grounded (to
which it is subordinate), but rather with persuasion with
respect to what this prior conception of the nature of
political life entails. It therefore presupposes
divergent views of the way in which the principles
constitutive of political life may be effected, as well
as a context within which this may be accomplished. Its
close connection with the other modes of political
discourse is obvious: strategic discourse is concerned
with *available* instrumentalities, and rhetorical
discourse is concerned with which is the best one, given
constitutive political knowledge.

In its role as a component of the discourse of world
order, rhetorical discourse invites several observations
that need to be subjected to further analysis. Because
of the primacy that strategic discourse gives to decision
making based upon a calculation of response, it preempts
rhetorical recourse to constitutive principles, thereby
narrowing what can be conceived as a credible argument.
A vivid example of this occurs in the debate between
proponents of disarmament and those of arms control.
Arguments for disarmament seem utopian or "irrational"
from the perspective of a global strategic order and at
the same time are forced to rely upon constitutive
principles that made the strategic calculus plausible in
the first instance: the notion that there is a universal
rationality that is representable in discourse and
thereby amenable to institutionalization.

Rhetorical discourse presupposes a context within
which divergent views can be shared about the best
instrumentalities by which to effect the constitutive
principles of political life. It thus relies upon formal
structures of communication and rules about their use.

Three such structures seem to me to be particularly important. One is the structure of communication that articulates, makes intelligible, delineates a particular "position" in relation to collective social life based upon the "truth" that discourse about it has produced. The communication occurs in a "public" way. It is the direct result of what a particular discourse (discursive practice) conceives to be of concern to all members of the society. Thus, it is not merely the "statement" of concerned scientists or businessmen on the SALT talks or on welfare reform. Rather, it is that articulation of discourse that "positions" its truth in relation to its self-understanding of society as a whole. Such a structure of communication would not exclude the examples mentioned above, but it would also include, for example, the psychiatric discourse that articulates a "definitive position" on homosexuality through recognized "texts" and professional consensus. The communicative act resides between the collective need for a "truth" (homosexuals "coming out of the closet") and its corresponding production by a specific discourse. Global systems theory and its popularization tends to provide this "truth" in relation to the consequences of challenges to Western economic power as well as to the problematical character of the Western "standard of life" itself. The result is to show, in effect, how we can all be "Western." This structure of rhetorical communication facilitates persuasion by an appeal to the authority of formal truth, the "knowledge" produced by discourse.

A second structure of communication for rhetorical discourse about world order is related to what Aristotle called *epideictic,* the ceremonial oratory of display. It provides for the communication of ethical signs, such as those of justice or injustice, baseness or nobility, prudence, wisdom, and so on. It takes the character of a political spectacle in relation to world order: the awarding of the Nobel Prize, the Presidential news conference, and quintessentially, such diplomatic displays as the signing of a peace treaty. What gives this form of rhetorical communication its specific significance is its nonreliance upon (even emptying of) substantive content. Its persuasive effect through demonstrable logic is subordinated to its appeal, through the interplay of signs, to myth, to "what should be."

A third structure of communication is established by the media of global mass (public) communication. This structure serves to order rhetorical production in accordance with the conventions by which discourse is controlled, selected, and organized in the particular society in which it is produced, albeit with reference to a global ordering through the hierarchical control of the communicative structure. Three principal criteria seem to exist: Who is competent to speak? What may be spoken (and what is prohibited)? When and how may it be spoken (under what circumstances: "news," "editorial commentary," "entertainment," etc.)? For example, the use of this structure in reporting the Iranian hostage crisis to the U.S. population was pivotal, I think in the expulsion of the U.S. media from Iran. Yet this phenomenon is not "partisan" or "conspiratorial." Rather it reflects the ordering of discourse itself, as in a general emphasis upon leadership instead of rank and file, or in an emphasis upon legality and procedural rather than substantive issues in the Iranian crisis. This structure of rhetorical communication, especially through the use of photographs and film, to which the verbal message is subordinate, permits persuasion through a nonreflective appeal to "common sense," to Walter Cronkite's guarantee: "and that's the way it is."

Finally, I would suggest that the significance of rhetorical discourse as constitutive of world order is not to be underestimated, my remarks on strategic discourse notwithstanding. Rhetorical discourse is progressively becoming more of a "language of connotation" than it was in its classical understanding. As it has become less reliant upon direct and verbal communication, it has become more invested with the covert communication of meaning. That is to say, it employs not just gestures, tone of voice, and other nonverbal elements, but cultural symbols that do not rely upon rational or critical faculties for their communication. Thus, scenes of protesting Iranians in front of the American embassy, in the absence of any opportunity to persuade the American people about their view, communicated a covert image of religious fanaticism, oriental despotism, and the breakdown of international law and order.

Rhetorical discourse as constitutive of world order, is, I suggest, of two principal "styles," each of which has profound political implications. Following a cue from literary critic Roland Barthes, it can be either repressive or terrorist. As repressive discourse, it is not explicitly linked to the rhetoric of law and order, but rather to the permeation of language by the law, the conventions of the social order for which it is constitutive. As Barthes states, "the Law here enters language as equilibrium: an equilibrium is postulated between what is forbidden and what is permitted, between commendable meaning and unworthy meaning, between the constraint of common sense and the probationary freedom of interpretations."[14] Repressive rhetorical discourse is characterized by a discursive balancing act: being impartial, objective, ostensibly neither for this nor for that, it is in reality for *this*; that is, for the status quo. "Repressive discourse is the discourse of good conscience, liberal discourse." As terrorist discourse, rhetorical discourse is not necessarily associated with the "peremptory assertion" or "opportunist defense" of a faith but rather attempts to show the true violence of language, "the inherent violence which stems from the fact that no utterance is able to directly express the truth and has no other mode at its disposal than the word."[15]

It is possible that "world order" is becoming a "sign" in public consciousness for the political itself. The existing world order increasingly constitutes the contemporary problematique for political analysts, and the idea of a world order is becoming a historically significant way of ordering our understanding of the nature of politics, as the *polis* was for the Greeks and the state has been for modern theorists. To the extent that the concept of world order can be employed to represent certain dimensions of human experience that cannot be understood through other categories of analysis, it may be part of a conceptual breakthrough analogous to Aristotle's discovery of "the economy" as a way of understanding social life.

To the extent that the concept of world order is introduced into the rubric of laws and institutions, into the programs of political movements, and into political reflection in general, it becomes an issue for political struggle at all levels of social life. On the basis of the foregoing analysis it is important to stress that this concept refers to a specific discursive practice. Theory, strategic or operational rationality, and rhetoric are all components of this practice. Like a Wittgensteinian language game, the discourse by which we talk about the practice is the practice itself.

Thus all discourse is a strategy of creating the real. Strategic discourse is often conceived narrowly as discourse *about* strategy, as about strategies of nuclear deterrence. But the discourse of world order *as* strategy is the rationality used to govern others and ourselves in constituting a world order. In this context, theory is the aspect of this discursive practice that grounds governance in truth: a truth dependent for its effectiveness on a tradition of thought, in this case the tradition of political and international theory. Similarly, rhetoric is that discursive strategy by which truth and techniques of governance are consolidated through persuasion.

Thus we can say that the discourse of world order is cybernetic. It constitutes a plan of governance (strategy), grounded in truth (theory), which is self-sustaining through various means of persuasion and dissuasion. We can analyze the historical techniques or practices of governance in relation to the sciences of political economy and the balance of power. In addition, we can analyze how processes and means of persuasion or dissuasion operate to reinforce this relation of truth to procedures of governance through the creation of "subjects" (through the shaping of individuality based upon nation-states, cultures, classes, lifestyles, and so on) who rationally participate in world order as a discursive practice. The concern of some world order thinkers with cosmopolitanism and "planetary citizenship" is an attempt to counter the fragmenting individualization of world order discourse with an alternative subjectivity derived from a different ethic of human relatedness.

I have suggested that "the world order" is being introduced into modern political life to a large extent because issues of daily life are being problematized in relation to world order, as "world order issues." What happens when this occurs? In what sense is world order as a discursive practice a political issue? Four themes may be mentioned briefly.

First, world order as a discursive practice does not pose a critique of world order "in theory" because there is no transcendent rationality, no "Archimedian point," from which to formulate a critique or mount a challenge to the discursive practice of world order. Rather, it leads to an emphasis on politicizing the constitutive activity as such of daily life in the discourse of world order. An example of this might be the critique by feminists and gays of a domain of "personal life" that is supposedly free from, yet in reality is imbued through and through with, forms of governance that have political and, indeed, world order significance. Such critiques emphasize the continuous definition and redefinition of public and private given the changing tactics of governance--as with the recognition of power relations inhering in medicalization of daily life as a global phenomenon, with its relation to the management of domestic social insurance systems, migration patterns, eugenics, and so on.

Second, there is consequently a concern with the immediate effects of this constituting activity: not Power in its singular manifestation--the theory, the state, and the class struggle, which can only wait for "the revolution" and the establishment of a new world order at some indefinite future date--but power in its concrete exercise over individuals and groups, that is, how people can act in an immediate way by problematizing--recognizing, calling into question and changing--the relations of power within which the modern world order is constituted. Thus, more or less anarchistic, "self-help," "direct action" movements can be understood in this way.

Third, the experience of subjectivity itself becomes central. The question is posed as to how world order as discursive practice separates people from others based on class, race, nation, or "bloc," and how it separates people from themselves, internally. The experience of contemporary Jews and the question of "Jewish identity" in historical relation to the development of Zionism and

256

the government of Israel is an example of this kind of problematique.

The question of "nuclearism" as a regime of knowledge, as a technique of governance in both foreign policy and the domestic social order, and as political rhetoric in which it is posed as an imperative, provides an example of a fourth and final kind of problematique. This involves the abstraction or mystification of knowledge, techniques of governance, and the means by which these are persuaded and promulgated (through professionalization, ideology, and secrecy), so as to make the "question of world order" inaccessible and hence uneffectible.

NOTES

1. My use of this term is derived from but is also broader than that offered in Michel Foucault, *The Archaeology of Knowledge,* translated by A.M. Sheridan Smith (New York: Harper and Row, 1976); *see* especially pp. 194-195.

2. This and the following remarks of Gadamer are taken from "Notes on Planning for the Future," *Daedalus* 95 (2), Spring 1966:572-589.

3. Charles Taylor, "Hermeneutics and Politics," in P. Connerton, ed., *Critical Sociology* (Harmondsworth: Penguin, 1976), p. 180. Taylor approaches the relationship between language and community from a rather different direction, but our use of the term "discourse" is similar.

4. Michel Foucault, *Discipline and Punish: The Birth of the Prison,* translated by Alan Sheridan (New York: Random House, 1977), p. 27.

5. Michel Foucault, *The History of Sexuality: Vol. 1, An Introduction,* translated by Robert Hurley (New York: Random House, 1978), p. 100.

6. This paragraph draws on Sheldon Wolin, "Discourse and Collectivity," unpublished paper. Although Wolin's argument and conception of discourse are somewhat different from mine, I am indebted to his insights.

7. Hubert L. Dreyfus and Paul Rabinow, *Michel Foucault: Beyond Structuralism and Hermeneutics* (Chicago: University of Chicago Press, 1982), p. 109.

8. Sheldon Wolin, "Discourse and Collectivity." Here I draw upon Wolin's typology of political discourse as theoretical, rhetorical, and consiliary/advisory. I have employed "strategic" in lieu of the latter for a number of epistemological and methodological reasons, the most important of which is that in the context of modern society, "advisory" implies a certain centralization of the location of what is political, which I believe to be inappropriate for the analysis I am attempting here.

9. This typology is close to that of Robert Gilpin.

10. André Glucksmann, *Le Discourse de la Guerre,* 2nd ed. (Paris: Grasset, 1979), p. 94 (my translation).

11. Ibid., p. 130.

12. Foucault, *The History of Sexuality,* p. 89

13. Aristotle, *Rhetoric,* Book I, Chapter 2 (translated by W. Rhys Roberts).

14. Roland Barthes, *Image-Music-Text,* edited and translated by Stephen Heath (New York: Hill and Wang, 1977), p. 209.

15. Ibid., p. 208.

CHAPTER 12

Social Forces, States, and World Orders: Beyond International Relations Theory

Robert W. Cox

Academic conventions divide up the seamless web of the real social world into separate spheres, each with its own theorising; this is a necessary and practical way of gaining understanding. Contemplation of undivided totality may lead to profound abstractions or mystical revelations, but practical knowledge (that which can be put to work through action) is always partial or fragmentary in origin. Whether the parts remain as limited, separated objects of knowledge, or become the basis for constructing a structured and dynamic view of larger wholes is a major question of method and purpose. Either way, the starting point is some initial subdivision of reality, usually dictated by convention.

It is wise to bear in mind that such a conventional cutting up of reality is at best just a convenience of the mind. The segments which result, however, derive indirectly from reality insofar as they are the result of practices, that is to say, the responses of consciousness to the pressures of reality. Subdivisions of social knowledge thus may roughly correspond to the ways in which human affairs are organised in particular times and places. They may, accordingly, appear to be increasingly arbitrary when practices change.

International relations is a case in point. It is an area of study concerned with the interrelationships among states in an epoch in which states, and most commonly nation-states, are the principal aggregations of political power. It is concerned with the outcomes of war and peace and thus has obvious practical importance. Changing practice has, however, generated confusion as to the nature of the actors involved (different kinds of state, and non-state entities), extended the range of stakes (low as well as high politics), introduced a

----

Reprinted by permission from *Millenium: Journal of International Studies* 10:2, 1981.

greater diversity of goals pursued, and produced a greater complexity in the modes of interaction and the institutions within which action takes place.

One old intellectual convention which contributed to the definition of international relations is the distinction between state and civil society. This distinction made practical sense in the eighteenth and early nineteenth centuries when it corresponded to two more or less distinct spheres of human activity or practice: to an emergent society of individuals based on contract and market relations which replaced a status-based society, on the one hand, and a state with functions limited to maintaining internal peace, external defence and the requisite conditions for markets, on the other. Traditional international relations theory maintains the distinctness of the two spheres, with foreign policy appearing as the pure expression of state interests. Today, however, state and civil society are so interpenetrated that the concepts have become almost purely analytical (referring to difficult-to-define aspects of a complex reality) and are only very vaguely and imprecisely indicative of distinct spheres of activity.

One recent trend in theory has undermined the conceptual unity of the state by perceiving it as the arena of competing bureaucratic entities, while another has reduced the relative importance of the state by introducing a range of private transnational activity and transgovernmental networks of relationships among fragments of state bureaucracies. The state, which remained as the focus of international relations thinking, was still a singular concept: a state was a state was a state. There has been little attempt within the bounds of international relations theory to consider the state/society complex as the basic entity of international relations. As a consequence, the prospect that there exist a plurality of forms of state, expressing different configurations of state/society complexes, remaind very largely unexplored, at least in connection with the study of international relations.

The Marxist revival of interest in the state might have been expected to help fill this gap by broadening and diversifying the notion of state and, in particular, by amplifying its social dimensions. Some of the foremost products of this revival, however, either have been of an entirely abstract character, defining the state as a "region" of a singularly conceived capitalist mode of production (Althusser, Poulantzas), or else have shifted attention away from the state and class conflict towards a motivational crisis in culture and ideology (Habermas). Neither goes very far towards exploring the actual or historical differences among forms of state, or considering the implications of the differences for international behaviour.

Some historians, both Marxist and non-Marxist, quite independently of theorising about either international relations or the state, have contributed in a practical way towards filling the gap. E. H. Carr and Eric Hobsbawm have both been sensitive to the continuities between social forces, the changing nature of the state and global relationships. In France, Fernand Braudel has portrayed these interrelationships in the sixteenth and seventeenth centuries on a vast canvas of the whole world.[1] Inspired by Braudel's work a group led by Immanuel Wallerstein has proposed a theory of world systems defined essentially in terms of social relations. The exploitative exchange relations between a developed core and an underdeveloped periphery; to which correspond different forms of labour control (e.g., free labour in the core areas, coerced labour in the peripheries, with intermediate forms in what are called semi-peripheries).[2] Though it offers the most radical alternative to conventional international relations theory, the world systems approach has been criticised on two main grounds: first, for its tendency to undervalue the state by considering the state as merely derivative from its position in the world system (strong states in the core, weak states in the periphery); second, for its alleged, though unintended, system-maintenance bias. Like structural-functional sociology, the approach is better at accounting for forces that maintain or restore a system's equilibrium, than identifying contradictions which can lead to a system's transformation.[3]

The above comments are not, however, the central focus of this essay but warnings prior to the following attempt to sketch a method for understanding global power relations: look at the problem of world order in the whole, but beware of reifying a world system.[4] Beware of underrating state power, but in addition give proper attention to social forces and processes and see how they relate to the development of states and world orders. Above all, do not base theory on theory but rather on changing practice and empirical-historical study, which are a proving ground for concepts and hypotheses.

ON PERSPECTIVES AND PURPOSES

Theory is always *for* someone and *for* some purpose. All theories have a perspective. Perspectives derive from a position in time and space, specifically social and political time and space. The world is seen from a standpoint defineable in terms of national or social class, of dominance or subordination, of rising or declining power, of a sense of immobility or of present crisis, of past experience, and of hopes and expectations for the future. Of course, sophisticated theory is never just the expression of a perspective. The more sophisticated a theory is, the more it reflects upon and transcends its own perspective; but the initial perspective is always contained within a theory and is relevant to its explication. There is, acordingly, no such thing as theory in itself, divorced from a standpoint in time and space. When any theory so represents itself, it is the more important to examine it as ideology, and to lay bare its concealed perspective.

To each such perspective the enveloping world raises a number of issues; the pressures of social reality present themselves to consciousness as problems. A primary task of theory is to become clearly aware of these problems, to enable the mind to come to grips with the reality it confronts. Thus, as reality changes, old concepts have to be adjusted or rejected and new concepts forged in an initial dialogue between the theorist and the particular world he tries to comprehend. This initial dialogue concerns the *problematic* proper with a particular perspective. Social and political theory is history-bound at its origin, since it is always traceable to an historically-conditioned awareness of certain problems and issues, a problematic, while at the same time it attempts to transcend the particularity of its historical origins in order to place them within the framework of some general propostitions or laws.

Beginning with its problematic, theory can serve two distinct purposes. One is a simple, direct response: to be a guide to help solve the problems posed within the terms of the particular perspective which was the point of departure. The other is more reflective upon the process of theorising itself: to become clearly aware of the perspective which gives rise to theorising, and its relation to other perspectives (to achieve a perspective on perspectives); and to open up the possibility of choosing a different valid perspective from which the problematic becomes one of creating an alternative world. Each of these purposes gives rise to a different kind of theory.

The first purpose gives rise to *problem-solving theory*. It takes the world as it finds it, with the prevailing social and power relationships and the institutions into which they are organised, as the given framework for action. The general aim of problem-solving is to make these relationships and institutions work smoothly by dealing effectively with particular sources of trouble. Since the general pattern of institutions and relationships is not called into question, particular problems can be considered in relation to the specialised areas of activity in which they arise. Problem-solving theories are thus fragmented among a multiplicity of spheres or aspects of action, each of which assumes a certain stability in the other spheres (which enables them in practice to be ignored) when confronting a problem arising within its own. The strength of the problem-solving approach lies in its ability to fix limits or parameters to a problem area and to reduce the statement of a particular problem to a limited number of variables which are amenable to relatively close and precise examination. The *ceteris paribus* assumption, upon which such theorising is based, makes it possible to arrive at statements of laws or regularities which appear to have general validity but which imply, of course, the institutional and relational parameters assumed in the problem-solving approach.

The second purpose leads to *critical theory*. It is critical in the sense that it stands apart from the prevailing order of the world and asks how that order came about. Critical theory, unlike problem-solving theory, does not take institutions and social and power relations for granted but calls them into question by concerning itself with their origins and how and whether they might be in the process of changing. It is directed towards an appraisal of the very framework for action, or problematic, which problem-solving theory accepts as its parameters. Critical theory is directed to the social and political complex as a whole rather than to the separate parts. As a matter of practice, critical theory, like problem-solving theory, takes as its starting point some aspect or particular sphere of human activity. But whereas the problem-solving approach leads to further analytical sub-division and limitation of the issue to be dealt with, the critical approach leads towards the construction of a larger picture of the whole of which the initially contemplated part is just one component, and seeks to understand the processes of change in which both parts and whole are involved.

Critical theory is theory of history in the sense of being concerned not just with the past but with a continuing process of historical change. Problem-solving theory is non-historical or ahistorical, since it, in effect, posits a continuing present (the permanence of the institutions and power relations which constitute its parameters). The strength of the one is the weakness of the other. Because it deals with a changing reality, critical theory must continually adjust its concepts to the changing object it seeks to understand and explain.[5] These concepts and the accompanying methods of enquiry seem to lack the precision that can be achieved by problem-solving theory, which posits a fixed order as its point of reference. The relative strength of problem-solving theory, however, rests upon a false premise, since the social and political order is not fixed but (at least in a long-range perspective) is changing. Moreover, the assumption of fixity is not merely a convenience of method, but also an ideological bias. Problem-solving theories can be represented, in the broader perspective of critical theory, as serving particular national, sectional, or class interests, which are comfortable within the given order. Indeed, the purpose served by problem-solving theory is conservative, since it aims to solve the problems arising in various parts of a complex whole in order to smooth the functioning of the whole. This aim rather belies the frequent claim of problem-solving theory to be value-free. It is methodologically value-free insofar as it treats the variables it considers as objects (as the chemist treats molecules or the physicist forces and motion); but it is value-bound by virtue of the fact that it implicitly accepts the prevailing order as its own framework. Critical theory contains problem-solving theories within itself, but contains them in the form of identifiable ideologies, thereby pointing to their conservative consequences, not to their usefulness as guides to action. Problem-solving theory tends to ignore this kind of critique as being irrelevant to its purposes and in any case, as not detracting from its practical applicability. Problem-solving theory stakes its claims on its greater precision and, to the extent that it recognises critical theory at all, challenges the possibility of achieving any scientific knowledge of historical processes.

Critical theory is, of course, not unconcerned with the problems of the real world. Its aims are just as practical as those of problem-solving theory, but it approaches practice from a perspective which transcends that of the existing order, which problem-solving theory takes as its starting point. Critical theory allows for a normative choice in favour of a social and political order different from the prevailing order, but it limits the range of choice to alternative orders which are feasible transformations of the existing world. A principal objective of critical theory, therefore, is to clarify this range of possible alternatives. Critical theory thus contains an element of utopianism in the sense that it can represent a coherent picture of an alternative order, but its utopianism is constrained by its comprehension of historical processes. It must reject improbable alternatives just as it rejects the permanency of the existing order. In this way critical theory can be a guide to strategic action for bringing about an alternative order, whereas problem-solving theory is a guide to tactical actions which, intended or unintended, sustain the existing order.

The perspectives of different historical periods favour one or the other kind of theory. Periods of apparent stability or fixity in power relations favour the problem-solving approach. The Cold War was one such period. In international relations, it fostered a concentration upon the problems of how to manage an apparently enduring relationship between two superpowers. However, a condition of uncertainty in power relations beckons to critical theory as people seek to understand the opportunities and risks of change. Thus the events of the 1970s generated a sense of greater fluidity in power relationships, of a many-faceted crisis, crossing the threshold of uncertainty and opening the opportunity for a new development of critical theory directed to the problems of world order. To reason about possible future world orders now, however, requires a broadening of our enquiry beyond conventional international relations, so as to encompass basic processes at work in the development of social forces and forms of state, and in the structure of global political economy. Such, at least, is the central argument of this essay.

REALISM, MARXISM AND AN APPROACH TO A CRITICAL THEORY OF WORLD ORDER

Currents of theory which include works of sophistication usually share some of the features of both problem-solving and critical theory but tend to emphasise one approach over the other. Two currents which have had something important to say about inter-state relations and world orders--realism and Marxism--are considered here as a preliminary to an attempted development of the critical approach.

The realist theory of international relations had its origin in an historical mode of thought. Friedrich Meinecke, in his study on *raison d'état,* traced it to the political theory of Machiavelli and the diplomacy of Renaissance Italian city-states, which marked the emergence of a sense of the specific interests of particular states quite distinct from the general norms propagated by the ideologically dominant institution of medieval society, the Christian church.[6] In perceiving the doctrines and principles underlying the conduct of states as a reaction to specific historical circumstances, Meinecke's interpretation of *raison d'état* is a contribution to critical theory. Other scholars associated with the realist tradition, such as E. H. Carr and Ludwig Dehio, have continued this historical mode of thought, delineating the particular configurations of forces which fixed the framework for international behaviour in different periods and trying to understand institutions, theories and events within their historical contexts.

Since the Second World War, some American scholars, notably Hans Morgenthau and Kenneth Waltz, have transformed realism into a form of problem-solving theory. Though individuals of considerable historical learning, they have tended to adopt the fixed ahistorical view of the framework for action characteristic of problem-solving theory, rather than standing back from this framework, in the manner of E. H. Carr, and treating it as historically conditioned and thus susceptible to change. It is no accident that this tendency in theory coincided with the Cold War, which imposed the category of bipolarity upon international relations, and an overriding concern for the defence of American power as a bulwark of the maintenance of order.

The generalised form of the framework for action postulated by this new American realism (which we shall henceforth call neo-realism, which is the ideological form abstracted from the real historical framework imposed by the Cold War) is characterised by three levels, each of which can be understood in terms of what classical philosophers would call substances or essences, i.e., fundamental and unchanging substrata of changing and accidental manifestations or phenomena.[7] These basic realities were conceived as : (1) the nature of man, understood in terms of Augustinian original sin or the Hobbesian "perpetual and restless desire for power after power that ceaseth only in death";[8] (2) the nature of states, which differ in their domestic constitutions and in their capabilities for mobilising strength, but are similar in their fixation with a particular concept of national interest (a Leibnizian monad) as a guide to their actions; and (3) the nature of the state system, which places rational constraints upon the unbridled pursuit of rival national interests through the mechanism of the balance of power.

Having arrived at this view of underlying substances, history becomes for neo-realists a quarry providing materials with which to illustrate variations on always recurrent themes. The mode of thought ceases to be historical even though the materials used are derived from history. Moreover, this mode of reasoning dictates that, with respect to essentials, the future will always be like the past.[9]

In addition, this core of neo-realist theory has extended itself into such areas as game theory, in which the notion of substance at the level of human nature is presented as a rationality assumed to be common to the competing actors who appraise the stakes at issue, the alternative strategies, and the respective payoffs in a similar manner. This idea of a common rationality reinforces the non-historical mode of thinking. Other modes of thought are to be castigated as inapt, and incomprehensible in their own terms (which makes it difficult to account for the irruption into international affairs of a phenomenon like Islamic integralism, for instance).

The "common rationality" of neo-realism arises from its polemic with liberal internationalism. For neo-realism, this rationality is the one appropriate response to a postulated anarchic state system. Morality is effective only to the extent that it is enforced by physical power. This has given neo-realism the appearance of being a non-normative theory. It is "value-free" in its exclusion of moral goals (wherein it sees the weakness of liberal internationalism) and in its reduction of problems to their physical power relations. This non-normative quality is, however, only superficial. There is a latent normative element which derives from the assumptions of neo-realist theory: security within the postulated inter-state system depends upon each of the major actors understanding this system in the same way, that is to say, upon each of them adopting neo-realist rationality as a guide to action. Neo-realist theory derives from its foundations the prediction that the actors, from their experiences within the system, will tend to think in this way; but the theory also performs a proselytising function as the advocate of this form of rationality. To the neo-realist theorist, this proselytising function (wherein lies the normative role of neo-realism) is particularly urgent in states which have attained power in excess of that required to balance rivals, since such states may be tempted to discard the rationality of neo-realism and try to impose their own moral sense of order, particularly if, as in the case of the United States, cultural tradition has encouraged more optimistic and moralistic alternative views of the nature of man, the state and world order.[10]

The debate between neo-realists and liberal internationalists reproduces, with up-to-date materials, the seventeenth-century challenge presented by the civil philosophy of Hobbes to the natural law theory of Grotius. Each of the arguments is grounded in different views of the essences of man, the state and the inter-state system. An alternative which offered the possibility of getting beyond this opposition of mutually exclusive concepts was pointed out by the eighteenth-century Neapolitan Giambattista Vico, for whom the nature of man and of human institutions (amongst which must be included the state and the inter-state system) should not be thought of in terms of unchanging substances but rather as a continuing creation of new forms. In the duality of continuity and change, where neo-realism stresses continuity, the Vichian perspective stresses change; as Vico wrote, ". . . this world of nations has certainly been made by men, and its guise must therefore be found within the modifications of our own human mind."[11]

This should not be taken as a statement of radical idealism, (i.e., that the world is a creation of mind). For Vico, ever-changing forms of mind were shaped by the complex of social relations in the genesis of which class struggle played the principal role, as it later did for Marx. Mind is, however, the thread connecting the present with the past, a means of access to a knowledge of these changing modes of social reality. Human nature (the modifications of mind) and human institutions are identical with human history; they are to be understood in genetic and not in essentialist terms (as in neo-realism) or in teleological terms (as in functionalism). One cannot, in this Vichian perspective, properly abstract man and the state from history so as to define their substances or essences as *prior to* history, history being but the record of interactions of manifestations of these substances. A proper study of human affairs should be able to reveal both the coherence of minds and institutions characteristic of different ages, and the process whereby one such coherent pattern--which we can call an historical structure--succeeds another. Vico's project, which we would now call social science, was to arrive at a "mental dictionary," or set of common concepts, with which one is able to comprehend the process of "ideal eternal history," or what is most general and common in the sequence of changes undergone by human nature and institutions.[12] The error which Vico criticised as the "conceit of scholars," who will have it that "what they know is as old as the world," consists in taking a form of thought derived from a particular phase of history (and thus from a particular structure of social relations) and assuming it to be universally valid.[13] This is an error of neo-realism and more generally, the flawed foundation of all problem-solving theory. It does not, of course, negate the practical utility of neo-realism and problem-solving theories within their ideological limits. The Vichian approach, by contrast, is that of critical theory.

How does Marxism relate to this method or approach to a theory of world order? In the first place, it is impossible, without grave risk of confusion, to consider Marxism as a single current of thought. For our purposes, it is necessary to distinguish two divergent Marxist currents, analogous to the bifurcation between the old realism and the new. There is a Marxism which reasons historically and seeks to explain, as well as to promote, changes in social relations; there is also a Marxism, designed as a framework for the analysis of the capitalist state and society, which turns its back on historical knowledge in favour of a more static and abstract conceptualisation of the mode of production. The first we may call by the name under which it recognises itself: historical materialism. It is evident in the historical works of Marx, in those of present-day Marxist historians such as Eric Hobsbawm, and in the thought of Gramsci. It has also influenced some who would not be considered (or consider themselves) Marxist in any strict sense, such as many of the French historians associated with the *Annales*. The second is represented by the so-called structural Marxism of Althusser and Poulantzas ("so-called" in order to distinguish their use of "structure" from the concept of historical structure in this essay) and most commonly takes the form of an exegesis of *Capital* and other sacred texts. Structural Marxism shares some of the features of the neo-realist problem-solving approach such as its ahistorical, essentialist epistemology, though not its precision in handling data nor, since it has remained very largely a study in abstractions, its practical applicability to concrete problems. To this extent it does not concern us here. Historical materialism is, however, a foremost source of critical theory and it corrects neo-realism in four important respects.

The first concerns dialectic, a term which, like Marxism, has been appropriated to express a variety of not always compatible meanings, so its usage requires some definition. It is used here at two levels: the level of logic and the level of real history. At the level of logic, it means a dialogue seeking truth through the exploration of contradictions.[14] One aspect of this is the continual confrontation of concepts with the reality they are supposed to represent and their adjustment to this reality as it continually changes. Another aspect, which is part of the method of adjusting concepts, is the knowledge that each assertion concerning reality contains implicitly its opposite and that both assertion and opposite are not mutually exclusive but share some measure of the truth sought, a truth, moreover, that is always in motion, never to be encapsulated in some definitive form. At the level of real history, dialectic is the potential for alternative forms of development arising from the confrontation of opposed social forces in any concrete historical situation.

Both realism and historical materialism direct attention to conflict. Neo-realism sees conflict as inherent in the human condition, a constant factor flowing directly from the power-seeking essence of human nature and taking the political form of a continual reshuffling of power among the players in a zero-sum game, which is always played according to its own innate rules. Historical materialism sees in conflict the process of a continual remaking of human nature and the creation of new patterns of social relations which change the rules of the game and out of which--if historical materialism remains true to its own logic and method--new forms of conflict may be expected ultimately to arise. In other words, neo-realism sees conflict as a recurrent consequence of a continuing structure, whereas historical materialism sees conflict as a possible cause of structural change.

Second, by its focus on imperialism, historical materialism adds a vertical dimension of power to the horizontal dimension of rivalry among the most powerful states, which draws the almost exclusive attention of neo-realism. This dimension is the dominance and subordination of metropole over hinterland, centre over periphery, in a world political economy.

Third, historical materialism enlarges the realist perspective through its concern with the relationship between the state and civil society. Marxists, like non-Marxists, are divided between those who see the state as the mere expression of the particular interests in civil society and those who see the state as an autonomous force expressing some kind of general interest. This, for Marxists, would be the general interest of capitalism as distinct from the particular interests of capitalists. Gramsci contrasted historical materialism, which recognises the efficacy of ethical and cultural sources of political action (though always relating them with the economic sphere), with what he called historical economism or the reduction of everything to technological and material interests.[15] Neo-realist theory in the United States has returned to the state/civil society relationship, though it has treated civil society as a constraint upon the state and a limitation imposed by particular interests upon *raison d'état,* which is conceived of, and defined as, independent of civil society.[16] The sense of a reciprocal relationship between structure (economic relations) and superstructure (the ethico-political sphere) in Gramsci's thinking contains the potential for considering state/society complexes as the constituent entities of a world order and for exploring the particular historical forms taken by these complexes.

Fourth, historical materialism focuses upon the production processes as a critical element in the explanation of the particular historical form taken by a state/society complex. The production of goods and services which creates both the wealth of a society and the basis for a state's ability to mobilise power behind its foreign policy, takes place through a power relationship between those who control and those who execute the tasks of production. Political conflict and the action of the state either maintain, or bring about changes in, these power relations of production. Historical materialism examines the connections between power in production, power in the state, and power in international relations. Neo-realism has, by contrast, virtually ignored the production process. This is the point on which the problem-solving bias of neo-realism is most clearly to be distinguished from the critical approach of historical materialism. Neo-realism implicitly takes the production process and the power relations inherent in it as a given element of the national interest, and therefore as part of its parameters. Historical materialism is sensitive to the dialectical possibilities of change in the sphere of production which could affect the other spheres, such as those of the state and world order.

This discussion has distinguished two kinds of theorising as a preliminary to proposing a critical approach to a theory of world order. Some of the basic premises for such a critical theory can now be restated: (1) an awareness that action is never absolutely free but takes place within a framework for action which constitutes its problematic. Critical theory would start with this framework, which means starting with historical enquiry or an appreciation of the human experience that gives rise to the need for theory;[17] (2) a realisation that not only action but also theory is shaped by the problematic. Critical theory is consciousness of its own relativity but through this consciousness can achieve a broader time-perspective and become less relative than problem-solving theory. It knows that the task of theorising can never be finished in an enclosed system but must continually be begun anew; (3) the framework for action changes over time and a principal goal of critical theory is to understand these changes; (4) this framework has the form of an historical structure, a particular combination of thought patterns, material conditions and human institutions which has a certain coherence among its elements. These structures do not determine people's actions in any mechanical sense but constitute the context of habits, pressures, expectations and constraints within which action takes place; (5) the framework or structure within which action takes place is to be viewed, not from the top in terms of the requisites for its equilibrium or reproduction (which would quickly lead back to problem-solving), but rather from the bottom or from outside in terms of the conflicts which arise within it and open the possibility of its transformation.[18]

FRAMEWORKS FOR ACTION: HISTORICAL STRUCTURES

At its most abstract, the notion of a framework for action or historical structure is a picture of a particular configuration of forces. This configuration does not determine actions in any direct, mechanical way but imposes pressures and constraints. Individuals and groups may move with the pressures or resist and oppose them, but they cannot ignore them. To the extent that they do successfully resist a prevailing historical structure, they buttress their actions with an alternative, emerging configuration of forces, a rival structure.

Three categories of forces (expressed as potentials) interact in a structure: material capabilities, ideas and institutions. No one-way determinism need be assumed among these three; the relationships can be assumed to be reciprocal. The question of which way the lines of force run is always an historical question to be answered by a study of the particular case.

Material capabilities are productive and destructive potentials. In their dynamic form these exist as technological and organisational capabilities, and in their accumulated forms as natural resources which technology can transform, stocks of equipment (e.g. industries and armaments), and the wealth which can command these.

Ideas are broadly of two kinds. One kind consists of intersubjective meanings, or those shared notions of the nature of social relations which tend to perpetuate habits and expectations of behaviour.[19] Examples of intersubjective meanings in contemporary world politics are the notions that people are organised and commanded by states which have authority over defined territories; that states relate to one another through diplomatic agents; that certain rules apply for the protection of diplomatic agents as being in the common interest of all states; and that certain kinds of behaviour are to be expected when conflict arises between states, such as negotiation, confrontation, or war. These notions, though durable over long periods of time, are historically conditioned. The realities of world politics have not always been represented in precisely this way and may not be in the future. It is possible to trace the origins of such ideas and also to detect signs of a weakening of some of them.[20]

The other kind of ideas relevant to an historical structure are collective images of social order held by different groups of people. These are differing views as to both the nature and the legitimacy of prevailing power relations, the meanings of justice and public good, and so forth. Whereas intersubjective meanings are broadly common throughout a particular historical structure and constitute the common ground of social discourse (including conflict), collective images may be several and opposed.[21] The clash of rival collective images provides evidence of the potential for alternative paths of development and raises questions as to the possible material and institutional basis for the emergence of an alternative structure.

Institutionalisation is a means of stabilising and perpetuating a particular order. Institutions reflect the power relations prevailing at their point of origin and tend, at least initially, to encourage collective images consistent with these power relations. Eventually, institutions take on their own life; they can become either a battleground of opposing tendencies, or stimulate the creation of rival institutions reflecting different tendencies. Institutions are particular amalgams of ideas and material power which in turn influence the development of ideas and material capabilities.

There is a close connection between institutionalisation and what Gramsci called hegemony.

Institutions provide ways of dealing with internal conflicts so as to minimise the use of force. (They may, of course, also maximise the capacity for using force in external conflicts, but we are considering here only the internal conflicts covered by an institution.) There is an enforcement potential in the material power relations underlying any structure, in that the strong can clobber the weak if they think it necessary. But force will not have to be used in order to ensure the dominance of the strong to the extent that the weak accept the prevailing power relations as legitimate. This the weak may do if the strong see their mission as hegemonic and not merely dominant or dictatorial, that is, if they are willing to make concessions that will secure the weak's acquiescence in their leadership and if they can express this leadership in terms of universal or general interests, rather than just as serving their own particular interests.[22] Institutions may become the anchor for such a hegemonic strategy since they lend themselves both to the representations of diverse interests and to the universalisation of policy.

It is convenient to be able to distinguish between hegemonic and non-hegemonic structures, that is to say between those in which the power basis of the structure tends to recede into the background of consciousness, and those in which the management of power relations is always in the forefront. Hegemony cannot, however, be reduced to an institutional dimension. One must beware of allowing a focus upon institutions to obscure either changes in the relationship of material forces, or the emergence of ideological challenge to an erstwhile prevailing order. Institutions may be out of phase with these other aspects of reality and their efficacy as a means of regulating conflict (and thus their hegemonic function) thereby undermined. They may be an expression of hegemony but cannot be taken as identical to hegemony.

The method of historical structures is one of representing what can be called limited totalities. The historical structure does not represent the whole world but rather a particular sphere of human activity in its historically located totality. The *ceteris paribus* problem, which falsifies problem-solving theory by leading to an assumption of total stasis, is avoided by juxtaposing and connecting historical structures in related spheres of action. Dialectic is introduced, firstly, by deriving the definition of a particular structure, not from some abstract model of a social system or mode of production, but from a study of the historical situation to which it relates, and secondly, by looking for the emergence of rival structures expressing alternative possibilities of development. The three sets of forces indicated in Figure 1 are an heuristic device, not categories with a predetermined hierarchy of relationships. Historical structures are

contrast models: like ideal types they provide, in a
logically coherent form, a simplified representation of a
complex reality and an expression of tendencies, limited
in their applicability to time and space, rather than
fully realised developments.

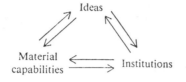

Figure 1

For the purpose of the present discussion, the
method of historical structures is applied to the three
levels, or spheres of activity: (1) the organisation of
production, more particularly with regard to the *social
forces* engendered by the production process; (2) *forms of
state* as derived from a study of state/society complexes;
and (3) *world orders, i.e.,* the particular configurations
of forces which successively define the problematic of
war or peace for the ensemble of states. Each of these
levels can be studied as a succession of dominant and
emergent rival structures.

The three levels are interrelated. Changes in the
organisation of production generate new social forces
which, in turn, bring about changes in the structure of
states; and the generalisation of changes in the
structure of states alters the problematic of world
order. For instance, as E. H. Carr argued, the
incorporation of the industrial workers (a new social
force) as participants within western states from the
late-nineteenth century, accentuated the movement of
these states towards economic nationalism and imperialism
(a new form of state), which brought about a
fragmentation of the world economy and a more conflictual
phase of international relations (the new structure of
world order).[23]

The relationship among the three levels is not,
however, simply unilinear. Transnational social forces
have influenced states through the world structure, as
evidenced by the effect of expansive nineteenth-century
capitalism *(les bourgeois conquérants,)*[24] upon the
development of state structures in both core and
periphery. Particular structures of world order exert
influence over the forms which states take: Stalinism
was, at least in part, a response to a sense of threat to
the existence of the Soviet state from a hostile world
order; the military-industrial complex in core countries
justifies its influence today by pointing to the
conflictural condition of world order; and the prevalence

of repressive militarism in periphery countries can be explained by the external support of imperialism as well as by a particular conjunction of internal forces. Forms of state also affect the development of social forces through the kinds of domination they exert, for example, by advancing one class interest and thwarting others.[25]

Considered separately, social forces, forms of state, and world orders can be represented in a preliminary approximation as particular configurations of material capabilities, ideas and institutions (as indicated in Figure 1). Considered in relation to each other, and thus moving towards a fuller representation of historical process, each will be seen as containing, as well as bearing the impact of, the others (as in Figure 2).[26]

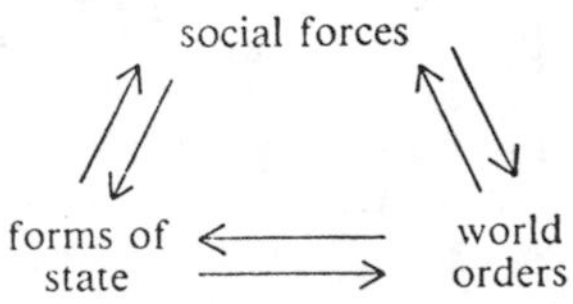

social forces

forms of state ←——→ world orders

Figure 2

HEGEMONY AND WORLD ORDERS

How are these reciprocal relationships to be read in the present historical conjuncture? Which of the several relationships will tell us the most? A sense of the historicity of concepts suggests that the critical relationships may not be the same in successive historical periods, even within the post-Westphalian era for which the term "state system" has particular meaning. The approach to a critical theory of world order, adumbrated here, takes the form of an interconnected series of historical hypotheses.

Neo-realism puts the accent on states reduced to their dimension of material force and similarly reduces the structure of world order to the balance of power as a configuration of material forces. Neo-realism, which generally dismisses social forces as irrelevant, is not much concerned with differentiating forms of state (except insofar as "strong societies" in liberal democratic politics may hamper the use of force by the state or advance particular interests over the national interest), and tends to place a low value on the normative and institutional aspects of world order.

One effort to broaden the realist perspective to include variations in the authority of international norms and institutions is the theory of "hegemonic stability" which, as stated by Robert Keohane, "holds that hegemonic structures of power, dominated by a single country, are most conducive to the development of strong international regimes, whose rules are relatively precise and well obeyed."[27] The classic illustrations of the theory discussed by Keohane are the *pax britannica* of the mid-nineteenth century and the *pax americana* of the years following the Second World War. The theory appears to be confirmed by the decline in observance of the norms of the nineteenth-century order which accompanied Britain's relative decline in state power from the late nineteenth century. Exponents of the theory see a similar decline, since the early 1970s, in the observance of norms of the post-war order, relating it to a relative decline in U.S. power. Robert Keohane has tested the theory in particular issue areas (energy, money and trade) on the grounds that power is not a fungible asset, but has to be differentiated according to the contexts in which a state tries to be influential. He finds that, particularly in the areas of trade and money, changes in U.S. power are insufficient to explain the changes that have occurred and need to be supplemented by the introduction of domestic political, economic and cultural factors.

An alternative approach might start by redefining what it is that is to be explained, namely, the relative stability of successive world orders. This can be done by equating stability with a concept of hegemony that is based on a coherent conjunction or fit between a configuration of material power, the prevalent collective image of world order (including certain norms) and a set of institutions which administer the order with a certain semblance of universality (*i.e.* , not just as the overt instruments of a particular state's dominance). In this formulation, state power ceases to be the sole explanatory factor and becomes part of what is to be explained. This rephrasing of the question addresses a major difficulty in the realist version signalled by Keohane and others, namely, how to explain the failure of the United States to establish a stable world order in the inter-war period despite its preponderance of power. If the dominance of a single state coincides with a stable order on some occasions but not on others, then there may be some merit in looking more closely at what is meant by stability and more broadly at what may be its sufficient conditions. Dominance by a powerful state may be a necessary but not a sufficient condition of hegemony.

The two periods of the *pax britannica* and the *pax americana* also satisfy the reformulated definition of hegemony. In the mid-nineteenth century, Britain's world supremacy was founded on its sea power, which remained free from challenge by a continental state as a result of Britain's ability to play the role of balancer in a relatively fluid balance of power in Europe. The norms of liberal economics (free trade, the gold standard, free movement of capital and persons) gained widespread acceptance with the spread of British prestige, providing a universalistic ideology which represented these norms as the basis of a harmony of interests. While there were no formal international institutions, the ideological separation of economics from politics meant that the City could appear as administrator and regulator according to these universal rules, with British sea power remaining in the background as potential enforcer.

This historical structure was transformed in its three dimensions during the period running from the last quarter of the nineteenth century through the Second World War. During this period British power declined relatively, losing its undisputed supremacy at sea, first with the German challenge and then with the rise of U.S. power; economic liberalism foundered with the rise of protectionism, the new imperialisms and ultimately the end of the gold standard; and the belated and abortive attempt at international institutionalisation through the League of Nations, unsustained either by a dominant power or a widely accepted ideology, collapsed in a world increasingly organised into rival power blocs.

The power configuration of the *pax americana* was more rigid than that of the earlier hegemony, taking the form of alliances (all hinging on U.S. power) created in order to contain the Soviet Union. The stabilisation of this power configuration created the conditions for the unfolding of a global economy in which the United States played a role similar to that of Britain in mid-nineteenth century. The United States rarely needed to intervene directly in support of specific national economic interests; by maintaining the rules of an international economic order according to the revised liberalism of Bretton Woods, the strength of U.S. corporations engaged in the pursuit of profits was sufficient to ensure continuing national power. The *pax americana* produced a greater number of formal international institutions than the earlier hegemony. The nineteenth-century separation of politics and economics had been blurred by the experience of the Great Depression and the rise of Keynesian doctrines. Since states now had a legitimate and necessary overt role in national economic management, it became necessary both to multilateralise the administrative management of the international economy and to give it an intergovernmental quality.

The notion of hegemony as a fit between power, ideas and institutions makes it possible to deal with some of the problems in the theory of state dominance as the necessary condition for a stable international order; it allows for lags and leads in hegemony. For example, so appealing was the nostalgia for the nineteenth-century hegemony that the ideological dimension of the *pax brittanica* flourished long after the power configuration that supported it had vanished. Sustained, and ultimately futile, efforts were made to revive a liberal world economy along with the gold standard in the inter-war period. Even in the post-war period, British policy continued to give precedence to balance of payments problems over national industrial development and employment considerations.[28] Another prime example is the case of the United States, where the growth indicators of material power during the inter-war period were insufficient predictors of a new hegemony. It was necessary that U.S. leaders should come to see themselves in ideological terms as the necessary guarantors of a new world order. The Roosevelt era made this transition, including both the conscious rejection of the old hegemony (*e.g.* , by torpedoing the world economic conference in 1933 and abandoning the gold standard) and the gradual incorporation of New Deal principles into the ideological basis of the new world order. There followed U.S. initiatives to create the institutions to administer this order.[29] Neo-mercantilists in the United States now warn against a danger of repeating the British error, urging U.S. policy-makers not to continue to operate according to doctrines appropriate to the *pax americana* when the United States can no longer afford to act as guarantor for a universalist world order. Their persuasive efforts underline the point that in these matters ideology is a determining sphere of action which has to be understood in its connections with material power relations.

SOCIAL FORCES, HEGEMONY AND IMPERIALISM

Represented as a fit between material power, ideology and institutions, hegemony may seem to lend itself to a cyclical theory of history; the three dimensions fitting together in certain times and places and coming apart in others. This is reminiscent of earlier notions of *virtù,* or of the *weltgeist* migrating from people to people. The analogy merely points to something which remains unexplained. What is missing is some theory as to how and why the fit comes about and comes apart. It is my contention that the explanation may be sought in the realm of social forces shaped by production relations.

Social forces are not to be thought of existing exclusively within states. Particular social forces may overflow state boundaries, and world structures can be described in terms of social forces just as they can be described as configurations of state power. The world can be represented as a pattern of interacting social forces in which states play an intermediate though autonomous role between the global structure of social forces and local configurations of social forces within particular countries. This may be called a political economy perspective of the world: power is seen as *emerging* from social processes rather than taken as given in the form of accumulated material capabilities, that is as the result of these processes. (Paraphrasing Marx, one could describe the latter, neo-realist view as the "fetishism of power.")[30] In reaching for a political economy perspective, we move from identifying the structural characteristics of world orders as configurations of material capabilities, ideas and institutions (Figure 1) to explaining their origins, growth and demise in terms of the interrelationships of the three levels of structures (Figure 2).

It is, of course, no great discovery to find that, viewed in the political economy perspective, the *pax britannica* was based both on the ascendancy of manufacturing capitalism in the international exchange economy, of which Britain was the centre, and on the social and ideological power, in Britain and other parts of northwest Europe, of the class which drew its wealth from manufacturing. The new bourgeoisie did not need to directly control states; its social power became the premise of state politics.[31]

The demise of this hegemonic order can also be explained by the development of social forces. Capitalism mobilised an industrial labour force in the most advanced countries, and from the last quarter of the nineteenth century industrial workers had an impact on the structure of the state in these countries. The incorporation of the industrial workers, the new social force called into existence by manufacturing capitalism, into the nation involved an extention in the range of state action in the form of economic intervention and social policy. This in turn brought the factor of domestic welfare (*i.e.,* the social minimum required to maintain the allegiance of the workers) into the realm of foreign policy. The claims of welfare competed with the exigencies of liberal internationalism within the management of states; whilst the former gained ground as protectionism, the new imperialism and ultimately the end of the gold standard marked the long decline of liberal internationalism.[32] The liberal form of state was slowly replaced by the welfare nationalist form of state.

The spread of industrialisation, and the mobilisation of social classes it brought about, not only changed the nature of states but also altered the international configuration of state power as new rivals overtook Britain's lead. Protectionism, as the means of building economic power comparable to Britain's, was for these new industrial countries more convincing than the liberal theory of comparative advantage. The new imperialisms of the major industrial powers were a projection abroad of the welfare nationalist consensus

among social forces sought or achieved within the
nations. As both the material predominance of the
British economy and the appeal of the hegemonic ideology
weakened, the hegemonic world order of the mid-nineteenth
century gave place to a non-hegemonic configuration of
rival power blocs.

Imperialism is, thus, a rather loose concept which
in practice has to be newly defined with reference to
each historical period. There is little point in looking
for any "essence" of imperialism beyond the forms which
dominance and subordination take in different successive
world order structures. The actual form, whether
activated by states, by social forces (e.g., the
managements of multinational corporations), or some
combination of both, and whether domination is primarily
political or economic, is to be determined by historical
analysis, and not deductive reasoning.

The expansive capitalism of the mid-nineteenth
century brought most of the world into the exchange
relations of an international economy centred in London.
The liberal imperialism of this phase was largely
indifferent as to whether or not peripheral countries
were formally independent or under the political-
administrative control of a colonial power, provided that
the rules of the international economy were observed.[33]
Canada and Argentina, for example, had similar positions
in real terms, though one had colonial and the other
independent status. In the phase of liberal imperialism,
local authorities, who were often pre-capitalist in their
relationship to the production process (e.g., traditional
agrarian-based rulers), kept their countries in the
commercial system. During the second phase, that of the
so-called new imperialism following the 1870s, direct
state control began to supplant the less formal patterns
of the commercial period. Capitalist production
relations under this political aegis penetrated the
periphery more thoroughly, notably in the extraction of
raw materials and the building of the infrastructure
(roads, railways, ports and commercial and governmental
administrations) required to link the colonies more
closely with the metropole.

Capitalist production relations generated new social
forces in the periphery. Outsiders came to play
important roles in the local society, some as agents of
the colonial administration and of big capital from the
metropole, others in smaller businesses, filling the
interstices between big capital and traditional local
production (for example, the Chinese in southeast Asia,
the Indians in east Africa or the Lebanese in west
Africa). A local workforce often numerically small and
materially better off than the majority of the population
was drawn into capitalist production. This politically
strategic group was opposed to capital on wage and labour
issues but aligned with it as regards the development of

the capitalist production sector. An indigenous petty bourgeoisie also grew up, occupying the subordinate positions in colonial administration and metropole-based enterprises, as well as in local small business. A local state apparatus emerged under colonial tutelage, encouraging the new production relations by methods ranging from the introduction of compulsory labour or a head tax as a means of generating a labour force, to reproducing, in the colonial context, some of the institutions and procedures of the industrial relations of the metropole.

The existence in the colonial territory of these new social forces, labour and the petty bourgeoisie, which could agree on a nationalist political programme, together with the introduction by the colonial administration of the elements of a modern state apparatus (control of which could be the aim of this programme), laid the basis for the anti-colonial revolt which swept the colonial world after the Second World War. This movement reacted against administrative control from the metropole, but not continued involvement in capitalist production and exchange relations. The anti-imperialist label on the forces which replaced the structures created by the second phase or new imperialism obscured their role in ushering in yet a third phase of imperialism.

James Petras, in his use of the concept of an imperial state system, has posed a number of questions concerning the structural characteristics of states in the present world order. The dominant imperial state and subordinate collaborator states differ in structure and have complementary functions in the imperial system; they are not just more and less powerful units of the same kind, as might be represented in a simple neo-realist model. A striking feature in his framework is that the imperial state he analyses is not the whole U.S. government; it is "those executive bodies within the 'government' which are charged with promoting and protecting the expansion of capital across state boundaries."[34] The imperial system is at once more than and less than the state. It is more than the state in that it is a transnational structure with a dominant core and dependent periphery. This part of the U.S. government is at the system's core, together (and here we may presume to enlarge upon Petras' indications) with inter-state institutions such as the IMF and the World Bank, symbiotically related to expansive capital, and with the system's periphery. It is less than the state in the sense that non-imperial, or even anti-imperial, forces may be present in other parts of both core and periphery states. The unity of the state, posited by neo-realism, is fragmented in this image, and the struggle for and against the imperial system may go on within the state structures at both core and periphery as well as among social forces ranged in support and opposition to the system. The state is thus a necessary but insufficient category to account for the imperial system. The imperial system itself becomes the starting point of enquiry.

The imperial system is a world order structure drawing support from a particular configuration of social forces, national and transnational, and of core and periphery states. One must beware of slipping into the language of reification when speaking of structures; they are constraints on action, not actors. The imperial system includes some formal and less formal organisations at the system level through which pressures on states can be exerted without these system-level organisations actually usurping state power. The behaviour of particular states or of organised economic and social interests, however, finds its meaning in the larger totality of the imperial system. Actions are shaped either directly by pressures projected through the system or indirectly by the subjective awareness on the part of actors of the constraints imposed by the system. Thus one cannot hope to understand the imperial system by identifying imperialism with actors, be they states or multinationals; they are both dominant elements in the system, but the system as a structure is more than their sum. Furthermore, one must beware of ignoring the principle of dialectic by over emphasising the power and coherence of a structure, even a very dominant one. Where a structure is hegemonic, critical theory leads one to look for a counter-structure, even a latent one, by seeking out its possible bases of support and elements of cohesion.

At this point, it is preferable to revert to the earlier terminology which referred to hegemonic and non-hegemonic world order structures. To introduce the term "imperial" with reference to the *pax americana* risks both obscuring the important difference between hegemonic and non-hegemonic world orders and confusing structurally different kinds of imperialism (e.g., liberal imperialism, the new or colonial imperialism, and the imperial system just outlined). The contention here is that the *pax americana* was hegemonic: it commanded a wide measure of consent among states outside the Soviet sphere and was able to provide sufficient benefits to the associated and subordinate elements in order to maintain their acquiescence. Of course, consent wore thin as one approached the periphery where the element of force was always apparent, and it was in the periphery that the challenge to the imperial system first became manifest.

It was suggested above how the particular fit between power, ideology and institutions constituting the *pax americana* came into being. Since the practical issue at the present is whether or not the *pax americana* has irretrievably come apart and if so what may replace it, two specific questions deserving attention are: (1) what are the mechanisms for maintaininng hegemony in this particular historical structure? and (2) what social forces and/or forms of state have been generated within it which could oppose and ultimately bring about a transformation of the structure?

THE INTERNATIONALISATION OF THE STATE

A partial answer to the first question concerns the internationalisation of the state. The basic principles of the *pax americana* were similar to those of the *pax britannica*--relatively free movement of goods, capital and technology and a reasonable degree of predictability in exchange rates. Cordell Hull's conviction that an open trading world was a necessary condition of peace could be taken as its ideological text, supplemented by confidence in economic growth and ever-rising productivity as the basis for moderating and controlling conflict. The post-war hegemony was, however, more fully institutionalised than the *pax britannica* and the main function of its institutions was to reconcile domestic social pressures with the requirements of a world economy. The International Monetary Fund was set up to provide loans to countries with balance of payments deficits in order to provide time in which they could make adjustments, and to avoid the sharp deflationary consequences of an automatic gold standard. The World Bank was to be a vehicle for longer term financial assistance. Economically weak countries were to be given assistance by the system itself, either directly through the system's institutions or by other states nominally certified by the system's institutions. These institutions incorporated mechanisms to supervise the application of the system's norms and to make financial assistance effectively conditional upon reasonable evidence of intent to live up to the norms.

This machinery of surveillance was, in the case of the western allies and subsequently of all industrialised capitalist countries, supplemented by elaborate machinery for the harmonisation of national policies. Such procedures began with the mutual criticism of reconstruction plans in western European countries (the U.S. condition for Marshall aid funds), continued with the development of annual review procedures in NATO (which dealt with defence and defence support programmes), and became an acquired habit of mutual consultation and mutual review of national policies (through the OECD and other agencies).

The notion of international obligation moved beyond a few basic commitments, such as observance of the most favoured nation principle or maintenance of an agreed exchange rate, to a general recognition that measures of

national economic policy affect other countries and that
such consequences should be taken into account before
national policies are adopted. Conversely, other
countries should be sufficiently understanding of one
country's difficulties to acquiesce in short-term
exceptions. Adjustments are thus perceived as responding
to the needs of the system as a whole and not to the will
of dominant countries. External pressures upon national
policies were accordingly internationalised.

Of course, such an internationalised policy process
presupposed a power structure, one in which central
agencies of the U.S. government were in a dominant
position. But it was not necessarily an entirely
hierarchical power structure with lines of force running
exclusively from the top down, nor was it one in which
the units of interaction were whole nation-states. It
was a power structure seeking to maintain consensus
through bargaining and one in which the bargaining units
were fragments of states. The power behind the
negotiation was tacitly taken into account by the
parties.

The practice of policy harmonisation became such a
powerful habit that when the basic norms of international
economic behaviour no longer seemed valid, as became the
case during the 1970s, procedures for mutual adjustment
of national economic policies were, if anything,
reinforced. In the absence of clear norms, the need for
mutual adjustment appeared the greater.[35]

State structures appropriate to this process of
policy harmonisation can be contrasted with those of the
welfare nationalist state of the preceding period.
Welfare nationalism took the form of economic planning at
the national level and the attempt to control external
economic impacts upon the national economy. To make the
national planning effective, corporative structures grew
up in most industrially advanced countries for the
purpose of bringing industry, and also organised labour,
into consultation with the government in the formulation
and implementation of policy. National and industrial
corporative structures can raise protectionist or
restrictive obstacles to the adjustments required for
adaptation of national economies to the world economy in
a hegemonic system. Corporatism at the national level
was a response to the conditions of the inter-war period;
it became institutionally consolidated in western Europe
just as the world structure was changing into something
for which national corporatism was ill-suited.

The internationalisation of the state gives
precedence to certain state agencies--notably ministries
of finance and prime ministers' offices--which are key
points in the adjustment of domestic to international
economic policy. Ministries of industries, labour
ministries, planning offices, which had been built up in
the context of national corporatism, tended to be

subordinated to the central organs of internationalised public policy. As national economies became more integrated in the world eocnomy, it was the larger and more technologically advanced enterprises that adapted best to the new opportunities. A new axis of influence linked international policy networks with the key central agencies of government and with big business. This new informal corporative structure overshadowed the older more formalised national corporatism and reflected the dominance of the sector oriented to the world economy over the more nationally oriented sector of a country's economy.[36]

The internationalisation of the state is not, of course, limited to advanced capitalist core countries. It would not be difficult to make a catalogue of recent cases in peripheral countries where institutions of the world economy, usually as a condition for debt renewal, have dictated policies which could only be sustained by a coalition of conservative forces. Turkey, Peru, and Portugal are among those recently affected. As for Zaire, a conference of creditors laid down the condition that officials of the IMF be placed within the key ministries of the state to oversee the fulfilment of the conditions of debt renewal.[37]

THE INTERNATIONALISATION OF PRODUCTION

The internationalisation of the state is associated with the expansion of international production. This signifies the integration of production processes on a transnational scale, with different phases of a single process being carried out in different countries. International production currently plays the formative role in relation to the structure of states and world order that national manufacturing and commercial capital played in the mid-nineteenth century.

International production expands through direct investment, whereas the rentier imperialism, of which Hobson and Lenin wrote, primarily took the form of portfolio investment. With portfolio investment, control over the productive resources financed by the transaction passed with ownership to the borrower. With direct investment, control is inherent in the production process itself and remains with the originator of the investment. The essential feature of direct investment is possession, not of money, but of knowledge--in the form of technology and especially in the capacity to continue to develop new technology. The financial arrangements for direct investment may vary greatly, but all are subordinated to this crucial factor of technical control. The arrangements may take the form of wholly owned subsidiaries, joint ventures with local capital sometimes put up by the state in host countries, management contracts with state-owned enterprises, or compensation agreements with socialist enterprises whereby, in return for the provision of technology, these enterprises become suppliers of elements to a globally organised production process planned and contolled by the source of the technology. Formal ownership is less important than the manner in which various elements are integrated into the production system.

Direct investment seems to suggest the dominance of industrial capital over finance capital. The big multinational corporations which expand by direct investment are, to some degree, self-financing and to the extent that they are not they seem capable of mobilising money capital in a number of ways, such as through local capital markets (where their credit is better than that of national entrepreneurs), through the Eurocurrency markets, through infusions of capital from other multinationals linked to technology and production agreements, through state subsidies, and so forth. And yet, particularly since the 1970s, finance capital seems to be returning to prominence through the operations of the multinational banks, not only in the old form of rentier imperialism administering loans to peripheral states, but also as a network of control and private planning for the world economy of international production. This network assesses and collectivises investment risks and allocates investment opportunities among the participants in the expansion of international production, that is, it performs the function of Lenin's "collective capitalist" in the conditions of late twentieth century production relations.

INTERNATIONAL PRODUCTION AND CLASS STRUCTURE

International production is mobilising social forces, and it is through these forces that its major political consequences *vis-à-vis* the nature of states and future world orders may be anticipated. Hitherto, social classes have been found to exist within nationally defined social formations, despite rhetorical appeals to the international solidarity of workers. Now, as a consequence of international production, it becomes increasingly pertinent to think in terms of a global class structure alongside or superimposed upon national class structures.

At the apex of an emerging global class structure is the transnational managerial class. Having its own ideology, strategy and institutions of collective action, it is both a class in itself and for itself. Its focal points of organisation, the Trilateral Commission, World Bank, IMF and OECD, develop both a framework of thought and guidelines for policies. From these points, class action penetrates countries through the process of internationalisation of the state. The members of this transnational class are not limited to those who carry out functions at the global level, such as executives of multinational corporations or as senior officials of international agencies, but includes those who manage the internationally-oriented sectors within countries, the finance ministry officials, local managers of enterprises linked into international production systems, and so on.[38]

National capitalists are to be distinguished from the transnational class. The natural reflex of national capital faced with the challenge of international production is protectionism. It is torn between the desire to use the state as a bulwark of an independent national economy and the opportunity of filling niches left by international production in a subordinate symbiotic relationship with the latter.

Industrial workers have been doubly fragmented. One line of cleavage is between established and non-established labour. Established workers are those who have attained a status of relative security and stability in their jobs and have some prospects of career advancement. Generally they are relatively skilled, work for larger enterprises, and have effective trade unions. Non-established workers, by contrast, have insecure employment, have no prospect of career advancement, are relatively less skilled, and confront great obstacles in developing effective trade unions. Frequently, the non-established are disproportionately drawn from lower-status ethnic minorities, immigrants and women. The institutions of working class action have privileged established workers. Only when the ideology of class solidarity remains powerful, which usually means only in conditions of high ideological polarisation and social and political conflict, do organisations controlled by established workers (unions and political parties) attempt to rally and act for non-established workers as well.

The second line of cleavage among industrial workers is brought about by the division between national and international capital (*i.e.*, that engaged in international production). The established workers in the sector of international production are potential allies of international capital. This is not to say that those workers have no conflict with international capital, only that international capital has the resources to resolve these conflicts and to isolate them from conflicts involving other labour groups by creating an enterprise corporatism in which both parties perceive their interest as lying in the continuing expansion of international production.

Established workers in the sector of national capital are more susceptible to the appeal of protectionism and national (rather than enterprise) corporatism in which the defence of national capital, of jobs and of the workers' acquired status in industrial relations institutions, are perceived to be interconnected.[39]

Non-established labour has become of particular importance in the expansion of international production. Production systems are being designed so as to make use of an increasing proportion of semi-skilled (and therefore frequently non-established) in relation to skilled (and established) labour.[40] This tendency in production organisation makes it possible for the centre to decentralise the actual physical production of goods to peripheral locations in which an abundant supply of relatively cheap non-established labour is to be found, and to retain control of the process and of the research and development upon which its future depends.

As a non-established workforce is mobilised in Third World countries by international production, governments in these countries have very frequently sought to pre-empt the possibility of this new social force developing its own class-conscious organisations by imposing upon it structures of state corporatism in the form of unions set up and controlled by the government or the dominant political party. This also gives local governments, through their control over local labour, additional leverage with international capital regarding the terms of direct investment. If industrial workers in Third World countries have thus sometimes been reduced to political and social quiescence, state corporatism may prove to be a stage delaying, but in the long run not eliminating, a more articulate self consciousness.[41]

Even if industry were to move rapidly into the Third World and local governments were, by and large, able to keep control over their industrial workforces, most of the populations of these countries may see no improvement, but probably a deterioration, in their conditions. New industrial jobs lag far behind increases in the labour force, while changes in agriculture dispossess many in the rural population. No matter how fast international production spreads, a very large part of the world's population in the poorest areas remains marginal to the world economy, having no employment or income, or the purchasing power derived from it. A major problem for international capital in its aspiration for hegemony is how to neutralise the effect of this marginalisation of perhaps one-third of the world's population so as to prevent its poverty from fuelling revolt.[42]

SOCIAL FORCES, STATE STRUCTURES,
AND FUTURE WORLD ORDER PROSPECTS

It would, of course, be logically inadmissible, as

well as imprudent, to base predictions of future world order upon the foregoing considerations. Their utility is rather in drawing attention to factors which could incline an emerging world order in one direction or another. The social forces generated by changing production processes are the starting point for thinking about possible futures. These forces may combine in different configurations, and as an exercise one could consider the hypothetical configurations most likely to lead to three different outcomes as to the future of the state system. The focus on these three outcomes is not, of course, to imply that no other outcomes or configurations of social forces are possible.

First is the prospect for a new hegemony being based upon the global structure of social power generated by the internationalising of production. This would require a consolidation of two presently powerful and related tendencies: the continuing dominance of international over national capital within the major countries, and the continuing internationalisation of the state. Implicit in such an outcome is a continuance of monetarism as the orthodoxy of economic policy, emphasising the stabilisation of the world economy (anti-inflationary policies and stable exchange rates) over the fulfilment of domestic socio-political demands (the reduction of unemployment and the maintenance of real wage levels).

The inter-state power configuration which could maintain such a world order, provided its member states conformed to this model, is a coalition centring upon the United States, the Federal Republic of Germany, and Japan, with the support of other OECD states, the co-optation of a few of the more industrialised Third World countries, such as Brazil, and of leading conservative OPEC countries, and the possibility of revived détente allowing for a greater linkage of the Soviet sphere into the world economy of international production. The new international division of labour, brought about through the progressive decentralisation of manufacturing into the Third World by international capital, would satisfy demands for industrialisation from those countries. Social conflict in the core countries would be combatted through enterprise corporatism, though many would be left unprotected by this method, particularly the non-established workers. In the peripheral countries, social conflict would be contained through a combination of state corporatism and repression.

The social forces opposed to this configuration have been noted above. National capital, those sections of established labour linked to national capital, newly mobilised non-established workers in the Third World, and socially marginal in the poor countries are all in some way or another potentially opposed to international capital, and to the state and world order structures most congenial to international capital. These forces do not, however, have any natural cohesion, and might be dealt with separately, or neutralised, by an effective hegemony. If they did come together under particular circumstances in a particular country, precipitating a change of regime, then that country might be dealt with in isolation by the world structure. In other words, where hegemony failed within a particular country, it could reassert itself through the world structure.

A second possible outcome is a non-hegemonic world structure of conflicting power centres. Perhaps the most likely way for this to evolve would be through the ascendancy in several core countries of neo-mercantilist coalitions which linked national capital and established labour, and were determined to opt out of arrangements designed to promote international capital and to organise their own power and welfare on a national or sphere-of-influence basis. The continuing pursuit of monetarist policies may be the single most likely cause of neo-mercantilist reaction. Legitimated as anti-inflationary, monetarist policies have been perceived as hindering national capital (because of high interest rates), generating unemployment (through planned recession), and adversely affecting relatively deprived social groups and regions dependent upon government services and transfer payments (because of budget-balancing cuts in state expenditures). An opposing coalition would attack monetarism for subordinating national welfare to external forces, and for showing an illusory faith in the markets (which are perceived to be manipulated by corporate-administered pricing). The likely structural form of neo-mercantilism within core states would be industry-level and national-level corporatism, bringing national capital and organised labour into a relationship with the government for the purpose of making and implementing of state policy. Peripheral states would have much the same structure as in the first outcome, but would be more closely linked to one or another of the core country economies.

A third and more remotely possible outcome would be the development of a counter-hegemony based on a Third World coalition against core country dominance and aiming towards the autonomous development of peripheral countries and the termination of the core-peripheral relationship. A counter-hegemony would consist of a coherent view of an alternative world order, backed by a concentration of power sufficient to maintain a challenge to core countries. While this outcome is foreshadowed by the demand for a New International Economic Order, the prevailing consensus behind this demand lacks a sufficiently clear view of an alternative world political economy to constitute counter-hegemony. The prospects of counter-hegemony lie very largely in the future development of state structures in the Third World.

The controlling social force in these countries is,

typically, what has been called a "state class,"[43] a combination of party, bureaucratic and military personnel and union leaders, mostly petty bourgeois in origin, which controls the state apparatus and through it attempt to gain greater control over the productive apparatus in the country. The state class can be understood as a local response to the forces generated by the internationalising of production, and an attempt to gain some local control over these forces. The orientation of the state class is indeterminate. It can be either conservative or radical. It may either bargain for a better deal within the world economy of international production, or it may seek to overcome the unequal internal development generated by international capital.

State classes of the first orientation are susceptible to incorporation into a new hegemonic world economy, and to the maintenance of state corporatist structures as the domestic counterpart to international capital. The second orientation could provide the backing for counter-hegemony. However, a state class is only likely to maintain the second and more radical orientation if it is supported from below in the form of a genuine populism (and not just a populism manipulated by political leaders). One may speculate that this could come about through the unfolding social consequences of international production, such as the mobilisation of a new non-established labour force coupled with the marginalisation of an increasing part of the urban population. The radical alternative could be the form of response to international capital in Third World countries, just as neo-mercantilism could be the response in richer countries. Each projects a particular state structure and vision of world order.

NOTES

1. Fernand Braudel, *Civilisation materiélle, Economie et Capitalisme XVe-XVIIIe Siècle,* 3 vols. (Paris: Armand Colin, 1979). Braudel's theory and method are outlined in his essay first published in 1958 in *Annales E.S.C.* "Histoire et sciences sociales. La longue duree" (republished in Braudel, *Ecrits sur l'histoire,* Paris: Flammarion, 1969).

2. There is now quite a large literature produced by this school. The basic work is I. Wallerstein, *The Modern World-System: Capitalist Agriculture and the Origins of the European World-Economy in the Sixteenth Century* (New York: Academic Press, 1974). A brief summary of the world systems theory is in Wallerstein, "The rise and future demise of the world capitalist system: Concepts for comparative analysis," *Comparative Studies in Society and History* (vol. 16, no. 4, Sept. 1974), pp. 387-415.

3. Among critics of the world systems approach,
note especially Theda Skocpol, "Wallerstein's World
Capitalist System: A Theoretical and Historical
Critique," *American Journal of Sociology* (Vol. 82, No. 5,
March 1977), pp. 1075-90; and more generally, her major
study, *States and Social Revolutions* (Cambridge:
Cambridge University Press, 1979). Also *see* Robert
Brenner, "The Origins of Capitalist Development: A
Critique of Neo-Smithian Marxism," *New Left Review* (No.
104, July-August 1977), pp. 25-92.

4. I use the term "world order" in preference to
"inter-state system" as it is relevant to all historical
periods (and not only those in which states have been the
component entities) and in preference to "world system"
as it is more indicative of a structure having only a
certain duration in time and avoiding the equilibrium
connotations of "system." "World" designates the
relevant totality, geographically limited by the range of
probable interactions (some past "worlds" being limited
to the Mediterranean, to Europe, to China, etc.).
"Order" is used in the sense of the way things usually
happen *(not* the absence of turbulence); thus disorder is
included in the concept of order. An inter-state system
is one historical form of world order. The term is used
in the plural to indicate that particular patterns of
power relationships which have endured in time can be
contrasted in terms of their principal characteristics as
distinctive world orders.

5. E. P. Thompson argues that historical concepts
must often "display extreme elasticity and allow for
great irregularity." His treatment of historical logic
develops this point in his essay "The Poverty of Theory"
in *The Poverty of Theory and Other Essays* (London:
Merlin Press, 1978), esp. pp. 231-242.

6. Friedrich Meinecke, *Machiavellism: The Doctrine
of Raison d'Etat and its Place in Modern History* trans.
by Douglas Scott (London: Routledge and Kegan Paul,
1957).

7. This is most clearly expressed in K. Waltz, *Man,
the State and War* (New York: Columbia University Press,
1954).

8. Thomas Hobbes, *Leviathan,* Part I, chap. xi.

9. Kenneth Waltz, in a paper presented to a panel
discussion at the American Political Science Association
in August 1980 for which a first version of the present
essay was written, asked the question "Will the future be
like the past?", which he answered affirmatively--not
only was the same pattern of relationships likely to
prevail but it would be for the good of all that this
should be so. It should be noted that the future
contemplated by Waltz was the next decade or so.

10. A recent example of this argument is Stephen
Krasner, *Defending the National Interest: Raw Materials
Investments and U.S. Foreign Policy* (Princeton:

Princeton University Press, 1978). The normative intent
of the new realism is most apparent as a polemic response
to liberal moralism. This was also the case for E. H.
Carr's *The Twenty Years' Crisis, 1919-1939* (London:
Macmillan, 1942) which offered a "scientific" mode of
thinking and about international relations in opposition
to the "utopianism" of the supporters of the League of
Nations in Britain. Dean Acheson and George Kennan, in
laying the foundations for U.S. Cold War policy
acknowledged their debt to Reinhold Niebuhr whose revival
of a pessimistic Augustinian view of human nature
challenged the optimistic Lockean view native to American
culture., Krasner's chosen target is "Lockean
liberalism" which he sees as having undermined the
rational defence of U.S. national interests.
11. *The New Science of Giambattista Vico* trans.
from the third edition by Thomas Goddard Bergin and Max
Harold Fisch (Ithaca and London: Cornell University
Press, 1970), p. 62, para. 349.
12. *Ibid.,* p. 6, para. 35; p. 32, para. 145; p. 25,
para. 161; p. 62. para. 349.
13. *Ibid.,* p. 19, para. 127.
14. *See,* for instance, R. G. Collingwood's
distinction between dialectical and eristical reasoning,
The New Leviathan (Oxford: Oxford University Press,
1942). Collingwood takes dialectic back to its Greek
origins and spares us the assertions of theological
Marxism concerning "Diamat."
15. Antonio Gramsci, *Selections from the Prison
Notebooks,* edited and trans. By Quintin Hoare and
Geoffrey Nowell-Smith (New York: International
Publishers, 1971), esp. pp. 158-168. The full critical
Italian edition *Quaderni del carcere* (Torino: Einaudi
editore, 1975) contains additional passages on this
point, *e.g.,* pp. 471, 1321, 1492. Gramsci saw ideas,
politics and economies as reciprocally related,
convertible into each other and bound together in a
blocco storico. "Historical materialism," he wrote, "is
in a certain sense a reform and development of
Hegelianism. It is philosophy freed from unilateral
ideological elements, the full consciousness of the
contradictions of philosophy." (Einaudi edition, p. 471,
my rough translation).
16. As in Krasner, *op. cit., and Peter Katzenstein
(ed.), Beyond Power and Plenty. Foreign Economic
Policies of Advanced Industrial States* (Madison,
Wisconsin: University of Wisconsin Press, 1978). The
United States is represented by these authors as a state
which is weak in relation to the strength of civil
society (or more particularly of interests in civil
society), whereas other states, *e.g.,* Japan or France,
are stronger in relation to their societies. Civil
society is thus seen in the U.S. case as limiting the
effectiveness of the state.

17.   The notion of a framework for action recalls what Machiavelli called *necessità,* a sense that the conditions of existence require action to create or sustain a form of social order. *Necessità* engenders both the possibility of a new order and all the risks inherent in changing the existing order ". . . few men ever welcome new laws setting up a new order in the state unless necessity makes it clear to them that there is a need for such laws; and since such a necessity cannot arise without danger, the state may easily be ruined before the new order has been brought to completion." Niccolo Machiavelli, *The Discourses,* (ed.) Bernard Crick (Harmondsworth, Middlesex: Penguin Books, 1970), pp. 105-106.

18.   In this regard, Stanley Hoffmann has written: "Born   and   raised   in   America,   the   discipline   of international relations is, so to speak, too close to the fire.   It needs triple distance: it should move away from the contemporary world towards the past; from the perspective of a superpower (and a highly conservative one), toward that of the weak and the revolutionary--away from the impossible quest for stability; from the glide into policy science, back to the steep ascent toward the peaks which the questions raised by traditional political philosophy represent."   In "An American social science: international relations," *Daedalus* (Summer 1977), p. 59.

19.   On   intersubjective   meanings,   *see*   Charles Taylor, "Hermeneutics and Politics," in Paul Connerton (ed.)   *Critical   Sociology*   (Harmondsworth,   Middlesex: Penguin Books, 1965), chap. VI.   Also relevant is Peter L. Berger and Thomas Luckman, *The Social Construction of Reality* (Harmondsworth, Middlesex: Penguin, 1971).

20.   C.   Taylor,   *op.   cit.,*   points   out   that expectations with regard to negotiating behaviour are culturally differentiated in the present world.   Garrett Mattingly, *Renaissance Diplomacy* (London: Cape, 1955) studied   the   origin   of   the   ideas   outlined   in   this paragraph which are implicit in the modern state system.

21.   Collective   images   are   not   aggregations   of fragmented opinions of individuals such as are compiled through   surveys;   they   are   coherent   mental   types expressive of the world views of specific groups such as may be reconstructed through the work of historians and sociologists, *e.g.,* Max Weber's reconstructions of forms of religious consciousness.

22.   Gramsci's principal application of the concept of hegemony was to the relations among social classes, *e.g.,*   in   explaining   the   inability   of   the   Italian industrial bourgeoisie to establish its hegemony after the unification of Italy and in examining the prospects of   the   italian   industrial   workers   establishing   their class hegemony over peasantry and petty bourgeoisie so as to create a new *blocco storico* (historic bloc)--a term which in Gramsci's work corresponds roughly to the notion

of historic structure in this essay. The term "hegemony" in Gramsci's work is linked to debates in the international Communist movement concerning revolutionary strategy and in this connection its application is specifically to classes. The form of the concept, however, draws upon his reading of Machiavelli and is not restricted to class relations but has a broader potential applicability. Gramsci's adjustment of Machiavellian ideas to the realities of the world he knew was an exercise in dialectic in the sene defined above. It is an appropriate continuation of his method to perceive the applicability of the concept to world order structures as suggested here. For Gramsci, as for Machiavelli, the general question involved in hegemony is the nature of power, and power is a centaur, part man, part beast, a combination of force and consent. See Machiavelli, *The Prince* , Norton Critical Edition, (ed.) Robert M. Adams (New York: W. W. Norton, 1977), pp. 49-50; Gramsci, *Selections op. cit.*, pp. 169-170.

23. E. H. Carr, *Nationalism and After* (London: Macmillan, 1945).

24. Charles Morazé, *Les bourgeois conquérants* (Paris: Colin, 1957).

25. A recent discussion of the reciprocal character of these relations is in Peter A. Gourevitch, "The Second Image Reversed," *International Organization* (Vol. 32, No. 4, Autumn 1978), pp. 881-911.

26. I have been engaged with Jeffrey Harrod in a study of production relations on a world scale which begins with an examination of distinctive patterns of power relations in the production process as separate historical structures and which then leads to a consideration of different forms of state and global political economy. Bringing in these last two levels is necessary to an understanding of the existence of the different patterns of production relations and the hierarchy of relationships among them. One could equally well adopt forms of state or world orders as the point of departure and ultimately be required to bring the other levels in to explain the historical process.

27. Robert O. Keohane, "The Theory of Hegemonic Stability and Changes in International Economic Regimes, 1967-77," in Ole Holsti, Randolph Siverson, and Alexander George (eds.), *Change in the International System* (Boulder, Colorado: Westview Press, 1981). Keohane cites as others who have contributed to this theory Charles Kindleberger, Robert Gilpin and Stephen Krasner. "Hegemony" is used by Keohane in the limited sene of dominance by a state. This meaning is to be distinguished from its meaning in this article which is derived from Gramsci, *i.e.*, hegemony as a structure of dominance, leaving open the question of whether the dominant power is a state, or a group of states, or some combination of state and private power, which is

sustained by broadly-based consent through acceptance of an ideology and of institutions consistent with this structure. Thus a hegemonic structure of world order is one in which power takes a primarily consensual form, as distinguished from a non-hegemonic order in which there are manifestly rival powers and no power has been able to establish the legitimacy of its dominance. There can be dominance without hegemony; hegemony is one possible form dominance may take. Institutionalised hegemony, as used in this essay, corresponds to what Keohane calls a "strong international regime." His theory can be restated in our terms as: dominance by a powerful state is most conducive to the development of hegemony. In the present text, the term "hegemony" is reserved for a consensual order and "dominance" *refers only to a preponderance of material power.*

28. Two classic studies relevant particularly to the inter-war period are Karl Polanyi, *The Great Transformation* (Boston, Mass.: Little, Brown, 1957) and E. H. Carr, *The Twenty Years' Crisis, op. cit.* The chapter by Stephen Blank, "Britain: The Politics of Foreign Economic Policy, the Domestic Economy and the Problem of Pluralistic Stagnation," in Katzenstein (ed.), *op. cit.,* comments on post-war British economic policy; as does Stephen Krasner in "State Power and the Structure of International Trade," *World Politics* (Vol. 28, No. 3, April 1976). *Also see* R. F. Harrod, *The Life of John Maynard Keynes* (London: Macmillan, 1951).

29. The international implications of the New Deal are dealt with in several passages in Arthur M. Schlesinger, Jr., *The Age of Roosevelt,* esp. Vol. II, *The Coming of the New Deal* (London: Heinemann, 1960). Charles Meier, "The Politics of Productivity: Foundations of American International Economic Policy after World War II," in Katzenstein, *op. cit.,* discusses the relationship between the New Deal and the post-war ideology of world order. Richard Gardner, *Sterling-Dollar Diplomacy: Anglo-American Collaboration in the Reconstruction of Multilateral Trade* (Oxford: Clarendon Press, 1956) shows the link between New Deal ideas and the institutions of world economy set up after World War II in the Bretton Woods negotiations.

30. The basic point I am making here is suggested by a passage in Gramsci's *Prison Notebooks* which reads: "Do international relations precede or follow (logically) fundamental social relations? There can be no doubt but that they follow. Any organic innovation in the social structure, through its technical-military expressions, modifies organically absolute and relative relations in the international field too." Gramsci used the term "organic" to refer to relatively long-term and permanent changes, as opposed to "conjunctural." *Selections op. cit.,* p. 176-177. In the critical Italian edition, the original is to be found in Vol. III, p. 1562.

31. E. J. Hobsbawn writes: "The men who officially presided over the affairs of the victorious bourgeois order in its moment of triumph were a deeply reactionary country nobleman from Prussia, an imitation emperor in France and a succession of aristocratic landowners in Britain." *The Age of Capital, 1843-1875* (London: Sphere Books, 1977), p. 15.

32. Among analysts who concur in this are Karl Polanyi, *op. cit.*, Gunnar Myrdal, *Beyond the Welfare State* (New Haven: Yale University Press, 1960); E. H. Carr, *Nationalism and After, op. cit.*; and Geoffrey Barraclough, *Introduction to Contemporary History* (London: Penguin, 1968).

33. George Lichtheim, *Imperialism* (New York: Praeger, 1971) has proposed a periodisation of imperialisms, and I have taken the term "liberal imperialism" from him.

34. "The Imperial State System" paper presented to the American Political Science Association, Washington, D.C., August 1980.

35. Max Beloff was perhaps the first to point to the mechanisms whereby participation in international organisations altered the internal policy-making practices of states in his *New Dimensions in Foreign Policy* (London: Allen and Unwin, 1961). R. W. Cox and H. K. Jacobson, et al, *The Anatomy of Influence: Decision-making in International Organisation* (New Haven: Yale University Press, 1972) represented the political systems of international organisations as including segments of states. R. O. Keohane and J. S. Nye, "Transgovernmental Relations and International Organizations," *World Politics* (Vol. 27 October 1974) pointed to the processes whereby coalitions are formed among segments of the apparatuses of different states and the ways in which international institutions facilitate such coalitions. These various works, while they point to the existence of mechanisms for policy co-ordination among states and for penetration of external influences within states, do not discuss the implications of these mechanisms for the structure of power within states. It is this structural aspect I wish to designate by the term "internationalisation of the state." Christian Palloix refers to "L'internationalisation de l'appareil de l'Etat national, de certains lieux de cet appareil d'Etat...." (*L'internationalisation du capital,* Paris, Maspero, 1975, p. 82) by which he designates those segments of national states which serve as policy supports for the internationalisation of production. He thus raises the question of structural changes in the state, though he does not enlarge upon the point. Keohane and Nye, subsequent to the work mentioned above, linked the transgovernmental mechanism to the concept of "interdependence." *Power and Interdependence,* (Boston: Little, Brown, 1977). I find this concept tends to

obscure the power relationships involved in structural changes in both state and world order and prefer not to use it for that reason. Peter Gourevitch, *op. cit.*, does retain the concept interdependence while insisting that it be linked with power struggles among social forces within states.

36. There is, of course, a whole literature implicit in the argument of this paragraph. Some sketchy references may be useful. Andrew Shonfield, *Modern Capitalism* (London: Oxford University Press, 1965) illustrated the development of corporative-type structures of the kind I associate with the welfare-nationalist state. The shift from industry-level corporatism to an enterprise-based corporatism led by the big public and private corporations has been noted in some industrial relations works, particularly those concerned with the emergence of a "new working class," *e.g.*, Serge Mallet, *La nouvelle classe ouvrière* (Paris: Seuil, 1963), but the industrial relations literature has generally not linked what I have elsewhere called enterprise corporatism to the broader framework suggested here (*cf.* R. W. Cox, "Pour une étude prospective des relations de production," *Sociologie du Travail*, 2, 1977). Erhand Friedberg, "L'internationalisation de l'économie et modalités d'intervention de l'état: La 'politique industrielle,'" in *Planification et Société* (Grenoble: Presses universitaires de Grenoble, 1974), pp. 94-108, discusses the subordination of the old corporatism to the new. The shift in terminology from planning to industrial policy is related to the internationalising of state and economy. Industrial policy has become a matter of interest to global economic policy makers, *cf.* William Diebold, Jr., *Industrial Policy as an International Issue* (New York: McGraw-Hill for the Council on Foreign Relations, 1980) and John Pinder, Takashi Hosomi and William Diebold, *Industrial Policy and the International Economy* (Trilateral Commission, 1979). If planning evokes the spectre of economic nationalism, industrial policy, as the Trilateral Commission study points out, can be looked upon with favour from a world economy perspective as a necessary aspect of policy harmonisation: "We have argued that industrial policies are needed to deal with structural problems in the modern economies. Thus, international action should not aim to dismantle these policies. The pressure should, rather, be towards positive and adaptive industrial policies, whether on the part of single countries or groups of countries combined. Far from being protectionist, industrial policy can help them to remove a cause of protectionism, by making the process of adjustment less painful." (p. 50). It may be objected that the argument and references presented here are more valid for Europe than for the United States, and that, indeed, the very concept of corporatism is alien to

U.S. ideology. To this it can be replied that since the principal levers of the world economy are in the United States, the U.S. economy adjusts less than those of European countries and peripheral countries, and the institutionalisation of adjustment mechanisms is accordingly less developed. Structural analyses of the U.S. economy have, however, pointed to a distinction between a corporate international-oriented sector and a medium and small business nationally-oriented sector, and to the different segments of the state and different policy orientations associated with each. *Cf.* John Kenneth Galbraith, *Economics and the Public Purpose* (London: Andre Deutsch, 1974) and James O'Connor, *The Fiscal Crisis of the State* (New York: St. Martin's Press, 1973). Historians point to the elements of corporatism in the New Deal, *e.g.*, Arthur M. Schlesinger, Jr., *op. cit.*

37. The Zaire case recalls the arrangements imposed by western powers on the Ottoman Empire and Egypt in the late nineteenth century, effectively attaching certain revenues for the service of foreign debt. See Herbert Feis, *Europe the World's Banker, 1870-1914* (New York: Kelly for the Council on Foreign Relations, 1961), pp. 332-341, 384-397.

38. The evidence for the existence of a transnational managerial class lies in actual forms of organisation, the elaboration of ideology, financial supports, and the behaviour of individuals. Other structures stand as rival tendecies, *e.g.*, national capital and its interests sustained by a whole other structure of loyalties, agencies, etc. Individuals or firms and state agencies may in some phases of their activity be caught up now in one, now in another tendency. Thus the membership of the class may be continually shifting though the structure remains. It is sometimes argued that this is merely a case of U.S. capitalists giving themselves a hegemonic aura, an argument that by implication makes of imperialism a purely national phenomenon. There is no doubting the U.S. origin of the values carried and propagated by this class, but neither is there any doubt that many non-U.S. citizens and agencies also participate in it nor that its world view is global and distinguishable from the purely national capitalisms which exist alongside it. Through the transnational managerial class American culture, or a certain American business culture, has become globally hegemonic. Of course, should neo-mercantilist tendencies come to prevail in international economic relations, this transnational class structure would wither.

39. Some industries appear as ambiguously astride the two tendencies, *e.g.*, the automobile industry. During a period of economic expaansion, the international aspect of this industry dominated in the United States, and the United Auto Workers union took the lead in

creating world councils for the major international auto firms with a view to inaugurating multinational bargaining. As the industry was hit by recession, protectionism came to the fore.

40. R. W. Cox, "Labour and Employment in the Late Twentieth Century," in R. St. J. Macdonald, et al, (eds), *The International Law and Policy of Human Welfare* (Sijhoff and Noordhoff, 1978). This tendency can be seen as the continuation of a long-term direction of production organisation of which Taylorism was an early stage, in which control over the work process is progressively wrested from workers and separated out from the actual performance of tasks so as to be concentrated with management. *See* Harry Braverman, *Labor and Monopoly Capital* (New York: Monthly Review, 1974).

41. Recent news from Brazil indicates restiveness on the part of Sao Paulo workers whose unions have been subjected to a state corporatist structure since the time of President Vargas.

42. The World Bank promotes rural development and birth control. The concept of "self-reliance," once a slogan of anti-imperialism meaning "decoupling" from the imperial system, has been co-opted by the imperial system to mean self-help among populations becoming marginalised--a do-it-yourself welfare programme.

43. I have borrowed the term from Hartmut Elsenhas, "The State Class in the Third World: For a New Conceptualisation of Periphery Modes of Production" (unpublished).

PART 5

Culture, Ideology, and Peace

Contemporary Militarism and the Discourse of Dissent

R.B.J. Walker

I

The widespread militarization of modern life in general and the instability of nuclear deterrence between the superpowers in particular is portrayed with increasing plausibility as the most pressing of the many dilemmas that confront us in the late twentieth century. Scenarios and technologies of limited nuclear war and counterforce first strike, and the proliferation of advanced weaponry across the globe, have led to a renewal of popular concern about a final collapse, an Armageddon without the Revelation.

It is not that the scale of the problem before us will compel any automatic leap into more rational and humane policies; necessity does not seem likely to father its own solution here. But neither can we acquiesce in the fatalistic and ahistorical discourse that speaks of the inevitable continuity of the current clash of powers under the charlatan label of realism. This has been a very influential formulation of the alternatives open to us. It is also deeply misleading. In fact it is a formulation that has done much to inhibit creative thinking about international politics for a long time. Rather, the analysis of and resistance to the militarization of the modern world must be understood as occurring within a historical and political arena--an arena of constraints, opportunities, and struggles.

It is this relationship between theoretical analysis and political action that concerns me here. The structures of contemporary militarism have now been the subject of a great deal of penetrating analysis and research for a considerable period.[1] Such analysis

----

Reprinted by permission from *Alternatives: A Journal of World Policy* 9:3, 1983-84.

provides a clear picture of a steadily deteriorating situation, a picture that seems to call ever more urgently for an interventionary as well as an analytic stance. Peace research, world order studies, and other similar orientations to this issue have always had a fairly strong policy orientation. They have now begun to merge with widespread popular movements that seek to generate resistance to current trends and to create alternative structures of peace and security. The peace movements themselves have even begun to be the subject of political analysis as one of the more interesting and persistant innovations in the otherwise fairly regularized political life of advanced industrial societies.

In this context, resistance to contemporary militarism raises many of the same problems that have confronted a wide range of radical social movements in this century. If anything has been learned from the experience of such movements, it is that the inherent rationality or justice of a cause does not guarantee its political effectiveness. Indeed, the very basis of justice and rationality on which claims for social change are made have to be established in a political milieu amidst a variety of counterclaims that favor the status quo. As a very wide range of theorists of modern political life have stressed, societies cohere around deeply structured patterns of consensus and legitimacy. These patterns are expressed in hegemonic or dominant ideological forms and discourses. In most Western industrial societies, it is precisely these ideological forms and discourses that have become an increasingly important instrument of political power and social control. The prevailing structures of knowledge are simultaneously structures of power. As a consequence, attempts to articulate critical and emancipatory positions--a discourse of dissent--become coopted, deflected, and even self-defeating.

This issue is usually posed as the "problem of ideology." It is undoubtedly one of the more important and most complex themes in contemporary social and political analysis. Although I do not intend to pursue it here in any great depth,[2] it is a theme that seems to me to have been unduly neglected by most critical discussions of contemporary militarism. Too often the assumption is made that it is enough to demonstrate clearly the insanity of the dynamics of arms races, to point to the brutal inhumanity of acquiring more and more weapons in a world of poverty, disease, and starvation, or to suggest that the supposed enemy is not quite as bad as has been assumed. These are indeed all points that need to be made with great force in the modern world. But although individuals are often moved by this reasoning, economies, societies, and states tend to be more resistant.

Hence my more narrowly conceived concern in this paper is to draw attention to the way in which various forms of the critique of contemporary militarism show quite different potentialities for undermining the hegemonic discourse that legitimizes and fosters militarism. My main focus is on the discourse of dissent itself. My starting point is a brief discussion of a number of fundamentally different forms of the critique of contemporary militarism as they have developed in the West in general and in North America in particular. This leads first to an analysis of some of the connections between the main theoretical assumptions and orientations of each form of critique and its characteristic fate in the political sphere. The discussion then proceeds to an analysis of the relations between each form of critique, and thus of the internal structure of the discourse of dissent to contemporary militarism as a whole.

II

Perhaps the most pervasive criticisms of contemporary militarism in the West draw upon some version of what can be called a *universalist moral argument*. Recognizing that so much of our contemporary predicament arises from the conflict generated in a fragmented system of states, critiques of the present and hopes for the future are often rooted in some understanding of the underlying community of humankind, either in fact or in potential. Many well established traditions are at work here, from pacifism to theories of natural law and various derivatives of Enlightenment rationalism. Some more recent versions stress the imminent danger of universal oblivion, and thus underline the increasing necessity of a global perspective on human affairs, particularly in response to the dangers of nuclear war or ecological degradation.

In one sense this kind of critique is unimpeachable. It has the angels on its side. It appeals to *one* humanity. It sides with civilization against barbarism. It embodies the aspirations of a broad range of social, political, and ethical doctrines, whether secular or religious, liberal or socialist, traditionalist or modern. It is an argument that has immense moral force and that lends itself to a powerful rhetoric. It is immediately understandable by people who, although having little grasp of historical or technical details, have a good intuitive sense that something is grievously wrong with the state of the world. Its broad appeal is precisely what makes this kind of critique a very effective mobilizing force, and explains much of the blurring of conventional ideological divisions that has been such an important characteristic of Western peace movements. Given that so much of the official rhetoric of modern states, not to mention modern international organizations, is also couched in this form, opponents of contemporary militarism are able to make good use of the exposure of hypocracy as a way of undermining official policy.

The very characteristics that have allowed this kind of argument to be so effective in mobilizing public support have simultaneously prevented it from having any very strong impact on state policies. For the appeal to normative and moral considerations on the one hand, and the universalist aspirations of the appeal on the other, are openly vulnerable to challenges from the dominant discourse about international politics. Against the appeal to normative principles it is only necessary to invoke the all-purpose charge of utopianism and idealism--to suggest that appeals to justice always get in the way of order, which of course is presumed to require hard-nosed policies of *realpolitik*. Against the appeal to universalism it is only necessary to invoke some great enemy to demonstrate that a community of humankind would be all very well if it were not for the aggressive/subversive/uncivilized/undemocratic/imperial-ist/etc., behavior of some other state. Whatever the claims of a cosmopolitan conception of humanity, of species survival, of a global system in which we all participate, conventional militarist rhetoric has only to tap some old Manichean doctrine about "them" in order to justify yet another increment in defense spending. And thus we get the most common form of public debate about contemporary militarism, in which a short, sharp reminder of--in the modern American case--the "Soviet threat," or the "realities" of international politics, is enough to puncture popular sentiments once they begin to impinge on the conventional rituals of foreign policy. In this sense, the universalist moral form of argument is highly susceptible to cooptation. It enables the peace movement to be portrayed in images and categories intrinsic to the hegemonic discourse. And the more the discourse of dissent corroborates the stereotype, the more it can be passed over as the inconsequential posturing of the emotional and uninformed.

In terms of its ability to generate effective political action, then, this kind of argument is deeply ambivalent. Its capacity to mobilize public support is considerable, but it has rarely been able to undermine the hegemonic discourse of international politics in any effective way. In some forms it may well reenforce that discourse. And in any case, this kind of argument does have important limitations just because it tends to leave so many important aspects of contemporary international politics out of account.

Some of these aspects are stressed by what can be called the *socioeconomic argument*. This argument, too, comes in many forms but essentially involves some understanding of the structures of contemporary militarism in terms of the socioeconomic forces that have given rise to them. Thus it points to the intimate connections between weapons procurement policies and national economic policies, international trade, the interest of particular corporations or cities, miltary-industrial (or bureaucratic) complexes, and the internationalization of capital. At a popular level it may stress the social sacrifices that are made in the form of schools, hospitals, and so on in order to build one more weapons system. At a more theoretical level it may emphasize the dual role that military hardware plays in the modern world as both weaponry and commodity, or it may enter into an ongoing debate about the precise economic consequences of military expenditures. The structures of contemporary militarism are here seen to emerge from a complex interdependence of economic and political relations, and the conventional picture of international politics as the collision of autonomous states comes to be seen as exceptionally oversimplified or even naive.

Where the universalist moral argument is grounded in somewhat metaphysical and abstract considerations, and is always in danger of degenerating into platitudes and collapsing in the face of supposed "realities," the socioeconomic argument derives from a firmer grasp of precisely what some of those realities are. And from this point of view it becomes clear that the critique of contemporary militarism implies a critique of socioeconomic structures on a massive scale, although the degree of radicalism varies widely according to the underlying theoretical or ideological assumptions of the analysis. It is in this context that much of the strength of this kind of argument in promoting effective action appears most clearly, in that it merges with related critiques made by progressivist social forces about a wide range of issues. Indeed, given that modern industrial societies have been so successful in defusing radical social protests and in undermining counter-hegemonic discourse in general, the critique of militarism in these terms has the potential to restimulate other more established forms of sociopolitical dissent. The mobilizing potential of this kind of critique is therefore more restricted but it may well be channeled into existing social structures and movements that can enhance its effectiveness considerably.

Conversely, this kind of argument brings a number of substantial liabilities with it into the political arena. As long as it retains any degree of theoretical sophistication it is difficult to communicate in simple terms. And once simplified it can degenerate into conspiracy theories, or direct attention to symptoms rather than to underlying dynamics. To point the finger at some cabal, some particularly insidious corporation or personality, is to direct attention away from more fundamental issues. More significantly, to dissent from the prevailing consensus on socioeconomic issues is to come face to face with the full force of hegemonic discourse, with its ingrained assumptions about economic growth, material accumulation, negative freedom, individual consumption, and political legitimacy. Thus those who benefit from the status quo may become torn between their own short-term self-interests and some more universally framed sense of injustice or disaster. And in any case, such forms of dissent are subject to the full force of counterrevolutionary rhetoric, from the more subtle constructions of "deviant behavior" to the more blatant indictments of--again in the American case--"Reds under the bed." In short, this kind of argument raises the general question of whether radical political and economic change is possible at all in advanced industrial societies.

The universalist moral argument tends toward radicalism at the level of consciousness. The socioeconomic argument tends toward radicalism in terms of the larger structures of political order. A third kind of argument is radical only in terms of implications that can be drawn from what is essentially a very conservative position. It is conservative precisely because it comes from within the establishment of those who more or less accept the basic assumptions on which many of the structures of contemporary militarism are constructed. Yet although accepting these assumptions, they argue that a number of "internal contradictions" in the contemporary international system have become intolerably tense and may be set to explode. This argument can be called the *strategic-geopolitical argument,* although it emerges primarily out of the specific difficulties created by strategies of nuclear deterrence.

Exponents of this view are given neither to illusions about the perfectability of human life on earth nor to radical schemes to overturn social and economic institutions. They view international politics as having always been a matter of quarrelsome states seeking to protect and extend their own interests. The central problem has been to create some minimum conditions of order in the international system so that states can at least coexist. To the extent that nuclear weapons have made direct war between the superpowers unthinkable, relations between them have been characterized by threats to use rather than the actual use of such weapons. Stability and order have come to depend on the fact that each side can still inflict unacceptable levels of damage on the other even after suffering an all-out first strike.

As this form of international order evolved it

became apparent that many factors could undermine the basic requirements of deterrence and return us to an inherently unstable situation in which war would become far more likely. And a great number of factors including technological innovations and the development of "flexible response" capabilities have now brought us very close to such a position. The new generation of counterforce first strike weapons and the various technologies that increase the likelihood of "launch on warning" policies or decrease the chances of effective arms control converge to reduce the stability on which security and international order have come to depend. The precise dangers posed by particular weapons systems may be in dispute, but the general tendency toward destabilization is very clear.

From this perspective, the very priority accorded to order has led an impressive array of conservatives, from academic strategists to the highest reaches of the military establishment, to suggest that our means of defense are becoming more dangerous than any potential enemy. It is the concern for order that has pushed them into a strange kind of alliance with people of radically different ideological persuasions. And it is a concern that has considerable potential for generating some kinds of effective political action. An appeal against militarism from those with some sort of military credentials is more difficult to deflect than appeals rooted in the more usual forms of progressivist thought. The appeal is capable of cutting through the technocratic jargon and can undermine the mystique of numbers and hardware that legitimizes and obscures the more fundamental strategic issues in the public sphere. To be warned of dire dangers by those who have in the past been partly responsible for bringing these dangers closer may provide an odd political spectacle, but it is certainly one that has added considerable credibility and power to the critique of current policies in the United States.

Moreover, to the extent that this kind of critique operates in terms of the prevailing assumptions of the hegemonic discourse of international politics, it carries greater weight within at least some policymaking structures. In some cases it may even constitute an orthodoxy that has become outflanked by political forces driven more by visions of victory and supremacy than by traditions of order and coexistence.

Conversely, this argument also has many liabilities. Its highly technical language and sophistication is difficult to communicate to a broader public, certainly not in a form that will mobilize widespread support. Moreover, despite its ability to undermine the hegemonic discourse on its own terms, it is eminently susceptible to cooptation by that discourse. In fact, destabilizing technology can be deployed and justified publicly in terms that seem to satisfy this kind of critique. More

significantly as a critique rooted in the dominant
discourse, it may well enhance the legitimacy of the
discourse. As a coopted critique, it is unlikely to
offer any alternative except those that have been ruled
out as impossible on grounds already established by the
hegemonic discourse. And thus, although it can be
disturbingly effective in identifying some of the more
immediately dangerous features of our current
predicament, it offers little in the way of guidance in
the search for a less dangerous form of world order.

III

The foregoing is a very simple categorization of the
main forms of dissent on contemporary militarism. The
categories themselves are fairly conventional, and they
could be elaborated at much greater length. There are
many important variations within each category
particularly with respect to the conception of
socioeconomic structures that underlie contemporary
militarist tendencies. In this case, for example,
significantly different analyses arise from liberal and
Marxist traditions. And in practice, dissent usually
draws on more than one of these three categories.
Indeed, the tendency to think in terms of all three is
becoming much more common. Nevertheless, this simple
categorization is sufficient for my present purposes and
it does capture the main lines of fracture within the
Western peace movement.
The most striking fact about the critique of
contemporary militarism viewed in these ways is that
although the three arguments emerge from and embody very
different theoretical and doctrinal positions, they
converge in a common indictment. Alliances between
different groups and the pragmatic cooling of doctrinal
differences in pursuit of some common interest may be the
very essence of political life, but the peace movement
seems to have become a rather extreme case. And this is
precisely because, for all the differences among them,
the three forms of critique outlined above each capture
important aspects of a very complex phenomenon. Although
it may be easier to adopt the model of the blind men
discovering an elephant and to confuse a part with the
whole, the most interesting questions posed by the
inherent fragmentation of the critique of contemporary
militarism concern the nature of the relations among the
various approaches. It does now make some sense to speak
of a single discourse of dissent on this issue, albeit
one marked at times by quite vigorous internal
disagreement and dialogue. And if the dialogue rather
than the disagreement is to be encouraged, then it seems
important to understand more clearly the relationship
between these different forms of critique both as they

are presently constituted and as they might be developed.

One way of pursuing this issue is to think in terms of levels of analysis. The strategic-geopolitical argument, for example, has a rather narrow focus on what used to be called "high" politics, the diplomatic, military, and technological relations of sovereign powers seeking to live with their "security dilemma." The socioeconomic argument has a much broader conception of modern political structures, one in which states have only a "relative autonomy" from other powerful economic and social forces. From this point of view, international politics takes on a vertical as well as a horizontal dimension. What is of interest here is still the state, but the state is conceived not as some black box labeled "state power" or "national interest" but as the principal mechanism integrating and regulating a much more complex "world system" or "international political economy." Where in an older tradition of international relations theory the notion of levels of analysis became a device for reifying various categories of supposedly discrete phenomena--particularly so-called national and international systems--more recent literature stresses their interaction, indeed their dialectical tensions. Thus it is possible to understand these two arguments as being related by a fairly coherent analytical model that is directly concerned with understanding the relationship between, say, the logic of deterrence and the logic of the internationalization of capital.

Similarly it is possible to think in this way of a number of even broader structures developing in the modern world that can provide a more concrete reference for the various kinds of universalist moral argument. Whether one speaks of a growing populist recognition of a common habitat and destiny, or of the frail beginnings of universally recognized standards of, say, human rights or international law, and so on, it is not entirely foolish to contemplate an emergence of some kind of global community of humankind. But this is to get into issues that are usually invoked not in the static analyses of structuralism but in terms of history and change. That is to say, the relations between the various forms of critique can be framed not only in terms of various "levels" of some all-inclusive structure, but also in terms of time.

Critiques that emphasize problems arising from the instability of nuclear deterrence provoke a sense of urgency and immediacy. The real problems are understood to be short term, or at least a matter of buying time so that some more lasting arrangement can be devised. The most frequent responses here involve a greater emphasis being placed on arms control, that is, on negotiations to minimize the dangers that are intrinsic to power-balancing systems in general and nuclear-deterrence systems in particular. This emphasis often goes hand in

hand with the advocacy of minimum deterrence policies, as
if the various pressures that have already undermined
minimum deterrence can be somehow swept away. One can
easily agree that policies like these might hold some
promise of constraining some of the more immediately
threatening weapons deployments between the superpowers.
Nevertheless, to suggest that this is all that can be
done is, in the face of the historical record, to admit
the high probability of eventual collapse. Hence the
appeal to longer-term solutions. For those operating
with strategic-geopolitical traditions, the options are
somewhat limited, and usually consist of suggestions that
some kind of "political" understanding can be found, that
some form of détente can be resurrected. More optimistic
solutions are forced to allow for the possibility of more
fundamental social and economic transformations,
transformations that embody some conception of "progress"
and radical action and that incorporate a vision of a
more desirable future. Hence the relation between the
three main forms of critique becomes structured in terms
of a historical progression: first things first, and,
hopefully, more fundamental transformations later.

Both of these ways of thinking about the relations
between different forms of the critique of contemporary
militarism seem inherently plausible. They offer a basis
for some kind of division of labor within the peace
movement, for structuring compromise and accommodation
between different doctrinal positions, and for organizing
research on alternative security policies. However, they
both contain an inherent ambiguity that raises important
questions about the direction in which such compromise
leads.

These three main forms of dissent to contemporary
militarism fall easily into a hierarchical pattern. The
strategic-geopolitical argument is highly specific and
focuses on the very short term. The socioeconomic
argument focuses on broader structures and has a much
longer time perspective. The universalist moral argument
is broader still and works with a more grandiose view of
the future, even if it often generates an impatient
desire to create heaven on earth as quickly as possible.
It is a hierarchy that seems to pose the familiar problem
of chickens and eggs. Do we need to solve problems at
the more specific or more immediate level before
beginning more far-reaching transformations? Or is it
necessary to revolutionize the prevailing socioeconomic
structures, not to mention the prevailing political
consciousness, before we can hope to escape from the
internal contradictions of nuclear deterrence? The
simplest way out of this dilemma is to reject the
either/or alternative and pursue all the avenues that are
available. But even here, an implicit value judgment is
inevitably made. Even though it may be necessary to
emphasize strategic-geopolitical issues in the short

term, the primary emphasis must be placed on some broader or "higher" level. At the very least, it is the possibility of some eventual solution at a higher level that gives meaning to work at a lower or more specific level. After all, a characteristic hallmark of the so-called realist tradition of international relations theory is that after repetitiously deflating universalist and moral aspirations of all kinds, the famous texts nearly all lose the courage of their convictions and conclude by invoking the possibility of something other than a continuous clash of state powers at some future time. Whether or not explicitly acknowledged, the discourse of dissent embodies a normative doctrine of "emergence." Priority is ultimately accorded to the more general, more universalist forms of argument. We cannot have a lasting peace, we might say, unless we reorganize our socioeconomic structures, and more particularly, unless we develop some more deeply grounded community of humankind. All else can only be a stop-gap measure.

In practice, however, it is the strategic-geopolitical argument that has become the dominant aspect of the discourse of dissent and that has become the focus of debates about current policies. The tendency has been not toward "emergence" but toward "reductionism." The reason is not that the strategic-geopolitical argument is the most popular or best known but that it has a long tradition of asserting itself over and coopting on its behalf both other forms of dissent. That is to say, it is not enough to suggest that all the main forms of the critique of contemporary militarism have an important contribution to make, although they do. And it is not enough to say that analytical or time-sequence relationships between them can be worked out, although they can. It is also necessary to understand that the discourse of dissent contains its own internal "political" dynamics in which its most radical forms have constantly been subverted by its most conservative ones.

IV

The most immediately pressing aspects of contemporary militarism are undoubtedly those arising from the nuclear confrontation between the superpowers. It is certainly this particular issue, rather than the broader spread of militaristic tendencies, that has become the focus of public concern. Those who have been motivated primarily in universalist moral terms have come to be familiar with the arcane language of deterrence theory, to appreciate the difference between first and second strikes and the significance of counterforce technology. Similarly, socioeconomically oriented radicals have come to accept the need to make accommodation with advocates of minimum deterrence, and to assert the immediate priority of reversing and stabilizing the current arms race.[3] Despite the theoretical priority of universalist perspectives, in practice short-run survival comes first.

This position is hardly surprising, but it involves a number of problems. Although the critique of contemporary militarism that arises from the strategic-geopolitical argument does show very clearly the dangers that are intrinsic to nuclear deterrence, this same critique also accepts all the assumptions about the nature of world politics that are rooted in the dominant discourse about international politics. To attempt to develop any counter-hegemonic discourse at this level is to operate on terms already set out by the dominant discourse. These terms are not obviously the most productive starting point for developing a more coherent vision of world order or more appropriate modes of peace and security.

The strategic-geopolitical critique begins with the destabilization of the contemporary structures of nuclear deterrence. It dwells on two main difficulties in particular: the move toward counterforce doctrines and missile vulnerability at the level of strategic deterrence forces, and the difficulties created by technologies of extended deterrence or flexible response in Europe. The overall drift is from a strategy of war prevention to one of war fighting. The prescription involves some form of arms control. Some versions can be quite sweeping in their recommendations: hence proposals for nuclear free zones, pledges of no first use, comprehensive test bans, deep cuts, the substitution of conventional for some nuclear forces, and so on. Most advocates of this way of thinking would like to restore some kind of minimum deterrence. And on the whole such prescriptions seem inherently sensible--until we ask what happens next.

Beyond minimum deterrence lie suggestions for denuclearization, for the delegitimization of nuclear weapons in the resolution of international disputes. These suggestions always introduce the increased risk of conflict escalation associated with conventional weapons, which nuclear deterrence policies have to some extent been able to restrain. In any case, to see the problem of contemporary militarism only in terms of nuclear weapons is to be aware of only the tip of a large iceberg. So beyond denuclearization lies a more general demilitarization and the development of alternative forms of civilian defense and global peacekeeping. Yet in the conventional view, such things seem very, very far away, as they may well be.

It is thus necessary to ask whether the conventional view of things is the appropriate one to take, and at this point the issues get much more difficult. They take us into a vortex of complicated theoretical and, indeed,

philosophical problems with the main traditions of
international political analysis.

One of the most obvious but least noted aspects of
Western theories of world politics--and I am thinking
here primarily in terms of "the American science of
international relations"--is that like all sociopolitical
theories, they can be understood both as "theory" and as
"ideology." They function both as systematic attempts to
understand and explicate phenomena and, simultaneously,
as ways of obscuring the phenomena. Attempts to analyse
the nature of international relations theory as ideology
have been few and far between, certainly when compared
with other socioscientific disciplines. Yet there can be
little   doubt   that   the   dominant   discourse   about
international relations has served to legitimize as well
as to explain the prevailing international order.

To pursue this theme it is necessary to emphasize
the   way   in   which   the   prevailing   discourse   about
international politics embodies a particular ontology, a
particular   conception   of   the   nature   of   international
"reality."   Some aspects of this have already been noted
in passing.   Against those who think in universalist
moral terms, it is argued that the international realm is
essentially pluralistic and amoral.   It is a matter of
the continuous collision of particular states mitigated
only by fragile and temporary structures of diplomacy and
rules of accommodation.   Against those who think in
socioeconomic terms, it is argued that the state, the
most fundamental form of pluralist fragmentation, is to a
very large degree autonomous as a result of the "security
dilemma." Yet it makes very little philosophical sense
to speak of any notion of pluralism without also invoking
its universalist polarity. Historically, the fragmented
international political system seems to have developed as
part of an increasingly integrated economic system. Thus
in both cases, it can be argued that the predominant
tradition of international relations theory has, at best
operated with a highly selective vision of "reality."

The   problem   goes   deeper.   Philosophically,
traditions of pluralism are associated with those of
historicism. The idea that the world is "one" is opposed
by the idea that it is "many." The idea that the "one"
is unchanging is opposed by the idea that the world is
constantly changing. If the world is one and unchanging
then it is possible to have a certain and unchanging
knowledge of it; if not, then knowledge can only be
relative to the time at which it is grasped. The problem
goes back a long way. It is the pluralist and relativist
challenge of Thrasymachus the Sophist in the *Republic*
that sets Western political theory off in its most
characteristic quest.   It is Machiavelli's pluralist and
historicist challenge to the universalist claims of
Christianity that articulated the setting for modern
secular   political   thought   in   general   and   for

international political theory in particular. Where the
political theory of civil society has subsequently
managed to develop a more universalistic basis for
political life, starting with the secularization of
natural law and the development of social contract
theory, international political theory has remained
preoccupied by the problems of pluralism, relativism, and
historicism.

Ultimately it is on this philosophical basis that
the claims of the dominant discourse of international
politics over those who think in universalist moral or
socioeconomic terms have been made.[4]   And as a critical
weapon against universalistic pretensions, relativism can
be deadly. Ultimately, of course, it is self-defeating:
if everything is relative, then the statement itself is
contradictory.   Even so, there are important
philosophical issues here, issues that certainly do not
justify the general disrepute into which pluralism,
historicism, and relativism have fallen.

Unfortunately, this old philosophical puzzle is not
all there is to it. By the time the claims of
historicism, pluralism, and relativism became dressed up
in the garb of modern international relations theory,
they became distorted in several important ways.[5] First,
they became absolutized, either in terms of some concept
of an unchanging human nature derived from Hobbes,
ethology, or Protestant theology, or in terms of some
notion of the eternal verities of power politics.
Secondly, the claims of universalism and pluralism, the
"one" and the "many," came to be reified into a mutually
exclusive opposition rather than as moments of a
dialectic.   Thus on the one hand we have seen the
development of a "science" of international politics to
legitimize its claims to objectivity; and on the other we
have seen all the rhetorical devices of relativism being
deployed against any position that bases itself on some
claim to universalism. The theoretical issues that arise
from this are of great complexity. Considered in terms
of ideology, however, the consequences are much simpler.
Over a long period of historical development, one way of
thinking about international politics--what in its more
"authentic" forms can be called pluralism or historicism,
but now in a degenerate ahistorical form are known as
"realism"--has come to dominate all others. And it has
done so not because its conception of "reality" is more
accurate, but because its partial grasp of that "reality"
has been legitimized through some deeply rooted
intellectual trickery. Consequently other forms of
discourse have been delegitimized.   And the discourses
that have suffered most in this way are precisely those
that give rise to the socioeconomic and universalist
moral critiques of contemporary militarism.

The discourse of dissent to contemporary militarism
can therefore be dissected in two ways.   It is possible

to categorize the different forms of critique and to understand their characteristic impact in the political sphere. It is also possible to understand the internal dynamics of critique when considered as a totality. We then have two different ways of addressing the same basic issue of the extent to which the critique of contemporary militarism is able to undermine the hegemonic discourse of international politics. Although there is a clear convergence toward a common indictment of militarism from a number of different theoretical traditions, they are in danger of being channeled in ways determined by the dominant discourse. In effect, they all confront a hegemonic discourse that is able to define the kind of opposition it can tolerate.

Once the critique of contemporary militarism is trapped in this discourse it becomes vulnerable to a wide range of difficulties. Most obviously it is subject to delegitimation by being labeled as utopian or subversive. Such labeling is not simply a political ploy. It is rooted in the hegemonic discourse of international relations theory itself. Less obviously, the pluralistic ontological assumptions of this hegemonic discourse necessarily pose the "problem of the other," or what has more recently come to be known as orientalism. The pluralist assumptions of the discourse are constantly reenforced by the stereotyping of some other state in ways that justify aggression. The appeal to "realism" and the appeal to some "great enemy" constitute a self-justifying and self-perpetuating system of assumptions. Critiques of militarism can then be dismissed not only in terms of being utopian or subversive in general, but utopian and subversive with respect to some specific and historically constituted enemy. One is then not merely naive, but is a dupe of some devil personified.

Not only is the hegemonic discourse of international politics self-justifying and self-perpetuating, but to the extent that it recognizes its own limitations, it also circumscribes the solutions that are possible. More specifically, it undermines the idea of a possible progression from nuclear deterrence to demilitarization and prescribes only the stabilization of the status quo. The "realities" are said to indicate that nuclear deterrence of some sort will always be necessary, and that arms control is all that is possible, even if it is an arms control that can allow for some quite drastic reductions in the level of armaments. And in this way it is always possible to hide behind a rhetoric of arms control while continuing to play the game of bargaining chips and supremacy.

V

The critique of contemporary militarism, then, works

in a milieu that is simultaneously theoretical and political. It encounters a hegemonic discourse about international politics in general and strategic relations between states in particular--a discourse that is itself a form of power. In this way, the critique of contemporary militarism confronts a basic contradiction. Although appeals to some kind of universalist moral or socioeconomic argument can be very effective in mobilizing mass support, their impact on public policy is much more limited. To have any credible impact on public policy it seems to be necessary to articulate the critique in terms of some kind of strategic-geopolitical argument. And indeed it has been one of the great achievements of the peace movement to have popularized basic strategic issues sufficiently to create a well-informed skepticism about official policy statements. Nevertheless, the net effect of this achievement has been to predispose critiques toward some directions rather than others. Most basically it leads us to ask how we can attain enough "peace" to allow us to tackle the underlying causes of conflict, rather than the other way round. The very structure of the dominant discourse emphasizes notions of "negative peace," defined as the absence of war. If there is a single common denominator among those who have written on the subject of peace, it is an agreement that such a conception is deeply inadequate.

This recognition leads directly to the question of "what is to be done?" More specifically, given that the short-term strategic-geopolitical issues are important, what can and ought to be the proper relation between the critique of contemporary militarism at this level and critiques based on much broader considerations? Two options seem to present themselves. One is primarily "political" and involves treating the geopolitical argument instrumentally or tactically. The special leverage of this form of critique at the policy-making level can be used in the short-term political arena without necessarily compromising the broader visions that motivate calls for more far-reaching transformations. From this point of view, for example, we can derive injunctions not to get too caught up on the lure of the hardware, in the myriad technical details that can so easily obscure wider principles. The other option raises more difficult theoretical considerations but seems to me to go more deeply to the heart of the matter. It involves an attempt to counteract the way in which the dominant discourse about international politics has been so successful in delegitimizing the broader forms of critique of contemporary militarism. This option implies the demystification of the hegemonic discourse itself and the reconstruction of the theoretical/philosophical assumptions on which that discourse has come to depend.

Although this second alternative is itself an

immense enterprise, one way to approach it can be outlined fairly briefly. The dominant discourse of international politics begins characteristically with a series of differentiations. The crisis of nuclear deterrence is separated from structures of militarism in general. Military structures are understood in terms of the defense of the sovereign state, which is itself understood to be an autonomous sphere of action. "High politics" are thus separated from "low politics." And thus we are taken into all those discourses that depend upon an artificial separation of the "political" and the "economic." With the world articulated in this way, complex phenomena can be broken down into more straightforward analytical categories. Specific disciplines and fields of study can then be constructed. Indeed, the phenomena themselves become reconstituted. The analysis of international politics and international economics can be refined separately. "Militarism" and "development" emerge as seemingly unrelated events, each to be identified and analyzed according to internal an logic of its own.

So much is familiar. It can be taken further by examining this relationship between militarism and development more closely. The logic of militarism emerges most forcefully out of those philosophical-political traditions that emphasize fragmentation and pluralism. War is seen to arise from the structure of the fragmented international system, either from some instability in the system itself or from the attempt by one actor in the system to alter the nature of the system or its own role in it. If war is undesirable and arises from fragmentation, then the solution is to overcome fragmentation through some kind of integration. The problem is pluralism; therefore the solution must be universalism.

The logic of development can be portrayed as precisely the reverse of this. The very term development embodies a strong sense of unidirectional teleology. In economic terms it has absorbed a wide range of meanings associated with universalist philosophies of the European Enlightenment and the experiences of nineteenth-century capitalist development. Translated into a normative prescription for the future, it has come to be portrayed as the best remedy for most of the ills that beset humankind, including war. It has been particularly influential as a prescription for the "modenization" of the "less developed countries." However, such claims have in turn come to be viewed by many people as mere quackery. Under the influence of various theories of imperialism, underdevelopment, and so on, the issue has begun to involve ways of resisting the claims of the hegemonic universalisms proclaimed by the dominant powers. Hence we can see part of the motivation for principles of nonalignment, Third World nationalism, and autonomous development, and for calls for a reconstructed international economic order. The problem is precisely too much universalism, too much rhetoric about the good of all which is really a cloak for the interests of the stronger; here the solution becomes increased pluralism, even if only as a strategy of resistance.

Put another way, in terms of militarism the problem is to attain "peace," whereas in terms of development the problem is to attain "justice." But peace and justice for whom? How is peace possible without justice? And is justice possible in this world without struggle and conflict? Peace, after all, can easily become yet another concept legitimizing an unjust status quo. Therefore the prospect is raised that the call for peace and the mobilization of the peace movement itself might be an inherently reactionary exercise.

Issues like this arise precisely because the problem is posed incorrectly in the first place. In fact we know quite well that the kinds of differentiations made by the dominant discourse about international politcs are thoroughly misleading. The separation of the "political" and the "economic" is in fact ideologically rather than analytically inspired. We know that military structures respond to pressures that arise from both the "horizontal" interactions between states and the "vertical" interactions of the world economy. To assume that "militarism" and "development" are separate phenomena is, among other things, to fail to grasp the significance of weapons as commodities or the role of arms transfers in the modern world.

At least we have begun to absorb all this at the level of academic theory and empirical research. At the level of public action, things are not quite so clear. For here the dominant discourse about world politics has managed to construct its own discourse of dissent at the deepest levels. It has done so because it has managed to articulate a fundamental separation between the claims of universalism and those of pluralism. It has reified a dialectical relation into static categories. "Peace" has become identified with universalism, with the creation of a single global community, with an unchanging and therefore unattainable "one." The "moral" and the "universal" have in fact established a long-lasting relationship. The dominant discourse is thus able to undermine the universal moral argument just because it can claim all the virtues of the "many." But the claims of neither universalism nor pluralism can be sustained without the other. Philosophically, they are meaningless unless treated as a dialectic. Historically, this dialectic has been resolved in quite different ways in different societies.

It is this latter consideration that brings us to crux of the matter. I have suggested that the critique of contemporary militarism occurs in three quite

different forms, each with its own strengths and
liabilities in the political arena. I have also
suggested that together they form a fairly coherent
discourse of dissent despite the deep cleavages within
it. This discourse of dissent, however, has to be
understood as a reflection of, indeed a creation of, the
hegemonic discourse that it seeks to undermine. As such
it contains an inherent ambiguity. In theoretical and
normative terms, the most powerful prescriptions for our
long-term peace and security seem to emerge from the
various forms of socioeconomic and universalist moral
argument. In practice, however, they inevitably seem to
be subordinated to the inherently conservative strategic-
geopolitical critique, partly and quite understandably
because of the immediacy of the crisis at this level, but
more fundamentally because effective discourse *can* only
occur at this level. In one way or another, other forms
of critique are disabled by the dominant discourse. To
the extent that the discourse of dissent remains
structured in ways determined by the dominant discourse,
it will necessarily remain politically ineffective.

The key to the power of the dominant discourse, I
have suggested, is that it has appropriated to itself a
particular form of the dialectic of the universal and the
plural. In doing so, it has drawn upon categories
specific to a particular historical epoch. It is a
common enough political ploy to portray parochial
categories as if they are universal. Here we confront a
particular reification of the relationship between
categories, as if it is eternal.

The point is that the reification is a historical
reification, and even though this is a matter of immense
complexity it can be understood historically. In my view
the reification has to be understood in terms of the
dominance of being over becoming, and in terms of the
influence of religious and secular monotheism in modern
Western societies. If it is a historical reification
then it has to be overthrown in history. That is to say,
where we are normatively drawn to seek the universal and
the moral, and pragmatically drawn to deal with the
immediacy of pluralist fragmentation, an effective
discourse of dissent to contemporary militarism has to be
rooted most deeply of all in a clear understanding of the
socioeconomic structures from which both our current
forms of pluralist conflict and our visions of a
universal moral order have emerged. A more appropriate
and effective discourse of dissent to contemporary
militarism can only come from social forces that are able
to reconstruct a more dialectical vision of the "one" and
the "many."

VI

To pose the issue in this way is, of course, to get at only part of the story. Analyses of the internal structure of any theoretical discourse require complementary analyses that seek to situate such discourses in a broader sociohistorical context. Here the traditional categories of class, economy, and state suggest themselves, though with a warning about the dangers of reductionism and oversimplification, which always seem to follow these categories around. The role of the state in particular as a source of self-justifying militarist discourse is of great importance in this respect. Less obviously, perhaps, the cultural dimensions of contemporary militarism offer considerable scope for further research. This should include both the better known ploys of media distortion and the more subtle symbolisms that permeate so much of everyday life from popular entertainment to children's toys and games. Similarly, the relationship between militarism and language offers an exceptionally fertile field for the analysis of contemporary political culture.

Beyond the need for more research on such issues, however, is the problem of political practice. Following Antonio Gramsci, I would merely stress here the impossibility of directly opposing hegemonic discourse and the "resistances" of civil society. Rather, they can perhaps be deconstructed and reconstructed in ways suggested by Gramsci's notion of a "war of position." Given that, in my view, neither history itself nor any particular social class holds the key to some predetermined future, the creation of a new hegemony involves a process of political articulation that is quite radically democratic in its implications. The development of new political subjects in the West--feminist, ecological and peace movements, racial minorities, nationalist groups, and so on--as well as the broadening of the agenda of world politics to include resistance to Western political forms, provides some scope for political practices that emphasize the plurality and autonomy of social movements. In this way the need to avoid all authoritarian unifications and to pursue unity through diversity provides, in my view, a common agenda for both political practice and political theory in a world in which our shared fate is becoming all too obvious.

NOTES

1. *See* for example Haken Wiberg, "JPR 1964-1980: What Have We Learnt About Peace?," *Journal of Peace Research* XVIII (2), 1981:111-148; E. P. Thompson et al., *Exterminism and Cold War* (London: New Left Books, 1982);

Mary Kaldor and Asbjörn Eide, eds., *The World Military Order* (London: Macmillan, 1979); Asbjörn Eide and Marek Thee, eds., *Contemporary Militarism* (London: Croom Helm, 1979); Mary Kaldor, *The Baroque Arsenal* (London: André Deutsch, 1982); and Dan Smith and Ron Smith, *The Economics of Militarism* (London: Pluto Press, 1983).

2. My own approach is intended to be suggestive rather than rigorous. It is loosely influenced by a variety of somewhat incompatible texts, including Max Horkheimer and Theodor Adorno, *Dialectic of Enlightenment*, translated by J. Cumming (New York: Seabury Press, 1972); Georg Lukacs, *History and Class Consciousness* translated by R. Livingstone (London: Merlin Press, 1971); Michel Foucault, *The History of Sexuality*, translated by R. Hurley (New York: Random House, 1978); and especially Antonio Gramsci, *Selections from the Prison Notebooks*, translated by Quintin Hoare and Geoffrey Nowell-Smith (London: Lawrence and Wishart, 1971). For a general discussion *see* Jorge Larrain, *The Concept of Ideology* (London: Hutchinson, 1979).

3. For a version of this argument *see* Paul Joseph, "From MAD to NUT's: The Growing Danger of Nuclear War," *Socialist Review* 12 (1), Jan.-Feb., 1982:13-56.

4. For recent examples *see* Ian Clark, *Reform and Resistance in the International Order* (Cambridge: Cambridge University Press, 1980) and Michael Howard, *War and the Liberal Conscience* (Oxford: Oxford University Press, 1981. Cf. R.B.J. Walker, *Political Theory and the Transformation of World Politics* World Order Studies Program, Occasional Paper No. 8 (Princeton, N.J.: Princeton University, Center of International Studies, 1980).

5. On this and related themes *see* Robert W. Cox, "Social Forces, States and World Orders: Beyond International Relations Theory," *Millenium: Journal of International Studies* 10 (2), 1981:126-155. Reprinted with permission as the preceding chapter (Chapter 12) in this book.

CHAPTER 14

Peace in an Age
of Transformation

Rajni Kothari

THE PRESENT PHASE OF WORLD HISTORY

The unfolding dialectic of world history is entering its most comprehensive and perhaps most problematic phase--at once unnerving and creative. It heralds a process of mutation in the history of the human species, with far-reaching changes in the arrangement of human affairs: in the structuring of global power relations, in the encounter of civilizations, in several other areas such as class, region, ethnicity, and religion. And yet few, if any, seem to have a clue to the real nature of this transformation.

It is a phase in which the so-called peripheries of the world political structure are responding to the concepts of self-determination and sovereignty of peoples and nations that the leaders of great powers had proclaimed, but which those leaders now superciliously ignore or wantonly violate in order to defend the status quo and to stall the forces of change with all the resources and skills at their command--conducting negotiations calculated to tire the opponent into quiescence and eventual cooptation; erecting barriers to freedom of trade, communication, and movements of people; forging lethal weaponry; and waging or threatening war.

It is a phase in which domestic social structures are being deeply destabilized, with the poor and the oppressed both rising in revolt and being put down by populist rhetoric on the one hand and a repressive state apparatus on the other.

It is a phase in which the struggle for human rights is drawing upon deeper springs of identity and authenticity, against domination and alienation and for human and cultural dignity.

Reprinted by permission with minor revisions from *Alternatives: A Journal of World Policy* 9:2, 1983.

It is a phase in which the conflict between
tradition and modernity is being turned upside down--with
modernity, the creed of the establishment, having become
an orthodoxy against which older civilizations and so-
called traditional societies struggle to provide radical
critiques and alternatives, and to propel movements of
revolt. The outcome of such movements, as in the case of
the momentous Iranian revoltion, is by no means certain
but could well lead to a revival of old animosities and
produce a new spate of uncontrolled violence and
atrocities as the defenders of modernity--and its main
bearers within the states system--become ever more
adamant and fierce in a last-ditch battle for survival.
Encounters between civilizations under such conditions,
instead of pluralizing the human condition and rooting it
into authentic indigenous streams, each as valid as the
other, may lead to situations of deepening conflict and
violence, weakening and debilitating all the
civilizations in the process.

The struggle for survival is thus endemic
to--indeed, inherent in--the struggle for transformation
of the present world into a just world. The issue of
peace in our age is deeply embedded in this phenomenon.
There can be no peace until the process of such a
transformation is accelerated. And this task is not
going to be easy. For the age of transformation that we
are living in is also an age of mind-boggling paradoxes.

The most visible paradox, and the one that has the
most far-reaching consequences, is that the erstwhile
dynamic agents of change (both the *Pax Americana* with its
theory and model of modernity and the Soviet Vanguard
with its theory and model of revolution) have turned
status quoist, making both modernity and revolution sour.
One aspect of the paradox is that the modernizing elites
look askance at the slightest manifestation of peoples'
demand for their share in the process and fruits of
modernity. Another is that the battle for alternative
universals is turning into a series of particulars. Yet
another, and the most sinister, is that the search for
peace and security is turning into ever-expanding arenas
of strategic checkmates and military escalations.

If it is an age of transformation that we are in,
let us also recognize that it is an age in which the most
powerful actors (global, national, local) are pitched
against transformation and are ready to prevent it from
being fulfilled by resort, if need be, to
violence--external or internal or both.

THE PARADOX OF TRANSFORMATION

The paradox of transformation reveals itself also in
a series of other dramatic contrasts and contradictions:
It is found in the mounting piles of ever-more

deadly armaments, on the one hand, and the growing hordes of the very poor and undernourished living in conditions of extreme deprivation including starvation, on the other. We are witness to a great schism in the human community, dividing the world into extremes of affluence and deprivation, with concentrations of poverty and scarcity and unemployment and deprivation in one vast section of mankind and of overabundance and overproduction and overconsumption in another, very small, section of the same species. A century of unprecedented material progress has also been one of sprawling misery and increasing deprivation.

It is found in the fact that an age that has witnessed the end of empires and the dawn of independence for so many nations has at the same time turned out to be an age of increasing domination of the world by just a few powers.

It is found in the fact that despite world agricultural production having stayed ahead of population growth, food availability has become a serious problem for millions of people, and, on balance, there is a net flow of nutritional resources from the poorer and more populous to the richer and less populous regions of the world.

It is found in the fact that immigration policies of rich countries with low densities, instead of providing opportunities and refuge, have in effect become policies of sucking the most skilled technical manpower from the poorer regions.

It is found in the fact that policies of "aid" and transfer of technology and resources from the industrialized regions have in effect turned out to be a net drainage of their surpluses.

The paradoxes seem unending. Industrialization was expected to put an end to the condition of scarcity for mankind as a whole. In fact, it has made even basic means of existence more scarce and inaccessible for an increasing number of human beings. Modern education was expected to lead to continuous progress and enlightenment for all and thus ensure liberation for all. In fact, it has produced a world dominated by experts and bureaucrats and technocrats--a world in which ordinary human beings feel increasingly powerless and find themselves manipulated by forces beyond their control. Similarly, communication and transportation were expected to produce a small world in which the fruits of knowledge and development in any part of the world would be available to all the others. In fact, modern communication and fast-moving transportation have produced a world in which a few metropolitan centres are extracting a large part of world resources and depriving other regions of whatever comforts and skills and local resources they once used to enjoy. Similarly, modern mass media and the "electronic revolution" are threatening self-reliance and cohesion of

communities, cultures, and major civilizations. The
world we live in is indeed very badly divided, the
divisions going far deeper than the merely ideological,
military, or economic.

A Deeply Divided World

The most critical of these divisions is no doubt
political, between states and between sets of
states--East and West, South and North, Orient and
Occident. Underlying these divisions is a crisis of the
modern state in both its internal and its external
manifestations. The worst victims of the crisis are the
more vulnerable states of the Third World, which, it was
hoped, would be instruments of liberation from inequitous
social structures and would become new foci of identity
and dignity, but which have turned out to be willing
allies or unwilling tools of the global status quo.
Facing unprecedented demands on their resources and
leadership, their stability and security threatened both
internally (mass turmoil) and externally (global
pressures of energy and resources and of economic
recession), and caught in the arms race, these states are
increasingly unable to cope with their problems. A world
composed of a large number of such unstable and insecure
states cannot provide a framework of peace and security;
it can only produce growing cleavages and breakdowns.

Another division, potentially no less troublesome,
that thinkers are only now beginning to perceive--though
as yet rather dimly--is the division between generations.
By this I do not mean primarily what is usually known as
the generation gap between the old and the young, which
for all its seriousness has not received systematic
attention apart from a great deal of talk about it. What
I have in mind is something more comprehensive, namely,
the division between the present and the future, with the
future including both the very young among us and the yet
unborn. Never before has the need for a deep concern
with the future been so pressing and urgent.

Nor is the issue of survival limited to the human
species, present and future. For the human species is
inextricably bound in an organic bond not only with other
species and forms of life but also with what we know as
inanimate nature; and a threat to the health and survival
of any one of these puts the health and survival of all
the others at stake. Increasingly man is thoughtlessly
destroying, almost without let or hindrance, various
other species, vegetation, organic and inorganic building
blocks of life, and the oceans and other commons whose
bounty has been the cause of so much imagination and
sense of unity and joy and creativity among humans. In
the unending acquisitiveness of technological man and the
decline in his sensitivity to his own kind in other

regions and in future generations, no less than other forms of life, he has gone on a rampage that threatens the extinction of all forms of creation.

The Problematique

This, then, is the problematique of the human condition at the present juncture of world history--*survival*. At stake is the survival of the state as an instrument of change and liberation, identity, and dignity; the survival of civilization; survival of the species; survival of the whole of creation. The problematique is already affecting institutional structures, the behavior of people, their psychic responses. It is found in the currently widespread feeling of uncertainty and insecurity at all levels, which seems to overshadow the earlier sense of confidence and certitude--about the theory of development, about the prospects for peace, about the continuity of human progress, about civilization and its underlying unity.

In one sense the "problematique" is no different than the basic predicament of human existence faced in earlier epochs of major transformation: Will man-in-society survive? Will he be able to contain the seeds of conflict and violence that he has himself sown in the pursuit of civilization and turn them into instruments of change and reconstruction toward a new and different order? Or will he, instead, confine himself to ad hoc and piecemeal tinkering with reality through instrumentalities fashioned for a different age, in the vain hope that ultimate catastrophe will somehow be avoided, in the meanwhile permitting the cleavages to sharpen and fragmentation to deepen?

However, although the basic predicament that we face in our age is in its most elementary sense the same as in earlier periods of transformation, it is fundamentally different in both scale and depth. In scale, it encompasses the whole human species, now facing the danger of total eclipse. In depth, it goes beyond contending regimes and ruling classes to entire populations all the way down to the poor and the dispossessed. It is a new and dramatic phase in the struggle for human survival; the stakes are high, the arena is the whole globe, and the actors are the peoples of the world as well as the numerous states and nationalities in which they are encapsulated. It is this all-encompassing canvas of new and unprecedented forces of change that should engage the minds of those who seek to achieve peace. For one thing is clear: "peace," unless it emanates from, and is rooted in, a structure widely seen to be just and fair, can be highly stultifying. Peace means different things to different groups. The victims of the system see in the present

structure of inequity and exploitation the very
embodiment of the worst kind of violence, the primary
cause of conflict. For them, peace means a just order
that ensures an equitable sharing of the power of
decision making. For the privileged, on the other hand,
peace means a congealing of the present structure. In
their views, therefore, any attempt to change it--even to
question it--is a disturbance of the peace.

These observations apply as much to the
international order as to the national and regional ones.
It is a characteristic of the world we live in that this
structure of inequity extends to both socioeconomic and
politico-strategic dimensions in a situation of
cumulative inequity in which a monopolistic command over
fantastic instruments of violence--military, paramilitary
and nonmilitary reinforces and supports a system of
economic and political domination. *Hence* the interest in
peace by those outside the dominant structure of power.
But the essential nature of this interest and striving
should be understood. It perceives peace as a component,
indeed an essential component, of a global effort toward
transforming the world polity with a view to building a
more just and equitable order. It is only on the basis
of such an order that a lasting structure of peace can be
achieved.

THE CRISIS OF THE SYSTEM

In large parts of the world there is increasing
evidence of growing incapacity to cope with problems and
crises, both domestic and international. The old
confidence has given way to a mood of concern,
perplexity, and confusion. We live in a period of
fundamental transition. The post-war world, which was
characterized by recovery from the ravages of war,
fascism, colonialism, and economic depression on the one
hand, and renewed competition for global power on the
other, had achieved a measure of stability through an
essentially managerial response to a new situation. The
chief architects of the managerial response were the two
superpowers with their rival systems of alliances and a
doctrine of deterrence, which, as the dangers of such a
doctrine became clear, was fortunately restrained by a
period of détente and a complicated balancing of world
power. Other expressions of the managerial response
included a modicum of development assistance for the
countries most affected by centuries of colonialism, and
a modest effort at creating an institutional framework of
conciliation, debate, relief, and welfare under the
United Nations system. This managerial response was by
no means satisfactory, as it ignored basic issues of
structural change and cultural diversity, but it did work
for a time in preventing conflict and tension from

turning into major catastrophes.

This system is no longer working. We are already in the throes of a growing breakdown of this system. It is breaking down not simply in respect to larger structural and cultural issues that are engaging sensitive minds everywhere, but even in respect to managerial efficiency, sustenance of growth rates, provision of certain minima of human survival, and maintenance of a framework of peace and security. The world economy has already entered a period of stagnation and paralysis; the old engines of growth in the industrialized world seem to have reached their limit; the energy crisis is taking a heavy toll everywhere; and the simultaneous onslaught of unemployment and inflation is fast eroding the framework of economic stability that had been constructed following Bretton Woods.

Major powers like the United States are fast losing influence, partly due to their economic decline in the world, partly to an incapacity to adjust to new political realities, and partly to major strains in the erstwhile Western alliance under the growing pressure of larger world forces. There is obvious danger when major centers of technological and military might find themselves unable to cope with a new situation, as they are likely to fall prey to irrational responses unless new and saner forces can inject a large measure of restraint and statesmanship.

Meanwhile, the socialist world is also in a state of flux, partly as a result of a fast-changing world economic and political situation that has cast a shadow on the framework of détente and has led to a new resumption of superpower rivalry, but partly also as a result--in their case, too--of older assumptions not working (such as the prognosis of imperialism and its nemesis; the socialist theories of planning and autarkic development; expectations of a new socialist man emerging; the theory of a world proletariat; and the tactical line of coexistence). New forms of nationalism are intervening at various points in the old edifice, and new and untidy alignments in regional contexts are undermining the cohesion of the socialist world and its special relationship with ex-colonial countries.

The Third World, despite a considerably heightened consciousness of political and economic power and its actual assertion, shows a whole set of disturbing signs. Although there is no reason to doubt that the new engines of growth and dynamism must come from the newly industrializing parts of the Third World, and although it is obvious that enormous resources must be provided by the poor of the world (both as productive forces and as new markets), the countries of the Third World are caught in deep conflicts both at home and abroad. They are unable to work in unison (except in verbal confrontations in the UN). Bewitched as they are by outworn assumptions about economic planning, technological transfers, and the model of a modern technocratic state--all of which they seem unable to control and which tend either to perpetuate older forms of neocolonialism or to foster new ones--the elites of the Third World are fast losing their leverage in world affairs. As latecomers to the game of world politics and to the processes of modernization and industrialization, the elites seem to view these matters in old power terms, whereas the real issues are of a different order. There is need to think anew of both development and power, but the elites are proving themselves incapable of doing it.

The nonaligned world, the Group of 77, the concept of collective self-reliance, and the call for a new international economic order all seem to be verbal constructs--useful perhaps in putting up the necessary resistance to Western domination, but insufficient bases for preparing the countries of the Third World to deal with their own problems either jointly or severally. They do not seem to agree on even setting up a powerful secretariat or sponsoring a major research and information system that can match the efforts of the OECD group of countries. Prisoners of their own rhetoric, which more often than not reflects relative powerlessness than power, and still immersed in archaic and often reactionary structures at home, the Third World countries present a picture of growing fragmentation and chaos. This is hardly a condition in which the Third World can join the North-South dialogue with confidence in its initial positions or strength. No wonder that the dialogue has become an empty ritual and has in effect all but collapsed. Nor does it seem likely that the much-talked-of South-South process will take off, given the shortsighted view of "national interest" in most of the South, the simmering regional conflicts leading to arms build-up in most regions, and the drive of the larger and stronger among the Third World nations toward playing hegemonical roles in their respective regions--a posture that suits the global corporate structures of both world capitalism and world militarism.

A Picture of Fragmentation

Such a picture of fragmentation all around, in which the superpowers have lost their capacity to provide any framework of stability and security, and in which the old alliances are disintegrating and new movements for structural change are failing to make headway, is serious enough; it is further compounded by an increase in the spate of violence, both domestic and international, and by the fast-spreading virus of militarization in all regions of the world, which some powerful countries of the North are fueling. There is also a much more

heightened competition for scarce resources, a growing
degradation of the natural environment, and a growing
erosion of the protective cover to the biosphere. The
craze for technological power, often wholly unrelated to
real needs of the people, has made the struggle for the
preservation of the sanctity and values of life--indeed,
human survival itself--truly desperate. Unless major
infusions of both knowledge and statesmanship intervene,
we are likely to witness a series of localized and not-
so-localized wars and unexpected mutations in power
relations among major states for which we may be wholly
unprepared. Large and uncontrolled movements of millions
of people across state boundaries, a process that has
already begun, is likely to further sharpen domestic
strife and economic collapse, challenging the stability
of regimes and producing a breakdown of civil society.
Failure to manage these accumulating sources of tension
and to intervene in them with necessary structural and
institutional changes may well lead us, without much
forewarning, to a psychic condition pregnant with the
ultimate nemesis of a nuclear war.

Forces of Change

The foregoing prognosis posits neither evil forces
working themselves out along some inexorable logic nor
evil designs and doings of mad and stupid men in power.
On the contrary, the causes of such a state of affairs
are to be found in some very positive and historically
inevitable forces of change: the stirring of
consciousness among millions of hitherto-submerged people
everywhere; the rise of Third World societies in the
global framework of power and position; the radical
shifts in the global structure of economic and political
power and in the demand for world resources; and the
resurgence and revitalization of ancient civilizations
and world religions and their assertion of alternative
perspectives on fundamental issues facing humanity.
Critical rethinking of values, perceptions, and
cosmologies are in the offing in the wake of new forms of
consciousness, new explorations of the human mind, and
new awareness that the old ways will not do and that
there is need to find new answers, produce new skills,
and generate new forms of knowledge to deal with a new
human problematique--in such a way as to restore vision
and perspective by taking cognizance of new secular and
spiritual forces at work. The long period of decline of
institutions and capabilities has also been one of new
expressions of the human spirit.

It is the huge and widening gap between the imminent
but still unclear mutations and the old and obsolete
institutional mechanisms of deliberation and decision
making that continue to persist at both national and

international levels that accounts for the present crisis. It is this birth of the new in the confines of the old that lies behind the conflicts and confrontations we are witnessing--many, though not all, of which are inherent in a process of rebirth and rejuvenation. The prevailing systems of management are patently incapable of fathoming the forces that are at work; they are therefore unable to provide the necessary restructuring of institutional, technological, and power relationships. Governments and political party machines are no longer able to aggregate interests, hold allegiances, and mediate between contending forces. The ubiquitous intrusion of the mass media and the virtual transfer of major political functions to bureaucrats and "experts" everywhere have transformed the nature of the state, in both liberal and socialist countries, and in the as-yet-nascent politics of the Third World.

Alienation

There is a growing alienation of the awakened masses at the bottom from the modes of conflict resolution that are still highly centralized and technocratic. Similarly, choices of technology and processes of social and political transformation are increasingly at odds, intensifying the alienation. But above all, the universities, scientfic bodies, and expert meetings (which have multiplied at a phenomenal rate in recent decades) are all lagging far behind in coming to grips with the new realities. Their places seem to be taken be purveyors of capsuled knowledge--the media, the smart salesmen of corporate interests, the experts and "advisers" from foreign aid agencies, and the phoney spiritualists and the gurus--who are unable to provide new answers but who have a mesmeric effect in a world of rapid changes and increasing insecurities. The alienation applies also to planning bodies and financial institutions, the economic pundits, the management specialists, and the disseminators of so-called innovations and inventions. This pervasive process of alienation that has produced a nonfunctioning structure of governance and decision making everywhere is above all to be traced to the deep schism between the world of knowledge and the world of reality; continuous and even exponential expansion of knowledge does not seem to increase the capability to deal with real problems. This is the biggest and sharpest alienation of all and one that lies behind the heightened sense of insecurity all around.

Crisis of Human Knowledge

Reflecting and reinforcing the fragmentation of the world discussed above is the fragmentation of the knowledge system produced by the modern conception of science. Even as elementary and integral an issue as survival in an era of strife is broken up into many fragments. Thus the social anthropologist's concern with the processes of strife within and between communities, the economists's concern with the material basis of world crisis, and the psychologist's explorations into the deeper springs of human destructiveness, all on the one hand, and the study of peace and security by experts in international relations and strategic studies, on the other, are hardly ever informed by a common conceptual paradigm or vision, and even less by a coherent framework of intervention in the historical process. The result is that reality is broken up into bits and pieces according to the logic of academics and technocrats, and then studied in separate and watertight compartments rather than comprehended by the logic of dialectical reality itself.

The fragmented approach to human knowledge is not unproductive, however; it has produced increasing specialization, making us witness to one of the biggest explosions of human knowledge of all times. But because of its fragmented character it is becoming increasingly divorced from the reality it claims to comprehend; the "explosion" has not increased our capacity to deal with the vital problems and crises that confront us. Thus, just at a time when researches at the frontiers of psychology and social anthropology have revealed the fragility of human collectivities, researches at the frontiers of other branches of knowledge have produced the most devastating engines of destruction, not just in terms of stockpiles of weaponry and other hazardous technologies but also in terms of doctrines of waging and winning catastrophic wars. Just at a time when social ferment and awakening at the bottom of the world pyramid are paving the way for fundamental democratization of societies, an increasing sophistication in the means of physical repression and genetic control of entire societies has spurred an equally fundamental assault on human freedom.

Underlying this schism in the world of knowledge, given its inherently fragmented character, is a deep arrogance that the modern scientific world view has given to man. Never before has the product of the human mind acquired so dominant a role as in modern times. It has changed the world beyond recognition and, according to some, produced a world beyond redemption. Its basic contribution has been to give to man a tremendous sense of power and manipulation. Nothing else could have made man so arrogant as this particular role of knowledge.

With it has also taken place a divorce between knowledge and understanding, knowledge and character, and knowledge and wisdom, undermining the conception of balance, the awareness of limits. The modern paradigm of knowledge is based on an assumption of infinity and of perpetual control and manipulation.

However, it would be quite an obscurantist position to take if one were to say that knowledge by itself has brought mankind to grief. The rise of science has been a great liberator of man from both the horrors of nature and the abuses of religious doctrine. But something happened to science in the course of its progress which blighted its original promisse. Because it flourished in a culture (viz., of the Occident) that looked upon it as an instrument of power and domination rather than as a liberator of the human spirit--which is how knowledge was looked upon by the ancient Chinese and the Indians and even the ancient Greeks--science soon became an instrument of technology, which, not content with overcoming hardships and fulfilling basic needs, went on a rampage for continuous domination, exploitation, competition, and perpetual tension, both between man and man and between man and the rest of creation. In the course of time it also became an instrument of monopolization, so that while the fruits of technology were diffused widely within some societies, they were denied to a great many other societies--many of which, it may be recalled, had provided the basic raw material for prosperity in those few societies.

Civilizational Thrust

Such an exploitative relationship between societies was inherent in the very process of civilization that was ushered in by the European Enlightenment. It was a civilizational process based on a materialistic world view. The Industrial Revolution in the West, followed by colonial expansion throughout the globe, were marked by a fundamental civilizational drive, informed by a clear doctrine emanating from the Enlightenment: the theory of progress and the idea of secular history. Arising from a dualism between the secular and the spiritual, the idea was subsequently legitimized by the conquest of a large domain of man's nature and territory through a materialistic interpretation of science and technology. This doctrine released tremendous energy and led, among other things, to a superiority in armaments and the art of warfare, which proved critical in extending the frontiers of Western civilization and its normative framework to almost the entire globe.

Colonialism entailed a new conception of universalism. The old universalistic conceptions found in China, India, ancient Greece, and Turkey in the

thinking of the Buddha and the Zoroastrian
teachers--despite their considerable
diversities--postulated the transcendence of the
immediate; the local, and the temporal through the
cultivation of the mind and a search for meaning in an
admittedly mysterious and complex reality, which fostered
moderation and containment of selfish and expansionist
drives in the human personality. By contrast, the
modernist conception of universalism that emerged in the
West fed the drive for expansion of a local civilization
and its dominance over the rest of the world, legitimized
by a belief in manifest destiny that was an outgrowth of
the dominant thrust of Judeo-Christian religiosity in the
post-medieval age.

Role of Technology

The Western imperial thrust stimulated by modern
technology and its accompanying economic expansion, as
well as by a psychological urge born of a conviction of
racial superiority was supported and spurred on by the
power balance in Europe. It thus extended the
competitive ethos of the growth of capital and territory
at home to the exploration, acquisition, and
consolidation of colonial empires abroad. The result was
global domination by European state power and its
economic infrastructure. Indeed, modern European
imperialism represented the first major effort at
unifying the entire globe under the dominion of a single
regional center.

In sum, then, largely because of the location and
efflorescence of modern technology in a particular
culture--a culture that was basically aggressive and in
which there was not enough moderation and self-
control--technology has become a Frankenstein. This has
begun to be realized only of late. And it has been
realized not because of the inequities to which modern
technology has given rise (after all, the problem of
poverty emanating from a pursuit of plenty was not posed
until very recently), but rather because the myth it was
clothed in has suddenly exploded: the myth of perpetual
progress, of the near-at-hand end of scarcity and of the
possibility of making this progress infinite and unending
and universal. Today, the affluent world itself, faced
with the specter of scarcity once again, is beginning to
see the excesses to which modern technology has brought
it--witness the current worldwide concern with the
environmental crisis. In fact, however, the
environmental crisis is only a symptom of a very basic
change in relationships: from man's reliance on nature
to man's dependence on machinery. The domination of man
by the machine--and his dependence on it for his
sustenance--means not just the constant and continuous

need for energy and raw materials (most of these obtained
by depriving the poor of their natural endowments); it
also entails less and less need for human beings. The
result is that there are in this world millions and
millions of what are called "marginal" men and women,
people for whom society has no use. The more serious
upshot is that man himself is becoming superfluous and
obsolescent; he is being looked upon as a burden not just
on nature but also on his own society. Paradoxical
though it may sound, the system that modern man has
produced is one in which the most dispensable element is
man himself.

The crisis that faces modern man is a crisis wrought
by science and technology taking a particular direction
under the impact of the age of positivism. The full
consequences of this are seen in our time as it envelopes
all the particular crises to which men of science and
philosophy have drawn our attention: the threat of total
war, the threat of extreme deprivation coexisting with
overabundance, the threat of the collapse of the
biosphere. As we realize this, we must also realize that
nothing short of fundamental rethinking about the human
enterprise will redeem man from these crises, and that
such rethinking will have to address itself to the world
as a whole. For what we face here is an extreme dualism
of the world, a world so divided that its survival itself
is at stake. Even if a nuclear war is avoided--and it
will be difficult to avoid if the divisions facing
mankind become sharper and deeper--can such a badly
divided species survive the continuous mounting tension
and violence that it will have to face? Many other
species under such conditions have perished even without
the instruments of mutual destruction that humans have.

Crisis in Values

Another manifestation of the crisis in the world of
knowledge, spawned by the prevailing paradigm of science
and the unbounded spread of technology, and related to
their incapacity to deal effectively with the problem of
survival, is the crisis in values as a result of the
obsolescence of earlier assumptions on the human
condition: (1) the assumption of a linear and continuous
march of progress benefiting all humanity; (2) the
assumption of the benign nature of government and
bureaucracy in mediating societal affairs (which was
further fortified after the collapse of empires with the
rise of colonies to independent nationhood); (3) the
"infrastructural" assumption about the aggregative role
of political parties and the federal process in liberal
democratic systems, and of the welfare state in both
liberal and socialist systems; (4) the broader and
culturally crucial assumption about the territorial

structuring of human loyalties and identities; and above all, (5) the assumption of peaceful relations between man and man and the close linkage between "development" and peace.

All of these assumptions and beliefs that underlay the modernist world view are today in a state of flux, if not disarray, that has produced a normative and moral vaccum. The various paradoxes of transformation mentioned earlier arise out of this characteristic of the contemporary human condition. There is also a political reason for this disarray of the paradigm of thought that held sway for so long. It was essentially an apolitical paradigm because it left out the crucial component of power and the problem of distributive justice. Yet the paradigm worked so long as the imperial cushion enabled management of demands from the lower classes in the metropolitan centers and kept out of view the emerging chasm between those centers and their colonial outreach. Even after the emergence of newly independent countries, problems were obfuscated by the dominant theories of development and modernization--no less apolitical than the theory of progress--according to which massive poverty and inequity could be handled through a managerial model of economic transformation. The theories were further buttressed by a conception of state and nation-building according to which erecting cohesive centers of power in each country would also provide a firm basis for genuine independence and autonomy.

Today, following the collapse of these theories and the startling evidence of increasing inequity and exploitation between and within societies, the problem of power relationships has emerged as the central issue in defining the human condition, and it is affecting the consciousness of people as well as states. It is a condition of sharpening dualism (1) between the imperial centers and peripheral societies and (2) between the rich and the poor of the world, these two dimensions converging in an intricate and all-encompassing battle for survival at several levels.

THE SPECTER OF INSECURITY AND THE STRUGGLE FOR SURVIVAL

The issues of peace and security need to be viewed in this context of a struggle for survival at every level--all the way up and all the way down--and the accompanying sense of insecurity that pervades all these levels.

Survival of Life

For millions of people around the world (the bulk of them concentrated in the South) a struggle for a simple physical survival exists, although for them, too, the struggle is also for defense of social and cultural values against external encroachments. One-third of the world has no access to potable water, no purchasing power to buy food even though it may be available in markets, no shelter worth the name, and no defense against erosion and plunder of community resources--land, forests, and rivers. Natural calamities are on the increase in these regions, each subsequent flood or famine proving more disastrous than the last, the primitive life-support systems collapsing under the onslaught of a mindless technology, and the prospects of real starvation of millions of people long before the turn of the century looming large. The peasant rebellions and lower class struggles sparked by these conditions are being ruthlessly suppressed by an increasingly repressive state apparatus supplied with technology from imperialist powers keen on maintaining "peace" (a euphemism for the authority of ruling juntas).

Survival of Life-Style

For some others, however, the struggle for survival takes a different form, namely, the defense of living standards and life-styles already achieved, and control over and cornering of resources needed for this end. There is evidence of anxiety and insecurity in this respect in the North, too, where the "challenge from the Third World" is perceived as a threat to the North's affluence. This new and dangerous conception of "national interest" lies behind the strident resource diplomacy of the Western powers, as well as behind the new strategic doctrines for the maintenance of global supremacy. This feeling of insecurity of the powerful in the face of challenge is reflected also in a similar insecurity of the privileged within individual societies of the South. Perhaps more wars will be fought on this single issue than on any other. Far more repression and atrocities will be committed on the poor and the oppressed for the same reason, notwithstanding all the rhetoric of a new economic order at the international level.

It is the issue of contending life-styles--and their politics. The prevailing conception of life-styles has given rise to a global structure of political and economic power that has become increasingly inequitous and that is therefore riddled with conflicts. It has led to a bottling up of world resources in a few centers, providing one of the major sources of stratification of the species--both internationally and domestically.

There are three aspects of this scenario of growing conflict. The first is the global structuring of the relationship between resources and human beings in which

a minority of nations has, in pursuit of a parasitic and
wasteful style of life, grabbed a large part of world
resources. The second aspect is the spread of the same
style of life among the dominant strata of the Third
World, which has produced deep divisions both within and
between its societies. The third aspect arises out of
the first two and consists in the growing conflict over
access to, and distribution and control of, world
resources for maintaining and raising standards of
consumption and life-styles as achieved by the industrial
world and, through emulation and prompting by the
privileged strata of the developing countries.

Survival of States

Based largely on this schism over control of
material resources and productive forces, but also
somewhat independent of it, are the sources of insecurity
and threats to survival of social and political
structures in various regions of the world both in
respect to local hierarchical orders and in respect to
the integrity and survival of national economies and
nation-states themselves. In Zaire and Chad, in Pakistan
and Afghanistan, in the Gulf area generally, in parts of
Central America, in Zimbabwe and Uganda, and as years go
by and with the growing movement of peoples *across* legal
boundaries, in India, in the Vietnam peninsula, and in
Southeast Asia as a whole, the issue of survival and
viability of existing political entities may prove
crucial to the stability and security of the states. Nor
is this phenomenon of internal convulsions of *new*
nationalities and their effect on the security of
existing states limited to the Third World. It is also
likely to affect the North: in the United Kingdom, in
Belgium, in Canada and, before long, in Eastern Europe.
The crises of an economic kind and the struggle of social
and regional components of existing states over scarce
resources will reinforce these political cleavages,
sharpen hostilities, and produce represssion and violence
under the established state structure (consider the
trauma of Irish nationalism). And all this will go on
without the need to cite as examples the tumultuous
changes in regional power equations that will be
occasioned by the highly convulsive and destabilizing
politics of countries like Israel and South Africa.

Survival of Power Structures

Quite apart from these sources of tension and
disaffection from within the social and territorial
structures of nation-states, and often sharpening them,
are international forces at work producing a sense of

uncertainty and insecurity about the political future of
major countries and their role in major world regions.
Partly caused by the intricate and intransigent politics
of energy and the consequent vulnerability of major
economies, and partly by continuing use of military means
in dealing with essentially political issues, many
countries are battling for survival on strictly political
grounds. Egypt, India, Saudi Arabia, Indonesia, the
European "great powers," Iran, and even Japan and the
till-now-unruffled socialist bloc face a convergence of
fast-changing geopolitical, demographic, techno-economic
and domestic political situations. Each of them will be
confronted by new mass awakenings, new challenges in the
spheres of intellectual grasp and ideological
orientations, and new expressions of dissent and revolt
against established ways of thinking about national
interest and national security. In the years and decades
to come, the global economic crisis caused by the twin
pincers of energy cost and military budgets is likely to
shake the complacency of the earlier alignments--and also
of the nonalignment of those who have so far refused to
fall in line--and push them along hitherto uncharted
paths. All this will add to the sense of uncertainty and
insecurity.

Survival of the States System

Finally, the superpowers themselves exhibit the same
sense of insecurity in the face of a variety of
challenges: the global realignment of forces, the
decline in credibility of erstwhile postures, the failure
of long-held doctrinal and ideological positions, and
above all the almost total unworkability of long-
developed strategies and theologies of national and
international security. Naturally resistant to change,
and lacking good sense and the will to undertake major
restructuring of the international system, the
superpowers will continue to cling to outmoded habits of
thought and patterns, hoping that somehow the status quo
will not be disturbed.
All of this is likely to give rise to a sense of
desperation and frustration in the various arenas of
international politics, transforming a steady competition
for power and scarce resources into erratic and
adventurist acts of preemption and checkmate on a world
chessboard, the ground rules repeatedly violated and the
number of players and their moves unpredictable.
In sum, lacking determined intervention for
restructuring the global enterprise, the various forms of
insecurity at all levels and the drives for hegemony by a
variety of actors, both on the one hand, and holding
operations and the politics of sheer survival, on the
other, will only accentuate the arms race, intensify

repression by the state apparatus, and aggravate violence and turmoil not only in the domestic socioeconomic foundations of state but in the states system itself.

Survival and Transformation

The crux of the foregoing overview of specificities of the emerging global problematique can be stated more simply: the twin basic dimensions of human prospects are survival and transformation or, to put it in conventional language, peace and development, and these two dimensions are inextricably intertwined. The contemporary human condition is characterized by recession on both dimensions, and the vision of an integral and unified human future based on bonds of solidarity and shared destiny is dimmer than ever.

Let us look more closely at this interrelationship. As we move into an age in which the superpowers will be unable to control the conflict between themselves or among their allies, and the United Nations itself more likely than not will be paralyzed by the growing world conflict between the North and the South, the East and the West, and within each of these world segments, the states system as it is presently constructed will be unable to provide peace and security, and all progress on disarmament and human rights will come to a standstill. Similarly, as the international system becomes even more precarious and further strains national and local resources and institutions, and as old engines of growth and dynamism begin to lose steam, there will be a need to pay special attention to the restructuring of the world economy, and to conceive new strategies of growth for the new industrializing countries by drawing upon the numerous resources of their vast populations and their rich and ancient civilizations and scientific traditions. The problems are fundamentally international and global in both respects.

I do not subscribe to any universal theory of human behavior or to globalism based on such a universalist view. It is rather the structure of interrelationships and linkages permeating the individual and social condition that interests me. I believe it is this that needs to be emphasized in our thinking about the human predicament and about the ways of dealing with it. It is this that I have tried to map in this paper. And it is from such a perspective that the close intertwining of the prospects for peace and the challenge of transformation emerges.

Global Structuring

Let us elaborate on this particular perspective on
the global spread of the human predicament. It will not
do any more to think in local, regional, or even North-
South terms. Though we strongly believe in the primacy
of the Third World in any strategy of world
transformation--both in respect to historical analysis
and in respect to a paradigm of action--we are convinced
that it is not any longer possible to think of either
development or peace in a narrow Third World sense; for
the developed world itself faces serious problems of
maldevelopment, exploitative structures, militarization
of science and technology, and cultural erosion.
Similarly, it is no use thinking of each dimension in
isolation. For example, although it is imperative to
deal with hunger, it is idle to do so without at the same
time ensuring physical survival to the poor and the
hungry. Again, unless one deals with and eliminates the
sources of war, the resources and political will needed
to deal with hunger and poverty will just not be there.
The contrary is also true: unless we develop the human
capacity to frontally attack and eliminate the worst
forms of misery and despair and the conflicts and
tensions inherent in such a human condition, we will
never succeed in removing the sources of violence and
war. The way to deal with this dual challenge facing
us--of war and poverty--lies not in some blind faith in
technology and its continuous expansion, but rather in
bringing the human being back to the center of the
development process, around whom and for whom to create a
peaceful and harmonious world.

RECONCEPTUALIZING THE PROBLEMATIQUE OF PEACE

It follows that the problems of peace and security
in our time must be tackled in a manner drastically
different from the one in which they have been pursued so
far. Although drawing upon the insights and
understandings provided by earlier traditions of thought
and practice in international relations, we must relate
the problems of peace and security to the profound and
turbulent changes of our time; the agenda must include
structural transformation and cultural change produced by
this turbulence, taking into account the still larger
mutations of religious, ecological, and aesthetic
consciousness at the popular level in large parts of the
world. The paradigm of peace includes the building of
human and institutional capabilities for carrying through
this major restructuring of the human enterprise with
minimum recourse to violence and human destruction, by
arresting the suicidal and self-destructive proclivities
in human culture and psyche.

Let us restate our conceptualization of the problematique in a summary form by enumerating the major contours of the unfolding human condition in this last leg of the twentieth century and the transition to the twenty-first. All of these contours or problems call for consideration and creative response:

(1) The fact that the superpowers, and the states system presided over by them, are unable to manage the sources of tension and instability in the international order, to respond in a responsible manner to the radical shifts in the global distribution of power that have taken place, and to provide a new basis of peace and security in the world;

(2) The fact that domestic political systems (across ideological differences and regime types) are increasingly unable to cope with the demands generated by mass awakening and the breakdown of the old "consensus;"

(3) The fact that the basic ideological thrust of our time is toward equity of an all-encompassing type, all the way from the power structure of the international order to the accessibility to sharing of world resources, to social and economic structures of diverse societies, to the world political process;

(4) The fact that the political, managerial, and technocratic elites of the world, faced by new challenges and threats to their hegemony, are feeling insecure and therefore resorting to archaic methods of dealing with revolutionary forces through repression, terror, and authoritarianism, all in the name of "stability," "peace," and "development."

(5) The fact that entrenched interests are fighting their last-ditch battle against the rising tide of the times by increasingly resorting to armaments and militarism, and by transforming civil societies into national security states and the international order into a balance of terror with ever more refined instruments of total destruction (and, of course, with military interventions and direct or indirect occupation of alien territories);

(6) The fact that this backlash is increasingly destabilizing and undermining the cohesion and security of the state in large regions of the world, especially in the fragile and vulnerable regions of the Third World. No formula of international security is possible without the security of the state, still the basic unit of human organization (even if it is in the midst of a long-term process of transition toward a different configuration of human structures);

(7) The fact that other components of the international order that were devised after World War II are collapsing, most strikingly the international monetary system, plunging the world into a global economic crisis. Then there are other international conventions and protocols, notably in the fields of

energy, ecology, oceans, and space which together have
given rise to a world energy crisis and an environmental
crisis of major proportions;

(8) The fact that the new interaction between
ethnicity and human rights, mediated by local wars and
regimes of occupation, is giving rise to movements on a
mammoth scale of peoples across states and ethnic
regions, which carries the potential of social
convulsions and the rise of new types of parochialism and
chauvinism;

(9) The fact that, with the decline in religious
feeling and the shared sense of community with all human
beings, under the impact of the information explosion and
the seductive ethic of consumption, traditional
restraints on violence and anomic behavior are giving way
in large parts of the world and at so many levels;

(10) The fact that in the meanwhile the
countervailing forces and alternative systems that showed
promise at one stage are in disarray, with the breakdown
of cohesion and solidarity of the Third World, the
erosion of youth and counter-culture movements, the
frustrations of traditional disarmament and peace
movements and "revolutionary" regimes to provide viable
alternatives to world capitalism and its technological
offensive;

(11) The fact that powerful nonstate actors and
corporate interests have emerged on a world scale with
access to massive resources, latest technologies, and
information. These too, alongside the world military
order, threaten the integrity and survival of the state
and reinforce monopolistic and authoritarian tendencies
inherent in a world system based on monopoly capitalism;

(12) And, in consequence of all these forces and
tendencies at work, the fact of an eventual collision of
North and South, endangering the survival of human
civilization as such;

(13) But also the fact that, on the other hand, new
and pervasive forms of awakening and renewal are under
way in large parts of the world; the reassertion and
regeneration of old religions and cultures is posing a
major challenge to the prevailing international order
and, by forcing a reformulation of the earlier conflict
between the sacred and the secular in a totally new
historical context, is also posing a fundamental
challenge to the capacity of all religions to contain the
forces of chauvinism, hatred, and violence and provide a
new basis for global consciousness and human solidarity.

(14) The fact that, alongside these deeper stirrings
of the human spirit, new movements are taking shape
within the secular framework of societies and the
international order--all the way from the assertion of
democratic rights by oppressed people and communities
within individual states to transnational movements for
transformation toward a more just world and for a model

of development that is conducive to such a transformation, to new and radical popular movements for peace and new regimes of security and for "people's security;"

(15) And finally, the fact that the phenomenon of nonstate actors in world affairs encompasses not just transnational corporations and the world military order but also the creative forces of change and transformation, at both national and transnational levels, outside the traditional framework of party organizations, interest groups, and intergovernmental structures, expressing itself both through spontaneous demonstrations of public weal and more organized and sustained agitations around issues and movements that transcend traditional region-based spaces and constituencies--such as the environmental and "green" movements, the feminist movement, the new upsurge of consciousness among the young against global inequities and exploitation, and above all the peace movements. All of these movements are seeking common ground and moving out of their earlier fragmented cloistered existence as well as ideological hang-ups. The focal point of this convergence could well be the issue of peace.

Multidimensionality

It is this multidimensional field of concern and perspective that we need to deal with. The problems of human survival, peace, and security must be addressed in terms of the most basic of all tasks facing the world community: evolving a strategy of purposive yet peaceful and by-and-large nonviolent restructuring of the prevailing international system as well as its various component structures within states. It is an essentially global task, but a global task that is simultaneously pursued in international, regional, and national--as well as subnational and grass roots--settings. The threats to human survival and peace are as ominous and brutalizing in the latter settings as in the international one. Indeed, it may well be that the unfinished structural transformations in national and subnational settings, and in the regional constellations of which they are parts, give rise to immense power vacuums, crises of legitimacy and confrontations between revolutionary movements and regimes of repression. All this may, in turn, trigger the destabilization of global strategic and military balances and, in the course of time, push them to the precipice. On the positive side, the rigid, insensitive, ahistorical, and unpolitic postures of the two superpowers--the United States more than the U.S.S.R.--on the one hand, and the growing movements of popular pressure for peace and democracy on the other, as well as the increasing divergence of economic interests within the North, are producing fissures within the old global monoliths and are opening up the possibility of new alignments within the states system itself, encompassing both North and South.

This, then, is the broad historical context of the problematique of peace and security in a world that is already in the throes of fundamental transformation and is in need of a comprehensive strategy of peaceful reconstruction toward an alternative social and international order, with appropriate technological and institutional underpinnings that while preserving the great diversity of cultures, ecologies, and moral and religious orders, moves toward a new sense of unity and common destiny.

Moral and Aesthetic Dimensions

Our conceptualization of peace and transformation involves such a perspective of unity in diversity. It involves much more: the evolution of an ethical and moral code, an ethic of survival that draws its basic sustenance from self-control and restraint in the ordering of human wants and demands, and that accepts the ecological constraints of a larger cosmology and pursues a religiosity and an aesthetic quality seeking fulfillment in what is at once self-regeneration and self-effacement. Translated in political terms, this involves a statesmanship that admits the role of wisdom and candor in the ordering of human affairs, and thinks of peace as a condition as much of enlightenment as of survival. Indeed, in such a perspective, even as survival of life and civilization remains the focal point of all endeavor, what is necessary at the bottom of it all is a new enlightenment and a new vision about the whole human enterprise, without which the struggle for survival cannot but become a losing battle.

RECONCEPTUALIZING DISARMAMENT

It is in light of this broad conceptualization of peace and transformation that the more limited issue of "disarmament"--on which so much intellectual effort seems to have been devoted--needs to be conceived.

A mood of pessimism has pervaded the campaign for disarmament over the last twenty-five years. Writing and pleading about it has seemed a futile exercise, failing to connect with the world of those who make decisions and take action. That world has moved along a different plane, totally insensitive to the very large body of opinion and number of popular movements in favor of disarmament. If there is one field where alienation of the world of thought from the world of action is total, it is the field of disarmament.

Could it be that the whole effort of promoting disarmament has gone on in an unrealistic manner, in a manner that is historically naive and conceptually empty? Could it be that, like efforts on behalf of development, a new international economic order, and other facets of global endeavor, disarmament efforts are being pursued in a rather abstracted and specialized manner instead of being located in a comprehensive and holistic perspective and strategy? To me at any rate, this seems to be the case.

There is something highly utopian in the manner in which we have approached the problem of disarmament--as if it could be achieved in and by itself. Although we should no doubt be greatly concerned about the terrifying magnitudes that the stockpiling and continuing refinement of ever-more deadly armaments are assuming, and the undeniable fact that the arms race is really getting out of hand, we should remember that in order to make any dent on this rather complex problem we must take cognizance of the larger historical context. It is a context of major transformation in several spheres of world reality, all of them taking place simultaneously--a transformation that could lead either to a world more peaceful and secure as well as more just and humane, or to a world wrecked by increasing turbulence, plagued by a greater sense of insecurity among the major centers of power. The latter will inevitably lead to a further tightening of the structures of domination and exploitation, producing in its wake an intensification of the arms race, on the one hand, and domestic repression on the other--through brutal preemptive countermoves against forces of change. The resulting domestic turmoil and regional conflagrations and pervasive chaos may eventually ignite a catastrophe that no one would be able to control.

Here, too, there is need for reconceptualization, for basic rethinking on the framework of assumptions that informs the field: as instances, the assumption of a bipolar world that used to inform our perception of world politics and to a large extent still does, consciously or unconsciously; the assumption that issues of peace and security are determined by existing technology, nuclear or nonnuclear, and prevailing military research and development; and the assumption of a balance of power and management of world affairs through such a balance. Similarly, the incremental conception of disarmament moving step by step through arms control and peace negotiations to ultimate general disarmament will have to go.

The Myth of Deterrence

We have to make a quantum leap in our intellectual perspectives. We have to explode the myth that has been steadily disseminated around the world, even among the strategic research community, that there can be a realistic nuclear deterrent based on the assumption of preparing for a nuclear war in order that it may not take place. The myth exploded, all the effort that goes into building parities in ever-escalating nuclear capacities, or building nuclear counterforce as a doctrine of defense, will become meaningless, and the halting of the nuclear arms race (as an initial step toward denuclearization) will then come to be placed as a first priority on the agenda of world security. It will have become clear that without this first and paramount prerequisite of achieving peace and security, no progress in disarmament is possible. And the problem of disarmament will be liberated from all the cobwebs of strategic thinking that have held the field for so long. For instance, the whole question of nuclear peace zones will have to be seen in perspective. Until the nuclear arms race between the superpowers is tackled, and tackled frontally, the prospect for disarmament will remain dim. Let us also not forget that it is as part of the superpower conception of security that clandestine transfers of nuclear armaments of varying degrees of sophistication to the most sensitive regions of the world--South Africa, the Middle East, and the Indian Ocean as well as Western Europe--are taking place. The issue of regional security cannot be seen in isolation from this global context.

Recession and War

Once the global context is recognized, many other issues will become highlighted, issues that are as clear as daylight but are somehow not grasped. For instance, it is clear by now that if the resources of the world are spent at the present rate on military technology and the arms race and on arms industries that keep producing and transferring ever more sophisticated armaments to the Third World, the cost to the people of the industrialized countries will be disastrous, with both inflation and unemployment breaking bounds and with wars becoming the only answer to economic recessions.

Poverty and Civilization

We have to think of peace and disarmament as critical to human survival and to the survival of civilization. At the present moment, the world is gripped at all levels by a rising sense of insecurity, from the superpowers themselves to the very bottom of societies among the world's poor who are being continuously denied their due by the rapacious character of modern technology, which is made more and more rapacious and menacing by the demands of militarism and military technology. We have to think of security in terms of people's security, and of peace as an aspect of people's participation in the building of a new human civilization. What we have today, instead, is people's insecurity and vulnerability in the face of mounting threats to their minimum sustenance, their lives, and their life-support system. Such people cannot participate meaningfully in the civilization process.

The State as an Instrument of Survival

We have to think of the nature of the state in our times, perpetually under the shadow of rising insecurity in the global context of regional wars and war-preparedness everywhere. There is an increasing pressure on national economies, consequent upon the withdrawal of vital resources for sustaining the arms race and high technology. This dimension of resources hurts the poor and the weak the most, and breeds unrest and turmoil that nascent states are unable to deal with except through more and more repression--hardly a condition for security and survival. In large parts of the world the state is weakening and collapsing as a framework within which to conduct human affairs, especially from the point of view of the people, their survival, their development, and their future. The issue of disarmament cannot be divorced from the need for security of the state, of all states, and of all peoples. Even the new phenomenon of the rise of various nonstate corporate actors needs to be reconceptualized so that their resources and skills are channeled toward providing security to the peoples of the world and to states, in particular the more nascent and poor. In the absence of such security, disarmament has no future.

Militarization

In the field of peace and security proper, the scenario is that the present danger is growing apace, at an alarming rate. The accelerating nuclear arms spread cannot be prevented except by the superpowers themselves changing course, i.e., being made to change course. Militarization is being globalized, engulfing the whole world. Worst of all, the most responsible powers in the world seem to be set on an extremely dangerous course. This peculiar brand of militarization, based on more and

more sophisticated weaponry, is becoming the largest drag
on world resources, undermining all efforts at growth and
development. Indeed, the only prospect it holds forth is
that of a continuous decline in human standards.

Military Research and Development

It is important to understand how militarization is
escalating. There is a growing system of military
research and development that is in fact quite unlike all
other researches in technology; it has become the
propelling mechanism of an arms race at once grotesque
and self-perpetuating. Obsolescence deliberately built
into every type of weaponry is the key to this research
and development. It does not permit an arms transfer to
be a one-time transaction. Unindustrialized recipient
countries (more accurately, their ruling elites) feel
insecure unless they have added the latest weapons to
their armory. Keen on acquiring these latest weapons
(even at the cost of declining domestic economies and the
consequent immiserization of growing numbers of their
populations, along with heightened tension with their
neighbors and within their regions), they find themselves
caught in an unending arms race and permanently hooked to
dependence on the industrialized suppliers. Important
and leading sectors of the national economies of the
supplying countries are structured around this nexus of
transfers of more and more sophisticated and expensive
armaments. This kind of perverse economic enterprise has
been facilitated by a barrage of hard selling of
conceptual talismans that has taken hold of politicians
and the mass media in both sets of countries; and even
the general public (especially from the educated middle
classes) is taken in by the pernicious propaganda merely
because it is so seductive (much like the advertisement
of aphrodisiacs and elixirs).

The Intellectual Challenge

It is necessary that thinking on disarmament rise to
the challenge of this empirical reality of widespread
apathy in the face of imminent danger. Underlying all
the major crises facing the world today is the crisis of
the intellect in the fields of development theory and of
peace and security alike. What is called for now is
thinking that goes beyond conventional approaches to
international relations.

The thinking will have to be innovative. Although
adopting a comprehensive and holistic approach, it should
focus on the specific problem of survival in an age of
transformation. It will have to deal with the nature of
the contemporary state, with the sources of violence,

with the conflict over resources (which will become very serious in the coming decades), with the sweep and consequences of military research and development, and, above all, with the role of the United Nations and ways of restoring it to its true categorical imperative from which it seems to have somehow strayed. The United Nations needs to be reminded that its principal task is to provide a framework of survival and security as a basis for a more humane and just world order. As set out in its Preamble, the primary purpose and raison d'etre of the UN is "to save succeeding generations from the scourge of war."

The new thinking on disarmament will have to take into account specific regional contexts along with the interrelationship of conflict, violence, and insecurity in domestic as well as regional and global settings. There is need for a new and comprehensive doctrine on the *ecology of disarmament*.

Debate

It should be emphasized that to leave all this to the realm of thought and discussion is not enough. Sustained analyses and debates should not be confined in conference halls of disarmament committees and commissions, but aired in public with the focus on the extremely hazardous nature and consequences of weapons technology as a whole.

There is also need to connect such public debate with action movements wherever they focus on the same issue. Indeed, it is necessary to view thinking and debate themselves as a part of the paradigm of action. A wide variety of popular movements against sources of deprivation, terror, militarism, and authoritarianism are sprouting around the world. There is need to relate to these grass roots micro-efforts, to macro-movements of antinuclear campaigning, ecology, and feminine liberation, to national self-determination efforts, and to the political perspectives and interventions of sensitive statesmen and intellectuals. The role played by the citizenry of the world, and of popular movements, in influencing the world political process has not been adequately stressed so far. It is high time it was.

In sum, there is need for public opinion, popular movements, and sustained debate in the UN forum, in regional and interregional organizations, and in the new forums of multilateral cooperation—sustained debate across regional and ideological blocs. The talents and resources in various spheres must all join in a common effort toward a global movement for peace and transformation.

The problems of peace and security in our time need to be tackled through a paradigm of scientific endeavor

that is different from those pursued so far. The
paradigm must draw upon the insights of peace research;
studies of disarmament, demilitarization, and
"disarmament and development," the considerable data and
analyses generated in fields like strategic studies,
international relations, and world order modeling; and
concepts from older schools of conflict resolution,
nonviolence, and containment of human aggression. While
doing all this, the paradigm must (1) adopt a more
integrated and holistic approach to the study of peace
and security; (2) relate it simultaneously to processes
at work at local (community), national (domestic), and
global; (3) locate it in the historical framework of
social and human transformation and political expression
of deeper cultural and religious stirrings of our time.

Methodologically, too, such a perspective should
combine historical, sociopsychological, policy-oriented,
dialogical, and action-oriented approaches. It should be
at once deeply sensitive to the civilizational crisis of
our time and the historical roots of these approaches,
and profoundly practical in terms of generating ideas for
action and intervention in different forums of decision
making, public opinion, dissent, and debate on
alternative futures and action profiles.

The principal task of such an endeavor should be, in
relation to the basic point of the profound and turbulent
changes of our time, to reformulate the agenda of
structural transformation and cultural change produced by
this turbulence (both within and between societies), and,
simultaneously, to restrain both linear and expansive
drives in human civilization and the potentialities for
violence that seem to be inherent in modern science.
Special attention must be paid to the tremendous dangers
to the sustenance of basic resources for the survival of
life.

KEY DIMENSIONS

Such an approach to locating the problem of peace in
the process of transformation, and the interrelationships
and paradoxes involved in this transformation, must lead
to a restatement of the dimensions of the contemporary
human condition.

The Role of the State

The first of these dimensions has to do with the
role of the state in processes of development and global
transformation. As in many earlier epochs of change,
there has been a large hiatus between objective reality
and political theory in our time: it has been in
evidence since 1945. This period was marked by the

collapse of colonial order and the successful culmination of national revolutions in many parts of the world, transforming in effect the world political structure and ushering in an epoch as momentous as the age of the Industrial Revolution and the age of imperialism. Yet the dominant paradigms in political theory were preoccupied with the notions of development and modernization (conceived in terms of transforming human diversity into the monolithic image provided by Western social science). It is only in recent years that the inequitous consequences of these models are being realized and that drives for national autonomy and the emergence of new centers of power are becoming the foci of theoretical work. Major human tragedies and the excesses of exploiting powers--in Vietnam, in the Arab World, in Czechoslovakia, in Chile--have stirred people to begin thinking in terms of taking command once again of their own destinies and reinstating their dignity and self-respect. During the same period, the disappointment with the dominant models of economic and political development, in combination with the realization that these models had in fact served the foreign policy interests of metropolitan powers and given a new lease of life to colonialism, has led to considerable rethinking among leaders and thinkers of the Third World--in Latin America, thinking on *dependencia*; in Tanzania, groping toward a new political model; in India, search for an eclectic model blending liberal, democratic, socialist, and Gandhian values; in China, search for a truly indigenous alternative (now in disarray); and in Africa, the still-continuing battles against the remaining bastions of European imperialism and for an authentic African political expression.

It is only in the very recent past that political theory has begun to respond to this compelling reality. The restatement of the problem of imperialism in terms of the center-periphery model, the rediscovery of Lenin's statements on the colonial and national self-determination questions, the growing recognition of Gramsci's emphasis on the importance of national political will in revolutionary advance, and, above all, Mao's adaptation of Marxist theory to the historic task of refashioning a national political culture with deep historical roots, are all examples of such an effort. Even more important is the search for new political formations based on traditional identities (forced on the agenda of political thought by the gruesome tragedies of fratricidal wars emanating from imposed colonial boundaries, as in Nigeria and elsewhere). No less important are the simultaneous stress on expanding people's participation (through decentralized state structures) and the protection of the state from external pressures, as well as the growing politicization of the debate on development (hitherto left to technocrats) and

the search for alternative visions of the state from
nonmodern sources of authority and legitimacy (Islam,
Gandhi, and others).

All this calls for a new paradigm that should take
account of the crisis of the modern state in both its
internal and its external manifestations. This is so
everywhere but especially in the more vulnerable states
of the Third World. Facing unprecedented demands on
their resources and leadership, these states are found to
be increasingly unable to cope, their stability and
security threatened from mass turmoil on the one hand and
global pressures of energy, the arms race, and economic
recession on the other. A world based on such unstable
and insecure states cannot provide a framework of peace
and security. It can only produce more conflicts and
more divisions.

Conflict over Natural Resources

Alongside the growth of conflict and violence in the
ordering of societies there has emerged another major
conflict to which inadequate attention has so far been
given. This is the growing and pervasive conflict over
natural resources at various levels of the world polity.
The rapid changes in the international division of both
resources and productive capacities, the relocation of
these and the growing scarcity *and high cost* of energy
and other resources, pose serious challenges to world
peace in the absence of a strategy of peaceful structural
change. The link between this most dramatic and far-
reaching development of our time and the process of
violence within and between nations has not been well
studied so far, and it ought to be taken up as a matter
of priority.

The conflict over resources provides perhaps the
most basic source of conflicts that plague today's world,
the most important basis of stratification in the
world--both international and domestic. It has brought
about the greatest of all confrontations in the world:
the developed world intent on maintaining and enhancing
the standard of living it has attained and the developing
world hard put to it to achieve minimum living standards
for its people.

There are three aspects of this scenario of growing
conflict. The first is the global structuring of the
relationship between resources and human beings such that
a minority of nations has, in pursuit of a parasitic and
wasteful style of life, shored up a large part of world
resources, especially energy and industrial raw
materials, generating intense conflicts over access to,
distribution of, and control over world resources.

The second aspect is the spread (no less through
prompting than through emulation) of the same style of

life among the dominant strata of the Third World, producing, in turn, deep divisions within and between these societies.

The third aspect, arising out of the first two, consists in growing inequality between rich and poor countries, between the tiny middle class and the large unorganized masses in the poor countries, and between the proletariat of the rich countries and the proletariat of the poor countries.

Global conflicts over natural resources also have a military-strategic dimension in that they are pushing the world in the direction of wars in various regions, by proxies so far, but threatening to culminate in nuclear war. Even in the absence of war, the quest for control over resources and the practice of stockpiling the so-called strategic resources goes on. In the Third World countries, resources are increasingly diverted away from development; national security considerations, often born out of a failure to build just societies at home and peaceful relations with neighbors, are given overriding priority over the minimum basic needs of the people. Military expenditures keep on mounting at a steady pace, fertile lands are taken over for military installations, and scarce foreign exchange is spent on enormously expensive weapon systems. This in turn gives rise to a preference for gigantism in the name of science and technology. In the name of "development," polluting industries are destroying nature and rendering large tracts of land unfit for cultivation. Large dams are displacing people who are eventually rendered landless. Forced migration of the poor to the urban areas has been going on for decades now. The destruction of ecology, community economies, the impoverishment of the people through the extraction of nonexistent "surplus" for military building and "development" has not only led to endemic social violence but to permanent destitution of an ever-increasing number of people. Worldwide, a large majority of the people are engaged in a daily struggle for sheer survival despite the fact that existing national and world resources are more than adequate to fulfill the basic needs of all.

Human Rights

Closely linked with the issues of physical survival are the issues of survival of justice, dignity, and freedom in the social existence of human beings. All three concepts are subject to definitional disputes, as is the concept of human rights. Yet, even after allowing for all the different interpretations, it is possible to arrive at a consensus about what should constitute minimum human rights in terms of justice, dignity, and freedom. But the trend in the present-day world is toward the increasing violation of even these minimum human rights. The threats to sheer physical survival--the most basic human right--have been outlined in the paragraphs above. Threats to, and violations of, other minimum rights come from many sources. At the national level, the collective rights of a people are threatened by the hegemonistic policies of the global and regional big powers, the erosion of a state's sovereignty and autonomy by corporate and supranational financial agencies, and by the incorporation of states into military alliances or spheres of influence. The situation is, however, much worse within nations. The spread of militarization has assumed alarming proportions. On the one hand, the developing countries are being subjected to political and economic penetration and military pressures, and so they are strengthening themselves militarily. On the other hand, the governments of these countries face the problem of social and political turmoil at home, to which they are increasingly responding with repressive violence. Distorted economic development has led to new unjust practices in addition to the injustices suffered by the poor in the past. Their forced migration and forced urbanization in festering slums has taken away whatever dignity they had in their ancestral locations. The law courts almost routinely deny justice to the poor; few poor have any access to the courts anyway.

There has been a tremendous growth in the police and paramilitary forces in most developing countries, and these forces almost invariably act on behalf of the rich and the powerful. Even in countries that have a formally democratic constitution, the culture of repressive violence is all-pervasive. But the increasing trend among Third World developing countries is toward the seizure of power by the military. Under such military regimes, even the fiction of any kind of freedom for the common citizen ceases to exist. Thus, the state, instead of being the protector of the rights of its citizens, is actually violating them on an increasing scale. And modern technology and modern communication have become its allies in this enterprise.

The Survival of Cultures

Yet another related area of immediate concern is the survival of cultures. The cultural penetration by the modern West of the rest of the world through artifacts, modes of production and consumption (life-styles), and one-way flows of information is a worldwide trend. But even within nations, cultural autonomy of communities (tribes, linguistic groups, religious minorities, etc.) has come under attack in the name of "nation-building;" diversity is being increasingly equated with disunity.

The educational system and the mass media have now become the major purveyors of synthetic official cultures. This has resulted in the alienation of the young from their cultural roots. New legal codes now directly interfere with age-old cultural practices such as marriage, property rights, religious celebrations, etc. But worse than all this is the destruction of tribal and minority cultures brought about through deforestation, desertification, forced migration, and urbanization--in short, through "development" as conceived by the elites. Agribusiness is forcing the people to change food habits. Deforestation and commercial forestry have been destroying the tribal ways of life. Government-controlled education and mass media are progressively extinguishing dialects with their rich folklore. Factory production and aggressive selling together have destroyed handicrafts and the aesthetic environment of the rural household. Urbanization has cut off the link between grandparents and grandchildren, which was so vital for the transmission of cultures to future generations. Modern communications have increased functional contacts beyond the community but have also reduced the cohesion and solidarity within communities. Such changes have still not reached the point of irreversibility, but there is an imminent danger that if the trend is not reversed immediately, traditional cultures will be totally destroyed without being replaced with anything worthwhile.

Global Militarization

Reinforcing these three trends, all of which severally and collectively threaten human survival, and making them all converge into a grim prospect, are the growing militarization and violence in the world at various levels of the human society, and the increasing insecurity and vulnerability felt by states on the one hand and people on the other.

Spurred by (1) internal restlessness and challenge, (2) the growing resource crunch, (3) widening regional and international inequities and power vacuums (including the vacuums created by the superpowers), and (4) the increasing possibility of nations of all types acquiring modern weapons (aided by developments in the global arms market), the world is set on an escalating and hazardous process of global militarization. A number of technical and analytical studies bear this out. What is needed now is to approach this all-too-important issue (1) by linking militarization to the whole issue of structural transformation, globally and within every society, (2) by analyzing deeper cultural and psychological factors that are perpetuating the structures and processes of global militarization, (3) by linking militarization of the international system to the militarization of the state apparatus as depicted earlier, (4) by focusing on the role and responsibility of the big powers as well as of the emerging regional powers in the spread of global militarization, and (5) by evolving strategies of first halting and then reversing the trend. The strategies must be responsible and credible strategies of demilitarization, which may then be presented to peace movements within countries, various international and regional forums, the UN system, and the citizenry of the world generally.

An important aspect of such a multidimensional approach to the problems of militarization and vulnerability of human societies is the whole field of military research and development and its consequences for other spheres of life. Whereas technical and specialized studies of research and development in the military sphere are available in plenty, there is need to think of military research and development as part of the overall problematique of peace as conceived in this essay. It is not only that military research and development absorbs almost 50 percent of the world's total research and development expenditures; it is also that as the arms race involves a qualitative (as well as a quantitative) competition in the whole field of research and development, as military emphases penetrate the sciences and engulf the whole world, and as the military increasingly controls developments in other technologies, it is becoming increasingly difficult to pursue an autonomous course of industrialization. The result is that all societies have willy-nilly to accept the domination of countries that control global technology through their control over military research and development. Unless military research and development is limited and brought under international regulation, no control on the arms race is possible, nor is it possible to delink development from militarism. The issue is far too serious to be left to specialists in military technology and think tanks for strategic analysis, for it has much wider ramifications that only a composite and multidimensional perspective can satisfactorily explore.

The World Economic Crisis

Similarly, the interlinkage between global militarization and the economic crisis facing the world (all parts of it) has been inadequately explored. Contrary to the conventional economistic explanations of the crisis of the world economy (such as those attributing it to the oil price increases and the monetary disturbances, or those tracing it back merely to the "normal" business cycle of the capitalist national economies), and also contrary to the usual fragmentation in the analysis of the crisis into regional and national crises, the world economic crisis that erupted in the early 19702 and has continued since then stems from certain noneconomic conditions as well; it has by now become a global, one-world crisis.

The crisis is deeply rooted in the *basic inequalities* and asymmetries in the world economic system, in the unequal pattern of ownership and control over resources, in international exploitation through an unequally structured international division of labor with built-in imbalances. One component of the complex process that has led to the eruption of the crisis is the increasing discrepancy between international and national frameworks of regulation. On the one hand, the capability of the state to manage the national economy is greatly reduced and, on the other, the state is overwhelmed by the resource-squandering "consumer society," both in the advanced countries and, via the demonstration effect, in the less developed ones. The arms race and militarization processes have also contributed much to "stagflation" and the slowing down of development in both the industrialized and the developing countries (though such "contradictions" can sometimes play a positive role). The economic crisis is related to a number of other things too: internationalization of production; transnationalization, through "compradorization" of some developing countries; unregulated activities of the transnational corporations that are not subject to any specific country's control; and spread of consumption patterns that cause economic imbalances and cultural destabilization.

Much hope was pegged to so-called "global negotiations." In the event, they have tended to fragment and isolate the interrelated elements of the global crisis and to blur substantial differences in views and interests by a "convergence of rhetoric."

CONCLUSION

The conceptual thrust of our analysis of the problem of peace in our time implies two methodological principles. First, the problem is multidimensional. So far, problems of peace and security, economic development, or human rights have been perceived as separate problems, each a subject of independent specialized study. Of course, we must draw upon the entire corpus of specialized knowledge and the insights vouchsafed by each, but then we must cut across the various dimensions of the global crisis to see the new questions and to find solutions that in order to be efficacious will necessarily be new. These questions and solutions will emerge out of a comprehension of the interrelationships and linkages between dimensions that have hitherto been treated as isolated and discrete phenomena.

Second, in the light of these interrelationships and linkages, the problem of peace has to be perceived as a set of dynamic paradoxes, as trends and countertrends that manifest themselves at once in the form of disintegration and destruction and in the form of new opportunities for equitable order, peace, and transformation.

The methodology can be expressed in the form of a matrix defined by the main dimensions of the problem of peace and global transformation--viz., military, ecological, economic, political, and sociocultural. By looking at the effects of each dimension upon each of the others, we can delineate a series of trends and countertrends that enable us to locate the focal points of crises--i.e., the points of greatest danger and also of the greatest possible efficacious action.

The theoretical task is to move toward a comprehensive analysis along these lines and then to conceptualize the dual outcome. *On the one hand,* the outcome is disintegration reaching the point of violence, which ranges from structural sociocultural violence to militarized violence (war). *On the other hand*, the outcome is the widely felt need to move toward a constructive set of alternatives based on emerging social movements such as the peace movement in Western Europe, the grass roots movements for civil and economic rights in the Third World, and possibly both types of movements in the socialist countries. The point is to grasp the phenomena of disintegration and violence in their various dimensions and, at the same time, to develop a new paradigm that would encompass the wide-ranging alternative forms of action. These alternatives must address themselves to different thresholds of the world crisis.

It is only through a multifaceted exploration of the causes of war and violence and their trends that a proper praxis of peace and transformation can emerge. As already indicated, such a praxis has to be located in the search for alternative structures, pedagogies, and paradigms of civil society at various levels of world reality. Empirically, it has to be located in the various countertrends that are already discernible, although not very clearly because they are as yet feeble, disjointed, scattered, and without any concentrated purposive thrust. Such countertrends have the potential of being knitted together into a philosophy of alternatives for purposive intervention and action. To work toward the formation of such a philosophy, to identify the agents of intervention, to do empirical work to locate the points of intervention and to inform the opinion-makers--and let us hope some receptive decision-makers--is the task that faces the community of peace researchers and activists, and the much larger community of opinion-makers and sensitizers of the public weal and consciousness throughout the globe.

Selected Bibliography

Abdel-Malek, Anouar, *Civilizations and Social Theory* (Albany, N.Y.: State University of New York Press, 1981).

Ajami, Fouad, *The Arab Predicament* (Cambridge: Cambridge University Press, 1981).

Amin, Samir, G. Arrighi, A. G. Frank, and I. Wallerstein, *Dynamics of Global Crisis* (New York: Monthly Review Press, 1982).

Anderson, Benedict, *Imagined Communities* (London: New Left Books, 1983).

Ayoob, Mohammed, *The Politics of Islamic Reassertion* (London: Croom Helm, 1981).

Bandyopadhyaya, Jayatanaju, *North Over South: A Non-Western Perspective on International Relations* (Brighton: Harvester, 1982).

Berki, R. N., *On Political Realism* (London: J. M. Dent, 1981).

Brewer, Anthony, *Marxist Theories of Imperialism: A Critical Survey* (London: Routledge and Kegan Paul, 1980).

Bull, Hedley, *The Anarchical Society: A Study of Order in World Politics* (London: Macmillan, 1977).

Cox, Robert W., "Ideologies and the New International Economic Order: Reflections on Some Recent Literature," *International Organisation* 33 (2), Spring 1979:257-302.

Cox, Robert W., "Gramsci, Hegemony and International Relations: An Essay in Method," *Millenium: Journal of International Studies* 12 (2), Summer 1983:162-175.

Dorfman, Ariel, *The Empire's Old Clothes* (New York: Pantheon, 1983).

Falk, Richard, *The End of World Order* (New York: Holmes and Meier, 1983).

Falk, Richard A., Samuel S. Kim, and Saul H. Mendlovitz, eds., *Towards a Just World Order* (Boulder, Co.: Westview Press, 1982).

Furtado, Celso, *Accumulation and Development* (Oxford: Martin Robertson, 1983).

Gellner, Ernest, *Nations and Nationalism* (Oxford: Basil Blackwell, 1983).

Hamelink, Cees J., *Finance and Information: A Study of Converging Interests* (Norwood, N.J.: Ablex Publishing, 1983).

Horowitz, Irving Louis, *Beyond Empire and Revolution* (New York: Oxford University Press, 1982).

Hourani, Albert, *Europe and the Middle East* (London: Macmillan, 1980).

Kiernan, V. G., *The Lords of Human Kind: European Attitudes to the Outside World in the Imperial Age* (London: Weidenfeld and Nicolson, 1969).

Laitin, David D., "Linguistic Dissociation: A Strategy for Africa," John Gerard Ruggie, ed., *The Antinomies of Interdependence* (New York: Columbia University Press, 1983), pp. 317-368.

Laclau, Ernesto, *Politics and Ideology in Marxist Theory* (London: New Left Books, 1977).

Larrain, Jorge, *The Concept of Ideology* (London: Hutchinson, 1979).

Larrain, Jorge, *Marxism and Ideology* (London: Macmillan, 1983).

Linklater, Andrew, *Men and Citizens in the Theory of International Relations* (London: Macmillan, 1982).

Maclean, John, "Political Theory, International Theory, and Problems of Ideology," *Millennium: Journal of International Studies* 10 (2), Summer 1981:102-125.

Mattelart, A., *Multinational Corporations and the Control of Culture* (Brighton, Sussex: Harvester Press, 1979).

Mayall, James, ed., *The Community of States* (London: George, Allen and Unwin, 1982).

Nandy, Ashis, *At the Edge of Psychology: Essays in Politics and Culture* (New Delhi: Oxford University Press, 1980).

Nandy, Ashis, *The Intimate Enemy: Loss and Recovery of Self under Colonialism* (New Delhi: Oxford University Press, 1983).

Nordenstreng, Kaarle and Herbert I. Schiller, eds., *National Sovereignty and International Communication* (Norwood, N.J.: Ablex Publishing, 1979).

Paul, Dianne, "'In the Interests of Civilization': Marxist Views of Race and culture in the Nineteenth Century," *Journal of the History of Ideas* 42 (1), Jan.-March 1981:115-138.

Piscatori, James P., ed., *Islam in the Political Process* (Cambridge: Cambridge University Press, 1983).

Pletsch, Carl E., "The Three Worlds, or the Division of Socio-Scientific Labor, Circa 1950-1975," *Comparative Studies in Society and History* 23 (4), October 1981:565-590.

Portes, Alejandro and John Walton, *Labor, Class and the*

364

International System (New York: Academic Press, 1981).

Preiswerk, Roy, "The Place of Intercultural Relations in the Study of International Relations," *Yearbook of World Affairs* 1978, pp. 251-267.

Reynolds, Henry, *The Other Side of the Frontier: Aboriginal Resistance to the European Invasion of Australia* (Harmondsworth: Penguin, 1982).

Ridley, Hugh, *Images of Imperial Rule* (New York: St. Martins Press, 1983).

Rodinson, Maxime, *Islam and Capitalism,* translated by Brian Pearce (London: Allen Lane, 1973).

Rodinson, Maxime, *Marxism and the Muslim World,* translated by Michael Pallis (London: Zed Press, 1979).

Said, Edward W., *Orientalism* (New York: Pantheon, 1978).

Skocpol, Theda, "Rentier State and Shi'a Islam in the Iranian Revolution," *Theory and Society* 11 (3), May 1982:265-304.

Shils, Edward, *Tradition* (Chicago: University of Chicago Press, 1981).

Smith, Anthony, *The Geopolitics of Information* (London: Faber and Faber, 1980).

Smith, Anthony D., *The Ethnic Revival* (Cambridge: Cambridge University Press, 1981).

Sullivan, Eileen P., "'Liberalism and Imperialism': J. S. Mill's Defense of the British Empire," *Journal of the History of Ideas* 44 (4), October 1983:599-617.

Tinker, Hugh, *Race, Conflict and the International Order* (London: Macmillan, 1977).

Turner, Bryan S., *Marx and the End of Orientalism* (London: George, Allen and Unwin, 1978).

Vincent, R. J., "The Factor of Culture in the Global International Order," *Yearbook of World Affairs* 1980, pp. 252-264.

Wallerstein, Immanuel, *The Capitalist World Economy* (New York: Cambridge University Press, 1979).

Wiarda, Howard, "The Ethnocentricism of the Social Sciences: Implications for Research and Policy," *Review of Politics* 43, 1981:163-197.

Williams, Raymond, *Culture* (London: Fontana, 1981).

Wolf, Eric R., *Europe and the People Without History* (Berkeley: University of California Press, 1982).

About the Contributors

Anouar Abdel-Malek: Centre National de la Recherche Scientifique, Paris, France.

R.N. Berki: Department of Politics, University of Hull, England.

Mark Blasius: City University of New York, U.S.A.

Joseph Camilleri: Department of Political Science, La Trobe University, Melbourne, Australia.

Robert W. Cox: Department of Political Science, York University, Toronto, Canada.

Celso Furtado: Ecol de Hautes Etudes en Sciences Sociales, Paris, France.

Rajni Kothari: Centre for the Study of Developing Societies, Delhi, India.

Ali Mazrui: Center for Afroamerican and African Studies, University of Michigan, U.S.A.

Ashis Nandy: Centre for the Study of Developing Societies, Delhi, India.

R. J. Vincent: Department of International Relations, Keele University, Staffordshire, England.

R.B.J. Walker: Department of Political Science, University of Victoria, British Columbia, Canada.

Immanuel Wallerstein: Fernand Braudel Center, State University of New York at Binghampton, U.S.A.